By Robert L. O'Connell

*Revolutionary: George Washington at War*

*Fierce Patriot: The Tangled Lives of
William Tecumseh Sherman*

*The Ghosts of Cannae: Hannibal and the
Darkest Hour of the Roman Republic*

*Of Arms and Men: A History of War,
Weapons, and Aggression*

*Soul of the Sword: An Illustrated History of Weaponry
and Warfare from Prehistory to the Present*

*Sacred Vessels: The Cult of the Battleship and
the Rise of the U.S. Navy*

*Ride of the Second Horseman: The Birth of Death and War*

*Fast Eddie: A Novel in Many Voices*

REVOLUTIONARY

# REVOLUTIONARY

★

## GEORGE WASHINGTON
## AT WAR

★

## ROBERT L. O'CONNELL

RANDOM HOUSE

NEW YORK

Published in the United States by Random House,
an imprint and division of
Penguin Random House LLC, New York.

RANDOM HOUSE and the HOUSE colophon are
registered trademarks of Penguin Random House LLC.

LIBRARY OF CONGRESS CATALOGING-IN-PUBLICATION DATA
NAMES: O'Connell, Robert L., author.
TITLE: Revolutionary: George Washington at War /
Robert L. O'Connell.
DESCRIPTION: First edition. | New York : Random House, 2019. |
Includes bibliographical references and index.
IDENTIFIERS: LCCN 2018013009| ISBN 9780812996999 |
ISBN 9780812997002 (ebook)
SUBJECTS: LCSH: Washington, George, 1732–1799—
Military leadership. | Washington, George, 1732–1799—Psychology. |
Washington, George, 1732–1799—Childhood and youth. |
Generals—United States—Biography. | United States. Continental
Army—History. | United States—History—Revolution, 1775–1783.
CLASSIFICATION: LCC E312.25 .O36 2019 | DDC 973.4/1092 [B]
—dc23 LC record available at https://lccn.loc.gov/2018013009

Printed in the United States of America on acid-free paper

randomhousebooks.com

246897531

FIRST EDITION

All maps courtesy of the United States Military Academy
at West Point Department of History

Title-page photograph courtesy of Mount Vernon Ladies' Association

Book design by Barbara M. Bachman

To the grandkids:
Raymond, Rose of Sharon,
Violet, Wren, and Zelda

# CONTENTS

LIST OF MAPS     xi

INTRODUCTION:
THE GENERALISSIMO     xiii

CHAPTER 1    **The Gentrification of George**    3

CHAPTER 2    **Living Large**    47

CHAPTER 3    **Rage Militaire**    75

CHAPTER 4    **Amateur Hour**    115

CHAPTER 5    **Out in the Cold**    166

CHAPTER 6    **Dangerland**    213

CHAPTER 7    **The Long Goodbye**    250

CONCLUSION     299

ACKNOWLEDGMENTS     305

NOTES     307

INDEX     343

# LIST OF MAPS

BOSTON AND VICINITY                   103

NEW YORK AND VICINITY                 135

TRENTON AND VICINITY                  157

TRENTON AND PRINCETON                 162

WESTCHESTER AND VICINITY              179

GERMANTOWN AND VICINITY               185

MONMOUTH AND VICINITY                 209

SOUTHERN COLONIES                     233

ATLANTIC SEABOARD                     278

# INTRODUCTION

# The Generalissimo

H E WOULD HAVE HATED THE CONCEPT "GENERALISSIMO," AND
all it implied. It was exactly the image he, and, above all, Congress,
didn't want to project. He was simply the commander in chief of a legitimate governmental entity's fighting forces, vested with the ano-
dyne moniker "His Excellency"—a generic term Washington regularly
applied to state governors in his own correspondence.

This was, of course, balderdash. "Generalissimo" would have fit the
bill. He was, as everybody knew, the central protagonist in a profound
national revolution, at once the ultimate director of all its violent ac-
tivities, and, through sheer force of will and decency, the chief brake on
its potential for excess. At the time of his investment, only Elbridge
Gerry was willing to admit Congress was "making him generalissimo,"[1] yet no other word comes close to the reality of Washington's
position and the magnitude of his task.

This was no ordinary war and he was no ordinary commander. This
was a revolution, and the Washington here emerges as cunning and
manipulative, a subtle puppeteer among intimates and a master cajoler
of those he did not command—but all in the cause of rectitude and
moderation. He draped himself over the Revolution, tamped down its
fires, and became its embodiment, until he and it were nearly inter-
changeable. Perhaps because it all turned out so well and he was carved
into Mount Rushmore, the revolutionary context—with all its melodrama, paranoia, and treachery—has been de-emphasized. Still, the

Revolution was GW's milieu; he was at heart a soldier, as much ir-regular warrior as regular one. And from this perspective he looks different.

So does the American Revolution, particularly if you consider its timing. Superficially, the revolutionary process can be understood as steadily accelerating from the Stamp Act crisis in 1765 to the Declaration of Independence in 1776, propelled all the while by a series of maladroit British measures to squeeze more revenue out of the colonists, who inevitably rejected them on the grounds of their rights as Englishmen. All true, but different if you look in detail.

While resentment was plainly building, the pattern was for things to settle down in the colonies once each incendiary event burned itself to embers. George Washington was hardly alone in early 1774 thinking the mob had gone too far in tossing the East India Company's tea into Boston Harbor.[2]

Then, in the summer of that same year, events exploded. In roughly the time it took to adjourn the First Continental Congress and assemble the Second—a period of less than a year—a network of revolutionary cadres known simply as the Association effectively eliminated royal authority from all thirteen colonies. Everywhere the process appears to have been similar. First, Association members took over colonial militias and revolutionized them.[3] This gave them the muscle to suppress Loyalists with ominously named "Committees of Observation and Inspection" and to grab the reins of government. In what amounted to a simultaneous burst of political alchemy, Patriots dominated locally and created independent state legislatures out of colonial assemblies, and the transfer of authority was complete.[4]

By any measure it was a stunning development. There is no ultimate model for revolution, but few have proceeded with such lightning suddenness, so little bloodshed, and then locked itself in place with such success. "The Revolution was effected before the war commenced," John Adams explained to journalist Hezekiah Niles more than forty years later. "The Revolution was in the minds and hearts of the people. . . . This radical change in the principles, opinions, sentiments, and affections of the people was the real American Revolution."[5] It was an essential observation. The Revolution never could have proceeded at such a pace unless vast numbers across all thirteen colonies were not simply in favor of it, but fired up. What, then, was the source of the flame?

This revolution was driven by ideas, and they raced across the colonies like a firestorm. Fortunately, we know a good deal more about the intellectual origins of the American Revolution than we used to, thanks to the pioneering efforts of historians Bernard Bailyn and Gordon S. Wood a generation ago. Previously, the conceptual framework of revolution was thought to have been built upon the writings of philosophers such as Montesquieu and Locke, along with suitable additions from the ancients—thoughtful and high-toned to the core.

But when Bailyn and later Wood looked into the sources of what the colonists were actually reading, they found something entirely different and a great deal more ironic. The names that kept turning up were not philosophes; they were polemicists—radical Whig critics of the political system in England, most particularly of the fantastically successful regime of Robert Walpole.[6] It was their cries against the perceived undermining of local say in determining tax rates, trial by jury, and, in general, the basic rights of Englishmen. Empire cost money, and it was their fingers that pointed to the huge and ever-expanding national debt, the price and dangers of a growing standing army, and the legion of politically appointed placeholders it took to run the whole thing, all of it suffused in a general aura of corruption. Critically, the radicals wove all these accusatory strands into a seamless fabric of conspiracy, one aimed at establishing a tyranny and basically removing all the rights of Englishmen.[7]

This was, of course, the worst case. From another perspective, it can all be seen as the unavoidable price of political stability and economic progress, both of which were undeniable. The radical critique was read and gained some influence, but never enough to make a real difference in the go-along-to-get-along atmosphere of Restoration England.

But not in the fated thirteen colonies. Here the effect combined elements of a time bomb and a poison pill. Separated from the source by three thousand miles of Atlantic Ocean and often hundreds of miles of rough territory, here information carried a surcharge of rumor and exaggeration as it spread. Colonists, only half of them literate, heard what they wanted to hear. These were edgy and emotional people, living in an environment far less socially constrained than Great Britain's. Thirty-five years prior, a wave of religious enthusiasms, the Great Awakening, had swept across the colonies; now a new, political tide was building to towering proportions. The message received—the bill of attainder against the parliamentary hegemon—came through stripped to its essentials and rendered explosive by its ineluctable bottom line: After they have flooded the place with brother-in-law officials and Anglican priests, taxed us at their discretion, cowed us with their redcoats, and stripped us of all our commerce, they mean to enslave us.

That was the nub. In England slavery was basically a concept and a commercial activity, not something you lived with. In the colonies slaves were everywhere. The South was suffused with them; they would have been a frequent sight in the mid-Atlantic and all cities. In upper New England and along the frontier they were rare, but hardly unknown. Pretty much everybody had a visceral and existential sense of what it meant to be enslaved. For many it was even more personal, since they had arrived indentured and knew what it was like to have their freedom constrained. These were people primed to react to a certain kind of argument aimed at a certain kind of conclusion.

It was, in essence, a conspiracy theory, and that, in large part, was its power to galvanize people into action. As GW succinctly put it, the British "are endeavouring by every piece of Art & despotism to fix the Shackles of Slavery upon us."[8] It's everywhere in the sources. From the beginning, as far back as the Stamp Act crisis in 1765, protestors had accused Parliament of aiming to enslave them.[9] The story never changed, and in the summer of 1774, when word reached the colonies of the parliamentary response to the Boston Tea Party, the Coercive Acts (the name said it all) triggered the American Revolution and the governmental clean sweep.[10]

Now, reducing a sophisticated political critique and the basis of our constitutional history to a conspiracy theory might easily be viewed as simplistic, particularly by those predisposed to a more Olympian view of the American Revolution. But at this level of social arousal, thoughts and emotions do grow simple; people become credulous and impulsive. What was termed at the time "the Rage Militaire,"[11] the impulse that set militiamen from all over New England marching toward Boston, basically described their emotional state.

Yet three thousand miles east, the fact remained that Parliament, though not at this point well disposed toward the colonists, had absolutely no intention of enslaving them. This was undeniably delusional. Meanwhile, the remaining sliver attaching the colonists to England turned on an equally fantastic notion that George III was really on their side, and if only better informed, would put an end to the dastardly scheme pronto. Objectively speaking, it amounted to magical thinking.

Yet as a revolutionary mechanism, the conspiratorial mindset was an extraordinarily potent call to action. Plainly, one key to enlisting people to overthrow a standing regime is to convince them that they are being systematically disadvantaged by those in control. Generally, the more lurid the portrayal, the better. Once the conceptual framework is in place and a sufficient state of arousal is reached, incident has only to follow incident until a critical mass is reached. In most revolutions this takes place slowly, initially among tiny groups. In America it happened in a flash, backed by the great majority (roughly an 80–20 Patriot–Loyalist split),[12] in large part because the supporters and participants carried with them the notion that there was virtually no limit to the degradation their adversaries might inflict upon them.

British authorities, locked into an entirely different reality, were and remained clueless. Therefore, nearly everything they did from 1763 onward proved inappropriate and counterproductive, until, finally, things turned violent and all was lost.

This brings us to a second surprising departure from most military recounting of what took place—a perspective revealing that the British effort to crush the soon-to-be Glorious Cause was doomed from beginning to end. English armed forces never came close to winning, and never could.

To some degree this was simply a matter of scale, the conundrum of confronting a burgeoning population of two and a half million scattered across a band of territory nearly thirteen hundred miles long and three hundred miles wide. The futility of British military operations becomes starkly apparent when you realize that they can be largely summarized by the successive occupation of six cities (Boston, New York, Newport, Philadelphia, Savannah, and Charleston), the population of all likely to have not exceeded 110,000.[13] But this really only speaks to the magnitude of the problem.

In large part the British were defeated by the nature of the military instrument they applied, a classic eighteenth-century firefighting army, tethered by an elaborate logistics chain. It is a surprising fact that from beginning to end the British Army was almost exclusively supplied from across the Atlantic by sailboats.[14] This certainly speaks to their skill and determination, especially since one of George Washington's best tricks was making sure they were cut off from local supplies. But it also ensured that moving inland, to finally get a grip on this spacious revolution, remained problematic. Nor was this the kind of army to prudently let loose on the countryside to gather its own food— some would desert, and the rest could be expected to behave badly.

This begins to get to the heart of the matter. The men in such a fighting force had been subjected to a long, rigorous, and draconian training process aimed primarily at turning them into marching and loading automatons, conditioned to obey without question and to kill without thought or mercy. Having largely recruited from the hard-knock lower orders, this process left many brutalized, their moral compass reduced to what they could get away with when their officers weren't looking.

And the officers, in turn, made looking the other way a cornerstone of their vindictive agenda. It's safe to say that most British officers hated the American Revolution and everything it stood for; it's also important to add that they viewed its participants with studied disdain. The British officer class may have drawn on a slightly wider slice of society than its Continental European equivalents; but aristocrats and aristocrat wannabes set the tone, and in their eyes, these "Patriots" were, in the words of British secretary of state for the colonies George Germain, "country clowns"[15]—peasants who deserved to be taught a lesson in the grand tradition of rebellion suppression in Ireland and Scotland.

Parliamentary and ministerial debates over what to do about the fractious colonies featured a persistent theme: that of the rebellious child ruined by indulgence and the parent's duty to exert discipline.[16] In America, the British Army became the flail of that attitude. This was a fighting force that, against colonials, preferred bayonets to bullets. There were tactical reasons, but the psychological message of a slow, horrible death, after being stuck like a pincushion, should not be overlooked. With regularity, throughout the course of the war, this is exactly how many hundreds of Americans, attempting to surrender, met their end. Those who were taken prisoner were little better off; stuffed in fetid prison ships, over eight thousand were destined to die in captivity.[17] But it was hardly just combatants who suffered.

The arrival of redcoats was too often accompanied by the looting and burning of houses and other property, along with the physical abuse of citizens, especially women. While rape was likely to have been the most unreported of crimes, the evidence that remains indicates a consistent pattern from beginning to end. It's impossible to estimate how many women were assaulted, but Congress knew it was going on and even called for a report.[18]

All of this should not leave the impression of redcoats run rampant. The British Army in America was and remained a highly disciplined fighting force throughout. That's the point. Much of this was done with a wink and a nod. The officers knew what was going on; it was part of their punitive agenda. Many spoke about or at least alluded to it in their letters and diaries, couched in good grammar and elaborate justification. Nor was the magnitude of criminality that great, especially considered in light of what happened during the twentieth century. But whatever the context, dirty deeds reverberate, and those of the British were heard by Americans and used as prima facie evidence of their motives.

And this, as much as anything, kept the revolutionary fires burning. Most Americans remained safe and at home. But newspapers and pamphlets widely and luridly reported the stream of abuses as they transpired, and, in effect, the screams of every soldier bayoneted and women raped drove home the message "This is what is done to those without rights. This is what they have in store for us. Tyranny, utter degradation . . . slavery." As the war dragged on and grew more brutal,

British behavior only degenerated. So, in the face of a collapsing currency and all other manner of congressional mismanagement, the Revolution persisted, immunized, it seems, from any reconciliation by the acts of the British themselves.

But if the British had no chance of winning, George Washington's role obviously calls for some reevaluation, our third point of departure from most renditions of the Revolution. At heart, GW was a soldier; at least that's the conclusion of many who have studied him, including Martha. So, much of this will focus on his military exploits and evolution. The Glorious Cause would be resolved violently, and that ultimately was his role.

As with his earlier adventures along the frontier, a lot of the fighting involved irregular warfare; in fact, from the summer of 1778 to Yorktown it was almost all irregular warfare. Washington knew war at this level well and controlled it with the deftness and subtlety of a symphonic impresario.

His star-crossed career as architect and leader of the Continental Army remains important, but not so much in terms of whether he won or lost on the battlefield. The Continental Army was vital as a symbol of legitimacy, and it taught Washington much about the patriotism and possibilities of even the poorest and most transitory Americans, but it was hardly irreplaceable. Some have maintained—including Washington at his most depressed—that its destruction would have ended the Revolution. They were wrong. The British could have captured or scattered it, and it would have regenerated. This was true at the beginning of the war, and it was still true at the end. In 1780 in South Carolina the British managed to destroy two complete American armies, only to have a third arise under Nathanael Greene to torture them anew. It was like sowing dragon's teeth. Armies the Revolution could afford to lose; George Washington was another matter.

Biographer James Thomas Flexner memorably attached the label "indispensable man"[19] to GW's already storied list of descriptors. Looking at it from a perspective that emphasizes revolution, Flexner was close, but not quite on the mark. The American Revolution would have survived even the loss of George Washington. But it would have been a much worse revolution, quite possibly like Argentina's, where the inheritors of independence turned on each other, and the whole thing degenerated into decades of civil war. Instead, Washington lived and the Revolution thrived, guided always by his rectitude and moderation, but also his savvy, cunning, and, when needed, his ruthlessness. For no revolutionary leader lasts for long without the latter quality; it's inherently a treacherous environment.

Or not. It has been argued that in America's case the reason the revolutionaries seized power so swiftly was that, excepting royal officials, the emergent power structure was in most respects the same as the one it replaced—a kind of "meet the new boss, same as the old boss" approach. It's true in a sense. The colonists liked things the way they were; it was change in the form of British regulation and more systematic governance that they feared and ultimately demonized. Here lies the paradox of a moderate revolution: The radical Whig critique was filled with advice on the dangers of power and how it might be curbed—moderate stuff; but it came cloaked in fear and loathing, and that's how Americans reacted. And this was why the climate became and remained truly revolutionary.

Unlike in the Civil War, where enmity was essentially geographical, in revolutionary America anybody could be your enemy—a secret collaborator, an informant, a traitor, and, in certain areas where irregular warfare thrived, an arsonist, a rapist, a killer. This was Dangerland. As with all violent revolutionary environments, it was a psychological terrain suffused with paranoia. Fear can be a terrible enabler, and as the war dragged on, conduct plainly deteriorated; but, critically, it did not degenerate into mass slaughter.

Speaking from the perspective of the early twenty-first century— looking back over the revolutionary disasters of recent history—that looks impressive, especially when you consider what happened less than a decade later in France, when heads by the tens of thousands literally rolled. The argument here will be that the essential reason we avoided a similar fate can be summarized in two words: George Washington. Certainly the Founding Fathers, with the possible exception of Alexander Hamilton, were moderate men. But Washington held the sword. He decided who lived and died; only he could steer the Revolution away from a sea of blood. On these grounds alone it makes sense to study it through him—the medium of his life and the evolution of his character.

But that's not easy; it's never been easy. There is an elusive and contradictory quality to Washington, the contrast caught by the painter Gilbert Stuart between the stolid façade and the "strongest and most ungovernable passions" below.[20] In the revolutionary context, the mask of rectitude that he was forced to don became virtually indistinguishable from the real man. For GW to accomplish the herculean task of taming and guiding the Revolution away from his countrymen's worst instincts, the mask had to be as solid as Rushmore, which necessarily obscures the human being underneath.

But it also appears that he and those around him wanted it that way. It's been argued with some insight that George Washington was an invention; that from youth he made himself into what he wanted others to see.[21] Later it became a team effort as the image of Washington assumed paramount importance. It was in this spirit that Martha burned their personal correspondence.

Of course, there are plenty of his letters left, and they have never been more accessible. Thanks to a collaboration between the massive Washington Papers project at the University of Virginia and the National Archives' Founders Online program, over thirty thousand of his key letters are instantaneously available to anybody with an Internet connection.

Still, it hardly amounts to Washington revealed. There is a good deal to be learned. But frequently it has to be dredged up through a mass of obfuscation. A natural diplomat, he was almost never direct. Washington's instinct was always to get the point across without offense. He also liked to consider every option. So his sentences became syntactical roller coasters.

Being a man of action—a student of action, really, since basically he learned by doing—GW never spouted forth, Mao-like, anything resembling a theory of revolutionary warfare. Instead, you find a mass of requests and instructions that gradually can be assembled into an overall strategy: Keep the Continental Army alive. Enervate the British—bleed them through attrition, keep them away from local food supplies, never let them go inland, and always behave better than they do. That's about all you get from an innately tight-lipped generalissimo.

The letters raise other questions, as well as some similarly oblique conclusions. Was the voice here even Washington's? From the time he became commander in chief, GW relied on a series of "penmen," staff aides dedicated to transcribing his words and turning them into correspondence. Having an extraordinary eye for talent, especially young talent, Washington assembled a star-studded cast, including Alexander Hamilton, Joseph Reed, and John Laurens. All reached the stage when they could literally speak for Washington at the highest policy levels. Were the words then his or theirs? Not necessarily idle speculation, considering Hamilton's throwaway line that GW had served as "an Aegis very essential to me."[22]

He liked to work through others; he was a master at getting capable, willful people to do exactly what he wanted. All the better if they thought it was their own idea. The words are Washington's. Not only because the tone and circumlocution never change, but also because these men were overshadowed by George Washington; they were simply his mimics, though it never would have occurred to him to rub that in.

He was almost nauseatingly polite. In part this reflected his seamless personality, but it also should remind us that Washington was a man of the eighteenth century—that he and his equivalently decorous correspondents are separated from us by a vale of time. Just how far can be illustrated by his proclivity, when he really wanted to get people's attention, to hang somebody, usually an enlisted man. In part this was a matter of military convention, but upon reflection it's hard to avoid the conclusion that in George Washington's mind, all lives mattered, but some definitely mattered more than others, and always would—this at the head of a revolution dedicated to the idea that all men are created equal.

It's a paradox, but there is no turning Washington into anything resembling an egalitarian. He was and remained a self-conscious and unapologetic member of the gentry, and assumed that the imperviousness of the social structure would remain roughly as he had known it.

Unlike some of the more conservative Founding Fathers, Washington never doubted that the government arising from the Revolution had to rest upon popular sovereignty, nor did he object to the broad extension of the franchise in national elections.[23] But he assumed that franchise would be employed to elect people like him, the better sort. The openness of our current system, or for that matter, Jacksonian democracy, would have left him fuming and appalled.

The young, striving Washington, the one whose rise was based upon scaling Virginia's aristocracy and Britain's military, begot the man, who then never changed. This outlook separates us from him, but it's important to take into account, since it had a significant impact on the manner in which he waged war. It's important at the outset to realize that Washington and his closest military advisers were essentially amateurs. When they set about building the Continental Army, they applied the most familiar model, the British one; but they did so slavishly, as amateurs are wont to do. There were a few iconoclasts like Charles Lee, a former British officer, who questioned the need for a regular, or conventionally organized, army;[24] but Lee was also an eccentric misanthrope who missed its strategic and psychological necessity. The problem lay in adopting its aristocratic aura, the presumption of a tyranny of officers utterly dominating a brutalized rank and file. Washington was at the heart of this. His experience with the British Army during the French and Indian War had provided the template, and he pretty much applied it whole cloth.

It's clear from his writing that he viewed officers and common soldiers as almost two different species, one as social equals to be treated with deference and consideration, and the other as sort of human livestock. He would go to heroic measures to feed and clothe the soldiers, but believed they had to be coerced into doing what he wanted.

The results were not great. Soldiers in the Continental ranks resisted the training regimen, and consequently frequently scattered in battle. It was only after Baron Steuben arrived, ironically from the notoriously brutal Prussian army, and enlisted their pride and enthusiasm, that their combat skills and steadiness improved significantly.

Meanwhile, judged as a whole, the performance of the officer corps was never outstanding, and it's obvious from the sheer volume of his correspondence in their behalf that Washington spent too much of his energy focused on them. Life was tough for everybody in the Continental Army, but officers were a privileged minority. As time passed they grew more cranky and entitled, dueling with one another rather than the British, and eventually hatching a scheme that threatened the republican order. Washington slapped them down, but he didn't like doing it; they were his sort of people.

So were those he chose for command, not generally considered a superlative lot. Judging by the success of Nathanael Greene—who was quite capable, but also virtually Washington's alter ego—one might even say the more like His Excellency you were, the better you did. It's telling that one of his most trusted battlefield commanders had a plantation with slaves in New Jersey, and insisted on calling himself Lord Stirling (based on a shaky claim to a title in Scotland). Meanwhile, Washington was chronically forgiving of perceived social equals without obvious military talent—John Sullivan springs to mind—largely, it seems, because he felt comfortable with them.

Conversely, it caused him to undervalue a man who was arguably his most consistently lethal and innovative combatant, Daniel Morgan. He was a good old boy who called Washington "Old Horse" (not to his face), and a former teamster who once received four hundred lashes from the British for striking an officer.[25] Yet no matter how well he fought, nor how interesting his tactical solutions—he managed to create a uniquely adaptable force built around the long rifle—in Washington's eyes he would remain an illiterate and maybe a drunk.[26]

It's hard for us to reconcile these blind spots with his otherwise visionary leadership, but that's in part because he came from another age entirely, and in that respect he remains unknowable, his motives always slightly beyond us.

Finally, there is the matter of luck, the ultimate unfathomable. It would be imprudent to state flatly that George Washington was the luckiest human being who ever lived. But surely he remains at the pinnacle of good fortune. Some of this can be explained in simple terms: You make your own luck. GW was an exemplary person; it was natural that others treated him well and things broke his way.

But this is a tepid rendition of the fortunes of George, which regularly featured bullets and other heavy metal objects whizzing toward our hero at high subsonic speeds. Paying no mind to such things was certainly the way officers of the eighteenth century manifested courage, but Washington took it to a near suicidal level. He may have paid more attention to mosquitoes.

The price he paid for all of this bravado was exactly nothing, not so much as a single welt raised by a spent bullet. He remained impervious to harm. War is interesting in part because it is a game of chance and the stakes are so high. General Richard Montgomery, young and charismatic, had his face blown off by grapeshot at Quebec, just as the war was getting started.[27] Washington was no fool; he must have understood that the risks he assumed over and over made his own survival improbable. His reaction might be described as GW's sole and only religious revelation—that the power he alternately referred to as God, Heaven, Providence, or just Destiny was keeping him alive for bigger things—"protected me beyond all human expectation."[28] Certainly he was motivated by other impulses, but this thought had the majesty to keep him going when things really got grim.[29]

Still, that's not the most important role luck plays in Washington's legacy. The fact remains that his good luck is our good luck. This was a long and grinding revolution, packed with potential for internecine violence. Washington was the central bulwark holding that back. He was a soldier by trade; he took life when he had to and without any apparent remorse. But, with the exception of a single incident when he was barely out of adolescence—one that ended up starting the French and Indian War—he never presided over anything that could be called excessive killing. Washington's success at keeping the American Revolution from doing too much harm to itself was, arguably, key to facilitating the process by which the original radical Whig indictment was turned into the U.S. Constitution, and central to his epic first presidential term, leaving us with the best of starts nation-wise. "The moderation and virtue of a single character," Jefferson wrote, "probably prevented this revolution from being closed, as most others have been, by a subversion of that liberty it was intended to establish."[30]

Alternately, he could have met Montgomery's fate, the Revolution might have spun out of control, and we would have been left with a whirlwind of retribution. Societies do recover from truly bloody revolutions; France is an example. But it takes time and too often leads basically nowhere. It's been a century since the Bolshevik Revolution, and the government Russia has now, minus hereditary succession, looks much like what Russia had before. China is certainly richer now, but the system is probably best described as neo-dynastic.

The human urge for revenge is strong, and, at the very least, massive bloodshed militates against the kind of trust and compromise required to reach resolution and move on. Instead, the default position remains more violence, until a kind of sullen authoritarianism finally takes hold. In the meantime, the death toll has regularly reached into the millions, bloody spikes in an otherwise depressing bar chart. Obsessive death dealing has become almost emblematic of modern revolution.

FORTUNATELY, THERE REMAINS AN alternative revolutionary strain, brilliantly labeled "Velvet" in what is now the Czech Republic, but also the one that produced modern India, post-apartheid South Africa, and, most recently, perhaps a much-changed Myanmar/Burma. In each case the fate achieved has proved better than the fate predicted. And in each case the process was dominated by a towering individual, one critically dedicated to the proposition that it's a bad idea to start the new era with a bloodbath. To make this stick, Václav Havel, Mahatma Gandhi, and Nelson Mandela fashioned public masks of extraordinary virtue; they set a standard of behavior that forced followers to confront their own demons and beat them back. Their power, ultimately, was exerted through force of example. But it is very hard. Aung San Suu Kyi clung bravely to a similar profile, only to fail to speak out or prevent in any way the ethnic cleansing of Myanmar/Burma's Islamic minority, the Rohingya, demonstrating just how treacherous the path of revolutionary moderation remains, and that even the most celebrated revolutionaries can be turned away from the pursuit of justice.

George Washington was the archetype for this brand of leadership. Others like William of Orange may have hinted at such a figure, yet it's Washington's mask of rectitude that is best remembered, its success most salient. Viewed in this light, his stature only grows. But it also raises a number of interesting questions: not just how he managed to walk such a narrow path of moderation in the face of unrelenting temptation and difficulty, but how such a figure came to exist in the first place. Did George Washington really invent George Washington? Or did the trajectory of his life blast him into a largely predetermined revolutionary orbit? Or some of both? It's not just worth looking into further; it's a good story.

REVOLUTIONARY

# CHAPTER I

# The Gentrification of George

## 1

GEORGE WASHINGTON WAS BORN ON FEBRUARY 22, 1732, A TIME when the great British colonization project of the North American continent was really taking off—at least in terms of population and space occupied, if not exactly in imperial profits. The Washingtons characterized that fecundity and, especially, land hunger.

They were fourth-generation transplants, solid but definitely lower-rung members of the gentry class that ran things in Virginia, and by extension across the British Empire. The original American Washington, John, came over in 1657, and was sufficiently land hungry to be remembered by nearby Indians as "Caunotocarious," roughly translated as "devourer of Villages."[1]

GW's father, Augustine, was similarly inclined, remembered for his relentless land speculation, love of farming, and reproductive success, siring nine offspring, including one amazing genetic bull's-eye, George, the first son of his second wife, Mary Ball Washington.

There is no record of Augustine having had any inkling that he really nailed it with young George, or much of anything about their interaction.[2] His plain favorite and the apparent star of the family was George's half brother Lawrence, who was English educated, debonair, and soon to be a commissioned officer in the British Army. He must have seemed like a shimmering image of success to little GW, fourteen years his junior. And he was. For if it was George, not Lawrence, who was destined to prove the family's rocket to the top, it was the older brother, not the father, who undeniably acted as the first stage.

*Lawrence Washington: doomed to die young, yet not before pointing George toward the top.*

WIKIMEDIA COMMONS

In 1743, when he was eleven, everything changed for George Washington. In April, Augustine, apparently in good health, rode into a storm, sickened, and died, leaving Mary with six children to raise and a plantation, Ferry Farm, to run. The Washingtons were far from wealthy—their family assemblage of "plate" silver was worth only slightly more than £25.[3] By all accounts, this flinty, determined woman rose to the challenge, managing the 276 acres of Ferry Farm and its attendant slaves with an iron hand.[4]

By necessity, her oldest son, George, had to be part of the process, her right-hand man—at least in her eyes. As time passed, the responsibilities she placed on those slender but growing shoulders gradually evolved into a comprehensive plan for George's future: manage Ferry Farm and take care of her. George Washington, homeboy: The concept was as ridiculous as it sounds. But she held fast to it, boycotting his wedding and refusing to acknowledge his accomplishments in the French and Indian War and the American Revolution on the firm grounds that his time would have been better spent in her service.[5] For George, young or old, since he supported her for much of his life, Mary Washington emerges not as an idealized figure of Mom, but as a vindictive dependency, a quality to be avoided, especially in a mate.

On the other hand, Mary must have known her boy pretty well, or at least an early version of him. One reason she was so vociferous about his duties to her was likely an early recognition that he had no such intentions. What evidence there is indicates young George's eyes and ambitions were already locked on to something far above and beyond her and Ferry Farm. And this was not just an adolescent fantasy. It was a real possibility.

There had been a stunning turn for the better in the fortunes of the Washington clan, and in particular Lawrence's. When Britain and imperial rival Spain were drawn into conflict, today graphically remembered as the War of Jenkins' Ear, Lawrence had secured one of eighty-eight blank king's commissions and participated in the notoriously futile and disease-ridden siege of Cartagena, where malaria and yellow fever killed ten thousand of the fourteen thousand British.[6] By the time the fiasco was called off in 1742, Lawrence had distinguished himself in a skirmish and had had the good fortune to command marines kept in ships offshore, largely away from contagion. He returned to Virginia more or less a war hero; he would name Mount Vernon, which he owned before George, after his admiral, maybe to celebrate his good luck. And it only got better. For single Lawrence promptly struck the matrimonial jackpot.

In July 1743, three months after Augustine's death and just seven months after returning to Virginia, Lawrence married Anne Fairfax, daughter of Colonel William Fairfax, American agent for the vast

Virginia land-grant acreage of Thomas Fairfax, the sixth Baron Fairfax of Cameron.

It amounted to a whole lot of Fairfax. Lawrence had wed his way into one of approximately two hundred families who made up the titled nobility who largely controlled Britain and its empire, and in this case several million acres of Virginia. Exactly why the Fairfaxes so rapidly embraced Lawrence, given his relatively modest pedigree, has never really been explained, but the marriage seems to have worked well enough, and it certainly launched him into the absolute upper reaches of the Old Dominion's power structure. Meanwhile, he never forgot George.

He became, more or less, George's surrogate father; more, in that he generously opened the Fairfax path to potential power and influence, and less, in that he never sent his promising half brother to school in England as he had been sent, or even to William and Mary for college locally. Instead, the plan for George was a solid, though somewhat intermittent, preliminary education, emphasizing useful skills with numbers, basic literacy, and, it appears, character development.

For in 1745, George, now thirteen, jotted down a long series of social do's and don'ts, apparently dictated to him by his teacher, the Reverend Marye, from a French source, and labeled *The Rules of Civility and Decent Behavior in Company and Conversation.*[7] While there was nothing original here, the 110 precepts would have provided a useful guide to not appearing the buffoon in front of Fairfaxes; but also, looking back at them more than 250 years later, they seem to form a kind of verbal hologram of the person GW would become—infinitely polite, obsessed with the subtleties of rank and social distinction, dressed for success, utterly self-controlled, secretive, indirect, and ultimately strategic. Whether he ever took the list seriously is impossible to tell. But it did constitute a plan for the upwardly mobile, and ends on an interesting note: "Labour to keep alive in your breast that little spark of celestial fire called conscience."[8]

The next year Lawrence's real agenda for George was unveiled, and it was a good one. Apparently, through his connections with Admiral Edward Vernon, not to mention his newly elevated status, he had managed to secure a place for George as a midshipman aboard a British man-of-war, one anchored in Alexandria and ready to take him aboard. George promised "to be steady and follow your Advice,"[9] and started packing.

He had reason to be grateful. A successful military career as an officer was the most plausible avenue to the upper echelons of an otherwise tightly constricted British power structure. It was no guarantee, as England's military, on land and at sea, was still dominated in mind and spirit by aristocrats; but there was also no substitute for real talent at war, so they were always on the lookout for likely lads. Given George's capabilities, adaptability, and, of course, proverbial good luck, combined with Fairfax influence at suitable intervals, there is every reason to believe he would have moved smartly up the ranks . . . gone east rather than west, a life afloat rather than one planted on North American terra firma, Admiral George not Generalissimo George. It could have happened.

But it didn't. Mary Washington made sure of that. George was fourteen, an age appropriate to join the Royal Navy, but he remained a minor. She was his mother, and she was bound to prevail. Lawrence asked Colonel Fairfax to convince her that George would thrive at sea; instead she stalled until her half brother in England advised her that the Royal Navy would "Cut him & Slash him and use him like a Negro, or rather, like A Dog."[10] With that she put an end to young George's best shot at success, but she also inadvertently opened the way for the ground-based GW that thirteen rebelling colonies would one day need.

George's path turned out to be exactly the same as Lawrence's; it led through Belvoir, the home of Colonel William Fairfax and his son George William,[11] conveniently located just a few miles from Mount Vernon, where young GW was spending more time.

Likely to Lawrence's surprise and satisfaction, his brother slid effortlessly into the Fairfax social orbit. Though eight years his junior, GW managed to cultivate the intelligent but cringing George William, and the two rapidly became fast friends. The colonel himself was impressed and soon took a special interest in the boy. It's not surprising. Whether fortified or not by *The Rules of Civility*, GW was instinctively polite and perceptive, more likely than not to say and do the right thing. And then, of course, there was his presence.

George was growing up, filling out into an impressive young man. With the exception of those really bad teeth, Washington was as lucky in his body as he was in life. Though his head was small, his features were strong, pleasantly symmetrical, and almost inevitably looked up to. For even at sixteen he would have already towered over most adults, well on the way to a full stature of around six two.[12] His hands and feet were huge, his thighs already massive, the rest of him remaining lean but promising one monumental adult.

But he was not just big; the evidence indicates he was gifted with near perfect circuitry, the mind-body linkage that turns a rare few today into professional athletes. Throughout his life Washington amazed others with his physical grace and strength, exemplified by having thrown a stone to the top of Virginia's Natural Bridge, around 215 feet high. (It's interesting that while Jefferson celebrated the bridge with elegant prose in his *Notes on the State of Virginia*, Washington threw a rock at it.) Since there was no such thing as a late-innings fireballer in the eighteenth century, young George naturally focused his attention and coordination on the prince of sports among Britain's gentry and titled aristocrats: fox hunting. He would have turned heads immediately the moment he got on a horse. He was made to ride, the big hands and feet exerting absolute control, while the hefty thighs ensured vice-grip stability in the saddle. Likely, he would have flown to the head of the hunt, and, given the right mount, there were few obstacles he could not have cleared—a sight to behold, especially by the right people.

Things were changing rapidly among Fairfaxes. In 1745 the baron had obtained a bonanza of a court judgment that not only confirmed his much-disputed claim to the Northern Neck of Virginia, but extended it westward over the Blue Ridge into the Shenandoah Valley, a total of over five million acres.[13] The potential for rents, which were in the past trivial in Virginia, was suddenly enormous—by 1768 worth £4,000 a year, an income equal to that of the biggest landholders in England. Very plainly the Fairfax financial center of gravity was shifting dramatically westward, and it didn't take long for the baron to start taking his role as proprietor seriously and join the migration.

So it was that Thomas, Lord Fairfax, took up residence with his cousin's family at Belvoir in 1747, adding a whole lot of weight to the family presence and more interesting possibilities for George Washington. A grizzled former cavalry officer, the baron treated the American Fairfaxes, including Lawrence, with a combination of generosity and thuggish disdain. He has been described as a man consumed by three passions: an obsession with his own power, a hatred of women, and an unremitting desire to hunt foxes.[14] A personality profile doubtless rough on the residents of Belvoir, but foreordained to be impressed by GW. One look at him in vulpine pursuit, and he likely became a made man in the eyes of the Fairfax that really mattered.

This connection soon led to George's first big adventure. The proprietor wanted his acquisitions in the Shenandoah Valley exploited promptly. So in the spring of 1748 a surveying expedition was mounted over the Blue Ridge and into the wilderness. Included in the party of experienced surveyors were George William and the sixteen-year-old Washington, the youngest member. Still, he had an early interest in the subject and Lawrence had even obtained some professional instruction,[15] so GW, ever adaptable, made himself useful.

He kept a journal, giving us another glimpse of the early George. "Began my Journey in Company with George Fairfax Esqr."[16] read the first words of the first entry, revealing that along with work there was a social agenda. Most notably the expedition ran into a band of Indians, probably a war party since they had a fresh scalp. Everybody played to stereotype. "We had some Liquor with us of which we gave them Part it elevating there Spirits put them in the Humour of Dauncing of whom we had a War Daunce."[17] It could have been any dance and George wouldn't have known the difference. But it did mark his first exposure to the Native Americans who would play such a formative role in Washington's career as a warrior and would soon enough come to call him "Caunotocarious," like his great-grandfather.[18] But no sparks, other than those from the campfire, flew at this meeting.

More relevant to the business at hand, almost two weeks later, the Fairfax party, now in the deep wilderness, ran into "a great Company of People Men Women & Children that attended us through the Woods ... shewing there Antick tricks ... but when spoken to they speak all Dutch."[19] Washington may have made light of these German immigrants, but they constituted the competition—the bow wave of a tide of Mennonites and other Anabaptists who, having crossed Pennsylvania, were now intent on settling the Shenandoah Valley from the north. They considered the land free for the taking, not Fairfax's for the renting or purchase. George didn't seem concerned, though one day squatters would plague him.

Meanwhile, there is no sign that George William, the Fairfax on the scene, did much of anything constructive. When GW describes himself as part of the surveying team, his friend is never mentioned. But he is plainly not forgotten. As soon as the returning expedition reentered the zone of European settlement, young Fairfax had bolted to visit friends. GW remained with the work party, but upon learning George William was again in the vicinity, he immediately left to join him "at 1 Peter Casseys," where they slept. Upon return, exhausted and discovering short supplies, both took to their tent, sending the surveyors out plotting alone. The next morning, George and George William left the group entirely and headed home, arriving safely at Belvoir on April 13, 1748, just the two of them.[20]

This journey west, the first of five that would largely define Washington's initial military career, was likely the biggest event so far in George's short life. But in adolescence things happen fast. In December, Cupid struck without warning. George William married eighteen-year-old Sally Cary, the sophisticated and attractive daughter of a wealthy and prominent planter, and GW responded by falling in love with her, now the wife of his best friend.

We know this to be true because of a small series of mostly George-to-Sally letters, providing a unique glimpse into his emotional core.[21] Yet at the time his condition took hold, it would have become GW's darkest secret. The beginnings of a lifelong mask were already in place. George Washington was never a fool; he had to understand that the Fairfax connection was the key to his future. So he stifled his emotions, at least for a while, and got what he could.

George's career as a surveyor prospered. He specialized in working the frontier areas where he could find and later acquire the best bottom acreage. It didn't take long.[22] In three years, performing nearly two hundred surveys, he earned around £400 in fees, a substantial sum then in Virginia, especially for someone so young. More to the point, land-hungry George got his first real taste of real estate, acquiring 2,300 excellent acres of the baron's land in the Shenandoah Valley.[23] Things only got better.

Colonel Fairfax, with the proprietor's support, was pressuring the masters and president of the College of William and Mary to avail themselves of young George's services, and in July 1749 they accordingly appointed him official surveyor of recently established Culpeper County.[24] Quite a coup for a seventeen-year-old, yet it would soon

*Sarah Cary Fairfax: His heart belonged to Sally.*

WIKIMEDIA COMMONS

become apparent that George's true compass was pointed in an entirely different direction from what would one day be called suburban Washington. His career in surveying proved short, but the skills and knowledge of the frontier he acquired would soon prove crucial. Meanwhile, another crack was forming in the Fairfax bond, and all of this had to do with Lawrence.

2

Given George's physicality and ambition, it's easy to conclude that his role model was always Lawrence. If his half brother was but a minor war hero dependent on Fairfax largesse, this wouldn't have been apparent to a boy fourteen years younger in immediate need of a father figure. Lawrence, from the time he received his royal commission, through his short tenure as Virginia's adjutant general, always considered himself a military man at heart. He would have filled George's evolving consciousness with war stories, his own along with what history could provide from a growing library at Mount Vernon. Very probably he also exposed him to the rudiments of the profession, the nuts and bolts of soldiering. So the aspirational basis for a military career was there almost from the outset. And as fate would have it, George and Lawrence remained land speculators in an operation pointed toward international confrontation.

It all began in 1745 when the House of Burgesses granted the so-called Ohio Company, a group of acquisitive Virginians including Lawrence, two hundred thousand (later five hundred thousand) acres just south of present-day Pittsburgh, which even then was comfortably in Pennsylvania, making the grant at the outset dubious at best. The added fact that the land occupied one of the most sensitive border zones in the world—English, French, and Iroquois all disputing its possession—didn't keep the ball from rolling, and in 1749 the Ohio Company received a royal charter.[25] By 1751 it had planted a network of small forts and trading posts across the Ohio Valley, the superstructure for permanent settlement right in the face of the French and Indians. That year Lawrence rose to serve as the company's president—a personal triumph—but he had other concerns. Pulmonary tuberculosis, possibly picked up as far back as Cartagena, was eating up his lungs, and he was dying.

George Washington's early path, while brilliant, was also marked by acts of ingratitude, even betrayal, though this should not obscure his fundamental decency. He may have been a young man in a hurry, but his intentions were mostly good. Therefore, when the desperate state of Lawrence's health caused him to leave for Barbados, hoping a dramatic change of climate might lead to a cure, GW dropped everything and joined him aboard ship in September 1751, right in the middle of hurricane season.

The trip would do nothing for Lawrence's health, but it provided George with his only voyage outside of North America and several important life lessons. Given his efforts to enlist him in the navy, Lawrence likely was pleased when George took to seafaring with gusto, studying navigation and talking like a tar by the time they reached Barbados in early November.[26] A local merchant and planter whose sister was married to Colonel Fairfax promptly made the family linkup, though it soon proved virulent.

"This morning received a card from Major Clarke, welcoming us to Barbadoes, with an invitation to breakfast. . . . We went,—myself with some reluctance, as the smallpox was in his family."[27] He was right to worry; the soiree proved contagious, and within days George was "strongly attacked with the smallpox."[28]

This was obviously serious; the disease had a mortality rate of around a third for those of European origin. (It was much more lethal among Indians, who, lacking previous exposure, died by the millions.) But GW was unusually robust and his recovery proved rapid, leaving him with just a few shallow facial scars and a lifetime immunity, but also with the memory of how bad it felt to have smallpox. One day he would fight the Revolutionary War in the midst of a lingering smallpox epidemic; it does not seem coincidental that he quickly realized the danger to his army, and went to great lengths to have his troops inoculated.

Meanwhile, back in Barbados, after an initially favorable diagnosis, Lawrence only worsened, leaving a reinvigorated GW to soak up the environment and the social scene. His budding interest in things military led him to take notes on local fortifications and watch the British garrison drill. He attended a string of parties around the island, and besides a lot of dancing and dinners featuring pineapple and avocado, he discovered that slavery looked different here. The blacks outnumbered the whites by more than three to one, and their treatment was notoriously harsh. The planters were both utterly dependent on them and perpetually terrified of an uprising.[29] Washington says nothing in his diary about the brutality he might have observed, but he cannot have missed the paranoia of the place—a dystopian vision of where the peculiar institution might lead and quite possibly the initial template for his own unease with slavery.

For unknown reasons, George left Barbados early, sailing for home on December 19, 1751, leaving Lawrence behind. When he landed in Virginia he stopped by Williamsburg and immediately met with the recently installed lieutenant governor, Robert Dinwiddie.[30]

This was interesting. Dinwiddie was a veteran imperial official, a shrewd Scot with the "face of a longtime tax collector,"[31] taking the time to meet with someone barely out of his teens. Very possibly it had to do with the Ohio Company. Dinwiddie was a prime investor, and would take control of the operation in 1752. Trouble was brewing on the forks of the Ohio, and he may have discussed it with young Washington.

Another reason Dinwiddie became president of the Ohio Company was the demise of Lawrence. Lonely and miserable in Barbados, wanting one last glimpse of the Virginia countryside, Lawrence staggered home in early June with just enough energy to write his will, then died the next month at age thirty-four. Anne quickly remarried, and GW moved into Mount Vernon as manager and ultimately owner, when she and her only son passed nine years later.[32] The house overlooking the Potomac provided a secure perch and home base until the day he died. Washington's days of surveying were drawing to a close; he moved almost immediately into another void left by Lawrence, seeking to replace him as adjutant general.

This was a tall order. Until recently things had been peaceful along the frontier. As his health deteriorated, Lawrence could remain adju-

tant of the whole colony in large part because he had basically nothing
to do. His job was to raise volunteers for a militia that had deteriorated
into a social club. Now tensions out west were rising; troops might
really be needed. Dinwiddie and the burgesses reacted reasonably by
dividing the job into four geographic districts. Washington wanted the
Northern Neck, it being the closest to home, the richest, and the one
he considered the most prestigious—this from a twenty-year-old with
absolutely no military experience but plenty of chutzpah and connections.[33]

The prize went to a veteran of the Cartagena expedition. But Dinwiddie hardly stiffed Washington, giving him the Southern District,
which came with a £100 yearly stipend and the rank of major. Within
a few months, GW, instant officer, was exactly where he wanted to be,
installed on the Northern Neck, when the veteran resigned his post.[34]
All signs point to Robert Dinwiddie having been impressed from the
beginning: For such a young fellow George was exceptionally sober
and mature; he knew the frontier and was certainly up to its rigors; and
his legendary charisma and leadership skills were already apparent.
Most compelling, perhaps, the lieutenant governor would soon have
need of just such a person, for he was in the process of placing the
entire colony on the same collision course as the Ohio Company.

Dinwiddie had a strategic vision: Whoever controlled the confluence of the Ohio, where the Monongahela and Allegheny rivers meet,
controlled the entire valley. He had already sent scouts to the Forks of
the Ohio to site a fort, and armed construction parties hauling cannon
were sure to follow. The Ohio Company's royal charter was simply a
sheepskin for British expansion, and Dinwiddie in his dual role as
venture capitalist and imperial official personified the effort.

That the French would react was practically inevitable; they had
fought three major wars with England in the previous sixty years, and
they, too, were highly interested in expanding their North American
portfolio. So in June 1752, Canada's governor-general, the Marquis
Duquesne, sent a shot across Britain's bow, wrecking a large Ohio
Company trading post. And he had other plans. When spring arrived
in 1753, he dispatched a force of two thousand to build four large forts,
the southernmost being at the Forks, a chain that would not only link

the valley to Canada, but also to Louisiana by way of the Ohio and Mississippi rivers.[35]

The Indians were caught in the middle. They, too, were newcomers—a mixture of Delawares, Shawnees, and migrant Iroquois called Mingos—having moved into the depopulated valley at the beginning of the eighteenth century for the abundant game and as a refuge from not just the expansive Europeans, but also from the Six Nations of the Iroquois Confederation, who had spread out across present-day upstate New York and considered the Ohio Valley a fiefdom. A half century later this influence was far weaker, and the local tribes had leveraged their strategic location into a healthy trade in animal pelts with both the English and the French.[36] But for this to continue they had to keep European settlers at bay, which no longer appeared possible. They would have to make a choice to side with the French or the English, and the fact that the English usually arrived en masse, the French less so, stacked the deck.

Robert Dinwiddie wasn't the least intimidated. As the French forts crept southward until all that remained for them to build was the final link at the Forks of the Ohio, he monitored the situation and reported back to London. In late October 1753, the Crown's response arrived, a royal message that if any party, French or Indian, built a fort on Virginia territory, he, Dinwiddie, should first oblige them to leave in peace, and if that should fail, drive them out "by force of arms."[37] It was exactly what he wanted; all he needed now was a messenger.


# 3


He wasn't hard to find. Young George Washington, still just twenty-one when he heard the news, rode immediately to Williamsburg and "offered himself to go."[38] Dinwiddie showed no signs of surprise and just a week later formally handed Washington a commission and a precise set of mission instructions. He was to proceed, "with all convenient & possible Dispatch, to that Part, or Place, on the River Ohio, where the French have lately erected a Fort, or Forts." On his way he was to "address to the Half-King . . . & other the Sachems of the Six

Nations; acquainting them with Your Orders to visit & deliver my Letter to the French," and in the process win over "Sufficient Number of their Warriors to be Your Safeguard." Finally, having arrived among the French, GW was to "enquire diligently into the Numbers & Force of the French on the Ohio" to include details on the fortifications already erected.[39] The instant major was now expected to become an instant diplomat and spy.

Compounding the agenda was the terrain, and soon the weather. GW's errand into the wilderness involved a trek deep into the primordial forest with winter closing in; Mother Nature was perfectly capable of eating up those who chose such an itinerary, and spitting out only their bones. But not Washington's.

Instead, he staged the operation like a veteran, obtaining the best supplies available, remembering to include trade goods for the Indians; and critically, GW got the people he needed, the first glimpse of a lifelong talent. To address the language barrier he hired a trader named John Davidson as Indian translator and Jacob van Braam, a former Dutch lieutenant who was fluent in French and also a fencing master, to add a dash of self-improvement potential for GW.[40] But Van Braam proved far less instructive than Christopher Gist, a tough, experienced guide who knew the Indians and had led an expedition to the Forks the year before. Nearly fifty, Gist was deep-woods-wise, providing exactly the kind of maturity young Washington needed on what would prove a harrowing, life-threatening mission for both—but also the beginning of a continuing alliance with this Gist and later others. Finally, he took on four more backwoodsmen as "servitors," to round out the party at eight. All of this he accomplished in just two weeks.[41]

The little expedition left on November 15, 1753, and within nine days had reached Logstown, the Half-King's base of operations. He was away, but soon returned and collected what appeared to be "the Sachems of the Six Nations" for a powwow. The message Washington received over his six-day stay with the Indians was that the French were preparing to fight a prolonged campaign, and were pushing the Mingos, Delawares, and Iroquois hard to cooperate. This was basically true, but Washington also left Logstown with an exaggerated opinion of the Half-King, who had already taken to calling him "Caunotocarious" after his great-grandfather. Iroquois power was in decline here, and the Half-King was dangerously unstable, in the last stages of alcoholism. This would come to haunt Washington, but for the moment the Half-King offered himself and three chiefs as escorts, the "Safeguard" Dinwiddie had stipulated, so the first portion of the mission seemed complete.

His next objective was the French-controlled village of Venango, about sixty miles north of Logstown. A cold rain fell steadily as they pushed forward and arrived on December 4, only to find that the commander of the French garrison, a captain named Joncaire, had no authority to accept Dinwiddie's letter; for that, Washington would have to journey another forty miles north to the regional commander at Fort Le Boeuf. In the meantime, the French seemed friendly enough, offering an escort and inviting Washington to dinner. But soon he discovered Gallic treachery, recording in his diary—his first effort at intelligence reporting—that the wine "they dos'd themselves pretty plentifully . . . gave license to their Tongues" and they spoke of "their absolute Design to take Possession of the Ohio."[42] Joncaire also got the Indians drunk, and only Gist was able to persuade them to rejoin the party as they set off again.

Finally, on the twelfth of December, not having failed to include his dress uniform among the supplies, Major George Washington of Virginia formally presented himself to an even more officially garbed Jacques Legardeur de Saint-Pierre, Knight of St. Louis, and delivered what amounted to an ultimatum. The French officer did not react immediately, telling Washington he would have to convene a council of war to draft a reply, which would take several days. This left GW free to ramble in and through Fort Le Boeuf with Van Braam in tow, taking careful notes on all the military details Dinwiddie wanted. The last item on the agenda, the French reply, was presented to Washington on the evening of the fourteenth in the form of a sealed letter.[43] All that remained was to return home and deliver it to Dinwiddie. But getting out of the wilderness proved harder than getting in.

It was the middle of December; if Washington was going to get the letter back to Williamsburg before spring, his little team had to move fast. Without a military escort, they chose canoes to get them back to

Venango—six miserable days on dangerously swollen creeks. It only got worse. As they prepared to go inland on horseback, the Half-King apologized then abandoned them. He may have known something. Snow was starting to obscure the trails; the horses were underfed and sick enough for Washington to order everybody to dismount and walk. After three days the snow became deep enough to stop the horses entirely.

At this point George Washington did what he had on his first trip west with George William: He abandoned everything and everybody he considered superfluous, and proceeded with the only team member who could help him. Christopher Gist argued that GW had no idea what he was getting into, then loyally accompanied him when his warnings bounced off Washington.[44] There followed a bitter two-day slog through ice and snow to stumble upon, exhausted, Murdering Town, where they hired a shifty-eyed Indian guide, who turned out to be an appropriate ambassador for a place so named.

After some time, Gist began to realize the guide was leading them nowhere, except maybe into an ambush. Later, when they reached a meadow, the supposed guide raced ahead into a stand of woods. A shot rang out. Half asleep on his feet, George Washington looked up to see Gist racing toward the Indian before he could reload a second round. As he reached the two of them, Washington found Gist with his gun pointed at the miscreant's chest, ready to pull the trigger.[45] Quite unexpectedly, GW gasped out for Gist to hold his fire. Suspecting more mischief from Murdering Town colleagues, they held the Indian until nine at night, then let him go. It was a singular act of mercy under very bad conditions, perhaps another glimpse of George Washington's soul when everything else was stripped away.

Still, they were not out of the woods. Afraid the Indians were following, they walked all that night and most of the next day until they reached the Allegheny River, which stopped them cold. They had expected it to be frozen; instead it was flowing fast and deep. Their only choice was to build a raft, which "with but one poor Hatchet" took "a whole days Work." They launched the thing at sunset and were trying to pole across when they jammed into an ice floe, which, GW later reported, "Jirk'd me into 10 Feet Water, but I fortunately saved my Self by catching hold of one of the Raft Logs."[46] Still unable to get to the other side, Washington and Gist finally had to wade ashore in the freezing water to an island midstream. There they spent a dreadful night, but awoke to find the pack ice had formed a solid bridge to the far shore. Mercifully, they found their way to a trading post, and after a few days' rest were on the trail again on January 1, 1754.

Six days later, Gist left Washington, who was now on familiar territory and well mounted. GW pushed on toward Williamsburg, stopping not at Mount Vernon but Belvoir for a day, a respite he did not fail to report to Dinwiddie.[47] This was interesting, indicating that the Fairfaxes, the Ohio Company, and the provincial administration were basically one.

But it also spoke to a hidden agenda. George Washington arrived at Belvoir beat-up, but still in the bloom of young manhood, on the cusp of completing a very dangerous mission for the lieutenant governor. To Sally Fairfax he wouldn't have looked anything like the adolescent of five years past; he had developed into a presence, especially in comparison to the pleasant but unassuming George William. Likely young Washington was the man of the moment in all Fairfax eyes, but he must have relished Sally's praise most, for it was the basis for something that would begin to look like a relationship.

Meanwhile, on January 16, after a two-and-a-half-month trek, Washington entered the governor's mansion and delivered the letter (presumably still sealed, though its bellicose content would provide no surprises) into the hands of Robert Dinwiddie. It had been an amazing performance for someone not yet twenty-two. He had fulfilled to the letter Dinwiddie's every requirement, and had accomplished them with astonishing alacrity considering the weather and terrain. The fact that Washington had befriended exactly the wrong Indian wouldn't have been apparent to Dinwiddie, who'd recommended the Half-King in the first place. That GW had abandoned his companions would have only demonstrated a proper determination "to get back to make my report of my Proceeding to his Honour the Governor."[48] Likely George Washington left the mansion that day as Dinwiddie's secret weapon, a fellow who got things done. But if GW was thereby caught up in the tide of history, he would soon find himself way out over his head.

## 4

The belligerent tone of Saint-Pierre's reply, along with Washington's report of obvious French ambitions and penetration toward the Forks, was exactly the evidence Dinwiddie needed to persuade a reluctant House of Burgesses to fund his expeditionary force. In the end he squeezed out £10,000 to recruit three hundred volunteers, a pot he promptly sweetened with a promise of shares in two hundred thousand acres of Ohio Company land along the frontier. Dinwiddie probably had Washington in mind for command from the beginning, but his relative youth and GW's own reluctance[49] led to his appointment to lieutenant colonel, second to an older man, Joshua Fry, a fiftyish mathematics professor with some experience as an officer in the militia.

Still, Washington was the center of gravity from beginning to end. With reinforcements to follow, his immediate job was to train and equip an initial force, then march them immediately to the Forks, where a small advance party was already constructing a fort.[50] As he had on his previous assignment, he proved both a whirlwind of activity and a master of detail. He remembered to include Van Braam the translator, who showed up alive after GW abandoned him and became a lieutenant. He also gathered a credible team of other officers, including Cartagena veteran George Muse,[51] and two Scotch medical men, Adam Stephen and James Craik, with whom Washington would have very long-term relationships.

Together they drilled the men as best they could (GW found them "loose, Idle Persons," "selfwill'd," and "ungovnerable")[52] while he scrounged what passed for uniforms dyed appropriately red (Washington thought crimson would scare the Indians) and enough flintlocks to go around. Whatever else constituted training and preparation would have to wait. On April 2, 1754, just over a month after it had been funded, George Washington marched his little regiment of 159 men out of camp and headed toward the fated Forks.[53]

He might as well have been stepping off into the abyss. No doubt filled with self-confidence and perhaps even a glimmer of fortune's favor, GW was still utterly without operational military experience.

Beyond what he had picked up from Lawrence, other officers, and a few books, he knew nothing of war. Nevertheless, he was about to start one—an escapade from which he would be lucky to escape with his life.

The first indication of how badly the odds were stacked against him came about two weeks into the march, when GW, riding ahead, ran into members of the advance team on the trail. They told him that a fleet of canoes bearing a thousand French combatants had descended on the Forks. They had been given one hour to leave their mini-fortress, which, once evacuated, the French wrecked and began constructing their own, much bigger version. It's likely that Washington, in his hyper-motivated state, considered this some kind of act of war, overlooking the fact that the team had been let go without a scratch by Captain Claude Pierre Pécaudy de Contrecoeur, the Frenchman in charge. This also meant he was hugely outnumbered, but that didn't slow down GW.[54]

Instead, he got in touch with the Half-King. Calling himself Caunotocarious and claiming he was simply the advance element of a much larger force, Washington lobbied for support from the tribes the Indian supposedly represented. What he got was advice: If he and the English really wanted to show they were serious, Washington should advance to the Ohio Company storehouse at Redstone Creek about forty miles south of the Forks.

The Half-King might as well have read GW's amped-up mind. He was acting out the role of commander in chief, going around Dinwiddie and directly contacting the governors of Pennsylvania and Maryland, urging them to "rouse from the lethargy we have fallen into" and rescue "from the invasion of a usurping enemy, our Majesty's property, his dignity, and lands."[55] They passed, but Washington knew there were reinforcements coming—British regulars from South Carolina, an independent company from New York,[56] plus Joshua Fry with more Virginia volunteers—so he remained locked in attack mode.

Yet the route remained just as rugged as it was the previous winter, and now his force numbered in triple digits, so progress was slow. More than half of May was gone before they reached a soggy natural pasture called Great Meadows, still nearly thirty miles short of Redstone Creek. At this point the young commander received a message from the Half-King: "an acct of a French armey to meat Miger George Wassiontton . . . deising to stike the forist English they see."[57] GW finally took heed and decided to dig in, the beginnings of what he called Fort Necessity, a few muddy ditches and some overturned wagons dug into Great Meadows. The troops remained on alert and under arms; patrols were sent out; yet days passed and nothing happened.

Then on May 27, 1754, Christopher Gist walked into camp and announced that fifty French soldiers had just stopped by his cabin on the way to Redstone Creek, threatened to kill his cow and break "every Thing in the House," and were now headed toward Washington. Gist was right, but he, Washington, and the Half-King remained ignorant of French intentions.

The steady shift in tribal allegiance in a Gallic direction was providing the French with a significant intelligence advantage; Captain Contrecoeur knew exactly where Washington was, but Governor Duquesne had forbidden him from attacking unless provoked.[58] So he resorted to some provocation of his own, an equivalent to GW's earlier mission. He ordered his young subordinate Ensign Joseph Coulon de Jumonville to proceed with a detachment of troops and demand that Washington vacate French territory.

But as Jumonville moved through the blanket of woods toward Great Meadows, he was being watched by the young warriors the Half-King had left in the area, and when the troop bedded down, he sent one of them, presumably a fast one named Silver Heels, to tell George Washington. The news found GW in full bellicose mode, even at the risk of scattering his force. He had already sent out about half of his men looking for the French; now he left the Meadows at the head of another forty and on the heels of Silver Heels, who would lead him to the Half-King.

He found him at sunrise of the twenty-eighth with twelve warriors and plenty of bad intent. The French were nearby, camped in a rocky glen, still asleep. Opportunity knocked. Without stopping to consider the larger implications of an attack, or that these Indians represented another military reality entirely, George Washington "in conjuction with the Half King . . . formd a disposition to attack them on all sides, which we accordingly did and after an Engagement of abt 15 Minutes we killd 10, wounded one and took 21 Prisoner's, amongst those that were killd was monsieur De Jumonville the Commander"—his succinct version of what happened, sent to Dinwiddie the next day.[59] There was a lot more to it than that.

The evidence indicates that the French, finding themselves caught hopelessly in a crossfire, got off a few shots, then threw down their muskets and surrendered. As Washington's Virginians and the Indians closed in around them, the wounded Jumonville angrily protested that he was on a diplomatic mission. Washington wouldn't have understood the French, and it was abruptly cut short anyway. The Half-King, noting that "you are not yet dead, my father," split Jumonville's skull with his tomahawk, ripped out his brain and washed his hands with it.[60] Washington did nothing to prevent the murder, nor did he stop the Indians from scalping the dead and putting one of their heads on a stake. They all left the scene with the bodies unburied.

Back in Great Meadows with a chance to ponder the previous day's events, Washington showed no remorse, instead warning Dinwiddie about the "subtilty and cunning" of the survivors. "These Officers pretend they were coming on an Embassy, but the absurdity of this pretext is too glaring as your Honour will see." Then, concluding on a plucky note, GW informed him, "I shall expect every hour to be attackd and by unequal number's, which I must withstand."[61] Washington more famously captured his upbeat mood in a letter to his younger brother three days after the encounter: "I can with truth assure you, I heard Bulletts whistle and believe me there was something charming in the sound."[62]

No surprise, this line found a publisher, and that summer George II, who had seen lots of combat before monarchy, read it in *The London Magazine.* "He would not say so, if he had been used to hear many," he quipped.[63] Bon mot King, but more to the point was Horace Walpole, a generation the King's junior: "The volley fired by a young Virginian in the backwoods of America set the world on fire."[64] It was true; George Washington at age twenty-two had managed to start the Seven Years' War (it lasted more like nine), the first truly global conflict in human history. Of course, such impudence seldom goes unpunished.

Great Meadows was no place worth defending. He told Dinwiddie "we shall loose the Indians if we suffer ourselves to be drove Back,"[65] when in fact he had only the Half-King, who showed up with a few elderly tribesmen, assessed the situation, then departed to die a few months later of acute alcoholism.

But other reinforcements had started to arrive. In mid-June, George Muse brought two hundred Virginia volunteers and nine small swivel cannon, along with the news that Joshua Fry had fallen off his horse and was dead, leaving Washington definitively in charge, a full colonel by Dinwiddie's order.[66] A few days later, the promised one hundred British regulars from South Carolina marched into the meadows. At their head was Captain James Mackay, a royal officer with over fifteen years of experience and not happy at being commanded by a tyro. He took one look at Washington's defenses and set up a separate camp.[67] Fort Necessity—now a palisaded structure Washington had his men construct in back of the original ditching—was not only sited in a depression but also entirely too close to the surrounding woods. But that didn't seem important to GW; with almost four hundred troops behind him, he was ready to resume the offensive.

The concept hadn't changed much: fortify the Ohio Company's base at Redstone Creek, but now with swivel guns, which necessitated cutting a wider path. Mackay avoided committing his regulars, arguing over pay for such work but probably realizing how foolhardy the enterprise really was. The thrust was taking place in the face of consistent reporting that the French presence at the Forks was only growing stronger and would soon lead to an attack.

Washington soon began to realize how blind and vulnerable his force had become without Indians. When Mackay finally brought up the regulars, they agreed the time had come to withdraw, not just to Fort Necessity, but all the way back to the Ohio Company's base at Wills Creek on the Virginia-Maryland border.[68] Yet hauling the swivel guns slowed the retreat and exhausted the troops, so when they reached Great Meadows after three days, there was no going any further. They had only to await the attack.

It was already on the way, a force of six hundred tough, experienced French and Canadians, along with around one hundred Indians, all of them led by Captain Louis Coulon de Villiers, none other than Jumonville's older brother.[69] To keep him motivated, on the way to Great Meadows his troops discovered the mutilated and unburied victims of the earlier battle, including presumably the now brainless corpse of Jumonville.[70] If there was ever a recipe for revenge, this was it.

The French arrived at the meadows just before noon on July 3, 1754, eager for a firefight. They formed up, fired a volley, and then began moving toward Washington's men drawn up in front of their little fortress. George Muse and the Virginians bolted, and very soon Washington found himself caught in a deathtrap called Necessity. For instead of pursuing, the French filtered into the woods at a high point about sixty yards away and set up looking down from cover at the Popsicle-stick fortress. There remained only to shoot Brits in a barrel.

By late afternoon there were a hundred dead or wounded, then the skies opened up, soaking the men's powder and rendering their muskets useless. Few had bayonets, so there was no organizing a charge to escape. Washington's best option, at this grim moment, was to open some kegs of rum and feed them to his men against a very grim future.[71] From his perspective inside the fort's tiny, leaky shelter, annihilation must have seemed pretty much a sure thing, his own promising future cut short, a scalp for some Indian.

But then a miracle arrived. A French officer under a white flag came down to parley. Not wanting him to see how bad things were inside Fort Necessity, Washington sent Van Braam out to do the negotiating. He arrived back with amazingly good news. In return for surrendering the worthless fortress and all but one of the swivel guns, Washington's men would be granted the "honors of war": not made prisoner, but free to leave with their arms shouldered. Huddled around a single candle in the shelter with Mackay, GW listened as Van Braam translated the document's convoluted French, but the words *"l'assasinat du Sr de Jumonville"* probably did not register before he signed. War between England and France was now inevitable, but young Washington had just conceded bragging rights to Louis XV by admitting to the murder of a diplomatic emissary.

Compounding matters, the next day (unquestionably George Washington's worst July fourth) Coulon de Villiers demonstrated that his professionalism had limits, allowing the Indians to loot the defeated troops as they marched out of Great Meadows.[72] Beaten down and exhausted, they could barely make it three miles before they had to set up camp.[73] Here George Washington left them; once again choosing mission over minions, he raced ahead toward Williamsburg to deliver the grim news.

It must have been a miserable trip. He would ultimately shift the blame to the Half-King and Van Braam—the beginning of a lifetime habit when disaster struck—but the sting was still fresh, the sound of flying lead no longer "charming" but emblematic of defeat, being outmaneuvered and forced to surrender. His schemes to enlist Indian support had come to nothing; they all seemed aligned with the French. Just about everything had gone wrong.

But if George Washington expected a tongue lashing when he reported to Dinwiddie on July 17, he never got one. Likely he was reminded of an earlier warning against the advance to Redstone Creek,[74] but otherwise the canny Scot stood behind his protégé's conduct in defense of the Ohio Company agenda. Meanwhile, Colonel Fairfax was busy bending ears and twisting arms, describing Fort Necessity as a brave if futile gesture in the face of French aggression. In September, the House of Burgesses picked up the tune, singing the praises of Washington and several of the Fort Necessity officers "for their late gallant and brave Behavior in the Defense of their Country."[75]

But if Virginians insisted on putting a brave face on humiliation, others elsewhere were more candid. Governor Horatio Sharpe of Maryland attributed the reckless advance to a "pique" over rank between Washington and Mackay; the proprietor of Pennsylvania William Penn worried over GW's "imprudent conduct," while back in London Dinwiddie's titular boss, the governor of Virginia Lord Albemarle, attributed the loss to the colonials, who, though brave, were dismally ignorant of military affairs and required leadership by regular officers, not amateurs.[76] He may have known something.

In Williamsburg, Dinwiddie at first seemed eager to take up the sword, to stage a counterattack with Washington at its head. On August 1, 1754, he told him to bring the Virginia Regiment up to full strength and "immediately march over the Allegany Mountains, either to dispossess the French of their Fort, or build a Fort in a proper Place."[77]

But by October he had reversed himself and broken the regiment down into companies designated for garrison duties; he also decreed that in the future no provincial could hold a rank higher than captain. Quite possibly Dinwiddie realized something bigger was coming, but George Washington didn't think so, and resigned in a mood that approached petulance. "What did I get by this?" he complained to his younger brother Jack. "Why, after putting myself to a considerable expense in equipment and providing Necessarys for the Campaigne—I went out, was soundly beaten, lost them all—came in, and had my Commission taken from me."[78]

Narcissistically said, all about rank and status, but that didn't mean that he had soured on soldiering. If nothing else had gone right, young George Washington does seem to have found his calling at Fort Necessity. In mid-November he ended a long letter to planter William Fitzhugh explaining his resignation by stating flatly: "My inclinations are strongly bent to arms."[79] He would have ample opportunity to use them.

<h1 style="text-align:center">5</h1>

Imperial authorities in London were not about to take this drubbing in North America without responding. And they had good reason to be confident. For beneath everything lay some pretty definitive numbers. By mid-century the English colonies had reached a million and a half inhabitants, a number that was climbing fast, while the combined population of French Canada and Louisiana was just seventy thousand.[80] In the end, body weight was bound to prevail, especially when levered by the Royal Navy and its presumed ability to cut communications and reinforcement from France.

Bowing to that reality, the French basically assumed the strategic defensive, the Forks being the farthest south they ventured in significant numbers during the long and frustrating conflict—the Seven Years' War, known in America as the French and Indian War. Naturally enough, British military planners turned their attention there first, though they had other ventures in mind.

The Duke of Cumberland, who was the King's son and captain general of the army, had a four-pronged plan: a main expedition against the Forks, followed by subsequent thrusts against Nova Scotia, the forts at Niagara, and then Crown Point on Lake Champlain. Conceived to keep the French off-balance, ultimately driving them out of the entire Great Lakes basin, the plan may have briefed well but began so slowly that Governor Duquesne was actually able to release troops to reinforce the Forks and the now completed fortification bearing his name.[81]

Meanwhile, Cumberland picked one of his cronies, Major General Edward Braddock, to lead the first charge. He was a thirty-five-year veteran; but Braddock's specialty was training, not combat, plus he had never been outside of Europe, and had but the foggiest notion of North America's brutal geography.[82]

Together he and Cumberland put together the prospective force as if they were playing a board game. Since the main problem seemed to be the colonial volunteers' lack of military knowledge and experience, they chose professionals for the infantry component, but not combat-hardened veterans; instead they picked up two regiments of garrison troops, previously assigned to keep an eye on rambunctious Ireland.[83] Because Fort Duquesne was, after all, a fort, they presumed it would have to be pummeled by artillery. In reality, probably not, considering that it was constructed of tree trunks. They provided a lot more siege guns than they needed—a heavy metal proposition, especially if you had to drag them over mountain ranges and through primeval forests. But in London, hunched over a nice flat map, this must have seemed a perfectly appropriate force—two thousand men, three in every four of them regulars—on paper surely enough to turn this campaign into a promenade.[84]

The first components of the expedition sailed into Hampton Roads by February 1755, only seven months after Fort Necessity. But as Braddock reassembled his army through the spring, further padding it with independent companies from Virginia and elsewhere, he began to realize the magnitude of his military problems. Just to get the force in

motion demanded around 2,500 horses to pull the artillery, along with
the endless wagons full of supplies for the men, generating a column
that would eventually measure six miles long.[85] He was also learning
that beyond a certain point, there were no roads, only faint trails into
endless wilderness. Scotsman Braddock was a stubborn little bulldog
of a man, bent on accomplishing his mission, but he must have realized he needed local talent, someone with experience out past the Al-
leghenies. He didn't have to look very far, since George Washington
had already written him a welcoming note upon his safe arrival in
Hampton Roads.[86]

There ensued a period of courtship. Virginia's gentry were intensely
status conscious, and few things held more sway than military rank. So
when Washington lost his position as colonel he took it as a slur upon
his character. This was, perhaps, the beginning of a lifetime obsession
with rank that took too much of his time and energy. Plainly, he was
in a touchy mood. Earlier, when offered command of a company and
the chance to keep his title on an honorary basis, he replied: "You must
entertain a very contemptible opinion of my weakness, and believe me
to be more empty than the commission itself."[87]

The problem was not only that provincials couldn't be promoted
beyond captain; young Washington didn't seem to comprehend that
the rank of colonel usually came with a price tag of thousands of
pounds. Ultimately, Robert Orme, Braddock's suave chief of staff,
came up with a subtle marriage contract. Washington would have no
formal rank, but would be directly attached to the general as an aide-
de-camp—made a member of his military "family."[88]

This was significant. Washington told Orme, "I wish earnestly to
attain some knowledge of the Military Profession," and "families" were
the way it was done in eighteenth-century European armies—constant
contact with commanders, learning by osmosis through spirited conversation. Not everybody got this privilege; besides young aristocrats,
only those deemed comers were given the opportunity. Washington
understood. He told his brother Jack: "I have now a good opportunity,
and shall not neglect it, of forming an acquaintance which may be
serviceable hereafter, if I shall find it worth while pushing my Fortune
in the Military line."[89] This was an interesting addition, for however

strong his bent to arms, George Washington plainly had other irons in the fire.

Two weeks later he told Jack he was angling toward election to the House of Burgesses and instructed him how to prepare the ground.[90] His directions were classic Washington: Quietly canvass the local power brokers, and only if there is interest reveal his intentions. But first, it was necessary to clear it with the Fairfaxes—"as it is in their power to be very serviceable upon many occasion's to us as young beginner's"—in particular making sure that George William didn't want to stand for the same seat. (He did, and Washington backed off later that year.) Nor did he fail to note "to that Family I am under many obligation[s] particularly to the old Gentleman," from whom Washington, just the past week, had requested a loan of £40 or £50 for new horses.[91]

But all of this cautious deference and apparent gratitude has to be measured against another agenda entirely. Right around this time, apparently without George William's knowledge, GW was establishing a personal correspondence with Sally Fairfax, "embracing the earliest, and every opportunity, of writing to you."[92] Probably, this was some time in coming—there exists an earlier letter never sent along with some lovesick poetry[93]—but this was definitive. However innocent the content, the letters' existence mattered and still does. He must have known she wouldn't show them angrily to her husband. But this was still truly reckless behavior for a young man who valued his future, not to mention the ingratitude it implied. Thus far, Fairfax heft had made Washington; without it, his charmed existence might lose its charm. But he was in love, going to war, and about to join a new family.

All signs point to Washington having made a splash-free entry into Braddock's personal staff and among the larger pool of officers, networking seamlessly but ironically with a number fated to become outright enemies (Thomas Gage, whom he chased out of Boston) or treacherous friends (Charles Lee and Horatio Gates, both of whom worked to undermine his authority during the Revolution), but probably missing the presence of a young teamster named Daniel Morgan, who would receive four hundred lashes for striking an officer but survive to become among the best of his generals.

That aside, it was apparent that Washington was an impressive presence among what was ordinarily a very snobbish group. It helped that Braddock plainly liked him. He loved to argue and he found Washington an adroit and resourceful opponent, just the sort the army needed, promising him "preferment . . . agreeable to my wishes"[94] when the campaign was over—the regular commission that would forever fade into a mirage.

For his part, Washington seemed impressed with the inner workings of the British Army, carefully copying the daily general orders for future study;[95] but he also saw what was becoming glaringly apparent: This was no way to run a wilderness invasion.

Braddock, no doubt at the urging of Dinwiddie and the Virginians, had chosen Washington's route west through Great Meadows, but progress was ridiculously slow. Anchored to the massive artillery train, his road builders were making only around four miles a day, and it would plainly get worse when they hit the Allegheny range. At this rate they would never make Fort Duquesne before winter; instead they would find themselves stranded in the trackless forest.

The alternative—disengaging from all but a minimum of artillery and forging ahead with a flying column of infantry—was fairly obvious, and, according to Washington's recollection, it was his idea.[96] At any rate Braddock and his war council quickly embraced the plan, breaking off around 1,300 redcoats and sending them west, leaving the remainder to catch up later. Now moving much faster, they reached Great Meadows on June 25. But as they gazed on the unburied victims of Fort Necessity, some at least must have sensed another specter: Indians.

Braddock had only contempt for them. When Benjamin Franklin tried to warn him of their danger, he blithely replied: "These savages may be formidable to your raw American militia, but upon the kings regular and disciplined troops, sir, it is impossible they would make any impression."[97] Not surprisingly, when a delegation of chiefs probed him for his intentions in the Ohio Valley, he could not have been less diplomatic: "No savage should inherit the land."[98] With that, they left, taking with them any hope of Native American cooperation, along with most of the longest-ranging scouts.

This effectively rendered the army blind, or at least very nearsighted. Although the British proceeded cautiously from this point, sending out flanking parties to shield the main columns, this only extended their vision several hundred yards outward. Beyond that, there was no way of seeing what lay ahead. Meanwhile, the regular appearance of dead soldiers, killed and scalped the night before, made it ominously apparent that the Indians knew exactly where the British were.

GW was in no position to watch the situation unfold. He had come down with dysentery just as the flying column was taking off, forcing him to be carried by one of the wagons in the rear element. Now, aware that the main body was nearing Fort Duquesne and about to cross the Monongahela, Washington was sufficiently recovered to have himself strapped to a horse with a cushion on the saddle. Racing ahead to join the others, he reached them on July 8, 1755, and found everybody in an upbeat mood. Since their departure they had traversed over 120 miles of the dreaded wilderness with minimal losses, and now the quarry was within their grasp.[99] Unfortunately, they had the roles reversed.

The inmates of Fort Duquesne had originally contemplated Braddock's approach with foreboding, but by July 6 reinforcements from the French governor had brought the defenders' numbers up to a respectable total of six hundred. Almost simultaneously, another six hundred Indian warriors representing at least seven tribes allied to the French had gathered nearby and were spoiling for a fight. It was at this point that the fort's commander, Captain Contrecoeur, and his fervid young subordinate Daniel de Beaujeu decided that the best defense was now a good offense. On the morning of July 9, Beaujeu gathered up the Indians and about 250 French and Canadians and trotted out of camp, making a beeline for the British.

With his usual caution Braddock had crossed then recrossed the Monongahela to avoid an obvious ambush site, then proceeded slowly toward Fort Duquesne, taking care to send Thomas Gage with an advance party of 300 to probe out front. Washington was with Braddock and the main body when it happened—a sudden crescendo of shots, followed about five minutes later by a herd of terrified redcoats. The rout had begun.

As soon as Beaujeu had made contact with the British vanguard, the French and Indians ran into the woods, forming a semicircle around them. Then, from behind the trees, they started pouring accurate fire into the red mass, which soon broke and reeled backward. Beaujeu was killed in the first exchange, but it was a tactic that continued to work when they reached the main body of British. Completely surprised, and without combat experience to fall back on, Braddock's troops did practically everything wrong—failed to deploy properly, mowed down other redcoats with friendly fire, unleashed useless volleys at nothing in particular, and ultimately were "struck with such an inconceivable Panick, that nothing but confusion and disobedience of order's prevaild amongst them," Washington later wrote Dinwiddie.[100] Only the Virginia troops, many of them rangers,[101] reacted appropriately, breaking formation and running into the woods to fight on more even terms. But most were soon cut down in the crossfire between British and French.

Meanwhile, Braddock's officers tried desperately to restore order, but, being easy targets on horseback, they paid a terrible price, some sixty wounded or killed.[102] That was Braddock's fate; he rushed fearlessly into the maelstrom of fire only to be gunned down with shots to the shoulder and lung.

As one of his three aides, Washington had followed. Now, with his coat shredded from four near misses and the others shot off their horses, he rose to the occasion. The wounded and baggage abandoned, men running for their lives, what was left of military order at this point pretty much boiled down to George Washington. He had Braddock transferred to a litter and got him to the rear, in the process becoming a rallying point for the remnants back across the Monongahela. Fortunately, the Indians, now more interested in baggage and scalps, did not pursue. The mortally wounded Braddock next ordered Washington to reconnect with the army's trailing element, and order them forward to succor what was left of the broken force.

Washington rode into the gathering darkness, and never forgot "the shocking scenes which presented themselves in this Nights march. . . . The dead—the dying—the groans—lamentations- and crys along the Road of the wounded for help."[103] Except that he was well clear of the battlefield. What he remembered was the terrifying feedback of the day's horrors reverberating in his head. Finally, the next morning he made contact with the rear group and led them back to Christopher Gist's cabin, where they met up with the remnants. On July 11, they all began a slow retreat back—Washington and the volunteers to Virginia, and the regulars all the way to Philadelphia.[104]

Braddock died when they reached Great Meadows, and they buried him in an unmarked grave at Washington's suggestion. It was probably appropriate. His combat element, around 1,300 British and Americans, had suffered two-thirds casualties (the French reported twenty-three killed and sixteen wounded) and, like their commander, had basically disappeared.[105] Yet neither would be forgotten.

"The whole transaction gave us the first suspicion that our exalted ideas of the prowess of British regular troops had not been well founded,"[106] wrote Benjamin Franklin, giving vent to a myth that would imbed itself deep into the American Revolution.

# 6

Virginia's backcountry, not to mention Maryland's and Pennsylvania's, was now completely exposed and utterly vulnerable. Dinwiddie had to act fast and did. He used the emergency to reconsolidate the Virginia Regiment, and squeezed £40,000 from the burgesses to recruit, train, and equip 1,200 soldiers to man it. There doesn't seem to have been much question who would be the commander. The conduct of George Washington had emerged as about the only bright spot in the Braddock debacle. Though he remained just twenty-three, he was the closest thing to a war hero the colony possessed, and as such was designated colonel of the regiment and commander in chief of all of Virginia's forces in mid-August 1755.

It's notable that Washington used his enhanced reputation to bargain for power—authority to appoint his own officers and procure supplies independently—so that the emergent regiment would bear his personal stamp.[107] He was clear about wanting a multipurpose force, one capable of engaging Indians in irregular warfare, while at the same time retaining the capacity for conventional European firefighting. This was an ambitious agenda, though no one seems to have questioned his intentions, which were in fact complex.

Dinwiddie wanted regimental headquarters well forward at Fort Cumberland in Maryland, but Washington chose to hang back and base himself at Winchester, where he could concentrate on building the force to his own specifications. Recruitment proved problematic and desertions endemic, but gradually the motley group he gathered in camp began to look military. He ordered European uniforms for them and designed those of the officers, another manifestation of his life-long obsession with rank and military dress. He drilled them ferociously up to three times a day using the latest British military manuals, which he encouraged his officers to study until they were second nature.[108]

On top of that he piled instruction on woodland fighting, and stipulated "The Men are to be regularly practiced in Shooting at Targets,"[109] a heretical departure from European practice, where only volume of fire mattered. He even recruited Christopher Gist and made him a captain of a company to consist of "active Woodsmen."[110] Money and supplies were always short.[111] Washington kept insisting even harsher disciplinary measures be approved by Dinwiddie and the burgesses.[112] Indian warriors seemed to be lurking everywhere. But as winter neared, it was becoming apparent the boy wonder was creating a useful and uniquely flexible fighting force. Yet it was also becoming apparent that there were ulterior motives behind it.

That fall, GW had become involved in a dispute with an inexperienced captain, one John Dagworthy claiming command over all provincials at Fort Cumberland on the grounds that he held a royal commission and they didn't. This, of course, included the commander in chief of Virginia, who made no secret of his outrage. Dinwiddie and the burgesses took up his cause, calling for Governor William Shirley of Massachusetts, now acting head of His Majesty's Forces in North America, to settle the issue. But Washington had something more dramatic in mind.

Braddock's death had closed off his most direct avenue to a royal commission. And it's hard to believe that GW's insistence on twofold capabilities for the Virginia Regiment was not founded on that same pursuit. He was frank about it. From the beginning he wanted the regiment to be adopted by the British Army as a regular unit, and that meant commissions for its highest-ranking officers.

The Dagworthy dispute provided a pretext to take his case directly to Shirley in Boston, where justice would be done, or so it seemed in his overheated imagination. Dinwiddie did what he could to dampen Washington's enthusiasm, but ultimately approved the journey.[113]

He set off in fine style with two aides and a couple of slaves clad in elaborate livery featuring the Washington family crest. Braddock's defeat ensured that GW's name was known throughout the colonies, and he rode that repute northward, staging conspicuous arrivals and departures at Annapolis, Philadelphia, New York, and ultimately Boston, networking and using his social connections all the way, another preview of a lifelong preoccupation.[114] It was also a testimony to Washington's inflated sense of his own importance, something Governor Shirley soon punctured. He met with Washington, relieved him of some cash at cards, and even conceded that every provincial above captain outranked Dagworthy. But with regard to transforming the Virginia Regiment into a regular unit, or granting Washington and his subordinates royal commissions, he got nothing—the equivalent of a cold glass of water thrown in his face. He had only to return home and face the Indians.

In the spring of 1756, the Virginia frontier was lashed by a series of raids, culminating in the ambush of one of Washington's companies, killing Captain John Mercer and about a third of his men.[115] The entire Shenandoah Valley seemed at risk; settlers were terrified, some pulling up stakes and heading east. The strategic antidote prescribed by the authorities in Williamsburg amounted to constructing a chain of eighteen small fortresses along hundreds of miles of exposed frontier and calling out the militia.

Washington realized this meant atomizing the Virginia Regiment and turning his men into construction crews. "I look upon it that the protection of the Inhabitants, was the motive for ordering these Forts; and to lose them while we are at work, is perverting the intention."[116] The number of forts seems to have been whittled down to five, and that autumn Washington left Winchester for an inspection tour of the entire line, narrowly avoiding a deadly Indian ambush in the process. It was symptomatic; the raiders were easily bypassing the forts and striking where they wished. To compound matters there was continuing pressure from Dinwiddie to station what remained of the regiment's consolidated units at Fort Cumberland in Maryland, removing them farther from the Virginia frontier.

Washington wanted his troops concentrated where he could use them offensively to take the fight to the Indians, but this meant working behind Dinwiddie's back, enlisting the Fairfax connection and the burgesses to outflank him, and finally, in a "between us soldiers" letter to Lord Loudoun, the new North American commander in chief, denouncing them all as military incompetents.[117] Playing both ends against the middle is always tricky, and GW was still a novice at the game. Consequently, when Loudoun—the latest in what was proving to be a high turnover leadership—decided to hold a strategic summit in Philadelphia in February 1757, Washington saw another golden opportunity to win friends and influence the boss. Dinwiddie gave his reluctant permission to attend, and once again Washington hit the road.[118]

His results weren't any better—worse maybe. Always the social animal, he spent much of his time in Philadelphia connecting with key locals, gambling, dancing, and playing the role of eligible bachelor, but he had a definite agenda, and when Loudoun arrived he presented it: a "memorial" formally requesting his patronage in establishing the Virginia Regiment as a regular unit.[119] Also, Washington's experience along the frontier had convinced him that Fort Duquesne was the nerve center of the entire pattern of Indian raiding. It was imperative that another expedition be mounted to remove it; only then would the problem go away.

Loudoun saw things differently. He wanted an offensive aimed at the Great Lakes; after Braddock he had little appetite for another thrust at the Forks. In fact, he considered South Carolina to be in greater danger than Virginia, and therefore decided to divert several of the regiment's companies to that quarter. Otherwise, he had no interest in making the Virginia Regiment a regular unit nor in granting its officers royal commissions. The diversion would prove temporary, and the Virginia units' performance in South Carolina amazed even British officers on the scene,[120] but that would provide little solace for George Washington. He left the conference crestfallen, treated to another demonstration of the British military establishment's adamantine imperviousness.

By mid-1757, the war had gone badly in almost every quarter. On the Continent, England's ally Frederick the Great, sandwiched between France and Austria, seemed headed for certain defeat. Hanover had been virtually given up to the French. At sea, Admiral John Byng surrendered Minorca and ended up facing a firing squad. In India, with Calcutta's fall, the whole subcontinent seemed at risk of French conquest. And in North America, the cradle of the conflict, just about everything had ended in failure.

Besides the Braddock disaster, French general Louis-Joseph de Montcalm had driven the English out of Oswego on Lake Ontario, then forged on down Lake Champlain to take Fort William Henry (a surrender that led to massive atrocities).[121] Loudoun's campaign against Louisbourg on Cape Breton Island came to nothing, and he was soon recalled. Better days were coming, and better leadership in the person of William Pitt, but at the nadir it was tough to be optimistic.

Yet at this critical juncture, George Washington refused to give up; instead he faced down adversity and kept the Virginia Regiment alive, doing what it could to stem the violence on the frontier. Through sheer energy and administrative capacity, he managed to keep supplies flowing through the most tenuous of support structures.

But he had to have help; scattering his companies across the frontier demanded good subordinates. GW's personal magnetism made him a formidable team builder, and the officers of the Virginia Regiment were the first true manifestation of this talent. In addition to Christopher Gist, Adam Stephen (now his second-in-command), and James Craik, Washington added, among others, Hugh Mercer and Charles Scott—names that would follow him into the future, a small but ever growing band of brothers that prefaced a lifetime of such collection.

Washington was a rigorous and exacting taskmaster. He had to be; the regiment's mission was that demanding and diversified. While the

main role remained to protect the inhabitants "and keep them if possible easy and quiet," GW instructed his company commanders to
have at least one-third of the men constantly out scouting the wilderness.[122] Add to that his insistence that the regiment remain proficient
at mass maneuver, and you have a veritable three-ring circus of military missions. Judging by performance alone, Washington's leadership
team seems to have conscientiously addressed all aspects. He not only
got more out of them than might have been expected, he also inspired
their loyalty and affection. From beginning to end he was their guiding light.

Very likely the same could not be said for the regiment's rank and
filers. They were a bedraggled lot, dragooned into service from the
lower classes largely because they didn't have money to pay for an exception. On this rowdy bunch Washington was determined to impose
order, buying totally the eighteenth-century military maxim that "Discipline is the soul of an army,"[123] and inflicting it on his soldiers when-
ever he could. They responded by deserting in droves, sometimes
twenty or more a night.[124] Available manpower sank to as low as four
hundred, and was only around seven hundred in the early fall of 1757.[125]

Washington seemed to take desertions almost as a personal affront,
reacting with the conventional military solution for plugging force
leakage when he caught up with miscreants. "Your Honor will, I hope
excuse my hanging, instead of shooting them: It conveyed much more
terror to others; and it was for example sake, we did it."[126] He certainly
didn't hang all deserters, or even very many; but this statement epitomized Washington's psychology in dealing with common soldiers, one
he didn't begin questioning until Valley Forge, when he realized his
troops in all their misery were there by choice, not compulsion.

But Washington's view of war was hardly static; it was evolving fast,
morphing even. Personal experience was, as it always would be, his
primary instructor. His campaign against Indian depredations was
gaining traction; the Delawares and Shawnees were calling GW
"the Great Knife" and attributing most of their losses to him.[127] By the
summer of 1757 he was using Native Americans directly against the
French, with the Virginia Regiment's Lieutenant James Baker and a

party of Cherokees tracking and ambushing ten Gallic combatants a hundred miles beyond Fort Cumberland.[128] His scouting parties and small patrols were now routinely accompanied by Indian guides, and became equivalently timelier and less vulnerable.

There was something else: Constant exposure to the consequences of war was changing him. Besides connections, George Washington's upward path so far could be explained essentially by his capabilities and his ambition, driven toward the top, programmed for success. But there was another side to this young man, an empathetic one. As he came to know the victims, viewed too many times the sites of their suffering, he began to see himself as their champion, his duty to protect them. And when he found he couldn't, it brought forth an extraordinary confession to Dinwiddie: "Your Honor may see to what unhappy straits the distressed Inhabitants as well as I, am reduced. . . . But what can I do? If bleeding, dying! Would glut their insatiate revenge—I would be a willing offering to Savage Fury: and die by inches, to save a people! I see their situation, *know* their danger, and participate their *Sufferings* without having it in my power to give them further relief."[129] George Washington doesn't get much more abject, but it also reveals there was a lot going on beneath what would one day become an almost impenetrable façade.

In the fall of 1757, his unremitting exertions finally caught up with GW; the dysentery of the Braddock campaign returned, compounded by a racking cough that seemed to mark the onset of the tuberculosis that had finished Lawrence. As always, Dr. Craik was at his bedside, pronouncing "the whole mass of blood . . . corrupted"[130] and applying the usual solution. Having Craik as a lifelong physician was a lot like having a personal vampire: The bleeding left Washington so weak he could barely walk, and in that condition he was delivered back to Mount Vernon to occupy what he thought might be his deathbed.

It was at this point he wrote Sally Fairfax requesting jellies and tea, but implying a more personal response might be in order—a visit, some nursing even. The timing was certainly pregnant. Colonel Fairfax had died in September, and George William immediately departed for England to deal with the inheritance, leaving Sally alone at Belvoir.[131]

She had known George Washington for close to a decade, and carried on an intermittent personal correspondence with him for several years. She was probably lonely. A visit to a sick friend, even multiple visits, would not have seemed inappropriate.

What happened remains and always will remain a matter of speculation. But it's hard to deny that George's love for Sally was real, or that it provides one of the very few windows into this enigmatic man's deepest feelings. He was plainly at a crisis point; not only did he think he was dying, but all his efforts must have seemed in vain—only Sally, the love of his life, hovered before him. What a setup for yielding to temptation; it's worth considering what might have happened.

Nothing is one choice. There is no proof she actually visited him during this period. Even if she did, he was, after all, pretty sick. Both owed everything to the Fairfaxes, neither were fools, et cetera. Actually, this reasonable approach doesn't square with two of Washington's letters to Sally the following fall. Although the syntax remains convoluted, he speaks frankly in the tone of an embittered lover.[132] Flirtation is over. She certainly could have spurned his advances. But this, too, doesn't track well with their continuing friendship; a rejected Washington would have been a mortified Washington, one much more likely to have cut off all communication.

Which leaves the least plausible but most probable outcome: that they became lovers, if only briefly. George Washington lying in the arms of his best friend's wife—an intriguing circumstance to consider. Had he been a rake, he might have considered this a conquest. Yet GW was no libertine; this event more likely would be remembered as the greatest betrayal of his young life, a truly traumatic moment stretching out into weeks of anxiety over a possible pregnancy. That would have meant utter ruin, their only future being anonymity along the frontier. Neither had much to worry about; he was almost certainly sterile due to his bout with smallpox, and she'd had but a single child in her long marriage to George William. So nothing came of it, and in March 1758, a much-recovered GW was pronounced a healthy man by Virginia's most eminent physician. The crisis had passed, and it seems that George Washington emerged with a new lease on life, determined to take it in a different direction, certainly in terms of finding a mate.

7

For a while, though, he remained pointed at the Forks.

London was pursuing the war with new energy. Braddock's defeat had vaporized the Duke of Cumberland's influence, freeing the dynamic William Pitt, leading political light of the age, to devise his own plan—really a rigorous implementation of the original concept. The focus remained on North America. But now the Royal Navy would effectively sever supply and communications between France and Canada. Meanwhile, colonial cooperation would be enhanced through generosity, by opening the royal treasury and paying for the forces raised in America. Once again there would be simultaneous attacks on familiar targets, but this time the attacks really would be simultaneous. But most important for George Washington, besides Louisbourg and Fort Ticonderoga, Fort Duquesne was again targeted for a major expedition.

At the head of the force, slated to be twice the size of Braddock's, was another Scot with three decades of service experience. But Brigadier General John Forbes was a different breed. He had seen a lot of combat, and, working under Loudoun, had already spent time trying to adapt the British Army to wilderness fighting. Characteristically, Washington quickly tried to arrange an introduction, but Forbes already knew exactly who he was, requesting in late March 1758 that the Virginia Regiment be concentrated at Winchester under its colonel, whom he called "a good and knowing Officer in the Back Countries."[133]

Actually, Forbes didn't expect much of the regiment, which had recently been enlarged with Pitt-derived pounds. But, to his surprise, they showed up in new but very functional uniforms featuring leggings and hunting shirts, and then proceeded to demonstrate considerable expertise in precision drill.[134] This, combined with their experience as frontier fighters, exemplified what Forbes and his capable second-in-command, Colonel Henry Bouquet, had been trying to achieve with their own troops. Above all they wanted to avoid Braddock's fate. Young Washington had survived the experience and obviously had come up with some solutions, so suddenly he became their main source of advice on readying an appropriate force.

As a military planner, GW plainly now knew what was called for. First, he understood that Indians were critical, not only in terms of hiring friendly Cherokees as scouts but also in the larger sense as potential allies against the French. He had obviously turned around on the subject of red coats, and urged the adoption of what Forbes called "Indian dress" and, most important, tactics to match.[135] Pretty much all of this would be put into effect, plus the Virginia Regiment was integrated into the vanguard of the combat element, where their wilderness skills would be most telling. It must have seemed that George Washington's dream of having the regiment made a regular unit and himself the holder of a royal commission would surely follow. But, as usual, the situation was complicated.

In the eyes of both Forbes and Bouquet, GW's advice on preparing the force contrasted severely with his directions for getting it out to the Forks. Washington assumed they would take the old Ohio Company route from Virginia that Braddock had taken. But since the main elements of the army were located in Carlisle, Pennsylvania, Forbes's engineers and Bouquet favored cutting a new road straight west (roughly the course of the Pennsylvania Turnpike). Washington's reaction was apoplectic: "If Colo. Bouquet succeeds in this point with the General all is lost!—All is lost by Heavens!—our Enterprize Ruind."[136]

When Forbes did go in that direction, Washington persisted in sniping back to political allies in Virginia, calling the general an "evil genius" tied to Pennsylvania land interests, and repeatedly predicting disaster for the campaign. Forbes was already a sick man dying of stomach cancer; his sole interest, unlike that of his young colleague, was in the mission. He was also a patient and pragmatic man, and realized he needed the young American's skill set. So when Bouquet brought him proof of GW's double-dealing he replied that he "would consult Colonel Washington, although perhaps not follow his advice, as his behavior about the roads, was no ways like a soldier."[137]

So despite tailoring his force to Washington's specifications, Forbes's pace was far slower than the Virginian wanted. GW blamed it on the necessity of cutting a new road, but in reality it was calculated. Forbes's plan of attack was based on short supply lines between a series of carefully fortified bases. Should disaster strike, the army would always have shelter nearby, but these took time to construct. There was another side to his studied procrastination, as well—one Washington didn't fully understand: Things were changing in the forest.

The Royal Navy's success at rupturing the Atlantic link between France and Canada quickly left the French unable to supply allied Indians with the guns and trade goods necessary to keep them happy and fighting. Tribes were already feeling the costs of the war, and now the benefits were dwindling to nothing. Sensing the timing was ripe, Forbes, with the help of Quaker and Moravian missionaries, managed to gather representatives of the Ohio tribes, the Delaware, and the Iroquois to a great conference at Easton, Pennsylvania, which resulted in the signing of a peace treaty on October 26, 1758.[138] That accomplished, Forbes made sure the word spread quickly, dispatching scouts to the surrounding Native American villages: "The English are no longer your enemies." Now there remained only the French and their most stalwart Indians at Fort Duquesne.

They proved a plucky, frustrating bunch. By the second week in September, Bouquet was in the midst of constructing Fort Ligonier at Loyalhanna—still a considerable distance from the objective—when scouts reported that French activity in the forest had virtually ceased. An ambitious major, James Grant, offered to lead a reconnaissance in force—450 regulars and 350 provincials, including 150 members of the Virginia Regiment—in the direction of the Forks, and Bouquet unwisely approved. What Grant did was march his force right up to Fort Duquesne at dawn, then had his drummers beat out reveille.[139] Appropriately aroused, their adversaries promptly inflicted a mini-Braddock upon them. Using Indian tactics, they poured fire into the regulars until they broke, with only the steadfast resistance of the Virginians preventing an utter rout. But the cost was high; Grant was captured sitting on a log in despair after more than three hundred of his men, including sixty-two Virginians, had been killed.

Seeking to capitalize on their coup, the French staged raids of their own on Fort Ligonier on October 12, and again exactly one month later. In the latter instance, Forbes, who was now on-site though he had to be carried, ordered Washington forward with the Virginia Regiment to intercept. In the confusion that followed, the French ran, leaving the Virginians engaged in what amounted to a friendly firefight. Exactly who caused what has never been determined, but Washington remembered it as one of the most dangerous incidents in a life full of bullets, riding between his men, knocking their leveled muskets up with his sword.[140] By the time the firing stopped, fourteen lay dead and another twenty-six wounded.

But this time, the day's losses were compensated by an intelligence bonanza: Three prisoners with intimate knowledge of Fort Duquesne admitted, upon interrogation, that the place was undermanned, Indians were leaving, and the commander was even contemplating abandonment.[141] Forbes's reaction showed why he had been chosen to avenge Braddock; he saw his chance and took it. He put together a strike force of 2,500 picked men divided into three brigades, with Washington at the head of one of them, and set them loose on Fort Duquesne. Ten days later, just a few miles short of the target, troops heard an explosive rumble. That night, Indian scouts reported seeing a great cloud of smoke hanging over the Forks. When they arrived the next morning, November 25, 1758, the source became evident; the French had blown up the fort and were gone. All that remained was a smoking ruin, soon to be rebuilt and appropriately christened Fort Pitt . . . ultimately Pittsburgh.

For George Washington it constituted an ironic end to the first chapter of his military career, a sort of martial Groundhog Day, prefacing the Revolution that would see him obsessing on another target, Manhattan Island, only to arrive victorious without a shot being fired. For now, though, it plainly marked a turn toward a more peaceful and prosperous future for our hero. The frontier was safe, Virginia's role in the French and Indian War was effectively over, and the finishing touches on the gentrification of George were about to be applied.

That winter, much to the disappointment of the Virginia Regiment's officers, he resigned his command. The grateful inhabitants of the Shenandoah Valley, specifically Frederick County, had elected him to the House of Burgesses, and he would soon take his seat. As the year turned, on January 6, 1759, George Washington married Martha Custis, the richest widow in the Old Dominion, becoming, it seemed, a man in full.

# CHAPTER 2

# Living Large

1

S HE COMPLETED HIM. THE MARITAL UNION OF GEORGE WASH-
ington and Martha Custis was arguably the most successful and
consequential in American history. They eventually became the First
Couple, establishing a standard of domestic happiness and utility that
remained unquestioned until the mid-twentieth century. It was much
more of a true partnership than was obvious on the surface. But even
if she had been simply a hell of a helpmate, she would have remained
vital to George Washington's all-important revolutionary image of decency and self-control. His marriage to Martha enabled him to finally
become the man America needed and we all know. The opaque mask
of goodness snapped into place.

Because of its importance, it's worth stopping to consider the nature of the match, or at least what we know of it, given that she burned
their letters. She was unlike, maybe the opposite of, the two women he
first loved: Mom, the ever dependent; and Sally, who could only lead
to self-destruction. Martha could take care of herself.

Her sheer wealth (seventeen thousand acres, three hundred slaves,
a townhouse in Williamsburg—all of it assessed at £23,000, or about
$6 million today) is frequently enumerated as having launched George
Washington into the stratosphere of big-time Virginia planters.[1] But
Martha's mega-dowry also brought Washington independence both

tangible and psychological; for the first time an intimate relationship with a woman was not a drag but a boost. She even came with an instant family, Jacky (four) and Patsy (two) from her previous marriage, which was significant—GW was very likely sterile. Sadly, both children were destined to be short-lived, but even this would eventually work to Washington's advantage, since he could never be accused of wanting to found a dynasty. In the meantime, he settled into the family circle with obvious contentment. Martha was fiercely protective of the children, and GW always treated them with deference—this despite Jacky being clearly on the road to rake-hood. But otherwise the marriage suited him.

*Martha Washington:
center of his
domestic universe.*

GILBERT STUART/
LIBRARY OF
CONGRESS

Barely five feet tall with a plump, round face and large, wide-set eyes, she was more pleasant than attractive. Nor was Martha demonstrative, or known for her wit; "a quiet soul," GW described her.[2] Yet her genius was with people. Down-to-earth and unpretentious, she was open and friendly to all, no matter how revered she became. Washington loved to entertain, and she was always at his side, his never-failing bridge to outsiders. Remarkably, in her long life and countless acquaintances she doesn't seem to have accumulated any enemies, or at least none who were willing to put it into writing. There was another side to Martha, the side that kept Mount Vernon functioning when he was away at war, the side that continued trudging north to be with her husband when the armies went into winter hibernation. It's really hard to imagine Sally Fairfax at Valley Forge. But Martha, like her husband, was a bad-weather animal.

There are certainly mysteries that hang about their marriage, but nobody denies that GW and Martha achieved true intimacy. Contemporaries recognized it instantly. She was his ultimate ally and confessor, his last emotional redoubt. They were welded eventually nearly into one being, to the point that Washington plainly felt incomplete without her.

Since in human welding the heat agent is generally sex, it's reasonable to assume that part of this was because he enjoyed sleeping with her. He stocked up on Spanish fly for the wedding, and the couple's library included Daniel Defoe's *Conjugal Lewdness; or, Matrimonial Whoredom,*[3] so it's pretty hard to believe that their childlessness was due to lack of trying. George Washington gives every impression of having been a lusty guy, and he remained flirtatious throughout his life. Yet no one has ever made a credible case that he was ever unfaithful to Martha. Still, he described the relationship to one of the women he did flirt with, Eliza Powel, as "more fraught with expressions of friendship, than of *enamoured love.*"[4] He was sixty-five at the time, but it also hints at something more basic.

His heart belonged to Sally. She remained the great passion of his life. We know this because, a year and a half before he died, GW wrote to tell her that the events of his stupendous career had not "been able to eradicate from my mind, the recollection of those happy moments—the happiest of my life—which I have enjoyed in your company."[5] Had the relationship been consummated she would have known exactly which moments he was talking about. Either way, he carried the torch for Sally virtually to the grave.

This is important, because right around the time he gave up on Sally and married Martha, Washington changed significantly. From then on his self-control became extraordinary, virtually impenetrable.

It's not unreasonable to speculate that his marriage and subsequent sexual self-restraint became symbolic buttresses of his larger moderation—that doing the right thing here provided not just a shield, but an emotional guide extendable to the realm of politics and war.

Few things come without cost. Though the psychology remains controversial, it's pretty clear that frustration can lead to deep and continuing anger. Contemporaries besides Gilbert Stuart certainly noticed there was a lot going on beneath George Washington's placid façade. "Yet those who have seen him strongly moved," attested his friend Gouverneur Morris, "will bear witness that his wrath was terrible. They have seen, boiling in his bosom, passion almost too mighty for man."[6] How much and how potent GW's most intimate frustrations may have been in stoking his inner fires is difficult to tell. But the anger itself is plainly there and grows continuously during his life as a planter.

Revolution feeds on rage. Being merely miffed does not cause people to do all the crazy things involved in insurrection. Washington had a gargantuan capacity to hold a grudge, one of the key things that kept him going until Yorktown. Therefore, it's important to our story to see how it developed.

Whatever the role his love life may have played, it was at least diffuse. From this point the vector of Washington's rage pointed in a specific direction, toward the source of all manna: Great Britain.

His new career certainly had its advantages, but Washington from adolescence thought of himself as a soldier. He had emerged as one of the heroes of the French and Indian War, probably the most conspicuous native-born provincial, yet somehow a commission in the British Army, like the one that fell effortlessly into Lawrence's hands, had eluded him.[7] He refused to concede that commissions were basically commodities, normally bought and sold, or that simple bad luck had a lot to do with his failure to get one—both Braddock and Forbes, who could have fixed things, had died.

Instead, he concluded that the system was rigged against provincials like him, which of course it was, but less consciously so than he thought. In fact, it was rigged against pretty much everybody except those who ran it. Still, Washington's courage and leadership talents were obvious to many of the British officers who served with him; he was exactly the type the military was supposed to scoop up. This snub hit him directly in the self-identity, and he was the wrong man to disrespect. From this point he took almost everything personally, every insult another step in a conspiracy against not just America, but against George Washington.[8]

## 2

All was not fulmination. During the first decade of his marriage, GW devoted much of his energy to simply having a good time, and, in the grand Virginia planter tradition, living large. As usual, the foxes suffered, with Washington hunting them as many as forty-nine days a year.[9] He also attended balls and horse races, and he gambled regularly. But mostly he and Martha were prodigious hosts, estimated to have entertained around two thousand guests during the seven years preceding the Revolution.[10] That was obviously expensive, but not nearly in line with the estimated equivalent of $2 million to $3 million they blew through during just the first half of the 1760s.[11] Like so many Americans who would follow, George and Martha were addicted to stuff.

So were the other big-time Virginia planters, locked in exactly the pattern of competitive "conspicuous consumption" Thorstein Veblen described with devastating glee a century and a half later.[12] The key to everything was tobacco, which is about all they grew—much to the detriment of the soil, which largely explains their land hunger. While small growers generally disposed of their crop locally, Virginia's sotweed elite typically sold theirs by consignment through mercantile houses in England. The houses were closer to the smokers, so theoretically able to get the best price; but, more important, they offered access to a staggering variety of consumer goods, most notably the latest fashions from London. And they were willing to extend credit, lots of it. It was a rapturous combination, nearly impossible to resist for provincials starved for stuff, but many awoke later to find themselves ruinously in debt.

Washington's experience was almost archetypical. Anticipating his future countrymen's epic yen for floor space, GW repeatedly enlarged Mount Vernon, transforming it steadily from an oversized cottage to a stately mansion equipped with pediments, columns, and a cupola.[13] He scarfed up land, more than doubling his holdings in the area, from around 3,000 to 6,500 acres. His slave population also more than doubled.[14] All this expansion, all of this large living, depended on products generated an ocean away, paid for with tobacco, or with the promise of more tobacco.

His agent was Robert Cary, head of one of London's biggest and most respected mercantile houses. Reading through the invoices he sent the Virginian over the years is likely to surprise even the most product-glutted consumer today with the range of consumer goods Cary and his people were able to assemble and ship—the fruits of a gathering industrial revolution. Basically all the fasteners and specialized building materials required for the multiple enlargements of Mount Vernon, all the metallic agricultural implements, all household goods and furnishings, all medicines, all fine clothing, all spirits, and so forth—virtually every amenity that the eighteenth century considered necessary for good living—Robert Cary dutifully delivered to his big-spending client.

George Washington showed no gratitude whatsoever. Rather, he gave every impression in his correspondence of a man being serially shortchanged—bombarded with inferior products at high cost and then given inconceivably low prices for his top-quality tobacco.[15]

The bickering was epitomized by Washington's dissatisfaction with his flashiest purchase, sort of an eighteenth-century Bentley: "a new handsome Chariot, made of the best Materials, green Morocco Leather trimmed with Cuffey Lace . . . Plate Glass diamd cut, . . . the Body & Carridge, Whls paint a glazd green; all the framd Work of Body gilt . . . Iron Axletree . . . Patent worm Springs wt. brass Sockets"—all that and more, as described by Cary.[16] Without considering the differences between the streets of London and the rural roads of Virginia, Washington reported it a piece of junk: "I mean the Chariot . . . made of wood so exceedingly Green that the Pannels slipd out of the Moudlings before it was two Months in use—Split from one end to the other. . . . I expect very little further Service from it with all the repairs I can bestow."[17] It sounds like two different carriages.

His tone was typical of the correspondence, almost unfailingly testy and sarcastic, and then bewildered when he learned in the spring of 1764 that his balance was nearly £2,000 pounds (approximately $360,000 today) in arrears to Cary.[18] Like other members of Virginia's elite, Washington felt the shackles of debt and foresaw something that looked like slavery. One by one Chesapeake planters were concluding that tobacco was their overseer, and the only escape was radical change.[19] George Washington was among the first to make the break and may have been the most resourceful.

Beginning in 1766 he dropped tobacco as a cash crop, and began growing mainly wheat, which he ground in a mill he had his slaves construct, and then sold locally. He also sent his slaves out on the Potomac to net the copious herring and shad to be dried and turned into fish flour. Eventually he bought an oceangoing transport—calling it *The Farmer*—and marketed his grain and fish products as far as Portugal. Meanwhile, at Mount Vernon, he systematized spinning and weaving, and generated the capacity to clothe his own workers.[20] Others adopted similar strategies, but few pursued them as relentlessly as GW, and by the early 1770s he was almost free of debt.[21]

Washington's climb out from under his own obligations had to have sharpened his perception of the British mercantile system and the manner in which it discouraged local, or at least American, product sourcing, as well as the morass of rules and fees involved in trade even between the colonies, not to mention with the Caribbean or mainland Europe—all of it amounting to another set of pitfalls in his rapidly changing psychological landscape.

Turning the tables on his creditors did not leave GW feeling liberated; instead, he came to view every new rule or attempt to raise revenue on the part of Great Britain as a new cord in the Gulliverian web calculated to tie the colonies down and render them helpless and enslaved. And he was far from alone; soon enough most Americans would see it exactly that way. But they were provincials, and this was tantamount to viewing England from the wrong end of a telescope. Certainly the metropolitan elite wanted to squeeze more revenue out of the colonies, use them to keep the standing army up to strength, and shape them according to their own strategic needs, but enslaving them was plainly not on the agenda.

## 3

Britain concluded the Seven Years' War in fine fashion, but the worldwide scale of operations and Pitt's largesse, much of it directed to the North American colonies, had exploded the national debt. At the beginning of 1763, it stood at nearly £123 million and carried an annual interest of £4.4 million;[22] these were unprecedented numbers, the kind that made politicians and functionaries of practically all persuasions nervous and itchy for new sources of revenue. But Britain's population was already among the most taxed in Europe, and had taken to rioting when more excises were slapped on.[23] The colonies, on the other hand, were thought to be getting something like a free ride. Protection cost money and they should pay their way was the reasoning. It was not a conspiracy, just a pipe dream.

Given the mercantilist mindset, it's a wonder that the debt went uncelebrated, that so much money was available to be borrowed, or the trust implied in the government's willingness and ability to pay it back with interest went largely unnoticed. Anyway, they were merely symptoms of something much more fundamental.

For the second time in human history we were switching subsistence niches. We'd moved from hunting and gathering to agriculture and advanced pastoralism; now we were about to make the jump to the industrial revolution, and England would lead the way. The reason that Robert Cary could supply George Washington with all that stuff would one day change the lives of everyone and practically everything else, including the atmosphere. The future of the British economy was in Britain, not in its colonies. Despite losing them, within fifty years it would be strong enough to defeat Napoléon and his Continental empire. But at the time, the future—even in its most profound manifestations—remained elusive.

So imperial functionaries coped dimly, applying traditional solutions and patterns of behavior to new problems and possibilities; they tried as best they could to exert some control over the vast economic and social energy being unleashed.[24] As was traditional, the institutions waging war and collecting revenue stood first in line for shares of the increase in national wealth, and, accordingly, bureaucracies in both quarters leapt ahead in size and responsibility.[25] As usual, those in charge looked to their friends and dependents to staff the growing administrative apparatus, patronage being the critical lubricant of eighteenth-century British politics. A certain amount of monetary corruption—you might call it fiscal leakage—was inevitable; but on the whole the performance of these bureaucracies was astonishingly effective. The support of the effort to suppress the American Revolution stands as the greatest achievement in military logistics up to that point in history.

Yet an effective bureaucracy can still be wasteful and misdirected, and this proved largely true of the myopic men who crafted colonial policy. Still, they were no more to be blamed than mercantilism, the body of assumptions that defined state power largely in terms of economic relations between the metropolitan and its colonial possessions.[26] It was axiomatic; the colonies existed for the economic benefit of the mother country, designated suppliers of raw materials, markets for manufactured goods, and overall cash-generating mechanisms.[27] A great deal had been invested in North America, especially during the Seven Years' War; now it was expected it would begin carrying its own weight, generating revenues to cover the cost of empire.

There were also strategic considerations that ran against the grain of the colonists' ambitions. Planners in London wanted a long, thin North America stretching from eastern Canada down into Florida, but not too far into the hinterlands; that geography would maximize the protection the dominant Royal Navy could provide, keep the Indians quiet, and ensure market penetration and better administrative control.[28]

Meanwhile, the war with France may have ended in 1763, but not the rivalry. Future wars against future Louises, only some of them fought in Europe, seemed an easy call. The army was the King's, and he wanted to do right by it. It had been expanded during the emergency, but now there was pressure to economize. One way to avoid cutting some regiments was to stash them in the American colonies. That was apparently his only motive for this momentous decision,[29] just one more in a series of ad hoc moves intended to accomplish—at least until news of the Boston Tea Party arrived—nothing more sinister than to bring some order and profit to empire.

But, as noted in the introduction, there was certainly another way of looking at these matters, an utterly alternate frame of reference. Like mercantile thinking, it originated not in the colonies, but in the metropolitan, and this made sense because its critique was aimed at the heart of the entire system—at what it considered a fetid mass of corruption.

The so-called Country Party—an amalgam of the reform-minded landed gentry—was given voice in the early eighteenth century by a series of political writers, most notably John Trenchard, Thomas Gordon, and Viscount Bolingbroke. Their barrage of invective was aimed squarely at the fantastically successful political machine of Robert Walpole, which remained dominant for more than two decades, a run unparalleled in British history. But what his supporters viewed as political stability and the conditions necessary for economic growth, the Country Party saw as incessant corruption and manipulation to extend ministerial influence, with the ultimate aim of overthrowing the rights of all Englishmen.[30]

In large part they represented the rural gentry, the families who had led the Glorious Revolution in 1688 and then been forced to the margins of politics by Walpole's co-option of the center.[31] While he and his allies cashed in on the economy's leap forward, they were left to fume on the sidelines and explain their fall in terms of a vast and intricate conspiracy dedicated to stifling, one by one, the rights of Englishmen. The narrative they created was not only peppered with some of the most radical notions of the age as to what those rights actually constituted, but it was also highly moralistic in tone, viewing the lubricated politics of the time as a pox bound to infect the people: Public vice leads to private vice.[32]

To build their case they enumerated transgression after transgression, beginning with the public debt and the burdensome taxes necessary to service it, money extorted from Englishmen living in districts chronically underrepresented in Parliament. Meanwhile, the proceeds were used to support a legion of cronies, a malignant officialdom who employed their power to ruthlessly enhance their own interests at the cost of the traditional and hard-won rights of Englishmen. And to enforce their will, they would nurture a standing army, the hammer of the state, in Trenchard's words "capable of destroying all right, law and liberty that stood in their way."[33] As the leviathan grew, so would freedom be extinguished.

It was a gloomy description of a place on the edge of a brilliant future, but this was also the era of Hogarth, and progress is seldom tidy. There was a lot that was accurate about the Country Party critique. The dangers of power are real and can be deeply corrupting; their support of republican principles served as a beacon toward the future. But in general they looked to the past, to what Bernard Bailyn called "a half-mythical rural world of stable hierarchical relations."[34] Because they didn't understand what was really happening economically, they saw just the most traditional way out of the cycle of decay. "Only a Patriot King, the most uncommon of all phaenomena," ventured Viscount Bolingbroke, could "restore the public spirit essential to the preservation of liberty and national prosperity."[35]

At this level of argument, everything becomes personal—only a Patriot King can save England from the willful scheming of evil men. Things don't just happen. Finance, technology, and knowledge don't change conditions; it is the veil of conspiracy that waves its magic over the course of events. This was the central vibe of the Country Party, and while it had its virtues, it simply did not square with the real England of the early eighteenth century sufficiently to gain anything like a decisive political following. But it was influential enough to define the pattern of protest against the ministries that followed Walpole.[36] It was also infectious, should you be in a place far off, looking at London from the wrong end of a telescope.

4

George Washington's path toward rebellion likely began in earnest during the late months of 1763, when he would have learned of the royal proclamation banning colonial expansion beyond the Atlantic drainage basin, or, more specifically, cutting off the two hundred thousand acres of Ohio Valley land promised to veterans of the Virginia Regiment. Psychologically and tangibly this struck directly at a vital interest.

Washington was all about westward expansion; it was a major theme of both his career and his imagination. The future he envisioned was plainly one of an empire headed west. On these grounds he dismissed the proclamation as a "temporary expedient to quiet the Minds of the Indians,"[37] many by this time engaged in a series of attacks along the frontier from the Great Lakes region down to the Ohio Country, known subsequently as Pontiac's War.

But in GW's here and now, the proclamation acted as a roadblock, not just to the bounty lands that would one day be a key element of his fortune, but also toward a much more ambitious scheme. In June 1763, Washington and eighteen other land speculators from Virginia and Maryland, calling themselves very frankly the Mississippi Company, petitioned for a twelve-year option on a whopping 2.5 million acres of western land. Now the proclamation put that effectively on hold. They hired a London insider to lobby the Privy Council and Parliament, only to learn in 1770 that the ministry had turned instead to English investors who were planning a new colony, Vandalia, on the same huge parcel.[38] Two years later Washington would write off his investment entirely.

Meanwhile, his pursuit of bounty land was similarly obstructed. In late 1768, word came of two new treaties with the Indians that effectively reopened the Ohio Valley to white settlement. Washington joined the subsequent feeding frenzy in the name of the veterans, and by late 1769 had succeeded in getting Virginia governor Lord Botetourt to honor the original commitment and specify the confluence of the Ohio and Great Kanawha rivers as the site of the bounty acreage. The next autumn he personally led an initial surveying expedition, biting off a choice 20,000-plus-acre chunk of bottomland for himself.[39]

But, in 1774, GW, now far down the path to rebellion, learned that Lord Dartmouth, secretary of state for the American colonies, had ruled that the only veterans of the French and Indian War eligible to receive bounty lands were British regulars.[40] Looking back on the episode, Washington spoke in terms "of his Lordship's malignant disposition towards Americans."[41] By this time, he had seen a lot more of what he considered insidious ministerial behavior, for as a fifteen-year member of the House of Burgesses, at the jagged edge of the imperial crisis, he'd had a firsthand look.

Two months after reelection from Winchester, Washington told a visitor to Mount Vernon "I deal little in politics"[42]—always the impression he wanted to leave. In fact, GW was a conscientious, not a reluctant, legislator, methodically learning his craft and only gradually emerging as a leader in the House. Never comfortable with public speaking, he preferred to listen and master the issues, so when he did talk it was with authority. And in the process he came to accept the windy and dilatory nature of legislative politics, cultivating a stoic patience that would one day pay huge dividends in his dealings with the Continental Congress. Meanwhile, he would only grow angrier and ever more impatient with Britain.

The year 1765 proved a momentous one in Virginia politics. The stage had been set by a fiery orator not yet out of his twenties, Patrick Henry, when he suggested in a court case that the King, by disallowing acts of the burgesses, "degenerates into a Tyrant, and forfeits all rights to his subjects' obedience."[43] The citizens of Louisa County responded by sending him to that body in a special election held in the spring of 1765. He proved no reticent newcomer. He was as impulsive as Washington was calculating.

It was a matter of stamps: small things, but they spelled big trouble. Parliament passed a scheme to raise revenue by requiring officially stamped paper for not just legal documents, but pamphlets and newspapers as well—a sort of consumption tax on the mind, and one bound to offend, especially the educated elite. It did, all across the colonies, but the response in Virginia was particularly prompt and vitriolic.

Patrick Henry waited until late in the session, when over half of the delegates—mostly the older, more conservative ones—had left Wil-

liamsburg, to rise and introduce his blistering set of resolves. Because
Virginians hold "all the Liberties, privileges, Franchises and Immuni-
ties . . . [held] by the People of Great Britain," that included "Taxation
of the People by themselves." As for the colonies, "Laws, respecting
their internal Polity and Taxation . . . are derived from their own Consent, with the Approbation of the Sovereign."[44] Parliament is not
mentioned, which is the whole point. The Stamp Act is null and void
because a body without the right to tax under these circumstances
passed it. The intent could hardly be missed and wasn't.

There is no record that GW stayed to hear Henry's Resolves, but
because he was a conscientious legislator he may have. At any rate, it's
plain he was on board and more so. As he informed his personal piñata
Robert Cary: "The Stamp Act, imposed on the Colonies by the Parliament of Great Britain engrosses the conversation of the speculative
part of the Colonists, who look upon this unconstitutional method of
Taxation as a direful attack upon their Liberties." He then extended
the threat to a sore point between them. "Luxuries which we have
heretofore lavished our Substance to Great Britain for can well be
dispensed with whilst the Necessaries of Life are to be procurd (for the
most part) within ourselves."[45] Non-importation was to be a key component of revolutionary thinking; it's hard to say Washington wasn't
on the leading edge of it.

As for Henry and his resolves, they were no legislative aberration;
the people of Virginia were solidly behind them.[46] And so were the
rest of the colonies; hence the resolves set off a sort of chain reaction
when they were printed in their newspapers. By the end of 1765, the
lower houses of eight additional colonies had piled on with resolutions
specifically denouncing the Stamp Act and more generally denying
Parliament's right to tax them. Though all were less emphatic than
Virginia's, they did show thinking essentially along the same lines.

Even better evidence was the Stamp Act Congress, held in New
York City in October, when representatives from nine provinces managed to negotiate a common protest based on the same interpretation
of colonial thinking. The foundation of intercolonial politics was being
set in place. North Americans would begin looking to one another, not
London, in times of crisis.

It was not just elites; working-class mobs threatened stamp distributors and forced them to resign in a number of colonies. Resistance was particularly fierce in New England, where groups known as the Sons of Liberty orchestrated the riotous festivities. In Boston, prominent politician and rumored advocate of the Stamp Act Thomas Hutchinson was lucky to escape with his life. All this from colonists who just two years earlier had concluded a successful war in tight alliance with the mother country.

The firestorm of anger generated by the Stamp Act left political Britain astounded, and even today it gives pause. So do the repeated assertions that it was simply "the first step to rivet the chains of slavery upon us forever,"[47] or similar words to that effect. One prominent historian of the period, Robert Middlekauff, believes the crisis to have been sufficiently explosive that, had Parliament not repealed the Stamp Act promptly after five months, revolution could have come in 1766, not a decade later.[48]

There was little choice in the matter, since nobody was willing to dispense the stamped paper. But the point is well taken. The colonists' reaction was wildly out of phase with actual intent. And so, too, was their explanation for its repeal. For no good reason, they concluded that George III had come to their rescue and slew the Stamp Act. So convinced were the inhabitants of New York City they erected an equestrian statue of the young monarch, fashioned of lead and layered richly in gilt, to commemorate the event.[49]

All of this makes sense only if you conclude that the colonists were already conditioned by a stripped-down version of Country Party thinking and were applying it liberally to their own situation. Of course George III saved them; he was the Patriot King. When General Thomas Gage, British commander in America, began moving regulars eastward to make them available during the crisis, Americans were reminded not that the monarch had stashed them there in the first place, but of the dangers posed by regular armies and their potential role in enslaving them.[50] So, too, did their thinking on who had a right to tax whom reflect Country Party concerns over what it considered extortionist policies in England. Almost the entire bill of particulars was there from the beginning, and it had the ability to ignite a population.

*George III, Patriot King, soon to become the
Revolution's worst enemy.*

THOMAS FRYE/WILLIAM PETHER/LIBRARY OF CONGRESS

This was derived from weaving a mass of accusations and tips on
good government into a whole cloth of conspiracy, one fashioned to
remove the rights of Englishmen, which in America meant slavery.
Suffusing it all was a stench of corruption and moral decay deplored by
the Country Party and bound to catch the attention of the more puri-
tanical and austere colonists, filling their heads with visions of a para-
sitic officialdom about to descend on them. Britain was an ocean away;
time and distance only served to distort and magnify each effort to
bring order and revenue. Conceding anything meant eventually losing
everything. It's true that at this point practically nobody was thinking

of independence; instead they joined George Washington in breathing a sigh of relief that the crisis was over.[51] But nothing had changed. They were primed to react along certain lines. And it would happen over and over until they resolved to rip themselves free.

It seems important to ask why that was; what gave this narrative the power to capture so quickly the political dreamscape of so many colonists? Progressives and Marxists have long argued that there are always economic disparities—not to mention ethnic, linguistic, class, and religious ones—powering revolution.[52] But in the colonies in the late 1760s and early '70s there was no mass poverty or simmering social discontent, only a vast acute touchiness that frayed colonists' nerves to the point of paranoia, a corporate dread that their prosperity and liberty might soon be removed and replaced by conditions amounting to slavery.[53] This is not to say that the American Revolution was without a substantial element of self-interest—basically the prospect of controlling an entire continent under a government of choice—only that it was tripped by something even more elemental, and that was fear.

Conspiracy theories are not inevitable drivers of modern revolution—the French example better resembles spontaneous combustion—nor do they even have to rise above pure caricature, such as the Nazi portrayal of Jewish bankers. But in the cases of Marxist-Leninism and the Country Party, an outlandish tale of malign motivation combined with a sophisticated ideology aimed at an overall prescription for governance produced a revolutionary cocktail of extraordinary potency.

Part of that power seems to be vested in story itself, the ancient power of narrative, especially ones that forecast danger and ascribe causation in terms of human actors. The story can be digested at various levels of information, from catchphrases to legalistic terminology, but once the hook is set—that a conspiracy exists to achieve a predetermined end—almost any bit of additional information will be interpreted in that light. And as that occurs, frustration, anger, and fear grow to the point that violent rebellion becomes the sole means of release from the dreaded end-state.

As noted earlier, the prospect of enslavement had particular resonance in the American colonies. Slaves were everywhere; held by the hundreds of thousands in the lowland South, they were common throughout the middle colonies and even in New England, where one in five families in Boston owned a slave and almost 12 percent of Rhode Island was black and enslaved.[54] Nor was bondage limited to those of African origin. In the half century before the Revolution, approximately fifty thousand Irish and English criminals and indigents had been sent to America and bound in indentured servitude. On top of that were tens of thousands of young white Americans indentured as apprentices or servants for periods up to a decade. Freedom was hardly rare in North America, but reminders that it could be lost were everywhere.

Not everything was in the debit column. The power of the Country Party tale certainly had a positive dimension. The gloomy critique of the political landscape logically brought forth its opposite; a focus on the rights of Englishmen naturally stimulated speculation on what those rights might actually constitute in more just circumstances.

One of those areas was representative governance. Country Party ideologues certainly favored it, but wanted it cleaned up and expanded. At one point or another most endorsed broad-based manhood suffrage: getting rid of rotten boroughs and replacing them with regularized standards for representation directly related to population distribution. They also wanted to bind representatives to constituents with residential requirements and specific sets of instructions on how to vote.[55] To ensure rigorous scrutiny they favored changes in seditious libel law, so as to allow the press (and, by extension, anybody) full freedom to criticize those in charge. To cap it off they advocated an end to official support and control of religion, thereby providing Englishmen true freedom to choose how they worshipped.[56]

Besides generating a blueprint for better government, the emphasis on individual rights implied something more fundamental, something that might ultimately signify an entire reordering of society. For if the individual (at least the landowning male individual) was the basic unit of political power, this negated the basis for the traditional social and governmental hierarchy, sometimes called the "great chain of being." Rather than the King deriving his authority from God and passing it down through the various stations of society until it impacted the individual at the bottom of the pyramid of dependency, power is vested first with the people and passed upward. In other words, democracy.

Of course, this remained a hidden agenda, only to be gradually revealed and reaching a crescendo with the rise of Andrew Jackson. It was the truly radical part of the American Revolution. Yet it remained subordinate. George Washington would never accept it, nor would any of the key Founding Fathers embrace it completely. Still, it was there from the beginning, and flashes showed even in GW when he waxed idealistic. But what really guided him and the others was the dark side, the malicious conspiracy to strip colonists of their freedoms one by one, until they were the equivalent of their own slaves.

Admittedly, this line of thinking casts the American Revolution in a more particularistic light than is frequently seen by contemporary historians, those who prefer a less exceptional view, one which emphasizes the general similarities among the revolutions which took place roughly contemporaneously around the Atlantic basin.[57] From a distance of several centuries and at the level of generalities it's hard to argue with this Olympian approach. But revolutions also take place on the ground, down and dirty. Emotions here are vastly exaggerated. Fear, suspicion, and, ultimately, hatred prevail. This became the psychological terrain of the thirteen American colonies, a place where conspiracies woven out of homespun Country Party ideas provided the best explanation for their dilemma and also the malignant forces behind it. It is at this level that our story will proceed.

# 5

In 1767, when Charles Townshend, chancellor of the exchequer, with sublime misunderstanding of the situation, sought to wrong-foot the colonists by replacing an internal tax, the Stamp Act, with an "external" version, he not only set off another firestorm; he also provoked a reaction that prefaced real organization and leverage among the colonials. That leverage was non-importation. If the British were intent on collecting taxes on imports such as lead, glass, paper, painters' colors, and tea, then the obvious countermove was not to consume them, and as little as possible of anything else they had to sell.[58]

This meant working together, colony to colony, just as had happened during the Stamp Act crisis. When the Massachusetts House issued a circular letter addressed to the Speakers of the other colonial legislatures, urging them to "harmonize with each other," New Jersey and Connecticut agreed, and then in the late spring of 1768, Virginia upped the ante. On May 16, the burgesses responded with their own circular, this one arguing for a "hearty union" and joint colonial action against any and all British impositions that "have an immediate tendency to enslave them."[59] Almost exactly a year later, George Washington, for the first time taking a leading role among the burgesses, proposed a colony-wide boycott of key British manufactured products, along with a cessation of the trade in slaves.[60] From that moment he was seen as the center of the resistance among Virginia's consumption-happy planters.

Actually, non-importation didn't work consistently well. In the Middle Colonies and New England there were dramatic cuts in British imports, but in the South there are signs they actually increased.[61]

But it was really the spirit of the thing that mattered. The colonists were getting more and more connected. Enforcement meant organizing at the local level to identify merchants dealing in enumerated goods.[62] It also involved a great many individual decisions not to consume British products. Women, especially in New England, dragged out spinning wheels that had not been used for decades, and taught one another the ancient art, no doubt chatting about the bad intentions of those across the water.[63] So the story spread and gradually revealed its capability to trigger action. Before Parliament repealed all of Townshend's duties save the one on tea, non-importation associations had spread to every colony except New Hampshire.[64] One by one they collapsed once the crisis passed, but the precedent had been set, and they would be back.

Besides the tax on tea, there was one other portentous holdover. On September 30, 1768, a string of transports arrived in Boston Harbor and began disgorging two regiments of British regulars under the guns of a squadron of warships. The city was and would remain, of all places on the North American continent, the epicenter of suspicion and resistance. By placing these troops in Boston, the British didn't just virtually guarantee violence; they fed colonial paranoia in exactly the manner expected. Here it was, the standing army meant to enslave them.

Back in Virginia, George Washington had not only established himself as Mr. Self-Sufficiency; he had also clearly fallen under the influence of Country Party thinking. The Custis library had all the texts[65]—Trenchard, Gordon, Bolingbroke—and if he wasn't much of a reader at this point, his friend and neighbor George Mason was available to fill him in with the details of radical Whig ideology. Still, in the spring of 1769, when the burgesses passed a resolution that only they had the right to tax Virginians, and Lord Botetourt, the governor, responded by dissolving them, Washington was in a sufficiently thoughtful mood to purchase John Dickinson's *Letters from a Farmer in Pennsylvania*, a highly influential series of essays couched in Country Party gloom.[66]

GW was ultimately a man of action and not very well educated, something that bothered him all his life. But he was plainly very bright, and during this period there is a marked improvement in his writing and, it seems, his thinking. The air was filled with ideas, not just conspiracy but radical and sophisticated political ideas, and GW seems to have just soaked it all up. Much was contrary to his gentrified nature, but that didn't really matter. Country Party thinking would become the argot of the American Revolution. Because GW had internalized it, he fit perfectly, instantly made the right impression on true believers, and knew instinctively just how far he could go without transcending the ideology's many strictures on power. He became, in essence, the Patriot King—without the king part, which was critical.

George Washington was also, deep in his heart, a soldier. Writing George Mason during the Townshend crisis, he dismisses petitions to Parliament and the King as useless. "At a time when our lordly Masters in Great Britain will be satisfied with nothing less than the deprivation of American freedom, it seems highly necessary that something shou'd be done to avert the stroke."[67] He is certainly willing to try non-importation, but beyond that there is only one other recourse. He writes elsewhere "no man should scruple or hesitate for a moment to use arms in defense of so valuable a blessing . . . [but this] should be the last resource: the dernier resort."[68] Perhaps, but in this regard, he was out in front of many, already a true militant.

But he was also a patient one. The real action was far to the north in Boston, and he watched it with some skepticism. In March 1770, when the inevitable occurred and British troops, after a great deal of provocation, gunned down eleven riotous civilians in what would come to be known as the Boston Massacre, GW, never a fan of mob action, reacted coldly.[69] Yet he may have been simply biding time.

When Jacky Custis arrived at Mount Vernon in May 1772, accompanied by the young Charles Willson Peale, Washington at Martha's urging agreed to sit for his first portrait. Dress was always significant to GW, and for this occasion he donned his uniform from the long-disbanded Virginia Regiment, and slung on his back what appears to be a Pennsylvania long rifle.[70] This was appropriate since the regiment had primarily operated along the frontier, where such weapons were the norm, but subsequent actions indicate that this getup may well provide a window on GW's mood and thinking. His arrival in uniform at the Second Continental Congress would prove one of his most risky and dramatic gestures, while his use of backcountry fighters armed with highly accurate long rifles, formally under Daniel Morgan and as pure irregulars, was to be a key component of his complex strategy to defeat the British when war did come. On these grounds you might say that Peale's portrait was a kind of dress rehearsal for a general in waiting.

He was still waiting in mid-December 1773, when a mob, some disguised as Indians, dumped an entire shipment of East India Company tea into Boston Harbor, setting off a chain of events that would lead directly to the American Revolution. He may have initially disapproved;[71] but it didn't take him long to realize this was destiny calling.

6

From beginning to end the British, or at least their government, remained profoundly misinformed. Three thousand miles of ocean proved a formidable barrier, not just physical but also mental. Few of

*First portrait of a general in waiting.*

CHARLES WILLSON PEALE/WIKIMEDIA COMMONS

the ministerial officials designated to get more money out of the colonists had much idea what they were like, or how they might view the process.[72] The impact of the Country Party critique on the peculiar circumstances of North America appears to have missed them entirely. So they continued to blunder from mistake to mistake, from failed tax to failed tax, from riot to riot until the whole thing exploded in rebellion.

Part of this was plainly a matter of attitude. The colonies existed for the good of the home country, not vice versa. They were, by definition, subordinate, and so, by extension, were the people living in them. They could talk all they wanted about the "rights of Englishmen," but this was never a quarrel between perceived equals. It could be argued that they had a voice in court in the wily Benjamin Franklin, who in effect came to serve as America's representative in London, but in reality his role was simply a conduit and punching bag. At no point did imperial authorities reach out to members of the colonial elite in any substantial way and build their loyalty by including them in the metropolitan political establishment.[73] There were no parliamentary seats in the offing for this rambunctious bunch.

Meanwhile, within Parliament critical decisions such as placing regular troops in North America or levying taxes through stamps were made offhandedly with a minimum of debate.[74] Of the major political players during the crisis brought on by the Stamp Act, only the redoubtable William Pitt defended the North American position, and even he equivocated: "In my opinion this Kingdom has no right to lay a tax upon the colonies. At the same time, I assert the authority of this kingdom over the colonies, to be sovereign and supreme in every circumstance."[75] He caused quite a stir, but convinced few.

One should no more debate constitutional points with them, than one would with a child: This was the key metaphor the King's ministers applied to explain the recurrent eruptions of colonial wrath. They were children in the process of being ruined by indulgence. Lest they be lost forever, discipline was required: "Spare the rod, and spoil the child."[76]

There is a documented tendency for people, when faced with a unique and puzzling situation, to put together the first plausible explanation and then look for examples to reinforce it.[77] Something like this seems to have happened at Whitehall, leading officialdom to conclude that the colonists, like children, could only profit from a little physical chastisement. If in real terms this meant filicide, so be it, since the contagion was really limited to a few troublemakers, mostly located in Boston[78]—the other half of their jerry-built counternarrative.

This would prove a critical misconception with grave operational implications. From beginning to end, British authorities, both civil and military, underestimated just how widespread support for the colonial position really was, that it had penetrated across the entire landscape. Worse yet, they failed to see that support was couched in a narrative that portrayed them in the worst possible light, not just as oppressors but enslavers. Their behavior would consistently be interpreted in these terms, and this as much as anything kept the Revolution going when the eventual war dragged on interminably. That and the bad behavior of the British themselves.

Given their long tradition of harshly suppressing rebellion among the Irish and Scots, it would he hard to maintain the British were not predisposed toward brutality in such situations. As souvenirs of the last Highland revolt in 1745–46, some of the heads of Bonnie Prince Charlie's officers were still spiked to Temple Bar, overlooking Fleet Street, one of London's busiest boulevards, twenty years hence.[79] There is little reason to believe that rebellious Americans, or at least their leaders, would be treated much better.[80]

So it was when the inflection point was reached as news of the Boston Tea Party arrived on English shores in late January 1774. The reaction was near universal fury. Even friends of the colonists condemned the Tea Party. Pitt, now the Earl of Chatham, simply called it "criminal."[81] Lord North, the prime minister, concluded: "We are not entering into a dispute between internal and external taxes. . . . We are now to dispute whether we have, or have not any authority in that country."[82] And on this basis he introduced into the House of Commons the Boston Port Bill, the first of five the Americans would come to call the Intolerable Acts, together reducing Massachusetts to a royal dependency and Boston an occupied city, its port closed and troops to be quartered with private families.

Meanwhile, George III, the Patriot King in the eyes of many Americans, had consulted with his North American commander, who was in London on leave: "I have seen Lieutenant General Gage. . . . He says they will be Lyons, whilst we are Lambs but if we take the resolute part they will undoubtedly prove very meek."[83] Permission, in other words, to apply the parental rod. Whatever their preconceptions, Americans would receive little sympathy from this quarter.

At this point—the spring of 1774—it appears that every element of the British military and governmental establishment had lined up behind what amounted to a coercion-based strategy in dealing with the Americans. Deliberately escalating the crisis was founded on the assumption that the colonists in the main would back down and become, if not exactly meek and lamblike, at least compliant in paying for some of the costs of empire. And those who refused, it was more than implied, would receive a good spanking, a therapeutic thrashing that would cause the rest to come to their senses.

This was a policy conceived in anger and aimed at punishment as much as anything else. Worse yet, it was launched on a sea of misperception. Its architects in London had little idea of not just the magnitude of the colonists' anger, but that it was based on what amounted to a revolutionary body of thought. These were not spoiled children; they were resolute adults, already spun up beyond English imagination. They would not be cowed. And when confronted by the British cudgel, they would become convinced their worst nightmares were true, and then they would never give up. The British approach was doomed to failure, from beginning to end. They could have hardly come up with anything worse. But it also may be instructive.

Coercive anti-insurgency policies designed along similar lines have been used repeatedly, most notably by Americans in Vietnam, and the results have not generally been positive. They characteristically involve large armies, great expense, lots of suffering, and, in the end, futility and defeat. Something like swatting flies with a sledgehammer. Yet coming up with alternatives is not exactly easy. Real wars and revolutions are immensely complex and culturally individualized; it's hard to pin them down to any one pattern. Still, given the human costs involved, it's irresponsible to ignore consistent failure and not try to come up with something better.

In our case, this inflection point provides a logical juncture to generate an alternative—a substitute scenario in a parallel reality. What would it take to construct a counterfactual sufficiently dramatic to break through the cloud of Country Party thinking and restore Britain's reputation and legitimacy in the eyes of Americans? A huge change in attitude, but almost nothing in terms of resources.

Let us suppose that the young king had fallen under the sway of Pitt rather than archconservative John Stuart, 3rd Earl of Bute; that as a result he had become thoroughly familiar with Country Party thinking, and that together they hatched a scheme calculated to cement him into the role of Patriot King in the eyes of North Americans. For the cinematically inclined, the resultant scenario might be called *The Long Strange Trip of George III.*

The action would begin with our alternative monarch (GIII) instructing "Foul-Weather Jack" Byron, the best sailor in the Royal Navy and grandfather of the poet, to immediately assemble a flotilla at Portsmouth to consist of three of HRH's newest ships of the line, along with fifteen transports. "We're planning a visit."

The next scene might pick up our voyagers mid-Atlantic, with GIII (Pitt can be presumed too sick to travel) informing Byron and a very bewildered Benjamin Franklin—hustled aboard without explanation—that their first destination would be Boston.

Their arrival would come absolutely without warning and likely cause some initial trepidation on the part of Bostonians. But this would be short-lived when a royal proclamation announced that an abject monarch had arrived to apologize to his subjects and return the regiments that had been such a burden to them back to the British Isles, where they belonged. The last scenes here might feature the troops boarding the transports along with General Gage, and GIII hosting a banquet, including as honored guests John Hancock, and the Adams cousins, Samuel and John.

Then it would be on to Philadelphia. Here, before a similar gathering, our imagined monarch would proclaim Benjamin Franklin "leading Savant of the Age for his Experiments with Electrical fluid," and appoint him "My own Personal representative to all My North American possessions. Through his trusted Voice, yours shall be heard. I understand your position on Taxation. I will advocate it before Parliament; but I can make no Promises."

The last stop for the flotilla, now down to three ships of the line, would be Alexandria, Virginia, where GIII would request George Washington's presence at still another gathering of influential locals. Here he would do two things: rescind the Proclamation of 1763 (his prerogative, since it was a royal degree), and commission GW commander in chief of all GIII's troops in North America (there wouldn't be many left).

The finale would spotlight GIII dictating his explanation to Parliament, pointing out that thousands of colonists pouring over the Appalachians was proof enough that the proclamation was worthless, and that the returning regiments were needed at home. "France is the True Enemy. If We continue to alienate our subjects in North America, She will find Advantage in the quarrel. Are the Paltry revenues We derive here, worth turning One Enemy into Two?"

This was a question the real George III never asked. Had he been in the mood to do so, something like the scenario above might have helped clear colonial paranoia and bring to light some sort of path to resolution, though the revenue question would still have loomed. But, of course, the real George III was at antipodes with the envisioned Patriot King. He turned into what amounted to Americans' worst enemy, his adamancy likely extending the Revolutionary War significantly. The larger point here, though, is that there was nothing inevitable about the British predicament. Even at this late date a dramatic change in the thoughts and actions of just one key individual might have provided sufficient leverage to send history off in an entirely different direction, and done so, most important, without violence. But this fanciful excursion also serves to accentuate just how far the situation was from peaceful resolution. As noted earlier, the die had already been cast. A revolution had been born, and its destiny would be written in blood.

# CHAPTER 3

# Rage Militaire

## 1

IT WOULD BE AN UNDERSTATEMENT TO SAY EVENTS ACCELERATED dramatically in the summer of 1774. The American Revolution took place with stunning suddenness; and George Washington, with equal alacrity, thrust himself into the middle of it—transformed in a matter of eight months from a respected regional figure with a two-decades-old military reputation into the chief defender of what would come to be known as the Glorious Cause. And he did it all with a studied reticence that belied what amounted to a brilliant campaign of self-aggrandizement. But this was less a matter of calculation than intuition; GW had become a true believer. He moved, as another creature of destiny once said, "with the instinctive sureness of a sleepwalker."[1]

As usual, luck, or at least fate, played a role. The previous June, his beloved stepdaughter Patsy had died during an epileptic seizure. Washington's genuine grief appears to have further bonded him to Martha, who was inconsolable and wore black for a year. There was an upside, though. Patsy's estate amounted to £16,000, which GW split with her brother, Jacky Custis.[2] This cash injection of nearly a million dollars in today's money not only enabled Washington to pay off the last of his debt to Robert Cary;[3] it also provided the financial base for full-time participation in what really mattered: foiling what he now considered a "regular Plan . . . to overthrow our Constitutional Rights

& liberties . . . [one that] will make us tame, & abject Slaves, as the Blacks we Rule over with such arbitrary Sway."⁴

On Sunday, July 17, 1774, GW's friend and neighbor George Mason arrived at Mount Vernon for an overnight stay, a working visit to discuss their reaction to the latest crisis in Virginia politics. A month and a half before, Lord Dunmore, the governor, had dissolved the burgesses after they had declared June 1 "a Day of Fasting, Humiliation and Prayer" over the British shutdown of Boston's port. The evicted burgesses reconvened the next morning at Raleigh Tavern and called for all of Virginia's counties to send representatives to a special convention in August. George Mason had drawn up and, with Washington's help, refined what were essentially the instructions for Fairfax County's representatives.

Not only were they far more compelling than any other county's guidance, they also constituted almost a classic exposition of the Country Party case against Britain, and as such quickly reverberated as far as Boston.⁵ The Fairfax Resolves were also in the vanguard in terms of militancy, proposing a revival of non-importation associations, along with extra-legal means to enforce them, and recommending a continental congress to "concert a general and uniform Plan for the Defence and Preservation of our common Rights."⁶

When the Virginia Convention met on August 1, Washington was one of over a hundred delegates who attended, but because the Fairfax Resolves dominated the discourse, he was drawn into the spotlight. Not surprisingly, when it came time to elect delegates to the general congress, now slated to meet in Philadelphia, his name was included among the seven chosen, receiving more votes than all but Speaker Peyton Randolph. Thomas Jefferson thought he felt a "shock of electricity" as the ballots were counted; more likely what he experienced was the tingle of revolution.⁷

Patrick Henry and Edmund Pendleton spent the night of August 30, 1774, at Mount Vernon, where Martha told them: "I hope you will stand firm—I know George will."⁸ The next morning the three of them departed on the long ride to Philadelphia, and what would be known to history as the First Continental Congress. It's a safe bet that none of them realized what they were getting into, propelled only by their intellectualized rage at what was an obvious conspiracy against them, drawn north by the gut instinct to gather with others similarly threatened.

They arrived on September 4, 1774, the day before the Congress formally convened. Every colony save Georgia (facing a Creek Indian uprising) had sent a delegation. Most were chosen by extra-legal assemblies similar in concept to Virginia's, and soon would begin functioning as replacements for legislatures also dissolved by royal authority.[9] They were all in town for the same reason and spoke the same dialect of Country Party politics, but this was still very much a feeling-out process. Much of the action took place over drinks and endless dinners as this amped-up cast of characters got to know one another.[10] With a few exceptions they constituted the core element of what would become the American Revolution.

Everybody, it seems, was impressed with the Virginians. Patrick Henry dazzled with his oratory, as did Richard Henry Lee: John Adams called them the "Cicero" and the "Demosthenes of the Age."[11] Peyton Randolph struck Connecticut's Silas Deane as "noble."[12] But it was clear who was the alpha male among these self-assured Virginians. Nobody was more impressive than George Washington.

Barely into his forties, he still retained his magnificent physique and catlike grace, plus he likely towered over practically everybody. The same Deane saw a "hard" but "very young look, and an easy, soldier-like air and gesture" in Washington. Stories circulated that upon hearing of the Boston Port Bill, he had offered to raise and equip a thousand men for the common defense. Yet he was plainly no hothead. A fellow Virginian described him as "sensible & speaks little—in action cool, like a Bishop at his prayers."[13] The same quality also caught the eye of John Adams, already sick of congressional bloviation: "Washington would speak only when he had something to say and Then without Bombast."[14]

There was more to this than style points. As historian Paul Longmore notes, GW, consciously or unconsciously, was acting out a role cast by the Country Party essayists, who characteristically took a dim view of flamboyance and demagoguery.[15] His good sense and modesty were exactly what they recommended in a leader, and it would not be forgotten when the time came to choose one.

That would be sooner than practically anybody expected, in large part because of what happened at this first congressional gathering. To keep the colonies—both large and small—united, it was necessary that each should have a single vote, instead of proportional representation. As future events would demonstrate, this made it inherently hard to get anything done, since their interests on some issues were bound to clash. But, prodded by the arrival of Paul Revere with the news that the British had bombarded Boston,[16] delegates did manage to craft a Declaration of Rights by the middle of October, but this was simply a statement of their position, essentially boilerplate. They were intent on doing something.

It was plain that non-importation was their key point of leverage, and this time the desire was to extend it to non-consumption and non-exportation—a virtual severance of economic ties with Britain. This was a tall order. South Carolina received an exemption for rice exports,[17] but in the end all signed on to a body of trade restrictions now called "the Association." In modern times, "nuclear device" would have been more descriptive, since it was destined to set off a chain reaction.

The Association differed from previous efforts at restriction mostly in terms of fervor; this was non-importation on steroids. Real sanctions were intended, and they were meant to blanket the land. Congress called for the election of committees "in every county, city, and town" specifically charged with enforcement. These committees would have unprecedented powers to examine custom house books to root out offenders, publish their names in newspapers, and "break off all dealings" with these "enemies of American liberty"[18]—to ostracize them, in other words. And if more than moral force was required, the committees were encouraged to link themselves to local militia. Lines drawn in the sand, mandatory taking of sides: This was the stuff of revolution.

Did the delegates realize what they were doing? It doesn't seem so. At this point, very few members of the First Continental Congress wanted to break all ties with Great Britain.[19] They perpetuated the silly notion that George III remained the Patriot King, and all their troubles could be traced to his scheming ministers.[20] So they resolved unanimously to petition him directly. Admittedly this was done without much enthusiasm;[21] still, it demonstrated that they clung to the illusion the situation could be fixed, the conspiracy cast aside by friendly fiat.

But they don't seem to have thought through the ramifications of the Association for undermining all royal authority everywhere, since an overwhelming majority of the people was not only with them, but was also interpreting politics through a stripped-down version of the same conspiratorial tale that prophesized slavery as the intended end state. The Association was permission to do something about it, and as such it was explosive.[22]

Like those of many other delegates, GW's thoughts and actions remained disjointed, though they were sliding steadily toward pugnacity. Near the end of the Congress, Washington got a letter from Robert McKenzie, a former member of the Virginia Regiment and now a British officer in Boston, claiming that there was "a fixed aim at total independence . . . and how necessary it is that abler Heads and better Hearts shd draw a Line for their Guidance."[23] Washington almost immediately sought to assure him: "I think I can announce it as a fact, that it is not the wish, or the interest of the Government, or any other upon this Continent, separately, or collectively, to set up for Independence." But then in the next paragraph came a stark prediction: "& give me leave to add, as my opinion, that more blood will be spilt on this occasion (if the Ministry are determined to push matters to extremity) than history has ever yet furnished instances of in the annals of North America."[24]

Solid and conscientious George was one of only two Virginia delegates who stuck around until the First Continental Congress adjourned on October 26, 1774, agreeing to reconvene in six months if the petition to King George III had no effect. Before he left town and headed back to Mount Vernon he bought new epaulettes for his uniform, checked on the cost of muskets and military equipment in bulk, and ordered a book on military appointments, presumably with the assurance of a sleepwalker.[25]

## 2

While Boston and Massachusetts were certainly at the forefront of the action, Virginia and, in particular, Fairfax County can claim primacy in getting things organized; the whole congressional scheme was derived from the original Virginia Association, the blueprint for which had been the Fairfax Resolves. Now, within two months of the Congress's adjournment, around half of the Old Dominion's sixty-one counties had chosen committees of enforcement, with most of the rest to follow in the opening months of 1775, a veritable clean sweep.[26]

Yet Fairfax remained the epicenter of militancy. Even while Washington was still in Philadelphia, George Mason held a meeting of freeholders aimed at creating an independent company of volunteer infantry. Now that he was home, GW worked with Mason to get the company organized, and ordered the drill manuals, muskets, bayonets, and military accouterments he had priced earlier.[27] To pay for all this, plus the ammunition consumed in training, Washington and Mason initially advanced the money, then pushed through a three-shilling poll tax partially aimed at reimbursement.[28] As chairman of Fairfax's enforcement committee, GW exhorted residents to study military science, then divide themselves into sixty-eight-man companies as new volunteers signed up.[29] It was a template for what was happening throughout the colonies, a prototype for the coming takeover at the local level.

It also seems that Washington himself was looking further afield, toward something larger. During the winter of 1774–75 he hosted a stream of visitors anxious to talk politics and military matters, among them two members of what would become the leadership of the Continental Army. Both had shared the Braddock disaster with Washington, but more likely it was his personal magnetism that drew them there. It was as if, biographer Ron Chernow suggests, power was already shifting in his direction, the larger body attracting the smaller ones.[30]

If you could construct a polar opposite of GW, it would have looked a lot like Charles Lee. Scrawny and slovenly, lecherous and cynical, he was also brilliant, well educated, and a true military professional. After the debacle on the Monongahela he had distinguished himself in subsequent combat in Canada, Portugal, and Poland. Then, having insulted George III when the monarch declined his further services,[31] Lee returned to North America, where he took to lobbying delegates of the First Continental Congress with the message that with proper training colonials could stand up to British regulars.

Now at Mount Vernon for what must have been six long days, he probably pushed his case for an emphasis on irregular warfare and harassment. He was also doubtlessly pumped for military information

*Charles Lee, Esqr.*
*Major General of the Continental - Army in America.*

*Charles Lee: a true military professional and no one to trust.*

JOHANN MICHAEL PROBST/LIBRARY OF CONGRESS

by Washington, and just as likely not found wanting. Compared to Lee, Washington was a tyro at war. Yet he was highly perceptive, and after almost a week with Lee he must have sensed that any alliance with him would be a Faustian one. Lee was not to be trusted.

So, too, with his other key guest that winter, Horatio Gates. Likely the illegitimate son of the Duke of Leeds, Gates obtained a commission in the British Army and had risen to the rank of major before his ambiguous origins blocked further promotion. Small, plump, and bespectacled, he didn't look much like a soldier, but Washington was impressed with him from the Braddock days and remained so— enough to encourage him to immigrate to Virginia after he left the army.[32] Gates was far more subtle and likeable than Lee, with whom he shared a friendship; he also had real capability, particularly in military administration. But he was exceedingly ambitious and proved a serial backbiter. Washington, always a better judge of talent than loyalty, was plainly gulled by Gates at this point, but would learn "very early in the War"[33] that he was no friend.

Others came also, most notable another, unrelated Lee, one day to be known as "Light-Horse Harry." Where others saw a teenage Latin major at Princeton, GW sensed a nascent irregular warrior.

Back in Philadelphia, Washington had made a point of befriending young Thomas Mifflin and Joseph Reed, seeing not a merchant and a lawyer, but potential military aides. So it went. He was building a cadre, and grafting it to veterans of Fort Necessity, the Virginia Regiment, and the Forbes expedition like Adam Stephen, James Craik, Charles Scott, and Hugh Mercer, whom he also encouraged to move to Virginia. The process seems more intuitive than calculated, but it was pretty clear that George Washington was getting ready to go to war. It could also be inferred he was planning to take charge.

He would not have long to wait. A firestorm of revolution swept across the land, as the Association's enforcement arm, now called committees of "safety and inspection," replicated everywhere with astonishing speed. Once established, they didn't stop at listening for seditious talk, checking tax records, and investigating who was avoiding local military obligations; they got directly involved with governance, and, perhaps most critically, they revolutionized the militia.[34]

*Horatio Gates: a capable soldier and administrator,
but a thorn in Washington's future.*

JOHN NORMAN/LIBRARY OF CONGRESS

By rigorously requiring service they forced the hands of the male population, demanding that even the most apathetic show up and actively associate themselves with the cause. Officers with royal commissions or Loyalist sympathies were purged and replaced with those deemed trustworthy. Training was certainly intensified as the urge for resistance—the so-called rage militaire—surged; but in reality the revolutionized militias were always better instruments of control than they were effective fighting forces. Actively or simply as a presence, militias constituted the Revolution's muscle, its power to coerce.[35] Once locked into place, they provided a solid base on which to build a replacement government, and one the British would find almost impossible to remove, since it was basically draped over the entire landscape.

One by one the various elements of royal governance would fall, replaced with revolutionary versions of local authority: the courts, the legislatures, executive councils, the governors, even the press—all of it swept away with unprecedented speed and ease.[36] In part this was a matter of the replacement institutions and staffing being pretty much like what came before. Royal authority and authorities had always been scarce; de facto the colonists had ruled themselves. Now they were simply making it official. But this does not mean that the takeover was accomplished without opposition or emotion, or that the climate was less than revolutionary.

It was a time of taking sides and taking names, a time of paranoia and fear, one of emotions strung tight enough for friends to denounce friends of a lifetime. Suspicion of trading with the British, not showing up at militia muster, or simply loose talk could land you in front of a committee of safety to explain yourself, sign a loyalty oath, or face the consequences. Most complied, but a minority of under 20 percent never would;[37] they could not countenance the suppression of royal authority and ultimately independence. These were destined to become the Loyalists ("Tories" to the revolutionary "Whigs"); but for the time being they remained "persons of interest," watched and increasingly vilified during the winter and spring of 1775, as the Revolution became an accomplished fact. For many their sole crime was a failure of imagination; they simply could not conceive of life without king and empire. A decade or so before, that sentiment had been near universal, but events had raced past them. In the face of a purported conspiracy to enslave, they could only pronounce their loyalty. It was not enough; it never would be, and that, in turn, stoked their anger and incredulity.

3

During the spring of 1775 the situation only grew worse and also more promising. At two in the morning of April 19, British general Thomas Gage, instructed from London to round up the leadership of the provincial congress and intent on surprise, sent a column of around seven

hundred elite grenadiers and light infantry toward Lexington, where
Sam Adams and John Hancock were hiding.[38]

They might as well have paraded out in broad daylight. The ever-
watchful locals were on to them almost immediately, and as they
marched the British troops could hear alarm guns being fired in the
distance, sending the news forward at the speed of sound.[39] Paul Revere made it to Lexington in plenty of time to roust Adams and Hancock out of bed. They were long gone when the British arrived to find
only around seventy plucky militiamen arrayed before them. When
they refused to drop their guns, the regulars fired two volleys, killing
eight and wounding ten. Then it was on to Concord to seize a purported powder magazine. They never found it, although they did start
to pick up more serious resistance from gathered militia.

But nothing like the march back to Boston, which turned into a
sixteen-mile gauntlet of rebels firing from behind trees, rock walls, and
buildings, at times swarming them hand to hand with axes and clubs,
before being driven off by British bayonets. In response the redcoats
attacked noncombatants, looting and burning houses while their infuriated officers looked the other way. When pursuit ended in Cambridge, the British had accumulated 273 casualties, the Americans less
than a hundred.[40] The echo of these shots "heard round the world"
would not soon be forgotten by either side.

GW didn't sound surprised at either the news or the implications;
instead he waxed elegiac. "Unhappy it is though to reflect, that a
Brother's Sword has been sheathed in a Brother's breast," he wrote
George William Fairfax, predicting "that the once happy and peaceful
plains of America are either to be drenched with Blood, or Inhabited
by Slaves. Sad alternative! But can a virtuous Man hesitate in his
choice?"[41] Not Washington. All signs, including the clothes he packed,
indicate that when he left Mount Vernon on May 4, 1775—not to return until 1781—GW understood he was not just heading toward the
Second Continental Congress; he was going to war.

On the way his carriage joined a procession of other Virginia and
North Carolina delegates rolling north, but it was Washington the
citizens of Baltimore asked to review its four volunteer companies.
Outside of Philadelphia a crowd of five hundred had ridden out from

town to greet the delegates, and again it was GW who drew the most interest.

But this was just a ripple compared to the stir he caused when he entered the Congress, clad in the blue-and-buff uniform he designed for himself as head of the Fairfax County militia. Others may have worn military attire, but it was Washington's martial duds that everybody remembered.[42] In fact, it was a huge gamble. He might have been viewed as crassly theatrical or, worse, overambitious. Instead, it was a style statement exactly matching the mood of the hall. Benjamin Rush summarized the reaction: "He has so much martial dignity in his deportment that you would distinguish him to be a general or a soldier from among ten thousand people. There is not a king in Europe that would not look like a valet de chamber by his side."[43]

Not just a clotheshorse but a workhorse, Washington quickly demonstrated a take-charge attitude toward military planning. Five days into the session he was named chair of a committee to advise New York on defensive preparations against expected English reinforcements. Remain vigilant, but take no action unless the British attack, they were advised, only to hear two days later that Benedict Arnold and Ethan Allen, on orders from the Massachusetts Committee of Safety, had just captured Fort Ticonderoga, gateway to the Hudson Valley.[44]

This was hardly defensive, and Congress reacted by forming a second committee to consider the broader issue of an inter-colonial supply system for "Ammunition and military stores." Once again GW was named chairman, and once again its deliberations were interrupted to consider a momentous suggestion from Massachusetts's provincial legislature: "As the Army now collecting from the different colonies is for the general defence of the right of America, we wd beg leave to suggest to yr consideration the propriety of yr taking the regulation and general direction of it."[45] In other words, they were calling for a centrally controlled and directed force, an organization within shouting distance of the standing army so stigmatized by the Country Party as a key step on the road to political perdition. Yet this perspective was always more dogmatically applied to the imagined British conspiracy than it was to the actual steps taken by Americans to govern themselves.

In this case, Congress chose baby steps, a series of reactions that led inexorably toward the formation of a national army with George Washington at its head. First, it recommended that the artillery and military supplies taken at Ticonderoga be removed and inventoried "in order that they may be safely returned . . . consistent with the overruling law of self-preservation."[46] Still looking northward, it addressed a letter to "the Oppressed Inhabitants of Canada," calling them "slaves" and "fellow-sufferers," but then on June 1 passed a motion forbidding an invasion of Canada by any colonial forces, only to reverse itself a month later.[47] Meanwhile, on May 26, 1775, Congress urged all the colonies to take up arms, then eight days later voted itself authority to borrow £6,000 for gunpowder.

Next, it formed another committee, this time to estimate the cost of a one-year military campaign, chaired as usual by George Washington. Finally, on June 14, it took the inevitable leap of faith, calling for rifle companies to be raised in Pennsylvania, Maryland, and Virginia and added to the New Englanders surrounding Boston. To generate rules and regulations for these troops and others raised by Congress, it turned almost reflexively to a committee headed by George Washington.[48] On paper at least, the Continental Army was born, and GW's fingerprints were all over it.

All of this is best considered in light of the gradual realization on the part of Congress that the American Revolution was largely an accomplished fact. British governance at this point was virtually nonexistent in the colonies represented at the Second Continental Congress. De facto they were in charge, but it remained to make it official. Ultimately, this meant establishing sovereignty and recognition by the European community of states, or at least some of its members. And in this world dominated and balanced by military power, a key criterion of sovereignty was the possession of an army. At this point the exigencies of defense certainly predominated, but as time went on the existence and continued survival of the Continental Army became symbolic of the British inability to reestablish their authority. And when this failure became salient, leading the French to capitalize by striking an alliance with the Americans, the Continental Army proved exactly the receptacle needed to receive and channel Bourbon legions as they arrived. This would be a matter requiring deftness, diplomacy, and, above all, leadership, which brings us back to the middle of June 1775.

Several of George Washington's prominent biographers have concluded that he was a kind of compromise candidate as commander in chief of the Continental Army.[49] As always there was an undercurrent of congressional grumbling and several others who craved the job, including Charles Lee, and from Massachusetts, Artemas Ward and John Hancock. Of the three only Hancock was on the scene as a member of Congress—its president, in fact—but he was a businessman with gout, not a soldier.

More recently the trend has been to consider GW's appointment as somewhere between a foregone conclusion and a slam dunk.[50] It speaks volumes that the decision occurred exactly one day after the Continental Army was formed, and that the vote was unanimous, the first in a long string. Decades later, John Adams tried to claim responsibility for the decision; but in fact it was Washington himself who had sealed the deal with a virtuoso performance.

From the moment he arrived he struck exactly the right note. His sixteen years in the House of Burgesses put him in tune with other legislators, while his instinct to listen rather than speak was seen as a sign of sagacity in this gabby environment. But most important he managed to hide every trace of ambition and present himself in a manner that exactly matched Country Party conceptions.[51]

The true patriot never panders, and the only signs GW gave of his availability for command were visual: his bearing and, of course, that uniform. His acceptance speech on June 16 was a masterpiece of high-minded reluctance:

> Tho' I am truly sensible of the high Honour done me, in this Appointment, yet I feel great distress, from a consciousness that my abilities and military experience may not be equal to the extensive and important Trust. . . .
>
> As to pay, Sir, I beg leave to assure the Congress, that, as no pecuniary consideration could have tempted me to have accepted this arduous employment. . . . I do not wish to make any

profit from it. I will keep an exact Account of my expences ... and that is all I desire.[52]

Exactly what these legislators—conditioned to suspect all forms of power, especially military power—wanted and needed to hear. It was as if a republican version of the Patriot King had sprung to life, a substitute for the other, increasingly disappointing George. In the face of this bravura performance, only Elbridge Gerry back in Boston thought to call him "Generalissimo." Those on the scene were thoroughly won over—barely aware, it seems, that they were not simply giving him command; they were potentially giving him the fate of the American Revolution.

For if Washington's image of disinterest constituted masterful politics, it also appears to have been utterly sincere. He fervently believed in his own high-mindedness and was determined to conduct himself accordingly. Nothing compromises morality like a long, violent revolution, and George Washington over the next eight years remained a bulwark of decency, a remarkable achievement and quite possibly his greatest contribution to the Glorious Cause.

Nor does his reluctance to assume command and doubts about his military capabilities appear to have been in any way feigned. Washington the sleepwalker may not have missed a step, but at another level he was full of trepidation. In the only letter between the two Martha left us, her mate cried out almost in despair: "You may believe me my dear Patcy, when I assure you, in the most solemn manner, that, so far from seeking this appointment I have used every endeavor in my power to avoid it, not only from my unwillingness to part with you and the family, but from a consciousness of its being a trust too great for my Capacity."[53]

He was absolutely right. Compared to the British officers he would soon be facing, Washington was an amateur.[54] He had never commanded more than a brigade, and that only once. He had never fought a field engagement, his specialty being irregular warfare. He knew nothing of artillery and had never been involved with cavalry operations, two of the three components of the eighteenth-century battlefield.[55] He did have a proven flair for military administration, and, of course, he was George Washington. But militarily at least, he would prove very much a work in progress. There was one more thing. By taking this job he became a marked man. Should the Revolution collapse at an early stage he could count on losing everything—all that he had worked for and an untimely death at the end of a rope.[56] But at this point there was no turning back.

As if to ratify its fateful decisions, just a few days later word filtered into Congress telling of a massive British attack on Patriot positions along a rise known as Bunker Hill. George Washington was already on his way to Boston and the rage militaire.

4

Gage had lost the confidence of the King when he simultaneously called for twenty thousand reinforcements and the repeal of the Intolerable Acts,[57] and at the end of May the warship HMS *Cerberus* sailed into Boston Harbor carrying his replacements, three major generals carefully selected from more than one hundred candidates.[58] William Howe, John Burgoyne, and Henry Clinton were all destined to play major roles in Britain's epic failure to suppress the Revolution, and to get things off on the right note they participated in Gage's parting shot, an operation that devolved into an absolutely bone-headed frontal assault on the Americans.

As usual, word had gotten out about Gage's plans, this time to seize the high ground, causing the Americans to respond by hastily fortifying Bunker Hill. Clinton suggested going in behind them by landing troops on the south side of the Charlestown Peninsula. But Gage expected little resistance from the "undisciplined rabble"[59] atop the hill, and ordered the force of around 2,500 elite grenadiers and light infantry, commanded by newly arrived William Howe, to engage from the northeast tip of the peninsula, expecting to outflank the redoubt from that direction.[60] When they arrived on June 17, 1775, the fortifications proved more extensive than expected. The men began shouting "Push on, push on," so the officers led them straight up the hill with bayonets fixed into a deadly surf of flying lead that would soon leave the hill dotted with grotesque piles of dead and dying redcoats. Two times they broke and re-formed, before a third charge rooted out the Americans, most of whom, now out of ammunition, raced away.

But the thirty or so rebels trapped at the top were bayoneted repeatedly in a frenzy of retribution that would be seen again and again when Americans tried to surrender. Almost archetypical was the fate of Joseph Warren, the prominent Patriot under whose signature the original letter requesting consideration of a centralized army had come. Or at least that of his corpse was. Killed instantly by a musket ball to the head during the last assault, his body was stripped, bayoneted until unrecognizable, and pushed into a shallow ditch. A day or so later Lieutenant James Drew returned to "spit in his Face, Jump'd on his Stomach and at last cut off his Head."[61] Bizarrely exaggerated behavior, of course, but fueled by the same combination of rage and contempt that British combatants would demonstrate throughout the war, and also one huge reason why they lost despite dominating most of the battles.

Tactically, Bunker Hill counted as a victory for the English, but as GW, paraphrasing Pyrrhus, told his brother Sam, "a few more such Victories woul[d] put an end to their army and the present contest."[62] The British suffered a horrendous 40 percent casualties, around 1,150 redcoats killed or wounded, more than double those of the Patriots.[63] It was even worse among officers, not generally targeted in Europe; their dead amounted to over one-eighth of all the English officers killed in the entire war.[64] They would adapt militarily, but this was symptomatic. Bunker Hill was a disaster that could have easily been avoided. From top to bottom the British were decidedly more competent than their adversaries, but their arrogance and disdain drove them up the hill, and they paid the price.

On the Patriot side, Bunker Hill constituted a kind of climax to the rage militaire—that delusive state that confused martial zeal with real military skill and training. The Battles of Lexington and Concord were surely no fluke now that Americans had mauled British regulars twice in a row.

But the notion that colonists were somehow better fighters than royal regulars stretched as far back as the Braddock debacle, and had been bolstered by the belief that the frontier had produced a particularly hardy and lethal set of combatants in its pioneering westerners, versed in the elusive tactics of Native Americans and armed with uniquely deadly firearms. "Rifles infinitely better than those imported, are daily made in many places in Pennsylvania, and all the gunsmiths are constantly employed," an Anglican minister warned the Earl of Dartmouth in 1775. "In this country, my lord, the boys, as soon as they can discharge a gun, frequently exercise themselves ... making the Americans the best marksmen in the world. ... In marching through the woods, one thousand of these riflemen would cut to pieces ten-thousand of your best English troops."[65]

Like all powerful myths, there was some truth behind this one. Unlike in England or Continental Europe, a large percentage of colonists owned or had easy access to firearms, though most were probably short-range muskets and shot-firing weapons.[66] Americans could shoot, and some could do it extraordinarily well, but these were not in the majority. Nonetheless, when the Second Continental Congress nationalized the army, the first troops it recruited to join those surrounding Boston were specifically rifle companies from the western counties of Pennsylvania, Maryland, and Virginia.[67] "This province has raised 1,000 rifleman, the worst of whom will put a ball into a man's head at a distance of 150 or 200 yards," the Bradford brothers of Philadelphia cautioned *The London Chronicle*, "therefore advise your officers ... to settle their affairs in England before their departure."[68]

Riflemen would prove valuable, especially when led by a commander of real ability, like Daniel Morgan, and used primarily to attrite the enemy. But they were never that numerous and they had serious vulnerabilities. The tight bore seal that made their rifles so accurate also left them very slow to load; nor could the long, slender barrels mount a bayonet, so in an open field, riflemen were inherently unable to hold off charging British troops. That would also prove true of many other more conventionally armed Continental Army units. Victory would take training and fire discipline and the ability to maneuver in large groups without becoming just a crowd. None of this could be said of the motley assemblage wrapped around the hills surrounding Boston. But they had a lot of heart, still fueled by revolution and the rage militaire. And as amateurs at war they were not afraid to innovate.

Neither was George Washington. He, too, was an amateur at war, but he was much farther along the road to professionalism, and the goal here was, and always would be, a force that looked and acted like its British counterpart. Consequently, when he reached Cambridge on July 2 and got a glimpse of what he was supposed to command, his reaction was somewhere between shock and horror: "It would be far beyond the Compass of a Letter for me to describe the Situation of Things here on my arrival," he wrote one of his recently appointed major generals, Philip Schuyler. "Confusion and Discord reigned in every Department. . . . Most happily the Ministerial Troops have not availed themselves of their advantages."[69]

## 5

The more he looked, the worse things seemed, and also smelled. The agglomeration of New England militias that had gravitated around Boston was more a gathering than it was an army. The components did pretty much what they wanted, only conditionally subordinate to higher authority; so they shot off their weapons just to hear them fire, and treated drill as some sort of pointless lobsterback routine that could never help them fight real battles. Meanwhile, they were coming to live in their own filth; letting garbage accumulate and not bothering to dig latrines, they were creating, as virtually all sieges did in this era, a paradise for epidemic disease.[70]

George Washington understood all this, but he also knew he had to move cautiously. Upon arrival he constituted essentially an army of one, commander in chief on paper alone. These were practically all northerners who already had their own generals, ones they liked— Artemas Ward and Israel Putnam.[71] This was the moment George Washington had to assume the mantle of generalissimo; if he was going to sell himself here, it had to be as a revolutionary leader of supreme charisma. They didn't necessarily have to like him, but they had to be awed by his presence.

This was, of course, all a bluff. Like good poker players, revolutionary leaders have to have this skill if they want to survive, since they almost always have the worst hand. George Washington was about to reveal himself as a master of illusion, a bluffmeister extraordinaire. The Boston campaign may not have been his masterpiece, but it certainly was an impressive opening act. As usual he relied first on his best trick—looking and acting the part of George Washington.

Dr. James Thacher, who kept a remarkably literate and accurate journal through the entire war, and whose path crossed Washington's on several occasions without the two ever getting to know each other, still had no trouble picking up his aura in Boston. On July 20, 1775, he recorded: "I have been much gratified this day with a view of General Washington. His excellency was on horseback in company with several military gentlemen. It was not difficult to distinguish him from all others; his personal appearance is truly noble and majestic, being tall and well-proportioned. His dress is a blue coat with buff-colored facings, a rich epaulette on each shoulder, buff under dress and an elegant small sword: a black cockade in his hat."[72] The man was made to wear a uniform and ride a horse, and with the exception of Artemas Ward, who was soon pushed aside, the New Englanders more or less instinctively fell in behind him.

Washington's immediate objectives were pretty clear and interlocking. First, he had to establish that this was now a unified Continental Army, the militias being formally incorporated by Congress on July 4, 1775, and that it was now his prerogative to issue general orders.[73] This was never challenged; he was free to install his blueprint for command and force development to the degree possible under the somewhat squalid circumstances.

Next on his agenda was the strong urge to instill as much discipline and military order as was possible with the rowdy bunch he had inherited. In order to be militarily effective in any kind of field engagements, troops had to be able to maneuver and shoot with at least some degree of precision and alacrity.

Yet George Washington's persistence in trying to turn the Continental Army into a force basically mirroring its British adversary seems tinged by his earlier experience of craving but never quite getting a royal commission. Now he was determined to build a counterpart, and to do so with the same aristocratic social model, not realizing until at least Valley Forge that there was more to his men and to training than to "work up these raw Materials into good Stuff."[74] Even at this stage, he probably underestimated the enthusiasm and ingenuity of the men in the ranks, though much of it and them were destined to be short-lived.

His presence was felt almost instantly. "There is great overturning in the camp as to order and regularity," wrote regimental chaplain William Emerson, Ralph Waldo's grandfather. "New lords, new laws. The Generals Washington and Lee are upon the lines every day. . . . Great distinction is made between officers and soldiers. Everyone is made to know his place and keep it, or be tied up and receive thirty or forty lashes according to his crime. Thousands are at work every day from four till eleven o'clock in the morning. It is surprising how much work has been done."[75]

But more challenges to the kind of army Washington wanted kept marching into camp, some, ironically, from his home state. In late July, to everybody's surprise since they were weeks ahead of schedule, the first of the congressionally mandated rifle companies arrived. Led by Captain Daniel Morgan, whom Washington (and the reader) may have remembered as a young teamster nearly whipped to death for striking a British officer, these Virginians shambled in after a six-hundred-mile trek, many of them over six feet tall, clad in "white frocks or rifle-shirts, and round hats" and, slung across their shoulders, the ubiquitous long rifles.[76]

They caused an immediate sensation, and none more than Morgan himself, a rustic giant of a man who treated his soldiers more like younger brothers than minions—certainly not the Washington way. Soon they were freelancing, picking off British officers at two hundred yards to the amazement of the New Englanders, and generally acting as if they owned the place. Soldiers from coastal Marblehead, themselves clad in round jackets and fisherman's trousers, started making fun of the Virginians' rural attire.

*Daniel Morgan: a great leader and innovative
tactician, just not Washington's type.*

CHARLES WILLSON PEALE/WIKIMEDIA COMMONS

As the months passed, animosity grew and finally erupted in an
epic snowball fight in Harvard Yard. As remembered by Israel Trask—
then a ten-year-old, brought by his father to war in a rage militaire
version of day care—the Marblehead men confronted fifty to a hundred of the Virginians and started pelting them with frozen artillery:

> These soft missives were interchanged but a few minutes before
> both parties closed and a fierce struggle commenced with biting
> and gouging on the one part, and knockdown on the other
> part. . . . Reinforced by their friends, in less than five minutes,
> more than a thousand combatants were on the field. . . . At this
> juncture General Washington made his appearance . . . and
> rushed into the thickest of the melee, with an iron grip seized

two tall, brawny, athletic, savage-looking riflemen by the throat, keeping them at arm's length, alternately shaking and talking to them.... Its effect ... was instantaneous flight at the top of their speed in all directions ... [until] the general and his two criminals were the only occupants of the field of action.[77]

Impressive perhaps, but exactly what George Washington didn't want to have to do. Where was Morgan? He wanted these troops under his control, not rioting.

GW believed—as did the British and the entire eighteenth-century European military establishment—that the key to everything was the officer corps. They trained and disciplined the troops. They led them in battle and maintained order in the face of chaos and death. All of this ranged from unpleasant to horrible, so they had to enforce their will brutally, and keep their distance emotionally. They were the central instrument of control. And the loose informality GW saw between enlisted and officers among not only Morgan's troops but also these New Englanders was exactly what he wanted to stamp out: "I have made a pretty good grand slam among such kinds of officers as the Massachusetts government abounds," he wrote a fellow Virginian in Congress.[78]

So began George Washington's Revolutionary War–long project to build an officer corps comparable to its red-coated competitors. The results were far from ideal. While the officers did improve militarily, they also grew into an entitled minority, whose special revolutionary credentials (risking their lives under miserable conditions) would one day cause them to toy with threatening civilian supremacy.

As you might expect from a generalissimo in a revolution, he did far better with the highest leadership, the gathering of his intimate cadre of trusted henchmen to carry out his plans. He had always been a team builder, cultivating a personal element that went back to Fort Necessity. He had also struck up some regional acquaintances with individuals he sensed had military talent, most notably with William Alexander of New Jersey, who insisted on being called Lord Stirling.

But that wouldn't do now. GW had to generate alliances with cadre from all regions but especially New England, and build bridges so that his leadership element had roots that stretched across the entire revolutionary landscape. That process began in Boston, and very rapidly took shape. He had arrived with a core group: Thomas Mifflin and Joseph Reed, the first of his young "penmen" acting as his personal staff; and also two major generals, Charles Lee and Philip Schuyler. Except for the last, all would prove disloyal early in the war. It didn't matter. Washington attracted people like lint, and he had an extraordinary instinct for talent. This malodorous gathering surrounding Boston contained some extraordinarily motivated and capable individuals, and Washington amid his wanderings and perpetual inspections quickly fastened on several who would become permanent links in his inner circle.

Henry Knox was a fat, ebullient Boston bookseller who spent every spare moment before the war reading military history and engineer-

*Henry Knox: from bookstore to artillery, an amateur at war.*

GILBERT STUART/LIBRARY OF CONGRESS

ing. Washington liked his hands-on approach. Now a self-taught artillerist at the head of a surprisingly effective regiment, he wasn't afraid
to shoot the guns himself or resort to the unexpected. Knox, like
Washington, was a gifted amateur. He was an intuitive and almost immediate choice to head all things artillery—a necessary one, too, since
virtually no one on the Patriot side knew much of anything about the
care and feeding of cannon.

Knox also would prove a great friend, a true stalwart who stood at
Washington's side through all the war's major battles, and eventually
(with the help of the French) turned the artillery into one of the Continental Army's most efficient branches.[79] For now it was his optimism
and bravado Washington craved; this was a siege and he didn't have
much in the way of siegecraft.

Then there was Nathanael Greene, the classic right-hand man, a
spirit so akin to Washington's that he was practically a doppelgänger.
A Rhode Islander, like Washington he sprang from relatively privileged but undereducated circumstances, born a Quaker but drummed
out for his support of violent resistance.[80] When Washington found
him in Cambridge, he saw a younger version of himself, an autodidact
at war, but a fast learner soon to become the youngest general in the
Continental Army. He would make mistakes, bad ones like the loss of
Fort Washington; but Washington never lost faith. By 1777, he had
introduced him to Congress as virtually his alter ego: "This Gentleman
is so much in my confidence—so intimately acquainted with my
ideas . . . with everything respecting the Army, that I have thought it
unnecessary to particularize or prescribe a certain line of duty or en-
quiries for him."[81]

But of course he did. Giving him all the worst jobs, because he
could do them. Making him quartermaster general when the Continental Army was falling apart for lack of supplies, then sending him
south, after two major American forces had been obliterated, because
Greene understood his advantage lay in the countryside. There he ran
Cornwallis ragged, setting him up for Yorktown.

There was something else. Greene, like Washington, was a passionate man, but unlike GW he had married his Sally Fairfax, the beautiful
and relentlessly flirtatious Caty.[82] War in the winter months turned

*Nathanael Greene: Washington's designated alter ego.*

JAMES TRENCHARD/ LIBRARY OF CONGRESS

MAJ.ᴿ GEN.ᴸ GREENE.

into a co-ed activity in this era, and that first social season, not only Martha but also Caty came to Cambridge, instantly turning GW's head and becoming his favorite among service wives throughout the war. "His Excellency and Mrs. Greene danced upwards of three hours without once sitting down," reported Mr. Greene at one point.[83] But he was not the jealous type, and this was nothing more than a flirtation, almost like having Sally Fairfax around, but not. So the bond only grew.

Far less capable, but still destined to join the inner circle as a sort of proverbial weak link, was John Sullivan. A ruddy, voluble New Hampshire lawyer with a reputation for causing trouble, he was a delegate to the First Continental Congress, where GW may have gotten to know him. Now as a brigadier general, his first letter to Washington in Cambridge informed him of a severe, perhaps fatal, ammunition shortage.[84] That would always be the sort of news that came from Sullivan. He knew virtually nothing of war at this point and would not learn a great deal more, so his results as a commander usually ranged from mixed to grim. But he was always straight with Washington, who hated nothing more than being lied to about bad news. He was also utterly loyal, if temperamental, and could be counted on to do GW's bidding to the degree his limited talents availed him.

These were not problems for Benedict Arnold, the man who eventually proved the rotten link in George Washington's chain of command; but in Cambridge that summer he seemed exactly the sort of paladin the Revolution required. He had already shown himself a military opportunist by seizing Ticonderoga, just the kind of audacity GW instinctively admired. Now he was pushing to form a second pincer in the planned liberation of Canada in which Congress and GW placed so much hope. While Schuyler and his second-in-command Richard Montgomery prepared to head up Lake Champlain toward Montreal, Arnold wanted another expedition to assault Quebec by marching overland along the Kennebec River. It says something about the moment that Arnold believed this would entail a trek of around 180 miles, rather than the true distance of 350.[85]

Nobody had accurate maps; what Arnold brought to the table was rage militaire and an extra helping of testosterone sufficient to convince George Washington he was in the presence of a kindred martial spirit, that he would fight and die for the Glorious Cause. He turned out to be its Judas Iscariot, but that took time, and something like it was probably inevitable. Because revolutions are a matter of extreme belief, they are binary politically. There is no middle ground; you must be on one side or the other, which opens the option for treachery, or at least perceived treachery. So, just as the French had Robespierre, the Russians Trotsky, and the Chinese Madame Mao, we had Arnold, our Black Knight. But for Washington, always a better judge of talent than loyalty, this was enough for now, so he sent him north.

6

Operationally speaking, the strategic situation around Boston bordered on the absurd. Neither side arrived as a result of clear thinking, and because of the murky intelligence climate, both misinterpreted adversary capabilities, all the while trying their best to mask their own vulnerabilities. So a sort of blind man's double-bluff standoff ensued, not likely to produce much fighting, but still subject to rapid overturn by novel means. As military amateurs, the Americans proved the more creative, so they won yet again.

The British notion that the Revolution was a matter of a few ideological hotheads was what trapped them in Boston, which was viewed as the source of the infection.[86] So they poured regulars into the city to lock it down with a military quarantine. By the time General Gage, who had presided over much of this, realized that the Revolution was everywhere, it was too late. The troops just kept cycling in, accumulating from five thousand in July to almost ten thousand when they were finally evacuated the following March.[87]

A thrombosis of redcoats dedicated only to being there, a kind of crimson placeholder in a game where the opponent has swept the board: They were a decent fighting force, and they had a very well-placed spy in Dr. Benjamin Church, the Americans' chief physician;[88] but they were no threat to the rebels surrounding them. Certainly they could cut their way out, probably disperse them, but then where would they go? What would they do? Inland there was only countryside dotted with villages, each potentially hiding a coven of rebels. The same sort of fighters that had self-organized around Boston would simply form scattered bands of irregular warriors impossible to catch. So the British stayed plugged up and attempted to look ferocious to the lines surrounding them, staging raids to keep up appearances, and committing an occasional atrocity, like mounting on a gibbet the body of a Continental soldier killed in a skirmish.[89]

It was about all they could do in Boston. But their mood was better reflected along the realm where they could bring power to bear: the seacoast. On October 17, 1775, a force of five British ships moved into the inner harbor of Falmouth, Massachusetts (now Portland, Maine),

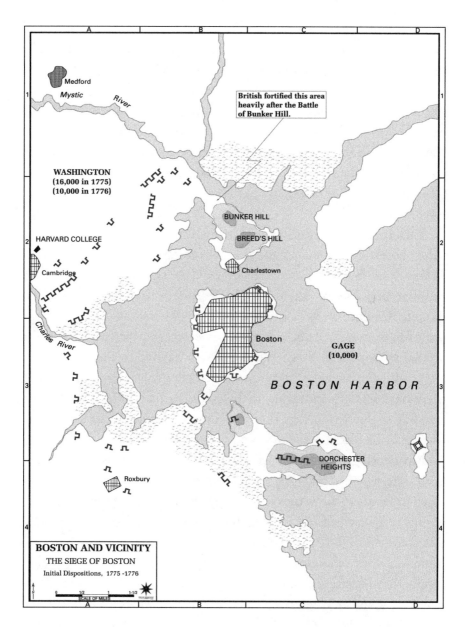

where a proclamation was issued informing the inhabitants that the flotilla was there to "execute a just punishment" for the town's support of the rebellion.⁹⁰ The townspeople could either swear an oath of allegiance to the King and turn over all their firearms, or they could evacuate. When they chose the latter, Captain Henry Mowat proceeded to level the place with an eight-hour bombardment that destroyed around four hundred structures and left more than a thousand people homeless on the brink of winter.[91] After a similar bonfire set by the Royal Navy in Norfolk on New Year's Day, 1776, such attacks trailed off but never ceased, as the residents of the Connecticut coast learned through repeated scorchings throughout the course of the war.[92] But even at this early date, raids like this revealed two enduring features of British power application in America: It never extended much beyond the reach of the Royal Navy, and it was fueled as much by an urge to inflict terror and punishment as it was by a desire to re-solve the crisis.

Back in Cambridge, George Washington nailed it when he wrote: "The Ministry have begun the Destruction of our Sea Port Towns ... with every Circumstance of Cruelty and Barbarity which Revenge and Malice would suggest."[93] But in this case he could do more than fulminate; Washington quickly obtained congressional ap-proval to arm and certify a number of vessels as privateers—basically pirates with papers. Since most of New England's merchant fleet, along with their capable and experienced crews, were now sitting idle, there were lots of candidates. If the colonists had nothing that could stand up to the Royal Navy, they could at least attack its commerce and wage guerilla war at sea.

Privateering proved one of the Americans' most useful acquired skills, one destined to work for the entire war, forcing British supply ships to resort to slow-moving convoys for protection, ones that still offered targets when bad weather blew them apart. And in GW's case this factor bore fruit almost immediately. On November 28, Captain John Manley's schooner *Lee* bagged the *Nancy*, a British ordnance supply ship loaded with a brand-new thirteen-inch brass mortar, sev-eral varieties of shot, and two thousand muskets with bayonets.[94] To an army chronically short on firearms, this constituted a godsend, and GW does mention "this Instance of divine favour;"[95] but in reality his army was still too short on powder to shoot them. From the point in August when Sullivan informed him the powder problem had become critical (down to thirty-six barrels, or less than nine rounds per man), recovery had been steady but gradual, far from enough in GW's eyes to stop a full-scale British assault.[96]

This was typical. About the best Washington could do at this point was a force built largely on flimflam, a time bomb of an army set to vaporize on New Year's Day if not before.

Given the unsanitary conditions, and the fact that most of its soldiers came from farms and villages unexposed to epidemic disease, it didn't take long for chronic illness to catch up with the Continental Army. Its members quickly came down with a range of respiratory and intestinal maladies, causing the number fit for duty to plummet to only a little more than half of the approximately ten thousand men surrounding Boston.[97]

And there was something more ominous. George Washington learned his old acquaintance from Barbados, smallpox, was picking off between ten and thirty of his men a day. It was destined to kill more than one hundred thousand Americans (about four times as many as the British managed) before the war was over.[98] With almost instinctive energy, GW quarantined those with symptoms and even considered inoculating the entire force, before backing off on the grounds that it might fatally reduce its already sagging readiness. Two years later he would inoculate his whole army at Morristown.[99] It proved to be one of his best strategic moves. Smallpox, if it ever picked up momentum among the rank and file, had a far better chance than the British of destroying the Continental Army.

So did the timer George Washington could almost hear ticking away in the background. The force around Boston was literally an army without a future, with almost its entire structure made up of men with a one-year term of duty scheduled to end on January 1, 1776.[100] In October, Congress sent a delegation including the savvy Benjamin Franklin north to meet their commander in chief and address the looming crisis. The man they found in Cambridge sounded less like Washington the revolutionary than Washington the general and British Army wannabe. He asked for authority to enforce stricter discipline with harsher and more frequent punishment. He wanted mutiny and desertion made capital crimes. He wanted to double the size of the force structure to around twenty thousand. But most disturbing in an ideological sense, he wanted it manned with long-term enlisted, which meant, in effect, that choker of liberty: the dreaded standing army.[101]

Congress endorsed it all, but they did so knowing that compliance depended on confirmation by state legislatures known to be solidly behind one-year enlistments, at this point on the grounds that the war was bound to be short (an assumption at the start of most wars).[102] So what historian Joseph Ellis calls "a military turnstile" was created by the states, and then kept revolving by a steady stream of newcomers arriving and veterans leaving, a heterogeneous mass of time obligations that kept George Washington nervously guessing through the course of the war what his force structure actually constituted.[103]

But his problem in the fall of 1775 was much more immediate. His army was set to abscond, and he had to get them to reenlist. But it was also plain that neither party much liked the other. Earlier, he had set off a firestorm in the Massachusetts legislature and the Second Continental Congress, when it was reliably reported he had described New Englanders as "an exceedingly dirty & nasty people."[104] It's a good bet that many held reciprocal opinions of their stiff-necked general.

At any rate, reenlistment remained sufficiently glacial for an October council of war to consider then reject the recruitment of slaves and free negroes, only to reverse itself on December 30 with regard to freedmen already serving.[105] As of November 28, only around 3,500 of his troops had signed up, a worried Washington reported, "and such a dirty, mercenary Spirit pervades the whole, that I should not be at all surprised at any disaster that may happen."[106]

But as December passed and the fatal date neared, enlistments picked up, and in the end 9,650 men signed on to the Continental Army's reincarnation.[107] You could almost hear GW exhaling sighs of relief as he wrote John Hancock: "Is it not in the pages of History perhaps, to furnish a case like ours; to maintain a post within Musket Shot of the Enemy for Six months together, without [powder] and at the same time to disband one army and recruit another within that distance of twenty-odd British regiments."[108] It was his biggest bluff since Fort Necessity, and it turned out a lot better. He was a natural at deception. After all, he lived inside a façade. But he still had a very shaky force structure and not much else. So he had to keep on improvising, campaigning with the equivalent of smoke and mirrors.

Washington's entire combat career had been spent on the frontier, a realm of raids, where surprise was the critical ingredient. During the course of the Revolutionary War, from beginning to end, he never strayed from that objective—to catch the enemy unaware. But it was one thing to stage a surprise attack with a force numbering in the tens or low hundreds, and another to move an entire army unnoticed into a position of decisive advantage; that took GW a long time to learn.

And at this point, necessity was the mother of invention. Back in September, he called a council of war and unveiled a plan for a sudden amphibious assault across Back Bay in flat-bottomed boats, a scheme that was certainly breathtaking in its audacity. But given that such operations are considered the most difficult of all military endeavors, and the training of his troops was not the greatest, his fellow generals roundly disagreed when he maintained that the plan "did not appear impractical, though hazardous,"[109] and quickly and decisively overruled him.

It was a good thing they did, because such an operation, to have any chance of success, had to be backed by continuous artillery support, and at this point Washington had little beyond the big brass mortar bagged from the *Nancy*. So he turned to Henry Knox, like Harry Houdini might turn to a stage assistant, and the twenty-five-year-old amateur artillerist soon began conjuring cannon from out of nowhere, it must have seemed to his British audience.

Actually it was from Fort Ticonderoga, where Knox and his men found and extracted forty-four guns, fourteen mortars, and a howitzer.[110] They then floated them down Lake George, transferred them to sledges propelled by eighty teams of oxen, crossed the frozen Hudson, and then pulled them up and over the Berkshires in an epic three-hundred-mile trek. By late January, Knox had passed Framingham, and by early February pieces were being put into position around Boston. As things turned out, it was probably the most important sleigh ride in American history. But George Washington at this point found it hard to be optimistic.

# 7

On January 13, 1776,[111] he had received word that Benedict Arnold's assault on Quebec had been turned back, and the Canadian invasion was crumbling into nothing. It was likely doomed from the beginning, undertaken at the edge of winter, and powered as it was mostly by improvisation and the rage militaire, both of which had limits. For one thing nobody seems to have asked whether French Canadians, though they may not have liked their English masters, would necessarily believe they were aiming to enslave them.[112]

That aside, the force structures on both pincers of the invasion were basically thrown together. On Philip Schuyler's side, initial success would eventually be confounded by his troops' departure, virtually en masse, when their enlistments terminated at the end of the year.[113] As for Arnold, the look of his eight hundred New England volunteers, mostly farmers, fishermen, and clerks, prompted Washington to fortify the force with three companies of the Virginia riflemen under Daniel Morgan. While Washington may have been happy to get them out of camp, these frontiersmen proved much better adapted to the Maine wilderness and provided the skills and endurance to keep the expedition moving. So did Arnold and Morgan, who quickly bonded into a team that would one day humble an entire British army, just not this time.

On November 9, 1775, after a forty-five-day slog, Arnold's army, now shrunk to 675,[114] had reached the Saint Lawrence River, just four miles from Quebec on the other side. A heavy storm prevented them from crossing for four days, but at last they stood before the city, protected on three sides by cliffs and to the west by a thirty-foot wall, but not much in the way of a garrison. Morgan wanted to attack immediately,[115] but Arnold thought their very presence might overawe. It didn't, and after a few days he pulled well back to try to recover from the march.

Patriot prospects brightened in early December, when General Richard Montgomery marched into camp. Having fought his way up to Montreal and taken it, he headed for Quebec with three hundred men and, more important, food, winter clothing, and the artillery needed to breach Quebec's fortifications. When Washington got wind of the juncture he was ecstatic, writing Arnold: "It is not in the power of any man to command success, but you have done more—you have deserved it,"[116] paraphrasing Addison's *Cato*, a key piece of the Revolution's inspirational rhetoric. For a moment it seemed that in spite of being in the middle of nowhere, the rage militaire might prevail.

It didn't. Things had changed in Quebec. Inside now was Governor Guy Carleton, a cool-headed military professional who had fled Montreal with a small element of British regulars.[117] Using them as a core, he organized the defenders who—though like the Patriot force consisted largely of fishermen and farmers—numbered nearly 1,800. Meanwhile, the calendar was forcing the hands of the Americans; the same year-end enlistment-completion date that bedeviled GW demanded an attack before everybody picked up and left.

After a false start on December 27, they were down to their last chance. The night of New Year's Eve featured a blizzard and screaming winds. "Our Detach't was drawed up and form'd a Square," remembered infantryman Jeremiah Greenman, "ware genl. Mountgomery asked us if we ware willing to storm the city & the biger part of them seam willing."[118] It wasn't hard to tell they were coming, and the British were waiting, having slept clothed for a week.[119]

The assault actually began well past midnight. Arnold led six hundred New Englanders against Lower Town on the north, while Montgomery's three hundred attacked the south, only to be greeted by cannon loaded with grapeshot. He led the charge, and the first blast blew his handsome face off.[120] After that things fell apart. Arnold's troops broke through the first British barrier but were stopped at the second, and as they reeled backward he was hit by a ball in the leg—a wound bad enough to leave him with a permanent limp—and had to be taken to the rear. Then Daniel Morgan, who took charge of the van, was cornered and, after waving his sword and daring anybody to take it, was forced to surrender, along with over four hundred other Americans, including Jeremiah Greenman.[121]

Arnold stubbornly hung on, pulling his camp back a mile from the city, picking up only a few reinforcements over the next several months. When spring finally came, the wound still bothering him, he ceded his command and left the scene, riding slowly toward Montreal. But he was far from a beaten man. Arnold was nothing if not resilient, so there would be further adventures. But the assault on Canada would never be repeated. It was a distraction and a waste of vital military resources.

## 8

The news from Quebec came on top of the winter blues for Washington. He and everybody else had invested a great deal of false hope in the venture, and it left him permanently soured on a redux when the French joined the cause. It also showed him rather definitively that revolutionary fervor and its military manifestation, the rage militaire, could only do so much. His opponent wouldn't just fold in its face: a lesson that was bound to remind him of the massive lump of redcoats who sat stolidly in Boston, his central problem being how to get rid of them. At least Martha had arrived and settled in, despite the rugged circumstances. "I confess I shudder every time I hear the sound of a gun," she reported home.[122] But her welcome appearance was cold comfort given Washington's other frustrations.

Both Charles Lee and Horatio Gates were by now playing important roles in the army surrounding Boston. Gates had immediately demonstrated his administrative skill and been named adjutant general;[123] besides, he was an affable sort popular with the New Englanders. Lee, meanwhile, had fallen into position as something like the army's general contractor, the man with the plans. He knew how to construct and train a force; he understood strategy and the capabilities of the British opponents at a level beyond Washington's at this point. He was acting as a de facto second-in-command, calling GW "My Dear General" instead of "His Excellency"[124] like everybody else— a slight not likely to be missed. Washington probably thought of Lee as a sort of useful idiot savant, an eccentric who had to be humored because of his military skills. He was more than that. He was treacherous, but still an idiot, so not too dangerous.

Gates was. A far more complete personality, his likeable nature masked an intense ambition that Washington sensed even at this early date. Alpha males survive in part because they keep an eye on their competitors, so relations with Gates very soon grew frosty, and with good reason as it turned out. Always in revolutions there are pretenders for the job of numero uno; to establish himself firmly Washington needed a stunning success here and now. But looking over his troops, that seemed like a long shot.

Nor were they any happier. It had been eight months since many of them had converged on Boston; life now was particularly miserable out in the cold, sleeping in huts. Just about everybody got sick at some point, and despite the Continental Army's miraculous reincarnation, desertions remained high. The rage militaire was wearing thin in the face of the elements.

But then in January everybody got a new shot of revolutionary energy, a renewed sense of purpose, and it came not out of the barrel of a gun, but from a printing press. Recent immigrant and brilliant propagandist Thomas Paine's *Common Sense,* the American Revolution's most influential single polemic, swept across the continent, selling 150,000 copies in just the first three months of 1776. The key to its power was that in clear, simple language it demolished the myth of the Patriot King, dubbing George III as "the Royal Brute of Great Britain," the chief tormentor of America.[125] The last link of loyalty to the mother country had been cut, and George Washington was quick to grasp the implications: "The sound Doctrine, and unanswerable reasoning contained [in] Common Sense, will not leave numbers at a loss to decide upon the Propriety of a Separation."[126] Suddenly the endless waiting around Boston snapped into focus with an objective, the same as Paine's: Get rid of the British.

Suitably infused, on February 16, 1776, Washington called his generals to a council of war again, and presented another plan based on surprise: an immediate attack across Back Bay, but this time with troops racing across the thick ice. Conducted at night with a cast of thousands ready to swarm, it might have worked, but it was inherently dangerous. Due to the continuing shortage of powder, none of Knox's newly acquired artillery had been emplaced on Dorchester Heights,[127] where they could cover the charging Continentals and keep them from being mowed down by British small-arms fire. Everybody knew this was true, but it was Gates who spoke up, calling the prospects of the plan "extremely doubtful" and questioning the whole premise of an attack: "I think there is no part of America where the Kings Troops can do so little injury to the United Colonies as the very spot they are now confin'd in."[128] This amounted to a stinging rebuke of Washington's entire plan, and as a concession the council offered an alternative: the fortification of Dorchester Heights alone.

Washington took it well, and in his crafty way worked methodically to bend the scheme to his own ends. There were signs the British were leaving anyway: cannon being removed from Bunker Hill and loaded aboard ships. But GW remained skeptical, and, besides, if the British wanted a quiet departure they could not allow Continental artillery on Dorchester Heights. The opportunity to provoke another, grander Bunker Hill was now in the offing. "If anything will Induce them to hazard an engagement," Washington assured John Hancock and Congress, "it will be our attempting to forifye these heights . . . provided we can get a sufficient supply of what we greatly want."[129]

This, of course was powder, and GW scrounged and begged the colonies until by early March he had enough to keep Knox's cannon and mortar firing for at least the time the plan required. Just as with the fortification of Bunker Hill, the idea was to seize it overnight. But Dorchester Heights was far harder, literally, since the ground was now frozen, making digging trenches nearly impossible. But practically no digging would be necessary, he had been assured by Lieutenant Colonel Rufus Putnam, whose experience as a millwright and surveyor convinced him that the necessary wooden frames, rock-filled wicker cylinders, and sharpened stakes "may be Carried on with safety to the people Employ'd and to the Cause in general."[130]

To mask his intentions Washington ordered the bombardment from his inexperienced artillerists to commence slowly over several days. (Before it was over they would still manage to burst five mortars, including the one taken from the *Nancy*.)[131] Then, as darkness fell on March 4, Knox and his men opened up full blast. The British took the bait, engaging in an unrestrained and utterly distracting artillery duel.

Meanwhile, under General Israel Putnam, who had commanded at Bunker Hill, eight hundred Continental infantry, a 1,200-man work party, and more than three hundred carts and wagons full of prefabricated materials headed up Dorchester Heights, on top of which they worked through the night. Dawn revealed two nearly finished redoubts looming over Boston and the British.

General William Howe, now in charge here, awoke to find himself in check . . . maybe checkmate unless he moved fast. Rear Admiral Molyneux Shuldham, his naval counterpart, informed him that once the colonists mounted artillery on Dorchester Heights the navy had to get out of the harbor, thereby removing his only means of escape.[132] His first instinct was to fight, and plans were laid for an immediate assault. But the memory of his disastrous day on Bunker Hill was still fresh in his mind, and Howe was nobody's fool; this was the last time he would fall for the colonists' version of the rope-a-dope, despite their fervent hope that he and his forces would remain just that predictable. A massive storm, which scattered his landing craft the next night, only ratified his decision to get out of town quick, so quick that the British left thirty cannon, three thousand blankets, and five thousand bushels of wheat. On March 17 the last of the redcoats quickstepped aboard ship, joined by many of the city's Loyalists in a flotilla of 120 ships that took ten days to get to sea, and eventually stretched nine miles out toward the horizon.[133] They were gone from Boston forever.

GW was the picture of modesty in victory. He even let the disdained Artemas Ward lead the vanguard into the city, following quietly, almost invisible to the elated multitudes of Bostonians. But as he wandered the half-wrecked and thoroughly plundered town, he must have been pleased with himself, though he would only confide how pleased to his brother Jack. "We have maintain'd our Ground against the Enemy . . . and, at last have beat them, in a shameful & precipitate manner out of a place the strongest by Nature on this Continent."[134]

He would have preferred a more sanguinary denouement decorated with heaps of dead redcoats. But strategists across time, including Sun Tzu and the Marshal Maurice de Saxe, have argued that the best victory is one in which the opponent is so disadvantaged that it is unnecessary to fight him. True enough, GW basically stumbled into this enviable position, dragged there by his own generals. But in war, as in cards, it's probably better to be lucky than good.

The Continental Congress ordered a gold medal struck for Washington.[135] It was really only endorsing what had now become obvious. With this stunning success George Washington became the heart and soul of the American Revolution, its primary human manifestation. The Patriot King had been replaced by a Patriot Generalissimo. To his everlasting credit Washington hated the concept, and did whatever he could to maintain civilian control, even when it was wrongheaded and mostly a fiction. But there were tough times coming, and he would be sorely tested.

# CHAPTER 4

# Amateur Hour

## 1

NOBODY DOUBTED THE BRITISH WOULD BE BACK, NOR WAS THERE much uncertainty as to their eventual destination.[1] Whereas Boston had been sterile strategically, its possession leading absolutely nowhere, New York was a positional jackpot, not only for its fine deep harbor, but also for the Hudson. Then known as the North River, it flowed straight up in that direction nearly to Lake Champlain, a potential water highway to British Canada and, more important, a means of severing New England from the rest of the rebellion.

Over a month before the British left Boston, GW had sent Charles Lee with a force of New Englanders to take possession of New York and formulate a plan for its defense. His professional eye quickly caught what could and could not be done. The entrance to the North River had to be fortified with heavy cannon. Lee planned to place four thousand troops on Brooklyn Heights in a "retrenched Camp, which I hope will render it impossible for 'em to get footing on that important Island," he wrote Washington.[2] "What to do with the City, I own puzzles me," he continued a few days later. "It is so encricle'd with deep navigable water, that whoever commands the Sea must command the town."[3] And as everybody knew, Britannia ruled the waves.

As if to remind him of that maxim, the day Lee arrived a flotilla of British warships carrying two companies of elite light infantry, under

Sir Henry Clinton and Admiral Sir Peter Parker, also pulled into New York Harbor. But there was no attempt to disembark; the object here was a conference with royal governor William Tryon, who at this point had been relegated by the rebels to an office aboard ship. Showing a bit of unbridled contempt for his adversaries, Clinton made no secret that he was headed south, where Loyalists were presumed numerous and potentially dominant with a little help from their friends in red coats—a persistent British illusion. "A certain droll way of proceeding," Lee observed acidly, "to communicate his full plan to the enemy is too novel to be credited."[4]

Very quickly Congress named Lee commander of the Southern Department, and just as quickly he left New York and headed toward Charleston to supervise its defenses. While this proved to be a good thing for that city, it removed from the strategic center of gravity the one general on the American side not only thoroughly familiar with British operational techniques, but also with the acumen to anticipate and potentially avoid their worst consequences. At a very critical point in the drama, the single true professional in the cast stepped out, leaving the stage to a pack of amateurs.

Meanwhile, George Washington remained one profoundly conflicted generalissimo. On one hand, he faced a series of purely military problems, responding predictably with a recourse to the standard eighteenth-century means of shaping up an army largely through punitive discipline. But on the other, GW was still every bit the committed revolutionary; he wanted a force that fought above all for the Glorious Cause. It would take him a long time and a fabulist Prussian drill instructor to begin reconciling these objectives, but at this point he operated as if the contradictions did not exist.

Militarily, the whole proposition of defending New York was dubious at best, and potentially catastrophic if the army got trapped on either Manhattan or Long Island; but from a revolutionary perspective it was entirely necessary as a demonstration of fervor. The Patriot narrative and Congress demanded that GW defend American territory from invasion by what was now a hostile foreign power.

But first he had to get there—move an army of ten thousand that had never marched anywhere to a point more than two hundred miles away—a logistical undertaking that dwarfed anything GW had previously attempted. Even Henry Knox's slender artillery train required three hundred teams of oxen.[5] Fortunately it was no race against the clock. Coast watchers had reliably reported that Howe's fleet leaving Boston had headed north toward Halifax, eliminating the possibility of an early strike against New York. So Washington and his ragtag army were able to shamble toward New York in a leisurely nine days.[6]

It was only when they arrived in mid-April that Washington must have realized what a formidable task awaited them. For one thing, the place was filled with Loyalists, thousands having fled, often from Connecticut across the sound, and taken up residence on Long Island or Manhattan itself. Washington despised them, joking back in Boston in a letter to Joseph Reed, when several were discovered to have killed themselves, that "it would have been happy for Mankind if more of them had done long ago—the Act of Suicide—By all Accts, a more miserable set of Beings does not exist than these."[7] Nevertheless, he scrupulously protected them from physical abuse and their property from plunder and destruction, finishing the missive: "Would it not be good policy to grant a general Amnesty? & conquer these People by a generous forgiveness?"[8] This became emblematic of George Washington's conduct during the entire course of the war. He always took the ethical high ground, never stooping to the excesses the British smeared over their attempts to suppress the Revolution.

In New York, it could have cost him his life. Although he didn't abuse them, GW kept the city's Loyalists under close watch, recruiting the first of what would become a substantial network of spies and designating a secret committee to ferret out and arrest Loyalist agents.[9] As it turned out, his suspicion was justified; danger lurked closer than he suspected. On June 17, 1776, a Loyalist counterfeiter under arrest revealed that two members of Washington's personal security detachment, Thomas Hickey and Michael Lynch, were involved in an arcane plot to sabotage the Continental Army. Soon the investigative dragnet drew in New York's mayor, David Mathews, who admitted funneling money from royal governor Tryon to help arm British sympathizers in a plot that was later revealed to have included George Washington's kidnapping or assassination.[10]

This was GW's first exposure to what is inevitably an occupational hazard to a generalissimo in time of revolution—betrayal, frequently with lethal implications. This one was pretty inept; still, it sent shock waves across America, ones that further alienated its citizens from Great Britain and welded GW into place even more solidly as the very embodiment of the Revolution.

His reaction was exactly what it should have been: decisive visuals but moderate in every other respect. A court-martial was held during which one witness stated that as many as seven hundred Patriots had vowed to take up with the British when they arrived, and that fully eight members of Washington's Life Guard were involved.[11] Unnerving stuff—the kind of occurrence that has stoked the paranoia of many a revolutionary, but not Washington; his reaction was measured. Mayor Mathews and a few of the apparently more culpable were shipped off to a Connecticut jail, where they either escaped or were let go without further trial. This left only Thomas Hickey as designated miscreant.

As noted in the introduction, when George Washington really wanted to get people's attention, he staged a hanging. This was one of his most notable. He brought out the entire army, every brigade, to witness the event. He had the gallows erected in a broad field near the Bowery so New Yorkers could watch. Twenty thousand of them showed up, just about the whole population. Hickey held it together, refusing even a chaplain, until, no pardon in sight, the hangman looped the noose around his neck, and he burst into tears—quickly cut short at the end of the halter.

Washington's general orders for the day further elucidated Hickey's demise, which he hoped would "be a warning to every soldier in the army" to turn his back on mutiny, sedition, and other transgressions "disgraceful to the character of a soldier and pernicious to his country." But then he got into causation. "And in order to avoid those crimes, the most certain method is to keep out of the temptation of them and particularly to avoid lewd women who, by the dying confession of this poor criminal, first led him into practices which ended in an untimely and ignominious death."[12]

This was no idle bit of moralism. As far as GW was concerned, he remained commander of an army still far too inclined to do whatever it pleased. In particular, wandering down to the Holy Ground—land owned by Trinity Church—to consort with the hundreds of whores who gathered there nightly.[13] In general, what George Washington wanted was an army made up of virtuous, impassioned Patriots, who were at the same time disciplined automatons obedient to his every command. And at this point it was pretty clear he had neither.

The force was growing, but really just accumulating. In March, Congress and Washington had agreed on a sketchy reinforcement scheme known as a "flying camp," by which designated militia units from a number of states would join the Continental Army in emergencies.[14] Now they came in droves, swelling the ranks to nineteen thousand by the end of June, and eventually to twenty-three thousand. But they proved nearly indigestible. Most had virtually no training, and the simplest orders had to be repeated unceasingly just to be comprehended, much less obeyed. For militia and Continentals alike, discipline was an obstacle to be maneuvered around. When soldiers found that firing their weapons really was forbidden and punished accordingly, they took to "snapping their pieces continually," thereby destroying the flints. Muskets were seldom cleaned. And bayonets—a rare military commodity, with only enough to equip a few regiments—were used as crowbars or simply thrown away, acts of carelessness many would soon desperately regret.

George Washington did what he could. If his troops lacked uniforms—something that bothered the forever dress-conscious GW—he advised recourse to easily obtained linen hunting shirts so the English might think they were facing a legion of frontier marksmen.[15] In fact, the army remained short on powder and ball, along with guns to fire them, prompting him to suggest that the Congress in Philadelphia borrow several thousand muskets from the Pennsylvania militia. He made the same sort of request to the governor of Connecticut, whom he also urged to get the lead out, literally, from a mine in Middletown.[16]

Troops were drilled regularly, using a manual called *An Easy Plan for a Militia*, cobbled together seven years earlier by a Massachusetts officer, Timothy Pickering, whom GW would soon make his adjutant general. How much good it did was open to question. Mostly, the men didn't take it seriously, clowning around and often ignoring their officers' commands. It infuriated Washington. He had already gotten Congress to raise the number of permissible lashes from the Mosaic thirty-nine to one hundred, and he would continue to lobby for more on the grounds the men remained defiant.[17] It also says something that by early July, when powder supplies were at last sufficient for live-fire exercises, each man was allowed just two rounds.[18]

That presumed he was well enough to shoot, or even still in camp. By summer approximately a third of the Continental Army around New York were too sick to perform their duties, with, as Nathanael Greene informed Washington, "great numbers taken down every day."[19] As usual, the new arrivals, being largely rural and unexposed to the common contagions that hung over military camps, suffered worst, further compounding the basic problem of turning them into effective soldiers.

But at least they were stationary; many simply left. As we saw with the Virginia Regiment, few things enraged George Washington like desertion; he seemed to take it personally, fearing the come-and-go, temporary-enlistment attitude might break his whole army apart. He may have underestimated their constancy, but it remained a stubborn fact that the Continental Army over the course of the war lost between a fifth and a quarter of its numbers to desertion every year, and that was after it had developed a core of long-term veterans.[20] In New York, it was a sieve.

This was particularly frustrating because there was a great deal more than training that had to be accomplished: Defenses had to be constructed. Getting soldiers to dig is never easy, but George Washington ran into a particularly hard case when the Connecticut Light Horse stormed into camp in early July, four or five hundred of them, all expecting their mounts to be maintained. But when asked to do some heavy lifting and digging—"fatigue duty" in Washington's words—they flatly refused, "or even to mount Guard, claiming an exemption as Troopers."[21] He therefore discharged them, and as fast as they had come, they were gone.

GW had better luck with those on foot, and, gradually, over the months leading up to the British arrival, fortifications took shape.

Washington, who had little training in military engineering beyond
Fort Necessity, appropriated Charles Lee's initial defensive plan without significant change. Accordingly, to guard the North River passage,
twin fortifications were built on either side: Fort Washington atop a
bluff at the northern end of Manhattan, and Fort Lee on the Jersey
side. Looking down on the river two hundred feet below and now
blocked with obstacles, the twin citadels, armed with as many cannon
as Knox could manage and stuffed with a brigade of 2,400, must have
seemed formidable. But they were more of a façade than anything else.
Fort Washington, in particular, was amateurishly constructed and
looked, in the words of one historian, like a "half-ruined sand castle"[22]
when completed. Even worse, it could be approached from three sides
by land.

At the southern end of Manhattan was the city itself, which everybody assumed would be attacked first and could not be held indefinitely. Here soldiers and Patriot volunteers threw together an
improvised string of redoubts and barricades around the outskirts.
Meanwhile, within the perimeter, officers planned for a house-by-
house, street-by-street defense. Around nine thousand Americans
waited, their objective to make the British pay another price in blood.

The linchpin of the entire rickety system lay across the East River,
on Brooklyn Heights, where Americans had constructed a series of
strongpoints, now bristling with Knox's cannon sighted to cover both
lower Manhattan and the passage to the Long Island Sound. Manning them and protecting Long Island were now the four thousand
troops Lee had recommended. But they were not good troops.
Throughout the spring, as soon as Nathanael Greene finished training
and familiarizing a combat element, GW seemed to grab it and send
it elsewhere, to Governors Island or Fort Washington.[23] Finally, in an
effort to keep one of his best units, Greene warned Washington: "The
most of the Troops that come over here are strangers to the Ground,
Undisciplined and badly furnish'd with Arms."[24] It didn't change
GW's mind.

He had his fingers in everything. He was an innately capable administrator and would soon master the art of delegation, but at this
point he was chronically shorthanded and felt compelled to burrow

into every detail—make every decision no matter how small. It chained him to his desk, and he lost track of what should have been his first priority, the actual operational environment. Land warfare is all about terrain: exploiting it, defending it—knowing it down to almost a photographic level of detail. The first thing a military professional does is check on the lay of the land. Washington didn't, or at least not adequately. Had he been out and about more, the dangers his force positioning posed would have been more starkly apparent. By placing troops on both Manhattan and Long Island, he had thoroughly divided his army, separating them by bands of water—a medium on which the British were bound to dominate. The chances of being trapped, in whole or part, were considerable. This was a complicated problem, and he warned John Hancock, the "contracted knowledge which any of us have in Military Matters stands in very little stead."[25]

On the other hand, the revolutionary GW was more in touch with the psychological environment. He never forgot that the crucial military terrain was in the minds of Americans. Likely he understood that successfully defending New York was a long shot, and in mid-May journeyed to Philadelphia to consult with Congress again on strategy. Both agreed. The Patriot narrative dictated that New York was sovereign territory, and a maximum effort had to be made to defend it from invaders intent on enslaving them. Nothing less would serve the purposes of the Revolution.[26] Despite all the suffering this would entail, they were probably right. The Glorious Cause, to be truly glorious, demanded sacrifice.

Washington intended to wage war at every level. And as he awaited the inevitable, he began looking into and even planning for a post-invasion environment of intrigue, irregular warfare, and interdicted food supplies. He took to skullduggery like a duck takes to water. In part this came from his background on the frontier, but also a personal penchant for secrecy and deception. It was hardly inappropriate at this point. Although Patriots were firmly in control, the area was already a magnet for Loyalists, and militants were at the point of coagulation.

And just as a shark smells blood, Robert Rogers smelled opportunity. Along with Washington he had been one of the most celebrated native-born combatants in the French and Indian War, an acknowledged master of irregular warfare along the frontier. Unlike Washington, he had subsequently fallen on hard times, moved to London, and landed in debtors' prison, all the time drinking heavily. Finally released and buoyed by a belated military pension, Rogers set sail for the American Revolution, arriving in late 1775, ready to sell his talents to the highest bidder.

A bit too obviously, it seems. Washington immediately suspected him of being a British mole.[27] He was briefly arrested, but upon promising not to wage war on America, released. In the spring Rogers applied to Congress for a commission, not knowing that GW—now certain he was a double agent—wanted him "strictly examined," doing the job himself on his trip to Philadelphia, after having him snatched. He remained in custody until early July, when he was sent under armed guard in the direction of New Hampshire, where he had grown up; he quickly slipped the leash and, living off the land, was soon back at ground zero. On August 6, 1776, General Howe wrote Lord Germain: "Major Rogers having escaped to us from Philadelphia, is empowered to raise a battalion of Rangers, which I hope may be useful in the course of the campaign."[28]

This is exactly what Washington didn't want to have happen. Control of the countryside and its corollary, the interdiction of local food and livestock, was to form a key element of his strategy to defeat the British. He was already arranging to have fresh provisions and horses sequestered virtually as soon as they arrived.[29] A combatant as subtle and dangerous as Rogers, who quickly set up shop on Long Island, could upset his entire calculation. Though at this point it's probably safe to say George Washington had bigger problems. New York Harbor was filling with a forest of English masts. The day of reckoning was not far off.

2

The British government's military response to the American Revolution was handicapped, from beginning to end, by several misperceptions, which substantially undermined any chance of success. The first of these was the most daunting—trying to figure out what exactly was going on, what the colonists were actually feeling at this point. Officials in London, especially at the top, never fathomed the depths of the colonists' suspicion of English intent. As usual, the truth was hidden right in the open, or at least available, in the homegrown Country Party critique of English politics. But those in charge of war planning and execution seem to have been almost cognitively blocked from understanding the power of this narrative when superimposed over America: that everything they did in the way of suppression would be filtered through its conspiratorial lens. And having missed its potency, they uniformly and consistently held to the fantasy that the rebellion was the making of a few loud-mouthed malcontents who had temporarily deluded a gullible but basically loyal population.[30]

As they sought to recover from the drubbing in Boston, it made sense to the strategists in London to react with what they assumed would be overwhelming force, an effort massive enough to break the rebellion and end the crisis quickly and forever. "America must fear you before they will love you," was the phrase Lord North had used earlier to describe the mindset, words that would come to haunt him.[31] But in actual fact, the attitude was more like that of James Grant, now a general (we last saw him as a major being captured by the French after losing most of his men in front of Fort Duquesne), writing on the eve of the New York invasion: "If a good bleeding can bring those Bible-faced Yankees to their senses the fever of Independence should soon abate."[32]

Superficially this strategy of overwhelming force bears a striking similarity to the American war in Vietnam; but what was missing from the more recent campaign, despite its many incidental cruelties, was an institutionalized spirit of revenge and retribution. Not so among the British, or at least among those at the pinnacle of power and at the sword's edge. While very much a part of Europe's stylized and relatively limited approach to conventional warfare, the English army had a long tradition of putting down internal revolts with singular brutality. The crushing of the Scottish Jacobites in 1746 at the Battle of Culloden and the subsequent lethal pursuit of the survivors was very much in character. And it can't have been forgotten three decades later by those putting together the great invasion of New York.[33] The Americans were disobedient children run riot in the face of reasonable efforts to share the burdens of empire, and now they would be swiftly and sharply punished.

There were cooler heads in London. William Pitt, now Earl of Chatham and always a friend of America, had attempted to fashion a grand compromise—basically conceding everything to the colonists in return for an affirmation of Parliament's sovereignty—but few legislators were in the mood for this sort of magnanimity, and the plan was quickly brushed aside.[34] There were other consistent voices of dissent, such as that of James Fox; but the course of events and the nature of the British power structure were pushing toward a punitive approach. The hawks were now in charge, and the higher you climbed, the truer this got.

At the peak perched the King. From mildly sympathetic at the beginning of the crisis, George III had turned into the colonists' worst enemy after the Boston Tea Party. He was convinced their behavior was a product of too much lenience, and as the Revolution grew more republican, the more passionate he became. The war to crush this rebellion would become his personal crusade.[35] He had already played a major role in the selection of generals Burgoyne, Clinton, and Howe; now he was instrumental in the appointment of Howe's brother Richard as naval commander in America to form an amphibious tag team. Henceforth, he would avidly follow every detail of the war effort, doing all he could to maximize its impact, including enlisting what amounted to military scabs.

Probably no measure of suppression enraged the colonists more than the injection of German mercenaries into the Revolutionary War environment, foreign thugs obviously introduced to break them, the perfect villains in their conspiracy melodrama—courtesy of George III. In his capacity as prince elector of Hanover, he had begun shopping Germany's grand mall of principalities in the summer of 1775,[36] and—after writing Catherine the Great about available Russians—put together a grab bag of five varieties of Teutonic hired guns, two-thirds of whom came from Hesse-Kassel, hence Hessians. From the invasion of New York to the end of the war, their numbers ranged from half to a quarter of British troops in North America, with a cumulative total of around thirty thousand.[37] In 1776, virtually all could be counted on to behave badly toward civilians—George III's personal kiss of death on the entire recovery project.

As secretary of the American Department and his personal warlord, the King had chosen George Germain, a controversial figure, having been court-martialed and convicted of not pursuing retreating French at the Battle of Minden in 1759. But he had been a determined presence in Parliament for thirty-four years, and within the cabinet he was alone in sharing George III's passion for the war and a determination to pursue it to the bitter end. While Germain was always among those who believed that most Americans remained quietly loyal—their version of the "silent majority"—he was convinced this condition was particularly true in the southern colonies. The initial Clinton-Parker expedition noted earlier was the first thrust in this direction, but Germain would retain a particular fondness for this "southern strategy" and fall back on it when nothing else seemed to be working.

But at this point he was of the mind that a "decisive blow" would do the job, a show of strength sufficient to quickly cow even the most fervently rebellious, and this would be aimed at New York.[38] He put together the largest expeditionary force in the eighteenth century: seventeen thousand German mercenaries, plus various contingents of British regulars, for a total of thirty-three thousand when they had all arrived.[39] The accomplishment was all the more impressive because of the distances involved. He kept them there, albeit in diminishing numbers, for seven long years, feeding, clothing, and equipping them in an age without steam or electricity from the other side of the Atlantic Ocean, surely the greatest feat of logistics in military history up to that point. But also one of the most wrongheaded.

Germain commanded no large following in Parliament when he became secretary for America, nor was the prospect of all-out war that popular. Lord North, the prime minister, was desperate for a negotiated settlement, and wanted the Howe brothers, known to be sympathetic to the Americans, named as peace commissioners with broad discretionary authority. Germain couldn't stop their appointment, but he did succeed in narrowing their scope to not much more than granting pardons,[40] thereby ensuring the invasion remained a big mailed fist clad in only a very thin velvet glove. This was a consistent pattern. Through the logic of inside position the King and Germain managed to perpetuate the war, while the opposition was at least partly muffled by the danger of appearing too sympathetic to an enemy, who was, after all, killing English soldiers.

Meanwhile, there is little question that the agenda of vindictive retribution was close to the hearts of those charged with actually conducting the war. The key generals were all handpicked men, either close to the King or anxious to please him. A number had titles— Richard Howe, Charles Cornwallis—and the rest were members of the aristocracy. In the face of massive societal change, the British military remained a firm bastion of the traditional ruling class, and the outlook of the aristocracy pervaded not just those in command, but also the junior officers who would do most of the fighting—men like Banastre Tarleton, John André, Patrick Ferguson, and Francis, Lord Rawdon.

"On every occasion during this war," German Jäger commander Johann Ewald wrote of his allies, "one can observe the thoughtlessness, negligence and contempt of the English toward their foe."[41] Coming from a Hessian, that was saying something. And their aristocratic disdain was compounded by ideological abhorrence of the American Revolution. It was, after all, meant to replace people like them. So from top to bottom, beginning to end, they reacted with cruelty— ordered it to be inflicted, or simply looked the other way while their soldiers stole the rebels' possessions, burned their houses, and raped their wives and daughters.

They were good at war, though. Clinton, Cornwallis, and the Howes were all exceptionally skilled professionals with tactical and operational capabilities honed by near lifetimes in the service. And they were flexible in their approach. The myth of the redcoats as a ponderous crimson wall of targets was just that; this proved a highly adaptive force. Almost immediately it capitalized on the opponent's lack of bayonets, and nearly as quickly adjusted to the rugged terrain, adopting a looser order.[42]

Whether British or German, these were well-trained and disci-

plined troops, able to maneuver rapidly in open country—marching in
column then shifting into broad, thin firefighting formations, usually
without a trace of confusion—capabilities the Continental Army
could only dream about at this point. They were professional soldiers,
unlike the twentieth-century American conscript army in Vietnam;
long-term enlistment allowed time for internal loyalty and unit coher-
ence to build. They were tough and used to miserable conditions; many
had combat experience and were used to killing coldly and without
hesitation. They were also spirited and confident, entering battle expecting to win, a notion the subsequent course of the war usually confirmed. The fact of the matter was that the British forces about to
descend on New York completely outclassed what George Washington had waiting for them. But it would not be enough to finish him,
his army, or least of all the Revolution.

There were lots of reasons why the British lost. Geography was
certainly against them. The place was an ocean away, and although the
Royal Navy could deliver troops, oftentimes unexpectedly, to any place
on the coast, the army proved consistently unsuccessful at penetrating
the revolutionary heartland, the rural environment where most Americans lived. Because Washington and the Patriots interdicted domestic
access to food and livestock, the British remained tethered to supply
lines that stretched three thousand miles, denying them, among other
things, the fresh horses needed to effectively run down and destroy
defeated rebel armies or just irregulars. It was also subject to inevitable
attrition. The force that invaded New York was the largest of the war;
from this point it only contracted. Professional troops like these demanded years to train and were therefore hard and expensive to replace. The Americans had a huge potential advantage in homegrown
manpower: Time was on their side; they had only to endure and keep
picking off hostiles one way or another. But in the end the British
failure was more a matter of psychology than a product of demogra-
phy, geography, or purely military factors.

Americans were in a revolutionary state of mind, brought there by
a narrative that cast the British in the role of tyrants and enslavers. The
behavior of the British Army lived up to all expectations, and kept

doing so throughout the course of the war. Revolutions are hard to sustain, the amped-up state of mind inevitably wearing people down with time. The rage militaire was already frayed. In this context, the British cavalcade of atrocity would operate like sequential jolts of electricity, recharging the Revolution's fervor and reinforcing the central narrative's bottom line. The British were already operating under severe disadvantages in North America, but it was in the psychological domain that their failure was truly foretold. Here they became, quite literally, their own worst enemies.

3

As if by magic they began to arrive. On June 25, 1776, the first ships of an armada that looked to one observer "like London afloat" reached Sandy Hook.[43] Right away they wrong-footed the Americans, disembarking on Staten Island, not Manhattan—nine thousand redcoats from Halifax along with William Howe, the overall commander of the land component. Thirteen days later, brother Richard's flagship, HMS *Eagle,* hove into view after a transatlantic passage, accompanied by almost 150 ships and eleven thousand more troops. As the month passed, the juggernaut only grew, with an additional three thousand redcoats and eight thousand mercenaries from Germany.

Among the later contingents to arrive were two thousand infantry under Major Generals Clinton and Cornwallis, participants in the first episode in the ill-fated southern strategy. It had not gone well. They had arrived too late to prevent the defeat of North Carolina Loyalists at Moores Creek Bridge; but wasted enough time for Charles Lee to complete the fortifications on Sullivan's Island across from Charleston. When the British attack finally came on June 28, the land contingent found itself blocked by the tide from supporting Admiral Parker's shipborne assault. Without infantry, ships with guns against dirt and cement with guns is never a good matchup, so Parker took a beating. Within three weeks the English had withdrawn to join their colleagues on Staten Island, leaving Charles Lee very much the hero ("A

*Lord Richard Howe: the nautical member of the Howe brothers tag team.*

LIBRARY OF
CONGRESS

victory it undoubtedly is," GW wrote him, "when an Enemy are drub'd, and driven from a Country they were sent to Conquer[44]") and far south, clear of the drubbing his boss was about to endure.

The Americans shouldn't have been surprised that British forces first headed for Staten Island. Upon arrival they were in no condition to fight. It had taken almost all of Britain's merchant fleet to transport them from Canada, Germany, Ireland, and England, all journeys measured in months. Packed in, six to a bunk, with minimal time on deck and short rations, they were guaranteed to arrive in a shaky state. Staten Island was just the place for them. The Americans had not managed to get the livestock off in time, so there was plenty of protein for the men and forage for the equally beat-up horses the British had transported.

But food and the opportunity to move around almost instantly revealed the dark side of the whole agenda. Young Lord Rawdon was part of the Charleston contingent, and soon after he reached Staten Island he was writing the Earl of Huntingdon:

> The fair nymphs of this isle are in wonderful tribulation, as the fresh meat our men have got here has made them as riotous as satyrs. A girl cannot step into the bushes to pluck a rose without running the most imminent risk of being ravished, and they are so little accustomed to these vigorous methods that they don't bear them with the proper resignation, and of consequence we have most entertaining courts-martial every day. . . .
>
> To the southward they behaved much better in these cases, if I may judge from a women who having been forced by seven of our men, [came] to make a complaint to me "not of their usage," she said; "No, thank God, she despised that," but of their having taken an old prayer book for which she had a particular affection.[45]

Rawdon was only twenty-two and apparently thought he was being funny, but he was no outlier; rather, he was already a competent commander headed for an eminent career as both a general and a politician—eventually royal governor of India. Oxford educated and, most important, a titled aristocrat, Rawdon was exactly the sort other British officers emulated, especially the ambitious ones, imprinting his cruel disdain for Americans and behaving accordingly in all too many instances.

While his men were busy terrorizing the women of Staten Island, General Howe was seeking to unfurl the kinder, gentler face of British policy in the form of a letter addressed to "George Washington, Esq., etc. etc." from his brother. The subsequent diplomatic dance revealed the American at his nimble best, every bit the politico-military maestro his job title demanded. After consulting with his generals, Washington instructed a three-man reception committee of Henry Knox,

*General William
Howe: a master
of war, a novice
at revolution.*

LIBRARY OF
CONGRESS

Joseph Reed, and Samuel Webb to intercept the officer attempting to
deliver the missive, and refuse to accept it until he named the ad-
dressee.[46] When he did, using simply Washington's given name, he was
told no such person existed so they couldn't take it off his hands.

The episode left Lord Richard's personal secretary fulminating: "It
seems to be beneath a little paltry colonel of militia at the head of
banditti or rebels to treat with the representative of his lawful sovereign because 'tis impossible for him to give all the titles the poor creature requires."[47] This reaction utterly missed Washington's point; he
was military commander in chief of a sovereign and now completely
independent state, and accepted a letter several days later only when
addressed to "His Excellency George Washington." It requested a
meeting with William Howe's adjutant general, Lieutenant Colonel
James Paterson. His point made, GW agreed.

Described by one biographer as "suavely implacable,"[48] Washington arrived in his best uniform and proceeded to give the overmatched

Brit a lesson in cagey statecraft. After hearing Paterson's prepared statement on how a benevolent king had sent them the Howe brothers to reach an accommodation, GW popped his hot-air balloon by simply denying he had the authority to negotiate such a settlement. And even if he did, he added, the Howe brothers were empowered only "to grant pardons; that those had committed no fault wanted no pardon; that we were only defending what we deemed our indisputable rights."[49] He then offered Paterson a snack and sent him on his way, writing Adam Stephen that same day "on the discovery of the vile Machinations of still viler Ministerial Agents."[50]

Of course, GW's behavior, particularly his insistence that he lacked the power to negotiate, has to be considered in light of the decision made in Philadelphia nearly two weeks prior. On July 4, 1776, the Second Continental Congress gave its unanimous consent to an official Declaration of Independence. Largely the words of Thomas Jefferson, it can be seen as a brilliant evocation of the basic conspiracy theory, with a new twist.

Having established "as self-evident, that all men are created equal, and endowed by their Creator with certain unalienable Rights," and having warned against changing governments "for light and transient causes," Jefferson got to the heart of the matter: "But when a long train of abuses and usurpations, pursuing invariably the same Object evinces a design to reduce them under absolute Despotism, it is their right, it is their duty, to throw off such Government, and to provide new Guards for their future security." To prove his point he then itemizes British transgressions, twenty-seven of them. The chief perpetrator is no longer "ministerial influence"; it is the King himself. Every item on the list begins with "He."[51] The Patriot King was now officially tyrannizer in chief.

Going on record with such an indictment was not to be taken lightly. Many years later Dr. Benjamin Rush recalled the mood of the later signing ceremony in a letter to John Adams: "The Silence & the gloom morning were interrupted I well recollect only for a moment by Col: Harrison of Virginia who said to Mr Gerry at the table, 'I shall have a great advantage over you Mr: Gerry when we are all hung for what we are now doing. From the size and weight of my body I shall die in a few minutes, but from the lightness of your body you will dance in the air an hour or two before you are dead."[52]

Back in New York on July 9, before a vast crowd of soldiers and civilians, George Washington watched on horseback as an aide read out the declaration to the silent multitude. After three cheers, the official ceremony was over. But soon enough a riotous crowd headed down Broadway toward the statue of George III, erected on the delusion that as Patriot King he had killed the Stamp Act. Now to set the record straight, they swarmed the statue, looped it with ropes, then pulled it to the ground. Here the gold leaf was stripped off, and later its four thousand pounds of lead would be melted to make 42,088 musket balls.[53] As it turned out, they would need every one.

# 4

Having dismissed the Howes' peace offer, Washington wondered where, along the fifteen-mile front he had to defend, the inevitable assault would come, and why it had not already begun. It had been almost a full two months since British ships had begun piling up in New York Harbor, and he wrote his cousin Lund, "another revolving Monday is arrived before an Attack upon this City, or a movement of the Enemy—the reason of this is incomprehensible, to me. . . . There is something exceedingly mysterious in the conduct of the Enemy."[54] It turned out to be meticulous military planning. There would be no Bunker Hill this time; General Howe was not about to go off half-cocked.

Finally on August 22, 1776, the morning after a violent thunderstorm, Howe ferried fifteen thousand British and Hessian infantry with artillery, not to Manhattan but to Long Island. Over the next several days, five thousand more came over from Staten Island, and Howe took command of the whole operation, with Generals Cornwallis and Clinton as his deputies.[55] The latter, although he didn't much like him, proved Howe's secret weapon.

Clinton had grown up in New York, where his father was royal

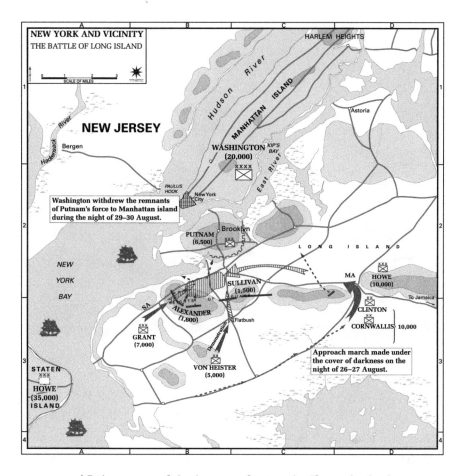

NEW YORK AND VICINITY
THE BATTLE OF LONG ISLAND

SCALE OF MILES

Hudson River

MANHATTAN ISLAND

HARLEM HEIGHTS

Astoria

NEW JERSEY

Bergen

Hackensack River

WASHINGTON
(20,000)

KIP'S BAY

East River

PAULUS
HOOK

New York
City

Washington withdrew the remnants
of Putnam's force to Manhattan island
during the night of 29–30 August.

PUTNAM
(6,500)

Brooklyn

LONG ISLAND

NEW
YORK
BAY

SULLIVAN
(1,500)

HEIGHTS OF

ALEXANDER
(1,600)

Flatbush

MA

HOWE
(10,000)

To Jamaica

CLINTON

CORNWALLIS  10,000

GRANT
(7,000)

Demonstration

VON HEISTER
(5,000)

Approach march made under
the cover of darkness on the
night of 26–27 August.

STATEN

HOWE
(35,000)
ISLAND

governor.[56] Like many of the best professional officers, he had an acute awareness and memory of terrain. He knew this ground; he knew there was a way around the Americans through the Jamaica Pass. This key bit of information allowed Howe to develop a classic battle plan.

First, General James Grant would lead his Highlanders and Lieutenant General Philip von Heister his Hessians in a two-pronged diversionary maneuver aimed at getting the Americans to commit their reserves in the wrong direction; meanwhile, the main attack would come after a daring night march of ten thousand infantry and twenty-nine cannon, led by Howe, Clinton, and Cornwallis, sweeping around and behind their opponents through the Jamaica Pass, which was guarded at the time by only five men.[57] By 8:30 A.M. on August 27, they were in position along the flank and rear of the main American formations, now commanded by John Sullivan—Nathanael Greene being

Lord Stirling at the Battle of Long Island, *by Alonzo Chappel.*

down with a raging fever—and the newly installed overall commander, Major General Israel Putnam, just four days on the job.[58] Killing time had arrived.

There is a painting—*Lord Stirling at the Battle of Long Island,* by nineteenth-century artist Alonzo Chappel—that captures, emotionally, at least, what happened next, the sheer panic as hundreds of Americans, many dressed in hunting shirts, are driven into what may be Gowanus Creek in a desperate effort to elude redcoats. The British cut through the Continentals on all fronts. Both diversionary attacks succeeded, with Hessians and Highlanders bayoneting many attempting to surrender, even leaving some impaled on trees.[59]

But it was on the exposed American left that the real damage was done. Sullivan's detachment, now caught between Hessians and redcoats, stood and fought near Flatbush Pass, ultimately surrendering around noon, their general taken prisoner hiding in a cornfield. Next came GW's friend and fellow planter, the self-titled Lord Stirling, and his two regiments. Both the Delaware and Maryland Continentals fought ferociously, trying to escape the trap with repeated counter-thrusts, but in the end only ten got away before the rest, including Lord Stirling, had to give up. An entire segment of the defense had collapsed; up to three hundred Americans were dead with many wounded. Over a thousand had been captured, with only those who managed to slog across the Gowanus Creek escaping.[60] Worse still, the way was entirely open to the American linchpin, Brooklyn Heights.

It was from these very heights that George Washington observed the battle develop, completely flummoxed as to why his left had evaporated. That was because he did not know Jamaica Pass even existed. He had been in the area for months, and he hadn't managed to reconnoiter his positions sufficiently to know a critical chink was left uncovered; neither had any of his generals. The visiting team knew home turf better than they did, or, as John Adams put it, "In general, our generals were out Generalled on Long Island."[61] Amateur hour of the day of reckoning was at hand.

In war, though, luck frequently trumps skill, and as usual GW had plenty. The day was young, casualties were light, and Howe still had twenty thousand troops exhilarated by victory and more than ready to take on the four to five thousand Americans atop the Heights. Yet he stopped short. He would do this repeatedly, as would Cornwallis a bit later at Trenton. It has never been entirely clear why.

The Howes were reputedly well disposed toward Americans but also known to believe conciliation could not come before rebel forces had been "roughly dealt with."[62] That had been done, and two weeks later a congressional delegation made up of John Adams, Benjamin Franklin, and Edward Rutledge met with Admiral Howe for what was billed as a peace conference, only to find his terms so unattractive they ended up publishing them as propaganda. "They met, they talked, they parted," wrote Howe's private secretary.[63] It was the last time delegates from the two governments conferred officially until war's end. The seriousness of the diplomatic component—even to the Howes, who were no fools—is open to question.

More central was a purely military consideration: Fighting uphill against fixed fortifications is bloodthirsty. "It is my opinion they would have carried the redoubt," Howe wrote Germain, "but . . . I would not risk the loss that might have been sustained in the assault and ordered them back."[64] Plainly he had not forgotten his bad day on Bunker Hill, but this also brings to mind the fact that even in victory, his army was an entirely finite and ultimately wasting asset; its future under such circumstances was bound to be limited.

Then there was probably complacency and overconfidence. These Americans would remain ripe for the picking, and their leader, "His Excellency," obviously didn't know what he was doing. If this was part of Howe's thinking, it was a mistake; Washington was always at his best and most dangerous with his back to the wall, or in this case, the East River. At first, he seemed inclined to try to hold the Heights, bringing over three regiments from Manhattan; but when he realized Howe was digging zigzag trenches for a siege he took the advice of his general officers.[65] It was hopeless. Were it not for a huge northeaster that blew in on August 28, Admiral Howe's frigates would have already trapped them.

GW's career on the frontier had taught him the leverage surprise can provide, particularly in desperate situations. This was no time for a prolonged withdrawal; he had to make his army vanish. On the night of the twenty-ninth a pea-soup fog descended like a magician's cloak.[66] One by one units were told to withdraw and march, without speaking, to the river landing, where crews of Marblehead men under Colonel John Glover were waiting in boats to ferry them across to lower Manhattan. All the while, the campfires were kept burning, an old trick, but good enough for the complacent British, who only discovered there were no troops left near dawn. Within six hours 9,500 soldiers and all but a few pieces of artillery were safely evacuated without a single mishap. Finally, just as British gunfire began to crackle, George Washington, after a long night of supervising every detail, stepped aboard the last American boat to disappear into the fog.[67] Like the foxes he loved to chase, GW could be fooled, but he was hard to trap.

With the artillery coverage from Brooklyn Heights lost, Washington must have known that New York City was no longer remotely defensible. If left to his own devices he would have burned the place to the ground.[68] But he also understood—as did some of his generals—

that the political narrative and his agreement with Congress demanded that he make some effort to defend it.[69] All of Manhattan was dangerous ground and he knew it, telling Congress's president, John Hancock, on September 6, 1776, "There is reason to believe they Intend to make a landing above or below Kings bridge [at the northernmost end] & thereby to hem in our Army and cut off the communication with the Country."[70]

Pinioned between the political and the military, Washington wavered until it was almost too late. It wasn't until September 10 that Congress got around to resolving that GW didn't have to remain in the city "a Moment longer than he shall think it proper for the publick Service."[71] Two more days passed before a council of war voted to begin moving the army to upper Manhattan. The evacuation quickly clogged the roads north, soon just a mass of slow-moving soldiers, civilians, and wagons. Meanwhile, though still admonished by Congress not to burn it, Washington had his men strip the city of useful supplies, in particular bronze church bells, which could be melted into cannon.[72] All of this took time, too much of it.

This was a defeated army. Morale was low; it needed a secure haven

The British Landing at Kip's Bay, *by Robert Cleveley.*

ROBERT CLEVELEY/WIKIMEDIA COMMONS

to regroup, and needed it quickly. Instead, it got the British, encouraged by their General Howe to place "an entire dependence upon their bayonets."[73] Brother Richard Howe was poised to help, bringing five warships up the East River to Kips Bay on the night of September 14, soon to be followed by eighty-four barges filled with four thousand redcoats and Hessians.[74] At eleven the next morning Admiral Howe's vessels let loose broadsides designed to, in GW's words: "scour the Ground and cover the landing of their Troops."[75] In short order, they beat down the Americans' flimsy earthwork defenses, and scattered the militia manning them like autumn leaves in a strong wind. The landing was unopposed.

GW was four miles north in Harlem, where he thought the attack might come. "As soon as I heard the Firing," he told John Hancock, "I road with all possible dispatch towards the place of landing, when to my great surprize and Mortification I found the Troops that had been posted in the Lines retreating with the utmost precipitation."[76]

Actually, it was more of a chain reaction. On the way he had been joined by about a thousand Continental reinforcements. Just as they crested Murray Hill, and Washington was in the midst of trying to deploy them, they were hit by a wave of fleeing militia from the south, followed closely by the British vanguard. Right in front of their commander in chief, the Continentals—officers and men alike—caught the contagion of panic and began to bolt. GW's reaction was memorable, but also ineffectual. "He laid his Cane over many of the Officers who shewed their men the Example of running," wrote aide Tench Tilghman. He "snapped his pistols, . . . three times dashed his hatt on the Ground, and at last exclaimed 'Good God have I got such Troops as Those.' . . . within eighty yards of the enemy, so vexed at the infamous conduct of the troops, that he sought death rather than life."[77] He didn't find it, of course. But reportedly he did have to be dragged from the battle, which left around fifty Americans dead and another three hundred captured.[78] As on Long Island the Hessians would take no prisoners, shooting the few dozen Americans who tried to surrender, and even mounting the decapitated head of one on a pike.[79]

By early afternoon Howe had landed another nine thousand fresh troops at Kips Bay, and having already taken Murray Hill, he could have easily sent them west to the Hudson, trapping thousands of Americans who remained in lower Manhattan. Yet again he hesitated. Legend has it he was slowed by an offer of wine and pastries from a patriotic Quaker woman; in fact, he understood how costly urban combat could be, and wanted to make sure his men were ready and fully organized before he moved.[80] Either way, it gave Bunker Hill veteran Israel Putnam an opening to save the Continentals.

Though never a favorite of Washington's, the grizzled "Old Put" was a renowned Indian fighter and at his best in emergencies, quickly locating less-traveled roads on the far side of the island, and driving and cajoling around 3,500 Continentals northward, reaching by night-fall the relative safety of Harlem Heights, where the rest of the army huddled. Just about everybody was wet, exhausted, and depressed.

Before the sun rose on September 16, Washington sent 150 rangers under Colonel Thomas Knowlton, and accompanied by key aide Joseph Reed, out through the Harlem woods to feel out British forward positions. They made contact at dawn, near what is now Broadway and 106th Street, exchanging light fire with several hundred Highlanders and light infantry. There was nothing light about them; these were shock troops trained to move fast and use their bayonets before their opponents could recover.[81] For the colonists, most without bayonets, they were a nightmare.

On this day, though, they were merely contemptuous. Knowlton moved slowly back toward American lines, and Reed was just reporting to Washington when "the Enemy appeared in open view & in the most insulting manner sounded their Bugle Horns as is usual after a Fox Chase. . . . It seem'd to crown our Disgrace."[82] This was not a wise riff to hurl in the face of the quintessential foxhunter. It would not go unanswered, nor would it be forgotten.

To lure the British element further forward, Washington sent a brigade out as bait, while reinforcing Knowlton with Virginia Continentals and ordering him to work his way behind the enemy so they could be surrounded and crushed. It almost worked, but Knowlton miscalculated and hit the Highlanders in the flank, not the rear. Now alerted to the trap, the British withdrew slowly, taking short stands in an orchard and a wheat field, during which both sides received reinforcements and sharp firefights ensued.

When it was all over each side had taken around 150 casualties, and Knowlton, a gifted commander and irregular warrior, lay dead.[83] But the fact remained the Americans had faced off against some of the best troops in the British Army, held their own, and forced them to withdraw. It was a small victory, but "this little Advantage has inspired our Troops prodigiously," Washington told Philip Schuyler[84]—exactly what they needed as they waited to see what would happen next.

Howe had moved into New York City unopposed. Loyalists were certainly happy to see him; but he wasn't exactly a conquering hero. While the most identifiable Patriots had fled, he must have been aware that many quiet sympathizers remained. Until the British could firmly establish themselves, the city remained a murky, suspicious environment, a place where nothing happened by accident.

And if you were Howe, certainly not on the blustery night of September 20, when a mysterious fire started near Whitehall Slip on the southern tip of Manhattan and raced out of control until dawn, consuming five hundred houses along with everything else between the Hudson River and Broadway. The absence of bells ensured firefighters were slow in coming. "Many circumstances lead to conjecture that Mr. Washington was privy to this villainous act as he sent all the bells of the churches out of town under pretense of casting them into cannon," the newly reinstalled Governor Tryon reported back to Germain in London.[85] Given his deference to Congress it's likely that the first that GW knew of the conflagration was the luminous glow he saw ten miles south of Harlem Heights. Yet he could still appreciate its impact and told cousin Lund "Providence—or some good honest Fellow, has done more for us than we were disposed to do for ourselves."[86]

It was in this context that Robert Rogers delivered a rumpled, terrified American, along with all the evidence needed to demonstrate he was a spy, to General Howe late the next night—more or less in the manner a cat delivers a mouse to its owner. It was true that the unfortunate young man, Captain Nathan Hale, had been recruited from Knowlton's rangers by Washington well before the city fell, to monitor

British forces on Long Island, the first in a long line of spies he would send in that direction. Like so much else that was happening at the time, the episode revealed GW as a tyro, a spymaster in training.

The open, affable, and loquacious Hale was the last person to send anywhere incognito. Rogers was in the midst of recruiting his band of Loyalist irregulars on Lloyd's Neck when he spotted Hale coming across the sound from Connecticut, followed him as he headed eastward, and introduced himself as a fellow Patriot, upon which Hale promptly told all. That night he met Hale at an inn with three of his henchmen as witnesses and bundled him off to Howe's headquarters on Manhattan, living evidence of his efficiency to his new patron. Hale was an American officer out of uniform caught behind enemy lines, so his fate was sealed. By military custom he deserved a court-martial; instead all he got from Howe was a death warrant.[87] He was hanged the next morning, probably without uttering the famous one-liner: "I only regret that I have but one life to lose for my country"; that one was lifted out of Joseph Addison's *Cato*, GW's favorite play. What does seem true is that the British left his corpse hanging for several days, swinging next to a soldier painted on a board and labeled GEN-ERAL WASHINGTON.[88]

As embarrassing as Hale's end must have been to GW, he was not about to renounce espionage. Besides harboring a personal fascination for the dark art, he instinctively knew that a revolutionary environment almost always provides an intelligence advantage to the revolutionaries, their followers being more dedicated and in this case much more numerous. So he continued throughout the war, with gradually increasing skill and success, to penetrate the shell of British secrecy, particularly at its core, New York City.

Meanwhile, being a military amateur was not always such a hindrance. As they had in Boston, Washington and his compatriots in the Continental Army's leadership remained on the lookout for military novelty, stratagems and devices that skirted tradition and allowed them to wage war on all levels. This was literally true in the case of David Bushnell.

Fire ships were a time-honored means of scattering an enemy fleet, and once the British arrived in New York Harbor it didn't take GW long to find a volunteer, one Silas Talbot, willing to sail a blazing vessel directly into the unwanted visitors. He tried it on the night of September 17 and succeeded only in severely burning himself.[89] The Royal Navy hadn't ruled the waves for centuries without being appropriately wary of fire ships and knowing how to deal with them.

But if a floating flambé was too obvious, GW found something entirely more underhanded—or, more correctly, underwatered—in a submarine conceived and constructed by David Bushnell. Like Hale a Yale graduate, he had been recommended to Washington by Connecticut's governor Jonathan Trumbull, and immediately impressed him with his prototype, the *Turtle,* a man-powered diving bell carrying an explosive charge designed to be attached to the bottom of a warship and detonated by a clockwork timed to allow the attacker to escape.[90]

In the midst of all GW's troubles in the autumn of 1776 it would have been easy to dismiss Bushnell and his *Turtle* as just another wild-eyed scheme, but instead George Washington's unerring eye for talent prevailed and saw "a Man of great Mechanical powers—fertile of invention—and a master in execution."[91]

The scheme was brilliant. A submarine vehicle promised near-total invisibility, while water, being noncompressible, ensured that explosions below its surface were inherently devastating, as they followed the line of least resistance up through the hull of the target. The fact of the matter was that Britannia ruled the waves alone; everything below was up for grabs, as she would eventually discover to her horror in the early months of World War I.

Even 138 years earlier, it came remarkably close to working in early October, with the *Turtle* managing to get underneath a sixty-four-gun ship of the line but unable to secure the charge, which later exploded harmlessly, much to the distress of Israel Putnam, who watched the whole thing from a wharf.[92] It would prove the *Turtle*'s only shot at British sea power. Patriot real estate within striking distance of its fleet was steadily diminishing. That's the way things were going as the days grew short and the fall of 1776 progressed—a few brilliant ripostes in the face of a string of failures filled with rookie mistakes.

5

Just days after his first beating at the hands of the British, George Washington sought to reassure John Hancock and Congress that they were all on the same page as far as fighting on the defensive: "It has been even called a War of posts, that we should on all occasions avoid a general Action.... With these views & being fully persuaded that It would be presumption to draw out our young Troops into open Ground against their superiors, I have never spared the Spade & Pickax."[93]

That may have been true, but Washington would soon be faced with the fact that there was a great deal more to defending strong-points against determined professionals than simply digging; military engineering in the eighteenth century was a highly developed art requiring a host of specialized skills, almost none of which anybody in the Continental Army possessed.

The exception was Charles Lee. He was no military engineer, but he had been around them throughout his long career in the British Army, and certainly knew the rudiments. Now he was back victorious from Charleston, with a congressional bonus of $30,000 and the delusion that he was being groomed as the new His Excellency.[94]

He was much more realistic about the Continental Army's position on Harlem Heights. It was hopeless: Either get off Manhattan quick or be cut off and destroyed. Howe had already tried to flank the Americans by landing at Throgs Neck, only to get bogged down in a marsh. A week later on October 18, thousands of British and Hessians poured ashore at Pell's Point in what is now the Bronx, well north of the American positions; but a determined retreat behind a series of stone walls by John Glover and his versatile Marblehead men along with Massachusetts Continentals slowed them just enough.[95] Virtually without a moment to spare, GW had marched his army across Kingsbridge at the top of Manhattan, and soon had them strung out in a three-mile line between a lake and Chatterton Hill near the village of White Plains on the mainland. Except for the several thousand Americans left behind guarding the rickety Fort Washington, it was another great escape.

But Howe kept after them. The morning of October 28 found GW up on Chatterton Hill, just realizing it was the anchor of his whole position and without prepared fortifications,[96] when an aide on a seriously winded horse rode up to inform him, "The British are on the camp, sir!"[97] Before racing back down, Washington reinforced the skittish militia atop the hill with around a thousand Continentals and a few artillery pieces under a young Captain Alexander Hamilton.

Howe had brought along thirteen thousand troops, most of them Hessians, along with plenty of artillery. He quickly sized up the situation and focused his efforts on Chatterton Hill, ordering two columns to attack it. The first scattered the militia it faced; but against the Continentals it was different. Firing grapeshot from a rocky ledge, Hamilton's cannon initially drove the Hessians and British grenadiers back down; the Maryland Continentals, shooting from behind stone walls and clumps of trees, held firm and even counterattacked before eventually succumbing to the weight of numbers and cannon blasts.

The hill may have been lost, but its taking gave Washington time to retreat to a line of even more rugged hills known as Mount Castle, a position recommended by Charles Lee. Meanwhile, the Americans had inflicted around 275 casualties on their adversaries, about twice the number they had suffered themselves.[98] It wasn't Bunker Hill, but this was exactly the sort of trade-off Howe had to avoid. His soldiers were precious; these locals could be replaced. The weather turned cold, and after about a week of glowering at the Americans, the British packed up and headed south, where there were easier pickings to be had.

Despite all his tactical and operational woes, the strategic importance of the North (Hudson) River corridor was never far from Washington's mind. Here, as elsewhere, things seemed only to go from bad to worse.

Far to the north, the redoubtable Benedict Arnold, his force ravaged by smallpox and down to three hundred, had been driven out of Montreal and Canada in the summer by the reinvigorated and reinforced British under Governor Guy Carleton and General John Burgoyne.[99] Their plan was to head down the water corridor south (from Lake Champlain to Lake George to the Hudson and eventually New York). But then Arnold built a fleet, albeit a ramshackle one, on Champlain, forcing Carleton to cobble together one of his own. They fought it out on October 11, and the British blew him out of the water, forcing Arnold to retreat to Fort Ticonderoga, which looked vulnerable in the face of Carleton's nine thousand troops, especially after he seized nearby Crown Point. Yet Arnold had bought a lot of time; winter was coming and Carleton would soon abandon his position and head north. But George Washington couldn't know that in early November, just as things were crumbling at the southern end.

Howe's sudden exit south left GW and his staff puzzled and worried; if he continued unmolested he could cross New Jersey and take the capital in Philadelphia, or, alternately, he could move against Forts Washington and Lee, the southern bastions of the North River, or he could even threaten New England directly.

Like amateurs they tried to cover all bases by dividing the army into four parts.[100] Lee was designated to stay at New Castle with seven thousand men to shield New England. Washington would cross the Hudson with two thousand troops to protect New Jersey, where he hoped to pick up recruits, and with the understanding that should the British commit in his direction, Lee would quickly support him. Finally, since Congress had urged the use of "every art and whatever expense to obstruct effectually the navigation of the North River"[101] they doubled down here, with three thousand men designated for forts built farther up the Hudson, and the garrisons at Fort Washington and Fort Lee reinforced to three thousand and two thousand respectively.[102]

Lee later claimed he'd objected to the scheme, arguing that Forts Washington and Lee should be abandoned. But since he got the largest slice of the army and considering his own personal ambition, it isn't likely he complained too loudly.[103]

While grizzled Israel Putnam was still nominal commander of all troops left on Manhattan, Washington took to ignoring him and turning to his young alter ego, Nathanael Greene, now fully recovered. In the case of the two forts presumed to be blocking the Hudson it didn't matter much, since Greene was as bullish as Putnam on the prospects of holding them.

Washington had his doubts. On October 9, with GW watching, the British had sent three ships upriver right through the Washington and Lee gauntlet of artillery and sunken hulks, and on November 5 they did it again. A worried Washington wrote Greene three days later: "If we cannot prevent Vessells passing up, and the Enemy are possessed of the surrounding Country, what valuable purpose can it answer to attempt to hold a post from which the expected Benefit cannot be had?"[104] But Greene reassured him—"I cannot conceive the Garrison to be in any great danger the men can be brought off at any time"[105]—and Washington backed off.

It was a terrible mistake. The cannon of both were trained on the river, and most were too ponderous to turn against a land assault. The most obvious target, Fort Washington, lacked barracks, or even an internal water supply, and was too small in the first place to shelter more than a portion of the garrison, leaving the rest with only a feeble outworks to fight behind—a problem Greene compounded by pouring in more men and supplies. It was the military equivalent of low-hanging fruit, ripe to be plucked.

The invaders might well have been salivating on the night of November 14 as thirty British flatboats stuffed with redcoats and Hessians slipped quietly up the river past Washington, who was sleeping at Fort Lee.[106] Unaware of what had happened, GW left the next morning to begin a general survey of conditions in New Jersey. He had just reached Hackensack when a messenger caught up to tell him the British equivalent of the wolf was at the door, demanding Fort Washington's surrender. He raced back to personally supervise the defense, such as it was.

The formal attack began on the morning of November 16, with five thousand British and Germans converging on the fort's outworks from three directions. GW was soon on hand with Putnam, Greene, and Hugh Mercer, observing from the ramparts as the enemy ground through the outworks. The Americans fought hard, in some places driving the attackers back with the lethality of their fire. Before it was over they would inflict over 450 casualties and manage to infuriate what were almost certain victors. By noon the issue was no longer in doubt, and his generals begged Washington to cross the river back over to Fort Lee. He left only when they agreed to accompany him;

from here they watched the rest of the disaster unfold, with Washington at one point said to have wept like a child.[107]

But the fate of the actual defenders was worse. By the time their adversaries, particularly the Hessians, reached the inner fortifications, they were truly enraged by their losses. Now in a virtual killing frenzy, they bayoneted wounded Americans and refused quarter to any they caught. At 3:00 P.M. the fort formally capitulated, and an hour later over 2,800 Americans stacked their guns and marched out as prisoners through a crowd of jeering Germans, who were soon beating and kicking them. "The Hessians were roused," wrote the American-hating General James Grant to a fellow officer. "They had been pretty well pelted, were angry & would not have spared the Yankeys."[108] Officers did intervene to prevent a general massacre, but for most of these prisoners it only amounted to the difference between a quick end and a long, agonizing one.

These men, along with the one thousand captured on Long Island, were destined for the hell-holds of British prison ships, a collection of the least seaworthy transports anchored in New York Harbor with absolutely no accommodations for permanent inhabitants. Here, packed in the darkness below deck, without fresh air, fed next to nothing, they lived a nightmare existence for years on end waiting for paroles that never came. The only way out was to join the British Army, or to die. Few enlisted, so typhus, dysentery, scurvy, or simple neglect eventually killed two-thirds of them. To put this in perspective, percentage-wise in World War II a German prisoner of the Russians or even a Russian prisoner of the Germans stood a better chance of surviving captivity than these marooned Americans.[109] Before the war ended, around 8,500 POWs died in British captivity, aboard prison ships, in New York and in Charleston, or in a variety of other wretched jails and places of confinement.[110]

It could be argued this was more due to mismanagement and corruption than to actual malign intent. But this would miss the point entirely. This is the way the British military leadership in America characteristically behaved; they turned their backs while their henchmen did the dirty deeds—the bayoneting, the raping, the looting, and the most miserable and deadly incarceration possible for the Yankees they managed to capture.

If that seems extreme, it's worth considering the case of General Howe himself. A world-class party animal as we will see, he got into the spirit of things by bringing his mistress, the Boston-born Elizabeth Lloyd Loring, with him to New York. Being a benevolent sort, at least for this time, he also found a place for her cuckolded husband, Joshua. He made him commissary of prisoners, the very man responsible for starving them.[111] Howe had a direct view of those fetid hulks; but he didn't care to look, Mrs. Loring being much more comely. That was the way it was done, a façade of civility over an agenda of cruelty and retribution. They were living up to the Americans' worst fears, and having such a villain in an otherwise hyperbolic narrative was a recipe for keeping the Glorious Cause alive and inevitable.

# 6

November 1776 was not a good month for George Washington, and as befit the revolutionary environment, treacherous backbiting began almost immediately. On November 19, Charles Lee wrote him blaming Greene for the loss of Fort Washington, calling his recommendations "wretched," and concluding: "Oh General why wou'd you be overperswaded by Men of inferior judgment to your own? It was a cursed affair—yours most affectionately."[112] Probably not, since Lee was also writing Horatio Gates: "There never was so damned a stroke. *Entre nous,* a certain great man is damnably deficient."[113]

And it was compounded before Lee's letter even got to Washington. On the morning of November 20, GW was again in Hackensack when he learned that the night before thousands of enemy troops had secretly crossed the Hudson and scaled the rock wall of the Palisades. Now they were rapidly converging on Fort Lee. He raced back, and managed to evacuate its two thousand–man garrison just in the nick of time. But he did so at the cost of two hundred cannon, hundreds of tents, and thousands of barrels of flour.[114]

Coming on top of a series of beatings, the loss of the Washington and Lee complex did not reflect well on GW's military reputation, even when viewed by sympathetic eyes. Yet characteristically he accepted no blame. Nor did he shift it over to Nathanael Greene; instead—much to his credit and future advantage—he retained him. If it was anybody's fault, Washington believed, the militiamen were to blame for chronic desertion and repeatedly running away from the enemy, thereby infecting the regulars with similar proclivities.[115] This was cold comfort, especially for the friends and relatives of those who had been captured or killed.

So the biting of Washington's back continued, and the gashes grew only deeper. It now looked like the central British effort would be focused on New Jersey, and Washington wrote Lee on November 21: "This Country therefore will expect the Continental Army to give what Support they can & failing in this will cease to depend upon or Support a Force from which no Protection is given them. It is therefore of the utmost Importance that at least an Appearance of Force should be made to keep this Province in the Connection with the others."[116]

After Chatterton Ridge, Washington left himself desperately short of troops, and even this "Appearance of Force" required that Lee and his Continentals join him immediately, which he asked him, ever so politely, to do. This was not only his prerogative as commander in chief, but reflected a very cogent analysis of the strategic situation. In return he got insubordination and treachery.

Joseph Reed, his closest aide, secretly slipped a note of his own to Lee into the same dispatch pouch. It sounded very much like a man switching horses in midstream: "I confess I do think that it is entirely owing to you that this army and the liberties of America ... are not totally cut off." As far as his own boss: "Oh! General—an indecisive mind is one of the greatest misfortunes that can befall an army." He therefore recommended: "As soon as the season will admit, I think Yourself and some others should go to Congress and form the Plan of the new Army."[117]

Toward the end of the month GW was working at his desk when he opened what he assumed was Lee's reply, not realizing it was actually addressed to Reed. In it Lee revealed that he was disobeying

Washington and not bringing his army to New Jersey, sending two thousand men instead to the upper forts in the Hudson Highlands. Ever indiscreet, Lee also made it clear he was quoting Reed on "that fatal indecision of Mind which in War is a much greater disqualification than stupidity or even want of personal courage."[118]

It probably hurt; GW liked Reed, and always had trouble fathoming why anyone would want to betray him. But it was moments like this that revealed Washington at his most controlled and calculating, always keeping his priorities straight. He was in the middle of a military emergency, fighting with another temporary army whose enlistments would start running out in December; neither he nor it could afford a purge. So GW simply dropped Reed a line apologizing for opening his mail, and when Reed sent his resignation to Congress, talked him out of it. You don't rock a leaking boat.

Meanwhile, the British were looking to sink it. Historians have repeatedly wondered at the dilatory campaign of the brothers Howe, their apparent lack of enthusiasm for finishing off Washington and the Continental Army. In part this clearly had to do with complacency and avoiding attrition; but it also seems Howe and the British were looking beyond a single climactic battle, to a longer-range plan to put down the rebellion, one that largely mirrored Washington's fears. The English hadn't been repressing uprisings for centuries without some idea of the basic approach, or as Henry Clinton put it in this case: "to gain the hearts and subdue the minds of America."[119]

With this objective, Howe issued a proclamation in early December, offering pardons to all who would take an oath of allegiance to king and empire; within weeks over three thousand Americans, including one signer of the Declaration of Independence, had taken up the offer.[120] In New Jersey the dominant Patriot militias were starting to be replaced by equivalents from the other side, and very quickly the whole place began to look like it could be flipped.

Having gotten that started politically, Howe then set about to run down George Washington, and in the process secure the countryside and lock Loyalism into place. He tasked the pursuit to Lord Cornwallis, with an elite mix of British grenadiers and light infantry, plus Hessian grenadiers and Jägers—green-jacketed rangers armed with rifles—a force plainly optimized to perform its hunter-killer role.[121] And as the last of Washington's troops left Newark on November 28, the British were just arriving. The chase was on.

Being who he was, it may have crossed George Washington's mind that he was now the fox. Afraid of being cut off by a landing on the Jersey shore at Perth Amboy, he scuttled his panting army twenty-five miles down to New Brunswick in one day, and kept going through Princeton, where he left two brigades under Lord Stirling (now repatriated) and Adam Stephen to watch for the British, finally reaching Trenton on December 2, 1776, where boats were waiting to ferry the army over the Delaware. He thought about baring his fangs and making a stand at Princeton but, warned that Cornwallis was circling around the town, got his rear guard out and down to Trenton. On the afternoon of December 8, the British entered to find all the Americans gone across the Delaware, and—at Washington's orders—no boats to be found to follow them.[122]

For the moment GW and his little army were safe. But that was about the only good news available. Grim tidings, they came like hammer blows. Howe had sent Henry Clinton and a fleet of eighty-three ships up to Newport to try his hand again at amphibious operations. It went better this time; on December 8, seven thousand British troops landed virtually unopposed and effortlessly took America's fourth largest city and another trove of precious artillery. Even more embarrassing, on December 13 Congress, apparently finding Washington's little army of three thousand not much protection against twelve thousand British, evacuated Philadelphia and headed for Baltimore.

It's hard to imagine this move not reminding Washington of his growing consternation with Charles Lee, whom he had been begging to join him along with the four thousand men still under his command. At last he had crossed the Hudson and was in New Jersey, but on December 8 Lee wrote him, purporting to be "extremely shock'd to hear that your force is so inadequate," and informing him "I have put myself in a position the most convenient to cooperate with you by attacking their rear."[123] When Washington continued to plead for reinforcement, Lee wrote back on December 11 from Morristown, still over forty miles away: "We have three thousand Men here at present but They are so ill shod that We have been oblig'd to halt these two days for want of shoes."[124] As it turned out, he, too, would be caught without shoes.

The next night, after moving his army all of four miles south, Lee forged ahead to an inn at Basking Ridge, his objective being a night in bed with a whore. In the morning, just finishing a letter to Gates detailing Washington's latest foibles, Lee looked out the window to find the place surrounded by British dragoons, led there by local Tories. He tried hiding in the fireplace, but after a notably handsome but utterly ruthless young trooper named Banastre Tarleton suggested that they put the inn to the torch, Lee surrendered—led away in a dirty night-gown and slippers for what would prove to be sixteen months in captivity.[125] The British were exultant; they thought they had snatched the brains behind Washington. "Victoria!" wrote Howe's aide. "We have captured General Lee, the only rebel general whom we had cause to fear."[126]

He may have been reprehensible, but Lee was the closest thing to a true professional combat officer the Patriot side had. George Washington and his band of amateurs were now really on their own, and in a moment of greatest perceived danger. On December 14, William Howe called a halt to further campaigning. He wasn't going to Philadelphia; instead, he would distribute the Jersey force in an eighty-mile chain of brigade-sized garrisons or cantonments running from Perth Amboy to the Delaware River.[127] His intent was obvious: to provide maximum protection for New Jersey's Loyalists, the security needed to restore and regenerate royal governance.

George Washington recognized almost immediately what was happening and how dangerous it was. Less than a week after Howe's order Washington warned Hancock and Congress: "The Enemy are daily gathering strength from the disaffected; This strength, like a Snowball by rolling, will increase, unless some means can be devised to check effectually, the progress of the Enemy's Arms."[128] He had to strike and do it soon, somehow coax a victory out of his beat-up disheartened army—an army, just like the one around Boston, scheduled to disintegrate on January 1, when most of the Continentals' terms of service ran out.[129]

Besides that miserable night at Fort Necessity, this period in the middle of December 1776 seemed about as desperate as it ever got for George Washington. So it's interesting that we have a record of what amounts to a gut check from right around the same time, a purported "what if everything went wrong" conversation between Reed and GW, at the end of which he brought his hand up to his throat: "My neck does not feel as though it was made for a halter. We must retire to Augusta Country in Virginia . . . and we must try what we can do in carrying on a predatory war, and, if over powered, we must cross the Alleghany Mountains."[130] There was no sign of quitting here. In fact, it was exactly at such moments that George Washington was most lethal.

# 7

Things were nowhere near as bad as they seemed, for the British with their epic bad behavior completely undermined their own strategy. Chasing Washington required the British force cut the cord of seaborne supplies and live off the land. And when they did, foraging for the English and Hessians amounted to an excuse to act out. "In their march through the Jerseys," James Thacher wrote a month later, "they have committed such licentious ravages and desolation, as must be deemed disgraceful by all civilized people."[131] He wasn't necessarily exaggerating.

It was a road trip fueled by threats, beatings, murder, multiple gang rapes, and plunder without regard for the political sympathies of the victims, a veritable rampage.[132] The loot was the most obvious sign of what was going on; at one point Jäger Captain Ewald ran into a caravan of several hundred wagons "all loaded with plundered goods."[133]

When the march began, the tide of loyalism seemed to be overtaking the countryside; by the time it ended the flow had reversed. The British had convinced those in their path that their worst fears, foretold in the Patriot narrative, were real. Militia ranks swelled, and soon enough foraging parties were regularly mauled by local irregulars; even communication between cantonments was becoming difficult.[134] For if the countryside was no longer secure, neither were they.

The fox was no longer trembling and out of breath. Instead of disintegrating, George Washington's little army was being fortified, gaining strength. Faithful John Sullivan (also exchanged and liberated) promptly pushed the two-thousand-man remnant of Lee's force through a snowstorm and delivered them to the commander in chief. Horatio Gates even brought down six hundred Continentals from Ticonderoga, though he quickly left for Philadelphia, claiming bad health. Meanwhile, the regional response was similarly encouraging, including a Continental regiment recruited from German settlers in Pennsylvania and Maryland and a brigade of well-armed and disciplined Philadelphia militia (among them Charles Willson Peale, for whom GW had sat for his first portrait in 1772) under the pugnacious Colonel John Cadwalader.[135] All together it amounted to around six thousand men, half the British total in the state, but significantly larger than any one garrison—big enough, therefore, to hunt.

On December 22, Washington called only his senior generals and aides to a secret council of war, which proved less than secret since one of the subordinates—never identified—was a spy. The time had arrived, GW told them, to seize the initiative. With the Patriot militias having the upper hand and effectively isolating the various garrisons, the Continental Army now had the opportunity to cross the Delaware and move through the countryside unobserved, descending on individual German and British cantonments and overwhelming them in detail. When he finished, though, only Lord Stirling backed the scheme; the rest equivocated, and the meeting ended without reaching a decision.[136]

As usual with George Washington, luck favored his Christmas surprise. The spy bolted and headed to New Brunswick to inform the overall commander James Grant that Washington had talked about an attack, but without much support. Ever disdainful of Americans, Grant didn't take the prospect too seriously, issuing nothing more than a pro forma warning to Colonel Johann Rall and his Hessian brigade down in Trenton.

Meanwhile, the secret meeting, no longer leaking, had reconvened late that night to approve the plan: "Christmas day at Night, one hour before day,"[137] they would descend on Trenton. The operational con-

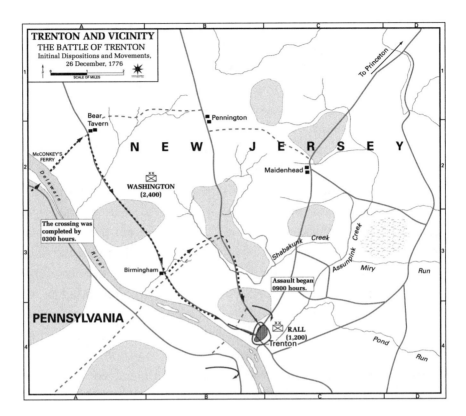

TRENTON AND VICINITY
THE BATTLE OF TRENTON
Initial Dispositions and Movements,
26 December, 1776
SCALE OF MILES

cept was redolent with Washington: heavy on surprise and way too complicated (featuring multiple simultaneous attacks coming from all directions), especially considering the nature of his troops and the miserable circumstances. Lots went wrong, but swept along by the last fumes of the rage militaire and their intrepid commander in chief, this tattered crazy quilt of an army made it work.

The crossings began at sunset, in the face of high winds and ice floes, but John Glover and his Marblehead men, rowing sixty-foot boats, managed to get the last men of the main force across by three in the morning. They were hours behind schedule, but Washington let the troops warm themselves around bonfires before forming them into columns for the nine-mile trek to Trenton. The weather got only worse; sleet and hail battered everybody. Most of Cadwalader's Philadelphia brigade and another Pennsylvania militia element never made it across the Delaware. Virginia troops under Washington's old comrade Adam Stephen prematurely attacked a Hessian picket, briefly alarming the garrison and jeopardizing the entire operation.[138] Halfway, the army split in two along parallel roads, Sullivan on the right, and Washington, Greene, Knox, and the artillery on the left. Somehow they all arrived just after dawn, blocking every road north out of Trenton, and when the attack began at around eight, Sullivan's and Greene's assaults came within three minutes of each other.

The Hessians were neither drunk on holiday cheer as legend has it, nor without warning. "Let them come," Colonel Rall had growled that afternoon. "Why defenses? We will go at them with the bayonet."[139] Still, they were profoundly befuddled when battalion after battalion of Americans led by Washington himself emerged from the woods and headed straight for the center of town. They arrived to find the Germans, just roused from their barracks, clumped together and only starting to fire sporadically. Knox's cannon—some commanded by Alexander Hamilton—put an end to that, scattering them with grapeshot and igniting a panic that sent Prussians scampering out of Trenton into the open fields to the southeast.

Here, with the help of a military band, Rall managed to pull two regiments together. He briefly considered retreating toward Princeton, but when he found his escape routes blocked by Americans, he de-

Battle of Princeton, *by John Trumbull.*

JOHN TRUMBULL/LIBRARY OF CONGRESS

cided on a counterattack, leading them back toward Trenton. They didn't stand a chance; artillery abandoned, the sleet having rendered their cartridges useless, all they had were their bayonets.

Meanwhile, Washington had five times their number waiting, powder dry, and deployed in defensive positions so they could fire at both the front and flanks of the advancing Prussians.[140] Mercifully, it didn't last long. Two musket balls shot Rall off his horse, and within minutes the better part of three regiments had surrendered. Though over six hundred managed to escape into the woods, almost nine hundred of the hated Hessians were now in American hands. The troops had been primed with plenty of stories of what they had done to New Jersey. If there was ever a get-even moment in the Glorious Revolution, this was probably it.

George Washington ignored it, and thereby revealed a key element in his grand strategy for winning, in this instance and throughout what would turn out to be a very long and vicious war. So he paid his respects to the dying Rall. He allowed no reprisals. After divesting German prisoners of anything that looked like loot, they were permitted to keep their baggage and eventually sent to the interior, where Washington ordered they be treated "with favor and humanity."[141] He even invited a few Hessian officers to dinner before they departed.[142]

Always be better than the enemy. Washington was instinctively magnanimous; but this was also a shrewd approach, one not just calculated to maximize the contrast between British and American war efforts, but also revealing a deeper understanding that this sort of war had an almost unlimited potential for violence. If truly unleashed it could consume the Revolution in an orgy of retribution. Only Washington could prevent this, and he did so with all the consistency the brutality of war allowed.

Washington knew his men were exhausted and quickly got them to shelter back across the Delaware. But he was not interested in just a single victory; he needed to drive the British out of inland New Jersey, so he led them back over the river beginning on December 29. Besides the British, his central problem remained that the lion's share of his army was still set to dissolve on New Year's Day, when all the New Englanders' enlistments expired.

There ensued a test of wills, a moment of political theater when George Washington briefly pulled off his mask of command and spoke to his soldiers as fellow citizens. He rode before them the next day, regiment by regiment, on his giant white stallion and implored them to keep it together just a little longer. Like a number of his best moments, he started flat, then grabbed their heartstrings.

As one sergeant remembered: "The General wheeled his horse about . . . and addressing us again said, 'My brave fellows, you have done all I asked you to do, and more than could be reasonably expected; but your country is at stake, your wives, your houses, and all that you hold dear. You have worn yourselves out with fatigue and hardships, but we know not how to spare you.'"[143] That did it. An army votes with its feet and nearly all stepped forward to stay. It helped that those steps were lubricated by a bounty of ten dollars to remain six weeks more, and also that two bags full of silver arrived from Philadelphia on New Year's Day.[144] But it was George Washington who had won over his soldiers. So the year 1777 found him still at the head of an army numbering 6,500 and ready to rumble.

Back in New York, William Howe was deep into the first cycle of winter banqueting when the news of Trenton arrived, so he delegated the response to Lord Cornwallis, who had been expecting to sail to England and his desperately ill wife. Cornwallis was an excellent soldier, but his motivation seemed to swing from having a very personal reason to eliminate Washington quickly, to not much interest in the whole operation. Meanwhile, General Grant, now taking the Yankee threat seriously, had moved forward to Princeton with reinforcements and, knowing the time limit on Washington's army, was awaiting an immediate attack. "They expect to make us quit the Jerseys before the Winter is over," he wrote in an intelligence assessment.[145]

But when Cornwallis arrived on New Year's Day with more troops, pushing the total number of Hessians and British to around eight thousand, thoughts instantly turned to fox hunting. The next morning, leaving three infantry regiments and some dragoons in Princeton to guard the rear, Cornwallis pushed off with the rest of his army down the road to Trenton and retribution.

GW knew he was coming, and to slow his progress sent out a

*Marquess Charles Cornwallis: He would spend the war chasing Americans, until finally they caught him.*

JOHN FIELDING/
LIBRARY OF
CONGRESS

thousand-man screening force divided into two brigades—Virginia Continentals under his longtime subordinate Charles Scott and Pennsylvania riflemen under Colonel Edward Hand.[146] They succeeded brilliantly, forcing the enemy columns to stop and defend themselves from constant sniper fire, and turning an eleven-mile march into an all-day event. By the time Cornwallis reached Trenton, he moved cautiously through the town and made contact with Washington's main line of defense at a stone bridge that was his obvious escape route; daylight was dwindling. A sharp firefight ensued, during which GW rallied his troops, while Knox's artillery drove the massed Hessians back. Darkness ended it, and Cornwallis fell back for the night, certain now that the fox was all but in the bag. In the morning a simple flanking movement would pin Washington and his army against the ice-choked Delaware and oblivion.

Sound thinking, except that it assumed the fox was out of tricks. He wasn't. Using information from a local sympathizer, the serviceable Cadwalader had drawn Washington a detailed map of the vicinity, including, crucially, the Saw Mill Road, a seldom-used farmers' path that provided a back door out of Trenton and right into Princeton.[147]

Washington called a council of war and convinced them that there was
no defense except to retreat and attack again. So once again they left
the campfires burning, while six thousand men and forty cannon hit
the road, but softly with wheels muffled, orders whispered, and torches
left unlit.

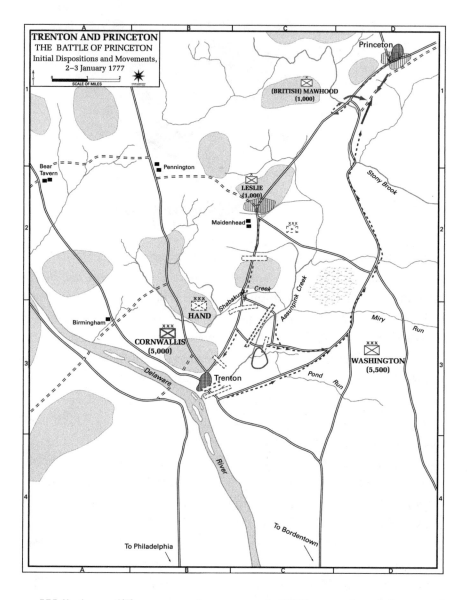

Well clear of Trenton as dawn neared, GW crossed and destroyed
a key bridge over Stony Creek to protect his rear from Cornwallis,

then split his own force for the assault on Princeton—Sullivan's three brigades of New Englanders would proceed on Saw Mill Road, while Greene's division would take the main route into town.

Almost immediately Greene's column ran into two regiments of redcoats marching toward Trenton. At the front, General Hugh Mercer moved his Continentals rashly ahead through shin-deep snow to make contact. They found the enemy arrayed behind a rail fence, and let loose an effective first volley, but then were savaged by the British, who not only shot accurately but had bayonets. Mercer was blown from the saddle and, when he refused to surrender, was clubbed and stabbed to death by the redcoats, apparently thinking he was Washington. Other wounded were similarly treated as the English charged into the now-leaderless Continentals and scattered them.[148]

Next in line was Cadwalader's Pennsylvania militia. As the militiamen advanced, the British took advantage of a second fence to let loose another devastating barrage, supported by two cannon firing grapeshot. The brigade was just breaking apart when Washington showed up, charging forward, barking out orders, and joining Cadwalader in trying to get the troops to hold their ground. Soon he was alone, caught yet again in a storm of flying metal. One of his aides, John Fitzgerald, put his hat over his eyes expecting the worst, only to find Washington as usual completely unscathed, having provided enough heroic glue to allow Cadwalader to re-form his troops just out of range.[149]

"Parade with us, my brave fellows!" one sergeant remembered Washington shouting. "There is but a handful of the enemy, and we will have them directly."[150] He was right. Greene and Cadwalader had only to bring up reinforcements and deploy them on the British flanks to render their position untenable. When the redcoats tried to take a stand the Americans scattered them. Perhaps remembering that humiliating moment on Harlem Heights, Washington joined the pursuit bellowing: "It's a fine fox chase, my boys!"[151]

That it was. When Sullivan and his New England Continentals arrived outside of Princeton, it was clear to the defenders that they had no chance of holding the town and they, too, were soon gone, scampering back toward New Brunswick. Washington's little army was short on just about everything, so he had his troops strip Princeton of all the supplies they could find in the hour or so he figured they had before Cornwallis got there. But when Continentals started stripping wounded redcoats of their provisions and uniforms, Washington stopped it immediately.[152] They were all gone by noon, and the British arrived in midafternoon. But instead of chasing the Americans, they spent the rest of the day looting the place themselves.

Washington wanted to hit the big British base at New Brunswick next. But his officers convinced him that his troops, many of whom had not slept in two days, were too fatigued to fight further. It's a good thing they did. Cornwallis, worried about his own supplies, had led his men on a forced march overnight and would have been waiting in New Brunswick the next morning.[153] Instead, Washington moved into the rugged wooded hills of north Jersey around Morristown, where Greene had already found a site for winter quarters. For now the fighting was over.

In purely military terms, the Jersey campaign was the most decisive of the war. The age's greatest soldier, Frederick the Great, was certainly impressed: "The achievements of Washington and his little band of compatriots between December 25 and the 4th of January, a space of 10 days, were the most brilliant of any recorded in the annals of military achievements."[154] Whether he simply adored Washington's audacity or grasped the true strategic significance remains unclear.

But GW certainly did. As he wrote Connecticut's governor, Jonathan Trumbull, on January 10, 1777: "They have called in all their out posts, so that their late possession of the greatest part of Jersey is reduced to the Compass of a very few miles."[155] He had forced the British octopus to draw in its tentacles, to centralize for safety's sake, and in doing so he drove them from the countryside where the Revolution lived. The British characteristically overestimated Loyalist support, but in New Jersey and three years later in South Carolina, they plainly understood that for their adherents to show their heads and contest control of the countryside there had to be security nearby, redcoats ready to intervene. When they failed at this, their chances of winning became minuscule.

Yet this is also largely irrelevant. Failure was less a matter of strategy than one of attitude and behavior. The British cut a swath of terror practically wherever they went, but most particularly in the countryside—burning, brutalizing, and gang raping as they moved. These were the houses and wives Washington was talking about when he begged his men to stay. These were the crimes that reverberated from Patriot newspapers to all corners of America, convincing people that the British were as bad as predicted by the Patriot narrative.[156] From beginning to end they provided a constant supply of lurid kindling guaranteed to keep revolutionary fires burning. This was the real reason they could never win.

# CHAPTER 5

# Out in the Cold

## 1

H AVING TAKEN SEVERAL SUBSTANTIAL BITES OUT OF HIS TOR-
mentors, the fox was in his lair for the winter. "Washington has
since taken post at Morris Town—where We can not get at Him,"
General James Grant wrote a friend back in England. "And as He can
move a Force from thence to any given Point we have been obliged to
Contract our Cantonments . . . in short it is the most unpleasing situation I ever was in."[1] That pretty much summed it up from a British
perspective.

But from Washington's it was also a respite during which he could
begin to develop the army he thought was necessary to challenge and
defeat the invaders. Just before the year turned Congress had granted
GW the extraordinary—a number said "dictatorial"—powers he had
requested at the height of the emergency.[2] While they were temporary
and Washington was hardly enthusiastic about assuming them ("desperate diseases, require desperate remedies"), his bottom line for the
Continental Army was replacing the yearly recruitment cycle with "a
permanent standing army."[3] Because the states continued to supply
the manpower, and their bounties and terms of service inevitably var-
ied, it never exactly came to pass. But he did get authorization to appoint all officers below brigadier general, along with the right to raise
sixteen new infantry and three more artillery regiments, three thou-

sand cavalry, and a dedicated corps of engineers. Perhaps most important, enlistments would begin to last for three years or the duration of the war.[4] Washington had at least the building blocks for the force he wanted.

The process of change began at Morristown. But it had to be done on the fly, because the British were continually venturing out from their now-centralized garrisons in search of extra food, wood to burn, and especially fodder for their horses. Washington used the opportunity to try a new approach, exposing his regulars to small doses of combat to continue building their confidence under fire, not to mention a growing expertise at raiding.[5] Back and forth they crossed New Jersey the winter of 1777, carving a pattern of near-daily skirmishes—the British and Germans in cumbersome multi-regimental units for protection, and the Yankees in packs of Continentals and militia, removing everything they could, and then laying ambushes for those seeking to take the rest. Not "a stick of wood, a spear of grass, or a kernel of corn could the troops in New Jersey procure without fighting for it," reported Loyalist Thomas Jones. "Every foraging party was attacked."[6]

As usual the redcoats and Hessians cut a swath of bad behavior wherever they went—looting, burning, and mistreating just about everybody they met up with, in their eyes all potential rebels.[7] "Ravages in the Jerseys' exceeded all description," wrote Nathanael Greene. "Many hundred women ravished."[8] Greene also heard a report that British soldiers had murdered "two of the Inhabitants . . . because they did not assist them with their Waggons to carry off their dead."[9] Redcoated corpses stacked like cordwood in carts were an increasing product of these hunting and gathering expeditions, a mute testimony to George Washington's strategy of on-the-job training.

His fighters were getting more lethal and accomplished, but GW also demanded they remain true to revolutionary principles. One extraordinary power granted him by Congress, "to take were-ever he mabe, whatever he may want for the Use of the Army,"[10] was exactly what he didn't want. As he warned John Sullivan when he heard his division was becoming notorious for property violations, such practices were "highly disgraceful and unworthy of the Cause in which we are engaged—Add to this that it has a fatal & obvious tendency to prejudice their minds and to disaffect 'em."[11] If they wanted to win they had to remain better than the British, no matter what the circumstances.

Washington's army that winter was a worn-down nub, numbering less than three thousand at this point.[12] And the prospect for its numbering a lot less jumped terrifyingly when GW realized in early February that smallpox was spreading among his troops. This time he went for the radical solution. On February 14, he informed John Hancock that the situation was sufficiently dangerous to warrant inoculating his entire force.[13]

This was very risky, not medically, but militarily. Mass inoculation meant weeks with soldiers quarantined and too sick to fight; GW realized if the British got wind of this the consequences could be catastrophic, warning his chief physician to keep "the matter as secret as possible."[14] It went well and almost all the soldiers were quickly back on the line, now smallpox-proof; but Washington's foresight was not limited to Morristown. Not only had he insisted that Martha, who was now in camp, be inoculated back in Philadelphia when he visited Congress, but, looking to an expanded Continental force, GW wrote the states, which would be contributing troops, to urge them to establish similar inoculation programs before sending them—a request that led to thousands undergoing the process at camps in Virginia, Maryland, New York, and Connecticut.[15] Freeing his army and his wife of smallpox's curse would pay big dividends, but at the time it was an act of faith; everything was.

The days of thousands converging, fueled by the rage militaire, were over. Getting men into camp now required sending officers and other recruiters to scour the countryside, raising bounties, and milking local militia of those willing to serve, or at least ready to act as bounty-lubricated substitutes for a dramatically increased term of duty. All of this took time, as did shepherding the recruits to Morristown. It was early May 1777 before the new regiments actually began to take shape with soldiers, but then they came in a rush; by the end of the month the army numbered nearly nine thousand.

This had happened before in New York, but this time Washington was much better prepared to equip them at least. Relations with France, the enemy of the Revolution's enemy, had been growing steadily warmer. The young King Louis XVI was suspicious of revolutions (with good reason, it turned out), but the minions of the ancien regime ached to overturn the results of the Seven Years' War.

So almost from the beginning, officers, guns, and money poured in, with court insider Pierre Beaumarchais even setting up a fictitious business, Roderigue Hortalez and Company, to speed the flow of arms and obscure the source.[16] In Washington's case the goods arrived in late March 1777—exactly what his under-armed army needed—eleven thousand high-quality French muskets with bayonets, to be followed by a "large quantity" of brass cannon, ammunition, and powder.[17] Uniforms remained in short supply, but quantities of hunting shirts along with blankets do seem to have been available to supplement the militia garb many recruits arrived wearing. It may not have been spit and polish, but neither would the new-model Continental Army go forward nearly naked and unarmed.

But it remained largely untrained, as green as the Jersey hills that spring. Most of those who had been through the battles around Boston and New York had left the army; even John Glover's Marblehead regiment had broken up to try their hands at privateering.[18] There remained a combat-hardened core making up about a third; but they had never mastered or even tried very hard to master battlefield maneuver. They were good at loading and firing their guns; but lining up to shoot them and moving rapidly in compact columns—the tactical maneuvers where the British and Hessians shined—continued to elude them. As for the rest, the newbies, they would have to pick up what they could, or cared to.

Knowing Washington, regular drill or some approximation likely took place at Morristown, but there is no evidence that the men took it seriously, much less embraced it as something that could save their lives.[19] George Washington had been through this before; he knew enough to keep them away from major combat until they had gotten used to full-time soldiering and marched around for a while. In the meantime, he continued to experiment and build what he could.

As GW had experienced during his time with the British army in the French and Indian War, a commander's personal staff was viewed in the eighteenth century as a "military family," the concept being that constant contact, on duty and over meals with the general, would allow his scribes to accurately reflect his wishes in written orders, and at best almost assume his personality, enabling them to represent him in other circumstances.

Washington bought in completely, and from his earliest days as commander in chief, he was always on the lookout for "penmen" with the right combination of deference and enterprise to become family members. Joseph Reed had been his first bright young man, but he had betrayed the generalissimo, and in revolutions such breaches are seldom forgiven, so in February he resigned and dove into Pennsylvania politics.[20] But Washington's eye for talent seldom blinked, and it had already fastened on someone much better: the young artillery officer who proved so handy at Chatterton Hill and Trenton, Alexander Hamilton.

On March 1, Hamilton was appointed aide-de-camp to the commander in chief, with the rank of lieutenant colonel: It was the beginning of a tumultuous and monumentally important relationship that would eventually culminate in the creation of a stable and effective national government. At this point Hamilton was barely into his twenties, but his brilliance and nearly unlimited capacity for work became almost immediately obvious. So, very likely, did his ego, which was both enormous and vulnerable, due to his obscure origins and illegitimate birth. Hamilton was always the proverbial "brightest boy in the room"; but he also had the hottest head. It took someone with the massive gravitas of Washington to not only control and bring out the best in Hamilton, but also to ensure that he played well with others.

The family would soon be joined by two additional luminaries, John Laurens, the astute son of Henry Laurens, John Hancock's replacement as president of the Second Continental Congress, and a twenty-year-old French officer, the Marquis de Lafayette, with sufficient connections in court to elicit a diplomatic protest from England when he arrived in America to join the cause.[21] This was a high-powered group with all the right connections, and Washington made sure that everybody got along—not just with one another, but also

*Alexander
Hamilton:
the most brilliant
of GW's "penmen,"
but also the most
egotistical.*

JOHN TRUMBULL/
LIBRARY OF
CONGRESS

with his key henchmen in the field, Greene, Knox, Sullivan, Lord Stirling, and the rest, one big happy family. It worked brilliantly.

Daniel Morgan, captured in the disastrous assault on Quebec, was back, released in a prisoner exchange. But he was never family. Unlike Hamilton, whose origins didn't keep him from being perceived as a gentleman, Morgan was a barely literate rustic, known to refer to Washington as "Old Horse."[22] He also seemed oblivious to faction, maintaining his rapport with Gates while remaining fiercely loyal to GW. All of this seems to have prevented Washington from realizing just how talented and innovative Morgan actually was, and taking full advantage of his potential.

But he still put him to good use. Even before he was cleared to rejoin the Continental Army, GW suggested to John Hancock that Morgan quietly be given permission to raise a regiment of "the sort of Troops he is particularly recommended to command."[23] A courier duly delivered a commission as colonel of the Eleventh Virginia, and in

January 1777 Morgan headed to the frontier in search of his kind of fighters. Only accurate marksmen need apply, and much to the chagrin of Governor Patrick Henry, by the end of March, Morgan had accepted only 180 candidates.

That didn't appear to matter when they arrived in Morristown that spring. They were a military multiplier, a lethal screen Washington could use to keep the British off his inexperienced troops as they moved tentatively into the field. This had not gone well initially. In early May, Adam Stephen, on his own initiative, attempted a raid on Bergen, was mauled by the British, and then lied about the results, causing Washington, who knew otherwise, to reply acidly: "The disadvantage was on our side, not the Enemy's, who had notice of your coming and was prepared for it, as I expected."[24]

Morgan, on the other hand, was plainly competent, and by mid-June GW had designated his command "the Corps of Rangers" and was fortifying it with riflemen from other backcountry regions, until they numbered around five hundred. They proved particularly useful when William Howe moved off Staten Island into New Jersey on June 17, 1777, and marched his army nine miles down the road to Philadelphia in a serious attempt to lure Washington into decisive combat. Instead they got "Colo. Morgan and his Corps of Light Troops composed of Rifle Men . . . hanging on the Flanks of the Enemy (doing) a good deal of damage,"[25] while Washington easily avoided the trap. A week later Howe tried a more elaborate ruse, a false embarkation designed to draw the Continentals forward. It worked better, but Washington and Lord Stirling still managed to withdraw largely unscathed, with losses under one hundred.[26] With that Howe lost all patience, loaded his fourteen thousand men on transports at Perth Amboy, and left New Jersey, forever as it turned out.

## 2

Through miscommunication and personality politics, the British strategic plan for 1777 was cleft into two uncoordinated efforts with separate objectives that did not necessarily reinforce each other. A policy disconnect of this magnitude is almost inconceivable in today's electronically connected world, and has been for almost a century, but in this war the fastest means of transoceanic communications was a sailboat. Messages back and forth had a time lag of months, so it was easy to get signals crossed and move in contradictory directions, which partially explains what happened. How much that mattered, though, is debatable, since neither plan had much chance of success.

Of the three major generals aboard the *Cerberus* when it pulled into Boston Harbor—William Howe, Henry Clinton, and John Burgoyne—the latter was decidedly the worst soldier, but also the most convincing. Germain and the King were unhappy with Governor Guy Carleton's progress down the water corridor to cut off New England in 1776 having only reached Crown Point, and had already decided to put Burgoyne in charge. The deal was cemented when Burgoyne temporarily cut the communications gap by sailing to London to confer. He spoke of big plans and bold strokes, exactly what they wanted to hear.[27] As it became clearer that General Howe back in America had his own ideas that did not include moving up the Hudson to meet and reinforce him, Burgoyne reassured Germain that he could go it alone.[28] So he got the go-ahead.

Meanwhile, William Howe had fallen back on that old standby of counterinsurgency: Crush the rebel army and take their capital city. It was the checkmate approach, but the plan ignored the fact that the Revolution was everywhere, a problem set more reflective of the labyrinthine Chinese game of Go. But the strategy was psychologically satisfying in terms of the conventional metrics of military success, battles won, places taken. Howe was good at this, a master of the operational art, and with the help of his brother he would put on a dazzling display. But it would prove fruitless. Meanwhile, Germain made him only vaguely aware that something big was planned up north,[29] not that it would have necessarily turned Howe away from his new set of objectives. Henry Clinton, also briefly back in England, quickly recognized the dangers of independent attacks but did nothing, at least not until it was too late. So "Gentleman Johnny" Burgoyne was left free to push his army off on its errant slide.

Early summer 1777 found George Washington racking his brain, his generals', his spies', and anybody else's who seemed to have a clue as to exactly what the British were up to.

Of the two, the move to isolate New England was the easier to predict, and by early July, GW had "a strong presumption that the Enemy have in contemplation a junction of their Two Armies by way of the Lakes & North River."[30] On July 6 the situation grew abruptly more dangerous, when Burgoyne, moving with surprising speed, captured Ticonderoga unopposed. When the news arrived, GW immediately recommended to Hancock that the region's militia be called out, and that his ace paladin Benedict Arnold be sent north to help lead them.[31]

But then Burgoyne headed into the woods, and circumstances reversed. His march slowed to a crawl, and resistance picked up. As the middle of August approached, GW now thought that given "the Alacrity with which the Militia have assembled . . . we may hope that General Bourgoyne will find it equally difficult to make a farther Progress or to effect a Retreat."[32] They could trap him, in other words. On the sixteenth, Washington learned that a large body of New England militia had gathered in Bennington, a force that was already in the process of confronting and annihilating an entire Prussian brigade, killing two hundred and capturing seven hundred.[33] This would certainly prove good news, but there was also a sense of urgency, since logic indicated that Howe must soon move up the Hudson to support Burgoyne.[34] Therefore, on the same day the battle took place, GW was already in the process of sending northward exactly what was needed to stop Burgoyne in his tracks: Daniel Morgan's Rangers, urging him to hurry and even arranging transportation.[35]

This was both a decisive and magnanimous move, since the politics had grown complicated. Horatio Gates wanted the semiautonomous Northern Department, and through his connections in Congress succeeded in supplanting Washington's man Philip Schuyler in March, only to see the decision reversed in May. But then Ticonderoga was taken; Congress blamed Schuyler, and Gates was back.[36]

Washington's letter of congratulations summed up the relationship at this point: "You will perceive . . . that they have appointed you to the command of the army in the Northern Department, and have directed me to order you immediately to repair to that post. . . . Wishing you success."[37] Nonetheless, GW also sent Gates just the team of leaders—Arnold and Morgan—and type of fighters that would bring him an astonishing victory. And in the interim, he did everything he could to cover Gates's rear, which meant figuring out when or whether Howe was coming or going.

On July 8 the murky situation seemed about to clarify. Washington watched as Howe loaded eighteen thousand troops aboard a huge flotilla of transports brother Richard had assembled in New York Harbor.[38] Assuming they were about to sail up the Hudson, GW shifted his army north, sending two divisions upriver to Peekskill to secure a vital pass. They were there more than two weeks when news arrived that the British had sailed, but not up the river; instead they had cleared Sandy Hook and headed out into the Atlantic.

Assuming this meant an eventual landing near Philadelphia, Washington sent his army racing toward the Delaware on an exhausting five-day forced march. Sure enough, on July 31 he received a report that the British armada had appeared off the Delaware Capes two days earlier. That news sent GW and his army across the river and toward the capital with all possible dispatch. He had just arrived at Chester, where he wanted to camp, when a message from coast watchers at Cape May reached him reporting that the British fleet had not headed up the Delaware but out to sea. Almost immediately a frightening thought crossed his mind: Howe's hegira had been a giant feint, and that "a sudden stroke [up the Hudson] is certainly intended by this Maneuvre."[39] So once again he pointed his army north, only to encounter still another message from the coast, this one stating that the British were sailing south.

Parking his force on the Neshaminy Creek twenty miles north of Philadelphia, Washington was by now thoroughly puzzled "being unable to account upon any plausible plan for Genl Howe's conduct in this instance or why he should go to the Southward rather than cooperate with Mr Burgoyne."[40] On August 21, GW called a council of war: His generals thought Howe's destination was Charleston, and since they could never get there in time, they should all head north. It sounded reasonable, but just hours after he had issued orders to that effect, Washington learned the British fleet had entered the Chesapeake Bay.[41]

It was another impressive sweep around the flank, the Howe-patented maneuver, only this time he'd enlisted his brother's fleet to enable him to vanish, reappear, then sail up the commodious estuary to within fifty miles of Philadelphia. On a map it must have looked like a stroke of genius—true operational surprise and then a short stroll through the soft underbelly of Pennsylvania, full of peace-loving Quakers, sympathetic Germans, and Loyalists. Reality, though, proved less hospitable. It was August 25—four days after Washington knew they were coming—before Howe could begin unloading redcoats and Hessians along the Elk River, and then they required a week's rest at Head of Elk because they were so beat up.[42] These troops were amazingly adaptable and resilient, but they had been packed aboard ship for two months in the middle of a hot summer and needed time to recover.

The same could not be said for their horses; hundreds had died at sea and many others arrived beyond recovery and dropped dead almost as soon as they landed.[43] Right away this imposed a critical weakness on the invading force's capacity to actually destroy its Continental equivalent. To do this the British force not only had to win on the battlefield; they then had to run down and either kill or capture the defeated survivors with cavalry. That's how armies were obliterated, and without healthy horseflesh Howe could not expect much more than sterile victories that left his opponent very much intact.

Nor did the invaders meet with much in the way of sympathizers. In the immediate vicinity, scouts—Ewald's Jägers and the Loyalist-manned Queen's Rangers—found the inhabitants gone, along with all the livestock, and, in their place, militia scattered in the woods picking off occasional redcoats.[44] When they did run into people "the prevailing disposition of the inhabitants," Howe complained to Germain, "seems to be, excepting a few individuals, strongly in enmity against us."[45]

As they left Maryland and moved through Delaware and Pennsylvania, they found Quakers willing to sell them food, but not much else in the way of a friendly reception. Many had fled, and those who remained could prove surprisingly hostile. Now among Germans, Ewald asked an old lady for a drink "in pure Palatine" dialect: "Water I will give you, but I must also ask you: What harm have we people done to you, that you Germans come over here to suck us dry and drive us out of house and home? We have heard enough here of your murderous burning. Will you do the same here as in New York and in the Jerseys? You shall get your pay yet!"[46] If there were hearts to be gained and minds to be subdued to the British cause, they remained well hidden.

George Washington put his army on the road directly upon hearing of Howe's location. But his first objective was political, and that was Philadelphia. On August 24 he marched his entire force, now numbering twelve thousand, down Front Street, then up Chestnut, leading the procession as always on a white horse and accompanied by new family members Lafayette, Hamilton, and John Laurens.

With men lined up twelve across, it took two hours for them, with "a lively smart step," to pass through town. The march demonstrated a visible commitment to defend the cradle of the Revolution, and also, GW told Hancock, would exert "some influence on the minds of the disaffected there and those who are Dupes to their artifices & opinions"—Tories, in other words. [47] Yet, even to the very civilian John Adams it all didn't look quite right: "Our soldiers have not yet quite the air of soldiers. They don't step exactly in time. They don't hold up their heads quite erect, nor turn out their toes exactly as they ought."[48] But ready or not, George Washington was intent on using them.

Despite his unfortunate experiences with an army not much different the year before, GW was again in a feisty mood, ready to roll the dice on the battlefield. He was in lockstep with Congress's determination that the nation's capital and birthplace had to be shielded. Combined with the bright prospects emanating from the Northern Department, Washington realized that a major victory over Howe in defense of the capital might very well break the back of the invasion, and he put it in terms his troops understood: "If they are overthrown, they are utterly undone, the war is at an end. . . . One bold stroke will free the land from rapine devastations, and burnings, and female innocence from brutal lust and violence."[49]

His optimism was plainly shared by the latest version of the Continental Army. They were much better armed, the French muskets (*avec* bayonets) were now in their hands, and, by this time, they were probably fairly good at loading and shooting them. They had also been marching hither and yon all summer and were now road hardened and used to soldiering. But besides a relatively small core of experienced fighters, along with some selective exposure to irregular warfare, this remained an army devoid of combat experience, and one that expected to defeat an enemy with lots of it. Meanwhile, their training at the key elements of tactical maneuver—moving from column to line and vice versa—remained at best sketchy and haphazard. In battle, especially at critical moments, this almost inevitably led to confusion and panic.

After a series of marches and countermarches that Howe easily had the best of, September 11, 1777, found the Americans strung out along the east side of Brandywine Creek, with most concentrated at what was apparently the only crossing, Chadds Ford, where the main road to Philadelphia ran.[50] It was the logical place to be, unless you knew, as Howe did and Washington didn't, that an adequate crossing existed at Jefferis Ford, well to the north of Washington's right flank. The ama-

*Brandywine Creek: the home team again outmaneuvered.*

F. C. YOHN/LIBRARY OF CONGRESS

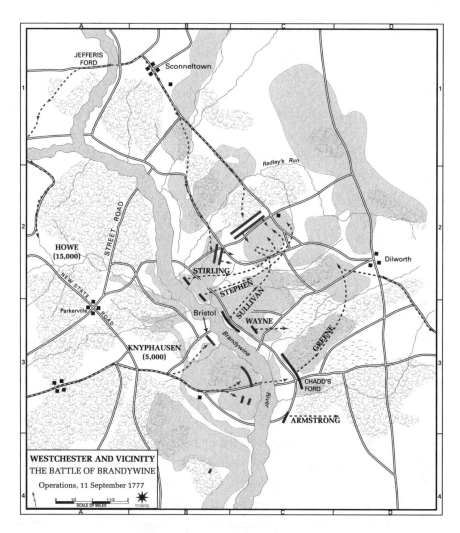

JEFFERIS
FORD
Sconneltown

Radley's Run

HOWE
(15,000)

STREET ROAD

NEW STATE ROAD

STIRLING

STEPHEN

SULLIVAN

Dilworth

Parkerville

Bristol

WAYNE

GREENE

KNYPHAUSEN
(5,000)

Brandywine

CHADD'S
FORD

River

ARMSTRONG

**WESTCHESTER AND VICINITY**
THE BATTLE OF BRANDYWINE

Operations, 11 September 1777

0    1/2    1    1-1/2    2
SCALE OF MILES

teur in Washington was again revealed. Once again the captain of the visiting team knew home turf better than the head of the locals.

It played out pretty predictably. Using General Wilhelm von Knyphausen's 6,800 Germans in a diversionary assault on Chadds Ford to grab and fix GW's attention, Howe led 8,200[51] redcoats in a looping twelve-hour march that left him at 4:00 P.M. staring at the hastily redeployed American right, consisting of·three uncoordinated divisions under Lord Stirling, John Sullivan, and Adam Stephen. Still, for two hours the Americans stood and fought before they collapsed backward, the only intact formation being Thomas Conway's Pennsylvania Brigade.[52]

Just prior to that happening, Washington, who had earlier ignored warnings of Howe bearing down on his flank, was at last drawn to the right by the intensity of the firing, bringing Nathanael Greene and a brigade of Virginians who were able to cover the fleeing Americans. Meanwhile, back at Chadds Ford, Knyphausen had come across to meet fierce resistance from brigades under newcomers William Maxwell and Anthony Wayne, a tough Pennsylvanian with a knack for the dramatic. But they, too, reeled back. Still, by slowing Howe, Greene's stand on the right allowed them to escape as well.[53]

Except for Conway—an opinionated Irishman who had previously made a career in the French Army—and Greene, American resistance collapsed at the Battle of Brandywine Creek. But the British were in no position to capitalize on their victory and destroy the Continental Army; night was closing in, they were exhausted, and they didn't have much in the way of cavalry in any case. The fox had been fooled again but had slipped easily from their clutches, bringing his army to rest and safety in Chester.

"Notwithstanding the misfortune of the day," Washington wrote John Hancock, "I am happy to find the troops in good spirits."[54] Meanwhile, he had exacted a toll in blood—almost 100 killed and 500 wounded—a price, in strategic terms at least, worth the cost of 200 dead Americans, along with 500 hundred wounded and 400 captured.[55]

One of these casualties, though, meant a great deal to Washington. The young Marquis de Lafayette—attached to Conway's brigade during the retreat and showing what even gonzo John Laurens thought of as almost suicidal bravery—had been wounded dangerously in the calf. He was now in the hands of a surgeon whom Washington had admonished: "Take care of him as if he were my son, for I love him the same."[56]

Without offspring of his own and stepson Jacky Custis lacking any discernible trace of martial ardor, Washington was always on the lookout for surrogates. But at this point he had known Lafayette for just over a month; figuratively speaking he'd been swept off his feet. This is no exaggeration: The record reveals that outside of Sally Fairfax, Washington opened up to Lafayette like no other person. But this bromance was not only precipitous and sincere; it was, like so many of GW's key relationships, profoundly in his own and, in this case, America's interest. Of course he didn't want Lafayette to bleed to death; he was the perfect conduit into the French court.

As usual, George Washington also might have died at Brandywine Creek, but in this case in a new and interesting way. Leading Knyphausen's column was Major Patrick Ferguson with a special team of sharpshooters he had been allowed to form, employing a remarkably accurate and fast-firing breech-loading rifle of his own design. This gun had the potential to dramatically change land warfare and, here, American history.

During the early portion of the battle, an officer on a large white horse, thinking he was far beyond the striking distance of conventional muskets, wandered well within the range of Ferguson's fire team. "I could have lodged a half dozen balls in or about him," Ferguson wrote.[57] Instead, he chivalrously refrained from blowing what might have been GW out of the saddle. Washington was in the same sector at this time, focused intensely on what Knyphausen might be doing; it was very much in his combat DNA to rush off impetuously before his staff could catch up. Whatever the case, GW emerged without a scratch; it was Ferguson who got shot, his elbow shattered by an American ball. While Ferguson recovered, Howe disbanded his unit and had his guns put in storage for good.[58] Like Bushnell's submarine, the breech-loading rifle would have to wait another century before it transformed war and reaped a grim harvest in human lives. At least the outcome at Brandywine was positive in this respect.

Nobody pretended it was an American victory. John Sullivan, who had presided over the collapse of the right, was something of a popular scapegoat, though GW defended him. No fingers, at least not yet, were pointed at the commander in chief, who blamed the whole thing on bad luck.[59] More penetrating was Thomas Jefferson's analysis of GW's mindset as a general: "If any member of his plan was dislocated by sudden circumstances, he was slow in readjustment."[60] Slow in the face of the fog of war: That was Washington at Brandywine. But then something happened just over a week later that must have drawn everybody's attention away. It was truly shocking.

As a means of slowing Howe's progress to Philadelphia, GW ordered Anthony Wayne and a brigade of 1,500 men to get in behind the British and harass them, "but take care of Ambuscades,"[61] he warned. Since the area was just a few miles from his own home, Wayne knew it well, and thought he could get his force in close to the British without them knowing where they were. He was wrong.

On the night of September 20, 1777, Major General Charles Grey led five regiments of lethal British light infantry on a three-mile march, their muskets with fixed bayonets but unloaded and without flints on his orders. For he had a very intimate kind of killing in mind. When they reached the brink of the camp almost unnoticed by the sentries, Grey called out with notable English understatement, "Dash on, light infantry."[62] They did a lot more than dash: It was a puncture-fest as the British descended on the Americans sleeping in their tents. Before they were through, between two and three hundred lay dead, most with multiple wounds.

In the morning, upon viewing the corpses, one British officer declared it "more Expressive of Horror than all the Thunder of Artillery & on the Day of action."[63] But not Howe; he officially thanked the general and his detachment "For their steddiness in Bayonitting the Rebels without firing a shot."[64] To the British he would be known subsequently as "No-Flint" Grey, and the episode remembered as the war's most successful special operation, producing casualties on the order of Brandywine. To Americans it remained the Paoli Massacre, the latest and most flagrant example of British inhumanity and despotic intent. So it was that horror hardened into enduring hatred.

Meanwhile, Howe continued to give Washington dancing lessons in operational maneuver, whirling him around eastern Pennsylvania, forcing him to choose between defending Philadelphia or the crucial American arsenal at Reading, and when GW picked the latter, pranced unopposed to the capital, into which Cornwallis—returned from an extended stay in England caring for his sick wife—marched, on September 26, "amidst the acclamation of some thousands of inhabitants mostly women and children," noted one observer.[65] Many must have been Loyalists, and as for the rest, there was little else they could do, George Washington and the Continental Army being forty miles away.

To the British this moment must have smelled like victory. The mission had been accomplished, the rebel capital almost effortlessly taken. True, the food supply had to be secured and the rebel army continued to exist. But it was obvious the British were intent on staying to enjoy a smashing social season. Within weeks the army's young social elite (Lord Rawdon, Banastre Tarleton, John Graves Simcoe, Thomas Musgrave, and John André)[66] had fanned out to network with rich Tories and move into abandoned rebel residences, where they took what pleased them. John André, a man of some considerable taste, was particularly fortunate in occupying the house of Benjamin Franklin, which he looted of its books, and scientific and musical instruments, along with Benjamin Wilson's portrait of the original occupant, which he gave to No-Flint Grey, presumably for his accomplishments at Paoli.[67]

A façade of civility, cloaking an agenda of bad behavior: It was the British calling card even among the chosen few. The entire mission was a charade. The Congress had simply moved out of town. George Washington lurked, and much worse news would be arriving from the North Country. Howe may have seized the birthplace of the rebellion, but the Revolution still surrounded him.

## 3

George Washington's prospects were in no way as forlorn as those of the British. Nevertheless, the results of Brandywine Creek would usher in a period during which his capabilities as generalissimo would be tested to their absolute limits. For a while even the good news was bad, since the contrasts it raised cast a shadow over his leadership, and led again to serious backbiting and eventually a concerted, if futile, challenge to his authority. GW was heading into the winter of his discontent.

Right about the time the British occupied Philadelphia, news would have arrived from the north of a bloody and potentially decisive action between the forces gathered by Horatio Gates and Burgoyne's invading army. The fate of the army, already weakened at Bennington, was probably sealed on September 14, when Gentleman Johnny marched it across the Hudson on a bridge of boats, thereby cutting the supply line to Montreal.[68] Gates knew his man well from their days in the British Army, and, expecting an attack, had been busy fortifying a ridge called Bemis Heights as the keystone to his defense. But as Burgoyne approached on the morning of September 19, it was Benedict Arnold and Daniel Morgan who seized the initiative.

Rather than await the attack, Arnold proposed and received reluctant permission from Gates to engage the enemy to the north in the primeval forest surrounding Freeman's Farm, the natural habitat of riflemen. Directed by Morgan with his turkey call, and under orders to take special aim at artillerists and anyone wearing the silver chest piece of an officer, Morgan's corps of sharpshooters, some of them hanging from trees, took a terrible toll. Before the day was over, Burgoyne had managed to take possession only of the worthless piece of real estate that was Freeman's Farm. The Americans under Arnold had inflicted over 550 casualties on the British regulars, the numbers particularly high for officers and anyone serving a cannon.[69] They cut the heart out of Burgoyne's army.

George Washington must have realized now that it was over along the Hudson, that a victory of astonishing magnitude—one for which he had supplied the key components, Arnold and Morgan—loomed for Horatio Gates. He, on the other hand, was on the outside of Philadelphia looking in, just as he had been cast out of New York a year earlier. In both instances his solution was a surprise attack. Yet the raids of the year before were plainly strategically driven; in early October of 1777, GW's competitive instincts seem to have gotten the better of him.

Howe appeared to be hibernating. He had split his army, with three thousand occupying the city, and five thousand camped in Germantown, five miles up the Schuylkill, without bothering to build fortifications.[70] To GW's overeager eye they looked ripe for the plucking.

By this time he had gathered eight thousand Continentals and three thousand militia and knew he had the advantage in numbers. There were four roads leading into Germantown, so a surprise along a broad front, the kind that paralyzes armies, was possible. A giant Trenton was in the offing, just so long as the four designated columns arrived at the same time after an all-night march. To put it mildly, it was an overcomplicated plan framed in overconfidence.

And in announcing to his troops the results of Freeman's Farm the day before the planned raid on October 4, George Washington revealed another element of his motivation: "This army—the main American Army—will certainly not allow itself to be outdone by their northern Brethren—they will never endure such disgrace. . . . *Covet!*

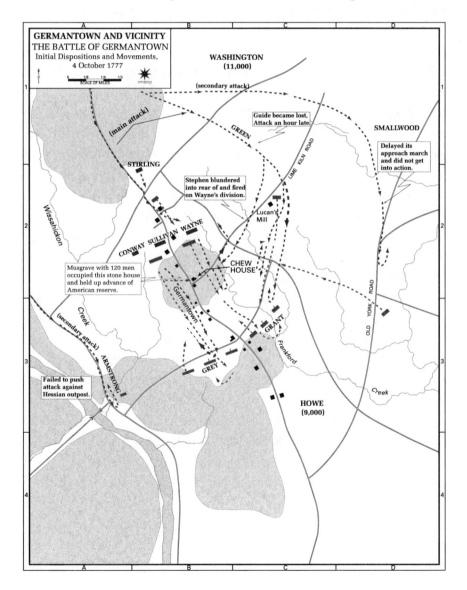

My Countrymen, and fellow soldiers! Covet! A share of the glory due to heroic deeds!"[71] And with these inspiring words he sent them marching into the fog of war and also a lot of real fog; it was not much of a climate for keeping precise schedules.

Just about everything went wrong. Initially the four columns—two militia and two Continentals led by Sullivan and Greene—made good time during their night march, but none arrived at the same time, and that lack of synchronicity set the tone for the day. To preserve surprise and likely remembering Paoli, Washington's orders called for "bayonets without firing";[72] but then, as he rode with Sullivan's force, his view obscured by a thick morning mist, he heard shots around a place called Mount Airy. He assumed they must be coming from the British, and since the volume seemed to diminish, he could also surmise a retreat. He continued forward with his reserve guard, and as he did, the tone deepened, indicating cannon and larger numbers of British engaged, still apparently falling backward. For the moment it seemed his plan was working.

Sullivan's column—some crying "Have at the bloodhounds! Revenge for Wayne's affair!"[73]—had run into several regiments of the dreaded British light infantry, and, as more Americans arrived, was steadily forcing them back through the fog toward Germantown. As he retreated, Lieutenant Colonel Musgrave took note of Benjamin Chew's particularly solid mansion, built with locally quarried schist, and decided it was an ideal place to take a stand. He ordered a hundred men inside, shuttered the windows, and turned the place into a human equivalent of a beehive, waiting for the Yankees hot on their heels.

It was not long before Washington and his coterie got there. What to do? Alexander Hamilton, an artillery officer who knew the structure would be hard to knock down, argued that they bypass it and keep up the momentum of the attack. But then über-artillerist Henry Knox, all three hundred pounds of him, rumbled forth with a verity from military history that "it would be unmilitary to leave a castle in our rear."[74] Exactly the kind of advice amateurs turned to in emergencies, and so, in this instance, did George Washington. When efforts to flatten it with four small field guns predictably failed, GW ordered three regiments to take it by assault. It turned into a futile bloodbath that left seventy-five dead Americans scattered around the place.[75] GW finally called it off, but he had lost more than troops; he had lost the initiative.

*Assault on Chew House: GW tripped up by a pile of stone.*

G. P. PUTNAM/LIBRARY OF CONGRESS

When Anthony Wayne, whose lead division had already passed, heard the firing to his rear, he assumed Sullivan was in trouble and turned back to help. Around the same time, Greene's delayed column of Continentals was just marching in, when one of its divisions under Adam Stephen pulled out and headed toward Chew House. Instead, amid the fog and smoke of gunfire, they ran into Wayne and began shooting, tripping a friendly firefight that spread confusion.[76]

It was at this opportune moment that Howe, now thoroughly aware of the danger, managed to stage a counterattack, sending several brigades under James Grant crashing into the disoriented Americans. Both Stephen's and Wayne's troops broke in panic, followed by Sullivan's, but more steadily. And with them gone, the remainder of Greene's forces, having pushed into Germantown proper, was further exposed. With neither of the militia columns having arrived for support, they fought hard, but in the end collapsed. Most made it out through the fog and smoke, except for the four hundred men of the Fourth Virginia, who were surrounded and captured. Cornwallis came up with reinforcements just as the retreat started, but the British didn't pursue with any great enthusiasm. By nine that night most of Washington's army had limped to safety at Pennypacker Mills over thirty miles away.[77] For many, October 4, 1777, had been the longest day of their lives.

For George Washington it was not one of his best. He had seized the initiative, then lost it with his dithering at Chew House. But there was plenty of blame to go around, and initially his command team took almost all of it, particularly the hapless John Sullivan, whose formations had fallen apart during two successive battles. Henry Knox was lampooned for historical blathering, and even Greene was nicked for being slow.[78] As for GW himself, he blamed two factors: the fog and the friendly fire incident, which devolved upon Adam Stephen.[79]

He was George Washington's oldest military associate, and as commander in chief GW had raised him to the level of major general. But Stephen had almost ruined the Trenton raid, lied about a failed sortie of his own, and had broken from Greene's column at Germantown without permission. George Washington could be accused of being loyal to a fault, but when a limit was reached and he went into vindictive mode, there would be no forgiveness.

Nathanael Greene presided over a preliminary court of inquiry, followed by a court-martial headed by John Sullivan. It found Adam Stephen guilty of "unofficerlike behavior" and being "frequently intoxicated," a verdict Washington immediately approved.[80] On November 20 he was drummed out of the army in the cruelest possible way, and his division was given to the now recovered Lafayette. It might have been a warning to others. The wrong side of George Washington was a very cold place to be.

If the results of Germantown made commanders squirm, the men of the Continental Army were hardly crestfallen; they saw themselves as fighting a lot better than the year before.[81] The cost had been high— almost 1,100 killed, wounded, or captured—but in return they had inflicted another 550 casualties on the invader's ever-shrinking army, another strategic trade-off well worth making. The men seemed to understand; at any rate, desertions hadn't spiked. Most had now been in mass combat with some of the best troops in the world and survived. The Continental Army was bruised, but still around. That was what counted, and would soon be tested by an even harsher enemy: the elements.

But meanwhile, GW had one more card to play before he gave up on Philadelphia. Howe, much as he had the year before, now retracted all his forces inside the city after his near disaster at Germantown. Washington reciprocated with swarms of irregulars, effectively denying the British foodstuffs from the surrounding countryside.[82] In the meantime, the Delaware remained blocked to the British by two dilapidated American forts, Mifflin and Mercer, and a network of river obstacles. If the Americans could keep the river closed, they could potentially starve the British into leaving Philadelphia.[83] Washington sent two hundred Continentals as reinforcements in late September, but the forts' condition and faulty design did not give him much hope they could be held. At any rate, when the British task force sailed up the river to confront them, the Continental Army was too far away to provide direct support.

Then things changed, at least for Washington. On October 18, the first of a string of messages reported Burgoyne's catastrophic defeat at Bemis Heights and subsequent surrender of his army at Saratoga. This was a huge development: an entire British army crushed and captured. Yet for GW it had to be bittersweet news. For a man of destiny, this was not the way things were supposed to work out. Gates was the hero, and he was looking like the goat.

Just days later the British sent a full regiment of Hessians to attack Fort Mercer, but the garrison under Colonel Christopher Greene, Nathanael's cousin, turned them back, inflicting over four hundred casualties, killing their commander, and even hanging the two pilots who brought them over.[84] The idea of the forts holding out, though still a long shot, suddenly seemed much more plausible to Washington. Around this time he conceived the idea of attacking the British warships with a flotilla of exploding kegs, and had the inventive David Bushnell begin constructing them.[85] But they wouldn't be finished until January, and ended up not working anyway, though the so-called Battle of the Kegs did provide the subject for a humorous song.[86]

Meanwhile, the British task force remained relentless. Despite losing a ship of the line, which went aground, was set on fire, and blew up,[87] they finally squeezed past the mass of river obstacles and reached a point where they could bring all their firepower against the already damaged Fort Mifflin. With Washington's permission, its evacuation began on the night of November 15 and was completed by morning. Five days later, Fort Mercer was also abandoned. Philadelphia was now securely in British hands, and George Washington had failed to defend it.

There was also more news from up north, none of it good if you were a generalissimo. It was now apparent to Washington that Horatio Gates had reported the victory at Bemis Heights directly to Congress and not first to Washington, an extraordinary breach of military protocol.[88] Then on November 4 he received a letter from Lord Stirling informing him that Gates's favorite aide had drunkenly mentioned a quote from a letter sent to the victorious general by one of Washington's own brigade commanders, Thomas Conway. It read: "Heaven has been determined to save your Country; or a weak General and bad Councellors would have ruind it."[89] The quote was all Washington forwarded to Conway the next day, a laconic warning the recipient would have been well advised to heed.[90]

There was more intrigue surrounding Gates. As the events of the Saratoga campaign made evident, there had been a major falling-out between him and Benedict Arnold (though not with Daniel Morgan, who managed to get along with both). Arnold had initially earned Gates's ire when he took on staff officers loyal to Washington's ally, the now displaced Philip Schuyler. Gates returned the favor by not even mentioning Arnold in his dispatches announcing the results of Freeman's Farm. This, in turn, led to a shouting match, during which Gates relieved Arnold of his command, leading him to request a transfer back to Washington.[91] But he did not leave.

Instead, Arnold sat in his tent like Achilles until October 7, when he injected himself into the middle of the battle for Bemis Heights and led a series of wild assaults that broke the British line. His frantic

bravery came to an end only when he was wounded again in his battered left leg and carried from the field. He certainly proved an inspirational presence, but also a wild, almost mutinous one. Washington
might well have wondered about Arnold's stability and the lengths to
which he might go if he felt himself slighted. But at this point there
were more elemental problems to consider, like where he would be
spending the winter.

4

When George Washington marched his army away from Philadelphia
in early December he did not yet know where he was going. He asked
his subordinates for suggestions, and got characteristic responses: Nathanael Greene, remembering Hannibal's enervating stay in Capua,
recommended a bracing rural location; while Knox, citing Frederick
the Great that "the first object in Winter quarters is Tranquility," favored the safety and comfort of Reading.[92] Meanwhile, Congress was
now convening in York, while the Pennsylvania legislature was at Lancaster: Both wanted Washington's army between them and Howe in
Philadelphia.[93] So he kept moving until he found a place that felt right.
On the nineteenth of December the troops were told GW had chosen
a site for the winter encampment, and then were marched the final
seven miles to a remote location in the heavily forested hills of southeastern Pennsylvania known locally as Valley Forge.

Strategically at least, he'd made an excellent choice. It was only
twenty miles from Philadelphia, so like Morristown the year before, it
provided a base to intercept and harass British foraging parties, while
at the same time shielding Congress and the Pennsylvania General
Assembly. To the south and east, open country made a surprise assault
by Howe improbable, while a convenient ford to the rear provided a
ready escape hatch, should all else fail.[94] There was plenty of water and
wood, so, as he assured the troops, "Huts may be erected that will be
warm and dry."[95] During the remainder of December the soldiers
waged war on the surrounding forest and, with the spoils, constructed
a city of log shanties divided by brigades and complete with a broad

open parade ground at the center of the camp.[96] The only thing missing was food.

Right from the beginning GW saw the problem as urgent, and on December 23 put it to the new president of Congress, Henry Laurens, in the starkest possible terms: "Unless some great and capital change suddenly takes place . . . this Army must inevitably be reduced to one or other of these three things. Starve—dissolve—or disperse."[97] He then proceeded with a jeremiad of logistical failures and administrative paralysis that left his troops not only hungry, but also dressed in rags and without even blankets—the responsibility for which he heaped on Congress. Much was deserved, but by this time in the war George Washington had gotten very good at making dire predictions, and these, in turn, were related to a larger tug-of-war going on between himself and the national legislature, one with major implications for the Revolution itself.

There were plenty of supplies available in southeastern Pennsylvania; what had changed was the money. Congress had floated a currency on little more than revolutionary fervor, and by this time in the war its buoyancy was nearing the "not worth a Continental" point. Pennsylvania farmers were now beginning to hide their produce from purchasing agents and refusing to accept their script.[98] The British, on the other hand, were offering pounds sterling, and as the contraband trade with Philadelphia appeared to grow, Washington fumed and wanted "to make an example of some guilty one."[99]

But members of Congress, aware of its inherent shortcomings as supply agent, saw a simpler recourse in the power they had given GW "to take . . . whatever he may want for the Use of the Army,"[100] and urged him to go ahead, even if it meant doing it at bayonet point.[101] Washington, having been in the field and seen the hatred engendered by the British, had a much clearer vision of how a policy of confiscation could undermine support. Whether the takers were English or claiming to represent the Glorious Cause, expropriation could only make enemies among those it was vital not to lose, the occupants of the countryside. So, in the face of what might be called temptation, or at least an easy way out, he kept his army purposely hungry for the sake of the revolutionary agenda—a signature act of a truly political general.

It was only in February 1778, when the men at Valley Forge had literally reached the point of starvation, that he authorized a massive foraging effort reaching as far as New England and the southern states, supervised by the trusted Nathanael Greene, Anthony Wayne, and the rising young cavalryman Henry Lee, whom Washington had known since he was a teenager.[102] Not only did they get results; they were given enough scraped-up specie to pay for, not confiscate, the goods. By the end of the month, convoys of wagons and herds of cattle were heading toward Valley Forge from practically all directions. As spring approached the food crisis passed, and reorganized quartermaster and commissary services were at last supplying quantities of shirts and breeches to cover the still-scrawny limbs of the remaining Continentals.[103]

To demonstrate his commitment, as March arrived Washington appointed Greene—by now one of his very best combat generals and as close as anyone came to an alter ego—quartermaster general, the man in charge of getting food and supplies to the troops so they didn't have to forage.[104] Meanwhile, malnutrition, exposure, and attendant diseases ended up killing around 2,500, or nearly one-fourth, of the occupants of Valley Forge[105]—concentration camp statistics, but the Continental Army survived and so did the Revolution.

But would George Washington? Congressional critics of his battlefield performance were getting vocal and now included both Adamses, John and Sam, Richard Henry Lee, and James Lovell, who wrote fellow member Jonathan Sergeant, "We want a general; thousands of lives and millions of property are yearly sacrificed to the insufficiency of our Commander-in-Chief."[106] But one member in particular, GW's former aide Thomas Mifflin, was ready to go beyond carping to active conspiring. His apparent objective: to slide Gates in and Washington out; his principal instrument: Thomas Conway.

Far from being cowed by GW's warning, Conway was now presenting himself to his commander's critics in Congress as a true professional soldier, one whose services were desperately needed to counteract the bumbling commander in chief.[107] Conceding Washington's continuing mystique with most members, Mifflin chose an oblique approach. He and Richard Henry Lee constructed a trap designed to so undermine GW's authority that he would resign, and built it out of two of Washington's own suggestions: that a standing board of war replace the cavalcade of congressional committees attempting to supply the army, and that an experienced foreign officer be appointed inspector general to establish a uniform system of drill and maneuver.

But in Mifflin and Lee's version, the Board of War transcended matters of supply, and was designated the ultimate military authority, even over Washington. Not surprisingly, it was stacked with his critics, including Mifflin, and Horatio Gates was named its president. But the real dagger was expanding the duties of the inspector general to supervising all of Washington's decisions and then naming Thomas Conway to the post with the rank of major general reporting to the Board of War. All of this Mifflin managed to pass through Congress, largely it seems because nobody was paying enough attention to think through the implications of undermining the generalissimo's authority.

This sums up what has come to be known as the "Conway Cabal," an interesting choice, since it avoids another c-word. Was this a conspiracy? A number of recent historians have dismissed it as little more than "a gossip network" among a handful of "disgruntled players"[108]; but this begs the question of the participants being in the middle of a Revolution and their aim being to depose its leader. That certainly sounds like a conspiracy, but perhaps the reason for dismissing it as such was that it was a ridiculous one. As John Adams assured Henry Knox at the time, GW "was the Center of our Union."[109] He and only he had come to personify the Revolution, and was, therefore, virtually irreplaceable. And as the days passed, that became increasingly obvious.

But less so to Washington and his team at Valley Forge. He had already been warned of the Board of War's intent by Dr. Craik,[110] and when Conway arrived to assume his supervisory function, GW brushed him aside with a technicality. Apparently, it didn't take long for Conway to realize that the reception went beyond frosty to potentially life-threatening among Washington's subordinates, since he left the Forge almost as soon as he arrived. He then made the mistake of resorting to quill and ink:

I Do not pretend, sir, to be a consummate General but as an old sailor Knows more of a ship than admirals who have never been at sea, Long experience . . . made me think that I could in some Measure be a helping hand in putting your army on a better footing . . . but . . . your Dispositions toward me, sir, have been clear, and the very Behaviour of some Gentlemen of your family did not permit me nor anyone else to entertain the Least Doubt of them.[111]

He was right about that. It's safe to say that George Washington hated Thomas Conway more than any human being he ever encountered.[112]

The wrath of Washington was monumental, and it echoed in army camps with rumors that he had been insulted and that underhanded schemers were vying to replace him.[113] It also was heard in Congress. Here the tide didn't just shift in GW's direction; the reversal was like a tsunami. A vote on his command, had they bothered, would have been unanimous.[114] His critics were loudest in their praise. Mifflin even announced that GW was the best friend he ever had.[115] If this sounds a little like the forced confessions of future revolutions, there's a reason for it. The environments were essentially the same. This was revolutionary politics; a move had been made on Fearless Leader, and now some retribution could be expected.

How much? Washington's answer was and always would be the minimal amount. For Gates it meant only disavowing his correspondence with Conway;[116] he was, after all, the titular architect of Saratoga, the biggest Patriot victory of the war so far.

Conway had no such redeeming virtue. He "conditionally" turned in his resignation from the Continental Army to Congress, and they accepted it unconditionally. But that wasn't enough. While there is no recorded "Will no one rid me of this meddlesome priest?" moment, it was clear that GW wanted Conway dead. Any member of his entourage would have gladly issued a challenge, but it was the serviceable John Cadwalader—being a general in the Pennsylvania militia and slightly removed—who got the honor. A duel was arranged, and he shot Conway in the mouth.[117] Standing over his bleeding opponent

Cadwalader supposedly remarked: "I have stopped that damned rascal's lying anyway." Conway, thinking himself mortally wounded, wrote Washington a pathetic letter of apology[118] and got only stony silence in return. He didn't die; but his role in the Revolution was finished.

It stands to reason that the Conway Cabal, coming when it did, served to further fuse Washington's command team and his military family, all of them gathered at Valley Forge for that momentous winter. The wives of Greene, Knox, and Lord Stirling[119] joined the redoubtable Martha and their husbands to initiate what resembled a social season in a charnel house—a bit grotesque, but bonding. It was also a time for the constellation of young talent—Alexander Hamilton, Lafayette, and John Laurens—to shine and forge further connections with Washington's more senior henchmen. By now there had been many shared moments of danger, mortification, and dejection, but no bickering. Washington simply did not allow it, and it was a tribute to his overpowering personality that not a whisper of dissention was heard among team members, even during this long, very grim winter.

But there were other military notables at Valley Forge, ones not necessarily on the team, and they posed special problems and possibilities. Daniel Morgan was back, thrilled that GW had sent Alexander Hamilton to fetch him from Gates.[120] Washington made good use of Morgan's corps of riflemen, directing them to guard the forested hills around Valley Forge, interdict British foraging parties, and keep track of Loyalist farmers' attempts to supply them provisions.

It was plain that the commander in chief valued Morgan as a military asset, but he remained a friend of Gates as well at a time when it was hard to be both. Morgan, as ever, retained the rough-hewed, egalitarian nature that rubbed Washington's class biases raw. Lafayette, the aristocrat, could afford to befriend Morgan,[121] but to the rest of Washington's gentrified retainers, he remained an outsider. This was unfortunate, since by this time it should have been obvious that Morgan was an innovative tactician and a natural leader on the battlefield—exactly what the Continental Army needed—in addition to being utterly loyal to Washington.

*GW and Lafayette at Valley Forge: keeping the
vital French connection close.*

PERCY MORAN/LIBRARY OF CONGRESS

That was not the case with Major General Charles Lee, last seen
sixteen months earlier being captured by the British under decidedly
unmilitary circumstances, caught literally with his pants down. As a
retired British officer fighting for the King's enemies, he might have
been hanged. Instead, his captors sought to turn him, and to an extent
succeeded. In return for a soft bed and the company of his beloved
dogs, Lee apparently provided suggestions on how to win the war.
Since it was unwinnable, how much he helped remains an open question. Meanwhile, his opinion of Washington was still tinged with contempt; he told the visiting American commissary of prisoners of "the
impossibility of our troops, under such an ignorant Commander in
Chief, ever withstanding British grenadiers and light infantry."[122]

How much of this had gotten back to Washington by the time a
prisoner exchange was arranged is impossible to tell. His information
network was excellent, and past behavior had given him reason not to

trust Lee; nevertheless, when the errant general finally rode into Valley Forge in early April, GW greeted him amiably and with all due ceremony. That night Lee was observed smuggling a whore from Philadelphia into his quarters,[123] not the kind of behavior that inspired confidence with His Excellency and his tight-knit, straight-laced cadre, much less their wives, sitting out the snow season in studied gentility.

Still, if pure eccentricity were a disqualifier for an important role at Valley Forge, it would be impossible to explain the success of the newly arrived Prussian general Frederick Wilhelm August Heinrich Ferdinand, Baron von Steuben, the Munchausen of the Continental Army. Recommended by Benjamin Franklin,[124] Steuben was neither a general nor a baron, but he was a seasoned military professional who had served on the staff of Frederick the Great, one of Washington's military heroes. GW liked him immediately, and as usual with Washington's friendships, the German possessed qualities he needed badly—in Steuben's case, a thorough familiarity with the latest European troop-drilling techniques and an infectious enthusiasm for teaching them. Time and again at the brink of victory or defeat, confusion had prevailed within the ranks of the Continentals. Yet no one had been able to get them to take drill seriously, so it kept happening.

Steuben was different. He was not pedantic about the new techniques; he knew the system well enough to strip them down to only the battlefield essentials. Despite barely speaking English, he also seemed to understand his half-starved charges better than Washington, providing a valuable link between the two. Explaining "the genius of this nation" as compared to Europeans, he told a former comrade: "You say to your soldier, 'Do this,' and he doeth it, but I am obliged to say, 'This is the reason why you ought to do that,' and he does it."[125]

He started small, with a 150-man model company, who drilled as the others watched. Then he let them join, company by company, injecting a competitive element. Gradually the maneuvers gained complexity and the formations grew larger until they reached full regimental scale.[126] Drilling twice a day, muscle memory began to take hold and individuals in the ranks felt the corporate solidarity that comes with marching in unison, a last-ditch pattern of movements

*Baron von Steuben: "Drill!" he said, and the Continentals actually did.*

CHARLES WILLSON PEALE/ WIKIMEDIA COMMONS

that has held together beleaguered military units since the first days of the Sumerian phalanx.[127] The men sensed it, too, knew they were not only getting better, but forged together in a way they hadn't been before. The fog of war might still prevail, but the next time they marched into battle, things would be different.

Thanks to modern historical research we know that the army had already changed demographically; the ranks were now made up of younger men, no longer property owners, but instead from the lower orders of society, who had been more or less bribed to sign up for long-term enlistments.[128] Many were recent immigrants, mostly Irish and Germans, and a substantial number at Valley Forge—one historian estimates up to 10 percent[129]—were black, their stake being the prospect of freedom.

But new personnel did not necessarily mean that the soldiers of this version of the Continental Army were less motivated or committed than their rage militaire predecessors, just different. As would become typical of such conflicts, a central group of "hard-core" revolutionary fighters and long-term survivors had emerged, men such as New Englanders Bill Scott, Jeremiah Greenman, and Joseph Plumb Martin.[130] As miserable as it was, these men were addicted to the life they led, its excitement and perceived importance. Their commitment to the Revolution was visceral; no matter what happened, they were there for the duration.

Others—probably the majority—not so much; but they looked to the hard-core in emergencies, especially combat; besides, just being there implied a considerable commitment. So did staying, and at Valley Forge, desertions don't appear to have climbed beyond the normal rate.[131] Foreign officers in camp were amazed that the Continental Army still existed. Any European force in such a spot, they agreed, would have long since mutinied or evaporated when pay and food failed to materialize.[132]

George Washington wasn't blind; he was completely aware of his men's suffering—had it rubbed in his face every time he reviewed the troops or just walked through endless lines of huts that defined the encampment. "Naked and starving as they are," he wrote in mid-February 1778, "we cannot eno[ugh] admire the incomparable patience and fidelity of the soldiery, that they have not been . . . excited . . . to a general mutiny and dispersion."[133]

Quite apparently GW understood that his army, whatever its social origins, was still held together by the gravity of the Glorious Cause, and it could be that Valley Forge marked a point when he began to suspect that the Revolution really could be trusted in the hands of the people. Also, the continuing presence of black faces at Valley Forge, enduring the miseries of that terrible winter along with everybody else, might well have suggested to GW, long in advance of his ultimate rejection of slavery, that the American Revolution could be for everybody.

But being George Washington, he cared more about his officers, and they, too, were changing. It was at Valley Forge that the Continental Army's officers began thinking of themselves as members of a nascent American aristocracy, their pedigree based on their superior commitment to the cause in the face of actual bullets. Perhaps as a distraction from their misery, Washington encouraged this sort of thinking; these were, after all, his kind of people, gentlemen.[134] It's unclear if table manners improved, but the presumably aristocratic custom of dueling came into vogue at Valley Forge.[135]

So did the idea of state support for their sacrifices—a lifetime pension at half pay to commence at war's end. When the officers first broached the idea to Washington in November 1777, he was dubious, thinking Congress's ideological suspicion of standing armies would kill it. But then at Valley Forge, faced with a wave of officer resignations, he became alarmed enough to put his weight behind the proposal, which Congress grudgingly passed, in May 1778, though limiting the benefit to seven years.[136] There were cries of extortion at the time, and it's not hard to see why.

It wasn't Washington at his best; even at Valley Forge he spent far too much time worrying about his officers, poring over the minutiae of their rank and precedence. They weren't worth it. There were plainly outstanding exceptions, but when measured against standards of their European counterparts and the decades it took to make even one of their number, these Americans remained a group of neophytes at the game of war, and whiny ones at that. This did not bode well for the future. But if they wanted to ape the nobility, they didn't have far to look at Valley Forge. The place was filling up with French aristocrats.

In November, when news of Philadelphia's fall reached Paris, Benjamin Franklin's hopes for a formal alliance seemed crushed. But then just as quickly they revived on December 4, when it was learned that Burgoyne and his entire army had been snatched at Saratoga. It proved the inflection point at Versailles. Within a few days Pierre Beaumarchais's boss, French foreign minister Charles Gravier, Comte de Vergennes, invited the American commissioners to resubmit their alliance proposal. Franklin did the drafting, and when they sat down on December 17, Vergennes told him that France would not only extend recognition to the United States, but would also enter into a full-scale alliance.[137]

By early February 1778, the two sides had formally signed both a commercial treaty and a military pact containing the crucial stipulation "they mutually engage not to lay down their arms, until the independence of the United States shall have been formally or tacitly assured by the Treaty or Treaties that shall terminate the War."[138] Nearly as significant but perhaps less convincing to skeptics was France's renunciation of any territorial claims on the North American continent.

By any calculation this was a huge development. France was at the center of European power and politics, its army was the biggest, and its population four times that of England's. America had suddenly acquired a very big brother, and also a rich one. French cash contributions should not be underestimated; specie at this point was in critically short supply, and French loans were based on a real currency, not to mention all the silver and gold that flowed in with Gallic military transplants. Lafayette himself was immensely wealthy, and on more than one occasion outfitted entire units out of pocket.[139] A steady supply of arms, ammunition, and even uniforms could now be expected; but probably even more important from George Washington's perspective, big brother had a navy, the very thing he lacked to trap the British, or at least stop them from bouncing at will up and down his coastline. All of this added up to a powerful stimulus for victory.

But could it win the war? This is an important question, since it has been argued here that the British military cause was hopeless from the beginning, and by the hatred it engendered had made only retrograde progress. The answer, it seems, lies in getting them to give up. Here French assistance was profoundly helpful. The longer armed revolutions last, generally the worse they get. Even with a leader like George Washington, the Revolution was gradually growing more brutal, destined to reach a crescendo in the final southern campaign. Without the French, the conclusion was just as inevitable.[140] But the Revolutionary War would have certainly gone on longer and the costs grown greater, perhaps too great to find forgiveness and found a stable government. Instead we got the United States of America.

As spring breathed some warmth into Valley Forge, things were definitely looking up. With Greene in charge, the supply system had stabilized and the troops were getting some meat on their bones, clothes on their backs, and enough French muskets to replace wastage, which was substantial.[141] Then on May 5, Washington confirmed what many had already heard; before his assembled troops he announced the French alliance. The next day to celebrate they paraded under arms, and, marching before Steuben's knowing eye, performed for their commander in chief a series of deployment maneuvers, culminating in modulated running musket fire, first right to left, then left to right, not a trick for tyros. They were then dismissed with an extra issue of rum, while 1,500 officers and dignitaries sat down with His Excellency and gorged themselves on a "profusion of fat meat, strong wine and other liquors."[142] As Washington rode off in late afternoon the guests broke out cheering: "Long Live George Washington," and spun what seemed a thousand hats in the air.[143] Had the British been invited, they would have left depressed.

# 5

News of the French alliance shattered any pretense of unity in London. But this time there would be no William Pitt to miraculously rescue a failed war effort; he died on May 11, 1778, shortly after collapsing during a speech in the House of Lords. This left the hawks and doves to go at it, while the moderates sought any political cover they could find. The doves, led by Lord Rockingham and Charles James Fox, argued that trying to fight America and France at the same time amounted to imperial suicide, while a grant of independence would rapidly restore the Atlantic trade and the British economy.[144] Likely this advice was given without fully comprehending the impact of what the British Army had been doing in America. But it didn't matter; however bad the news, the hawks still retained the inside track that would enable them to prolong the effort to subdue the rebellion up to and beyond all hope of success.

And George III, former Patriot King, remained the linchpin. When his prime minister, Lord North, abject and almost suicidal in his desire to resign, suggested the war was no longer worth the cost, the King countered "this is only weighing such events in the scale of a tradesman behind his counter," and then offered his own version of the domino theory, with American independence leading to the subsequent loss of the West Indies, presumably Canada, with Ireland soon to follow.[145] Meanwhile, his chief warlord, George Germain, remained solidly behind the proposition that thrashing the Americans into submission was the only satisfactory policy objective. And if the first lord of the admiralty, the Earl of Sandwich, kept insisting on drawing naval assets back to home waters to protect Britain now that the French were involved, it never caused the King or Germain to reconsider the American project; it only robbed them at key moments of the naval protection the army needed to survive in a hostile environment.[146]

Changing circumstances did demand some priority and personnel adjustments. Howe had lost favor and was out. He had won battles but not quelled the rebellion; his strategic schemes had led nowhere. "The war must be prosecuted upon a different plan," Germain informed designated successor Sir Henry Clinton. No more reinforcements would be lavished on the pursuit of Washington; instead, Clinton was to "relinquish the idea of carrying on offensive operations against the rebels within land," and detach eight thousand of his men to protect British possessions in Florida and the West Indies. Finally, "it is our will and pleasure that you do evacuate Philadelphia [and] proceed with the whole to New York."[147]

Meanwhile, as an alternative, the timorous and befuddled North persisted in sponsoring the idea of a peace commission as a sop to the doves. Within the cabinet George Germain hated the idea, but then manipulated it in his favor, first by the appointment of commissioners lacking experience, headed by the thirty-year-old Lord Carlisle, and then by making sure his instructions insisted that the rebels renounce their "pretensions to independence," a nonstarter if there ever was one. Together, the new plan and peace commission amounted to Revolutionary War Lite, a means of staying in the game until the prospects for suppressing the rebellion became more propitious. Of course, they never would: That was the basic problem.

The Carlisle Commission got the fate it deserved, six fruitless months in America. British officer John Peebles summed up its official reception: "the Congress's answere Short & Insolent." Washington's reaction to the commission was vitriolic, and it was also revealing.

As Washington became increasingly immersed in the details of fighting a war, revolutionary rhetoric largely disappeared from his correspondence, replaced by much more matter-of-fact terminology. Gestures like returning Howe's lost dog after the Battle of Germantown, along with his scrupulously good treatment of British wounded and war prisoners, could be interpreted as signs that he had mellowed, that his rage against Albion no longer burned as fiercely. His reaction to the Carlisle Commission pretty much puts that to rest. As he told Henry Laurens:

> The enemy are determined to try us by force, & by fraud; . . . I do not doubt but they will employ men in the second, versed in the arts of dissimulation. . . . It appears to me, that nothing short of Independance can possibly do—The injuries we have received from Britain can never be forgotten. . . . Besides, should Britain from her love of tyranny, and lawless domination attempt again to bend our necks to the yoke of slavery, and there is no doubt but she would, for her pride and ambition are unconquerable.[148]

If George Washington had anything to say about it, there would be no way out except conceding defeat on American terms.

In Philadelphia, the likelihood of such an outcome was becoming daily more apparent in rumors flying about that the British were getting ready to pull out of the city. But before that happened William Howe would make his own departure in the grandest possible manner—at least seen through the eyes of the ambitious young Captain John André, who orchestrated the whole occasion, called Mischianza, along with lining up the £300 to £400 it cost.[149] It began on the morning of May 18 with a river cruise on galleys bearing the Howe brothers amid a bevy of fashionably dressed ladies and other guests serenaded by naval cannon and 108 oboists; it then progressed to an afternoon jousting tournament featuring appropriately attired Knights of the Blended Rose and the Burning Mountain, competing for the favor of a number of equivalent damsels; the grand occasion then morphed into an elegant ball, followed by a vast late-night supper for over a thousand.[150]

Altogether, it amounted to a substantial day and night of entertainment, especially when you consider that it was highly unlikely that any of the city's Tories—or at least the ones who planned on staying— would have allowed their daughters to be seen cavorting with British officers at this point. More probably, the roles of damsels and other fashionably dressed ladies were played by the city's more comely and better-behaved prostitutes. And if guests like Lord Rawdon and Banastre Tarleton went home satisfied in both mind and body, they probably left clueless that the Mischianza was a veritable satire of the British war effort—as divorced from reality as their remaining hopes of suppressing the rebellion, and just as much of a cynical masquerade.

Now it was Sir Henry Clinton's turn. Of the three original voyagers on the *Cerberus,* Burgoyne and Howe were gone, having met their match in the American war; he was the last man standing. Clinton was conceded to be the most cerebral of the British generals in North America, and, having grown up in New York, knew it the best. But his personality was out of phase with leadership; he sulked and brooded

*Sir Henry Clinton:*
*no man to rescue a*
*war effort.*

NEWCASTLE UPON
TYNE/LIBRARY OF
CONGRESS

and quarreled with, rather than inspired, colleagues. "A shy bitch," he referred to himself aboard the *Cerberus*. Despite all his technical competence, he was not the type of person to rescue a war effort.[151]

But his problem at this point was more immediate. Since he lacked the ships to sail everybody to safety in New York, he was now faced with shepherding his army across New Jersey. The summer would only get hotter; there was no point in delay. So the retreat from Philadelphia commenced exactly a month after the Mischianza, at 3:00 A.M. on June 18, as a parade of 1,500 wagons, an army of 10,000, and 3,000 Loyalists trudged out of the city[152] and formed a caravan that stretched over twelve miles of countryside. It met the fate of all British armies that headed inland: constant harassment.

As he moved north, Clinton found all the bridges destroyed,[153] continuous irregular resistance, and even leaflets warning about "being Burgoyned." It took him six days to reach Allentown, around fifty miles from Philadelphia, before he lurched to the southeast toward Sandy Hook for more of the same. The heat was brutal, and the heavy wool uniforms and sixty-pound packs only made it worse. Since many wells had been poisoned by Patriots, water was in short supply, and a number of Clinton's troops dropped dead from heat exhaustion. Some six hundred soldiers, three-quarters of them German, deserted,[154] apparently aware that they were now better liked than their British counterparts. Clinton must have wondered if he was facing the same sort of nightmare that had befallen his comrades at Saratoga.

Meanwhile, George Washington was behind the scenes orchestrating this surreal walk in the country, populating it with militia, intent on making it as miserable as possible.[155] He had Daniel Morgan's rifle corps of six hundred waiting at Allentown, and they stung the British sharply enough that they brought up cannon to dislodge them.[156] This was exactly the sort of enervation everybody could get behind.

Washington wanted more. The fox remained a predator always; it was just an issue of scale and opportunity. The Continental Army now numbered twelve thousand, and thanks to the Steuben experience most in the ranks could now march, maneuver, shoot, and even use their bayonets. Washington's instinct was to pounce, and he called a council of war, even before Clinton left Philadelphia, to consider the question of a general action. Most of his leadership, including Henry Knox, urged caution. Notably, Charles Lee was passionate in his opposition to any action at all, arguing the faster Clinton got to New York the better.[157] So the compromise position had been to shadow Clinton with the American main force, which is exactly what it did, until the morning of June 24, when GW called another council of war with Lee, Greene, Lafayette, Steuben, Stirling, Knox, and Wayne among those attending.

Since the British were nearing the coast and safety, he asked them again if the time had arrived to "hazard a general action."[158] He was bitterly disappointed when they told him it had not. The most they would allow was that he detach just 1,500 men "to act as the occasion may serve, on the enemy's left flank and rear."[159]

But almost immediately GW got letters from Lafayette and Greene telling him that the real sentiments of the group were still for some form of concerted attack. "If we suffer the enemy to pass through the Jerseys without attempting any thing upon them I think we shall ever regret it," Greene wrote. "People expects something from us & our strength demands it."[160] GW promptly took him at his word, and effectively overruled the council by enlarging the detachment to four thousand, the kind of reconnaissance in force that almost always leads to a general action.

Unwisely but politely, Washington offered the command to his second, Lee, who promptly declined. So GW turned to Lafayette, who had been showing real talent as a commander, most recently escaping a British trap at a place called Barren Hill with an element of the now more nimble Continentals. The young Frenchman took the reins and moved quickly east to close in on Clinton, with Washington and the remainder of the army following in his wake. Lee, meanwhile, decided that he had misunderstood the importance of the command and wanted it back. Once again Washington's good manners overcame his good sense, and he gave Lee the command on the grounds of obvious seniority. He also sent him forward with a thousand more men, raising the ante for full-scale combat still further.[161] On June 27, when searing heat caused both armies to take a day's rest, it was agreed that the fortified vanguard would strike at Clinton's rear when he next moved from his campsite around Monmouth Court House (today's Freehold, New Jersey). Out of deference to Lee's military experience, Washington gave him no specific instructions, but he clearly was expecting at least a partial engagement.[162]

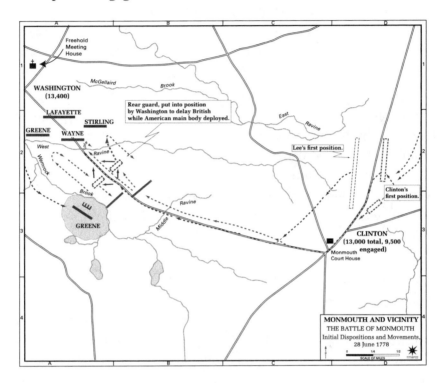

Freehold
Meeting
House

WASHINGTON
(13,400)

McGellaird

Brook

LAFAYETTE

STIRLING

GREENE   WAYNE

West

Rear guard, put into position
by Washington to delay British
while American main body deployed.

East

Ravine

Lee's first position.

Ravine

Wemrock

Brook

Clinton's
first position.

GREENE

Ravine

Middle

CLINTON
(13,000 total, 9,500
engaged)

Monmouth
Court House

MONMOUTH AND VICINITY
THE BATTLE OF MONMOUTH
Initial Dispositions and Movements,
28 June 1778

0      1/4      1/2
SCALE OF MILES

So was Clinton, who was looking for "a brush" with Washington at some point.[163] Now seemed the time. Consequently, as he packed up and re-formed the column around dawn of June 28, he gave the rear a lethal stinger in the form of the army's best units—Coldstream Guards, grenadiers, and the fast-moving light infantry—all under the command of the experienced and combative Lord Cornwallis.[164] This British army may have been thirsty, dog-tired, and down on numbers, but it was still made up of at least nine thousand professional soldiers who were nothing if not resilient, disciplined, and ready to fight.

Charles Lee found that and more as he moved his pumped-up detachment of five thousand in some disorder across a series of three ravines above Monmouth Court House, and, near the last, blundered into Cornwallis's waiting stinger, causing them to reel backward sometime before noon of what would prove another hellishly hot day. This was not like the epic panics earlier in the war; the troops were more confused and disoriented than afraid, and Lee's defenders claimed he kept them basically together as they slowly retreated toward the main American force.[165] His Excellency begged to differ.

As Washington moved forward in support of the vanguard, he began to encounter soldiers going the other way—first a terrified fifer, then clusters of Continentals, finally whole units, and with each his anger seemed to mount, until men near Private Joseph Plumb Martin heard him erupt: "Damn him."[166] The subject of his damnation became immediately apparent when he encountered Lee. "I desire to know the meaning of this disorder and confusion!"

"Sir! Sir!" Lee sputtered back in amazement before offering: "The American troops would not stand the British bayonets."

GW would have none of it. "You damned poltroon. You never tried them!"[167]

Further profanities followed, according to Virginian Charles Scott, before Washington sent Lee to the rear with Hamilton to keep an eye on him.

Just then a rider appeared with the news that the British were about fifteen minutes behind, and GW snapped from rage into rally mode. He told Anthony Wayne to hold off the British, while he rode off aboard his big white charger to steady and reorganize the troops. His presence was magnetic, and as Clinton moved to attack, the Americans were arrayed along a semicircle of ridges that created a crossfire along his avenue of approach.[168] A two-hour artillery duel ensued, during which Knox and Greene more than held their own. Meanwhile, GW was everywhere, buttressing positions, encouraging the troops, and having life-threatening experiences, including a brush with a cannonball that splattered him in the face with mud, but, as ever, without injury.

Finally, in the late afternoon, Clinton attacked the left side of the main American line, sending units across the west ravine and planting them in an orchard in front of Lord Stirling. After a one-hour firefight, Washington ordered three regiments of New Hampshire and Virginia Continentals forward to assault the British right. The well-

*Washington rallies the troops at Monmouth.*

FELIX OCTAVIUS CARR DARLEY/
GEORGE R. HALL/LIBRARY OF CONGRESS

drilled units advanced without wavering to within sixty feet of the enemy, before letting loose a devastating volley that scattered them back across the ravine.[169] At the other side of the semicircle, around the same time, Cornwallis sent his grenadiers and Coldstream Guards against Greene's position, only to be shattered and repelled by Greene's artillery. At 6:00 P.M., his troops utterly exhausted, Clinton withdrew to Monmouth, out of American artillery range. Around midnight, his redcoats arose and headed for Sandy Hook, leaving their campfires burning as the Continentals had once been forced to do in order to sneak away. It was a role reversal worth noting.

Washington spent the night beneath a tree near enough to see those fires, chatting with Lafayette about Lee's conduct until they both fell asleep. If nothing else, Monmouth Court House removed Lee as a source of annoyance and dissention. After a series of insolent letters to Washington,[170] he was court-martialed and convicted of disobeying orders, disrespecting the commander in chief, and presiding over an unnecessary, disorderly, and shameful retreat. In December

1778, Congress suspended him from the army, and that same month he fought a duel with Washington's aide John Laurens, who wounded him lightly in the chest.[171] He died before war's end in 1782, living in relative obscurity in Philadelphia, a victim, you might say, of revolutionary justice.

In more immediate terms, Monmouth Court House plainly constituted a victory in the field for Washington. British casualties were not only higher—around 500 to 350 Americans[172]—but battle is, in an elemental way, territorial, and on this day the Continental Army had finally driven their adversaries from the field.

On July 1, 1778, Clinton reached Sandy Hook, and five days later the Royal Navy had transported his entire army, along with wagons, supplies, and camp followers, to the safety of New York City,[173] a logistics feat that couldn't obscure how circumstances had changed since the fall of 1776. Now it was Washington who was looking to trap the British on Manhattan Island. Meanwhile, nine states had ratified the Articles of Confederation, and others were in step to create a single unified, if entirely inefficient, national government. And on July 8, a French fleet carrying more than eleven thousand soldiers and sailors arrived at Delaware Bay, the war's first tangible threat to the Royal Navy's omnipotence in America.[174] The British were far from giving up; but the handwriting on the wall now loomed the size of a billboard.

# CHAPTER 6

# Dangerland

## 1

THE NARROW POWER CHANNEL STRETCHING FROM GEORGE III through Germain to Clinton proved remarkably durable in the face of no clear path to victory in America—a situation prophetic of its rebellious former colony's eventual predicament in Vietnam. But at this point the British had worked their way into the strategic equivalent of a stalemate. They were stuck in New York, and the vital logistical necessity of holding on to the prototype Big Apple ensured that any future military effort would be compromised numerically. They could still capture ports on the Eastern Seaboard, and they would make one more great effort to go inland, but as usual the behavior of British commanders and troops and Loyalist irregulars guaranteed disaster. The situation was hopeless, but superior English financial, organizational, and military skills enabled it to be perpetuated for nearly half a decade more.

George Washington suffered through every one of those miserable years, swamped by congressional financial mismanagement and nearly frozen by the elements. There surely must have been times of true despair, but the record probably makes it look worse than it was, since Washington had long since become the master of gloom and doom in his endless effort to squeeze resources for his army from Congress and eventually the individual states. That's what we have left, the letters from his importuning period.

But his strategic situation actually remained viable throughout. If he continued to be frustrated in his efforts to get rid of the British permanently, there is a strong sense that he understood, at least, that he had them where he wanted them, pinned to Manhattan. "It is not a little pleasing, nor less wonderful to contemplate," he wrote a subordinate, "that after two years Manoeuvering and undergoing the strangest vicissitudes that perhaps ever attended any one contest since the creation both Armies are brought back to the very point they set out from and that which was the offending party in the beginning is now reduced to the use of the spade and pick axe for defence."[1]

There was more. Washington's ace in the hole was and would remain the French. Now he had the potential use of a French fleet that might chart the course to a truly decisive victory. But as Clausewitz reminds us, everything in war is hard, and getting somebody else to dedicate his own strategic assets to your purposes was a task of such ticklish magnitude that it required the emergence of George Washington into a master diplomat. But that took quite a while. And the first effort was a real bust.

When Charles-Hector, Comte d'Estaing and a fleet of twelve ships of the line and six frigates carrying four thousand troops arrived off Sandy Hook on July 11, 1778,[2] the first hope was that he would move promptly to engage Admiral Howe's outnumbered squadron, holed up in New York Harbor. But French capital ships were big and drew up to three more feet of water than their English equivalents, so, probably wisely, the comte did not attempt to cross the great bar, and sailed away after eleven days. Meanwhile, Washington and d'Estaing had decided to descend instead on Newport, the once-thriving commercial center on the Rhode Island coast captured by the British late in 1776.

It must have seemed like an easy target: a garrison of three thousand redcoats unshielded from seaborne attack. In addition to the French fleet and its infantry, John Sullivan quickly put together a force of ten thousand, most of them militia, but including John Glover's reconstituted Marblehead men to provide the amphibious capability to land on Newport island.[3] To help Sullivan command, Washington sent along Rhode Islander Nathanael Greene, whom he temporarily relieved from his quartermaster duties, and Lafayette to help relations with the French.

Washington, not Sullivan, should have led the expedition. Sullivan was a hothead and really nothing more than a henchman, not the sort you send on the honeymoon of a new strategic marriage. He promptly began giving d'Estaing, who outranked him, orders, a protocol faux pas of the first order with the hypersensitive French. Sullivan also failed to impress d'Estaing, who had considerable experience with amphibious operations, with his own professional competence, this being his first such attempt. Despite the friction, they did work out a plan of attack, which had Sullivan ferrying his force over from Tiverton and attacking the British under Sir Robert Pigot from the northeast, while d'Estaing would sail up and hit them simultaneously from the west.[4] It wasn't a bad plan, but it was formulated without knowledge of one vital bit of information.

In New York, Admiral Howe had been reinforced by Foul-Weather Jack Byron with thirteen British ships of the line,[5] and had promptly sailed for Newport. On August 9, the day the Americans landed, he appeared, packing almost one hundred more guns than the French. Rather than deposit his own troops, d'Estaing sought to capitalize on favorable wind conditions, and headed out to meet the British. For the next two days the rivals maneuvered warily, with d'Estaing retaining the advantage of having the wind at his back. Then an epic gale blew in, one of sufficient strength to scatter both fleets and probably cause more damage than if they had actually engaged.

Yet Sullivan remained hopeful and pressed on with his siege works, only to be repulsed during an attack on August 14.[6] Meanwhile, d'Estaing, having reassembled his battered fleet, and having heard that Howe would receive even more reinforcements, was pressing to leave, and did depart a week later for repairs in Boston. With the French gone and his militia disintegrating, Sullivan barely got off the island the day before Clinton arrived with four thousand troops, which he then used to raid and burn the New England coast under the supervision of Major General No-Flint Grey.[7]

Worse than the operational results were the diplomatic reverberations. As Nathanael Greene explained to Washington, "General Sullivan very umprudently issued something like a censure" of d'Estaing's departure.[8] "The Count's Sensibility was much wounded," reported the savvy French speaker John Laurens.[9] And well it should have been. This fleet was a huge responsibility, the result of France's massive effort to enlarge and modernize its navy after the maritime disasters of the Seven Years' War. Each ship of the line required two thousand mature oaks to construct.[10] And then there were the thousands of crew members and infantry, all of whom had been aboard ship for months and needed rest and proper nourishment. The Royal Navy, even under ideal circumstances, was nothing to play with recklessly. D'Estaing had every reason to get out of Newport.

Lafayette was quickly deployed to Boston to explain the rough-hewed ways of his new brothers-in-arms to the comte.[11] But you can almost hear Washington grinding his remaining teeth as he explained to Sullivan: "First impressions, you know, are generally longest remembered, and will serve to fix in a great degree our national character among the French."[12] In the future Sullivan would be used for tasks requiring only blunt instruments, while Washington would scrupulously orchestrate relations with the French. He gradually won them over, but it took time and a deft touch.

GW clearly understood that the French and their fleet constituted his best prospect of getting rid of the British for good;[13] but it's also apparent that he was wary of trading one European infestation for another. This remained the man who presided over the massacre of Jumonville that started the Seven Years' War, and it shortly became apparent that he still had few illusions about French good intentions.

In its enthusiasm over the French alliance, Congress had revived its long-held scheme to reinvade Canada, this time as a combined operation. This was exactly what George Washington didn't want to happen. And to further complicate the situation, one of the biggest advocates of heading north was Lafayette, the French connection Washington could not afford to lose. What ensued provides a rather graphic illustration of how the man operated, his first instinct being to disguise his real motivation behind a wall of words and obfuscation.

So it was in early November when he replied to Henry Laurens's request for comments on the proposed invasion. While "always happy to concur in sentiment with Congress," GW warned against participation "without a moral certainty of being able to fulfill our part." He then launched into a truly monumental discourse on the financial, logistical, geographic, and operational reasons why participation on this basis was impossible.[14] But when that seemed insufficient, three days later Washington wrote Laurens again "to unbosom myself to you on a point of the most delicate and important nature. . . . This is the introduction of a large body of French Troops into Canada, and putting them in possession of the Capitol of that Province—attached to them by all the ties of blood, habits, manners, religion & former Connixion of Government. I fear this would be too great a temptation to be resisted by any power actuated by the common maxims of national policy."[15]

The Canada reinvasion never came to pass, and GW adroitly managed to keep Lafayette busy in more constructive directions, but the message was clear. Beware the French. But he also needed the French. And as if to remind him, word would soon arrive that in late December a British amphibious force had landed near Savannah.

In the same letter directing him to detach eight thousand of his troops to the Caribbean, Germain had ordered Henry Clinton to wage comprehensive war in the South, where it was presumed Loyalist sentiment was high.[16] After absorbing those cuts Clinton still managed to put together a thousand-man scratch force under Lieutenant Colonel Archibald Campbell, which promptly descended on Georgia. A local slave told Campbell of a path through the swamp that enabled him to flank the American line on December 29, 1778, and almost instantly the mixed force of Continentals and militia disintegrated.

Savannah was now British, and a few days later so was the rest of coastal Georgia, with only a force under General Benjamin Lincoln blocking the redcoats from marching to Charleston.[17] Just like that, the triumphant Campbell bragged, he had "ripped one star and one stripe from the rebel flag of America."[18]

And it remained missing nine months later, when emissaries from d'Estaing sailed into Charleston to inform the Americans that the French fleet was on the way for a combined operation. This was news to everybody. His weather-battered ships finally repaired back in Boston, the French admiral had left for the Caribbean without telling Washington where he was going,[19] captured the rich island of Grenada, more than held his own against the avenging squadron of Foul-Weather Jack Byron, and was now primed to root out the British from Savannah.

Just over a week later, on September 12, 1779, d'Estaing began landing troops below the city, as around three thousand Americans under Benjamin Lincoln arrived overland. The British commander thought about surrender, but decided to hold on when reinforced. A short siege was followed by a disastrous d'Estaing-inspired assault, which was beaten back at a cost of over eight hundred American and French casualties, including the admiral, who was shot twice.[20] D'Estaing had had enough. Just over a week later the siege was lifted, and the French fleet sailed away and headed back toward Europe. So ended the first tranche of Franco-American combat operations, along with George Washington's initial lesson in just how hard it is to wield somebody else's sword, or at least the Gallic version of Neptune's trident.

Meanwhile, the botched Savannah siege energized increasingly militant southern Loyalists, who promptly won a string of small-scale engagements over the Patriots, leaving wide swaths of the rural South in apparent anarchy.[21] Back in London all of this seemed entirely encouraging, a prototype of the path to victory, especially to the eyes of Lord Germain: "Indubitable proof of the indisposition of the inhabitants to support the rebel government,"[22] he told Clinton. "The possession of Charleston would . . . be attended with the recovery of the whole province. Probably North Carolina would soon follow."[23] With a flourish of what amounted to an offensive version of the domino theory, Germain doubled down on the southern strategy, Britain's last shot at avoiding the inevitable.

2

Back on Manhattan, Henry Clinton would cooperate, but was inclined to a more skeptical assessment of the situation, the most critical ele-

ment of which was staring him in the face. George Washington sty-
mied him in every direction but out to sea by deploying the major
elements of the Continental Army in a great arc extending from Dan-
bury in the hills of western Connecticut, to the Hudson Highlands
close to West Point, then into northern New Jersey at Middlebrook.[24]
Because these positions were mutually supporting and far enough away
to avoid precipitous surprise, Washington was able to stabilize his position and avoid Clinton's attempts to lure him into major combat.[25]

These deployments defined the outer boundaries of an area of un-
ceasing conflict; the same was true of Long Island. This constituted
what might be called Dangerland, the world of irregular combat and
terror. It's important to realize that George Washington wanted it that
way. This sort of fighting was hard to control and could easily lead to
excess, but this netherworld of dirty deeds was a keystone of his strategy. For these areas could have easily raised the food and fodder the
British needed to perpetuate themselves. Instead, they became a place
of continuous dispute, of rival bands of Patriot "Skinners" and Tory
"Cowboys," of whaleboat raids across Long Island Sound, and of agriculture falling into suspended animation.

Much of this—though certainly not all—was sponsored by George
Washington, in a concerted effort to ensure the British invader's lifeline remained transatlantic. While the record certainly does reveal his
frustration with those who broke the embargo,[26] there is little doubt he
succeeded. Through most of 1778, the British Army lived what one
author describes as "a truly hand-to-mouth existence," and when the
transport fleet finally arrived from Cork in January 1779, they were
down to four days' provisions.[27] The situation did not change markedly
for the rest of the war. British eyes were always on the horizon, looking
for something to turn up.

Meanwhile, GW's eyes remained fixed on Manhattan. We last left
Washington's first effort at Gotham intelligence gathering, Nathan
Hale, swinging from a tree. But Washington was not deterred. The
Hale episode served only to convince him that he needed a more comprehensive and professional approach, a real intelligence network capable of infiltrating and perpetuating agents in the heart of redcoat
country.

Washington was fascinated, almost obsessed, by intelligence and its possibilities. Instinctively he grasped its importance in a revolutionary environment where knowledge of the enemy was power, but it also played to the furtive side of his personality hidden behind the mask of rectitude. Washington himself was good at keeping secrets; so, much of what he did and whom he dealt with in his intelligence efforts was never recorded.

He seems to have developed several entirely discrete channels, leading Light-Horse Harry Lee to mistakenly claim he was Washington's "primary agent for the spy department" and Charles Scott to think he had the same job.[28] They didn't. Washington remained the master puppeteer—the intelligence Geppetto—who created, then orchestrated, the effort to learn as much as possible about British plans and then disrupt them. The second part is important. Dangerland was an area of continuous irregular warfare, and Washington plainly fashioned his intelligence elements in conjunction with young officers we would characterize as special operators. Light-Horse Harry was plainly one example, but in terms of the intelligence component, more is known about the so-called Culper Ring.

The Culpers formed around two young Continental officers, Caleb Brewster and Benjamin Tallmadge, who volunteered themselves, along with their contacts on Long Island willing to go behind enemy lines and report.[29] Under Washington's supervision the ring began to function in the fall of 1779 and persisted throughout the war. While these agents' subsequent reporting on the state of the British Army and the comings and goings of their ships was of intense interest to Washington, he remained equivalently concerned with the intelligence implications for irregular warfare.

The Culpers provided information, but their leaders were also directly engaged in low-grade combat, and the two were inextricably entangled. So when Banastre Tarleton surprised Tallmadge's unit in July 1779, capturing some Culper-related documents, GW and his spook protégé were left to worry over not only the fate of an agent mentioned, but also whether the unit's information security had been compromised.[30] Fortunately it wasn't, and Tallmadge and Brewster continued their special operations, becoming involved in a series of raids on Long Island from across the sound, the so-called whaleboat wars.

These culminated in November 1780, when Brewster proposed to Washington an incursion directly aimed at the enemy's efforts at local supply. GW was on board. "The destruction of the Forage collected for the use of the British Army at Coram, is of so much consequence that I should advise the attempt be made."[31] It was and resulted in more than three hundred tons of hay being burned by Tallmadge and eighty dismounted dragoons acting temporarily as whaleboat warriors.[32] Such operations usually involved similarly small numbers, pulled together on an ad hoc basis, but their cumulative effect was great, less perhaps in terms of the destruction they wrought than in creating a climate of chaos that acted to stifle agriculture in the affected areas.

Channeling irregular warfare through the military also allowed GW to keep a lid on things. He was hardly naïve; he always seems to have understood how quickly this sort of combat could degenerate into slaughter. He wanted Dangerland simmering, not boiling, and to a remarkable degree he succeeded. There would be a body count, but it would remain low.

The British and their supporters were also inhabitants of Dangerland. As we saw in chapter 4, the place was a magnet for Loyalists. Early in the Revolution many had fled from Connecticut,[33] and to these were added a steady flow from other colonies that spiked when Clinton evacuated Philadelphia. Because they never understood or could accept the Patriot narrative, their reaction was largely on the level of emotion—an abiding anger that quickly ripened into rage. They had no other defense except that they were loyal and they were mad.

The British had moved quickly to harness this fury in the summer of 1776, when General Howe authorized Robert Rogers to raise a battalion of rangers and base them on Lloyd's Neck facing Long Island Sound. He was the most experienced and probably the most talented irregular warrior of his time, but he quickly fell afoul of British sensibilities by choosing former henchmen from the French and Indian War as officers, and then by recruiting "Negroes, Indians, Mulattos, Sailors and Rebel prisoners"[34]—exactly the sorts of things special operators do. But it didn't go down well with authorities. Desertion and

voracious pillaging were also problems, so Howe asked for his resignation. He was gone in the spring of 1777, replaced by Oxonian John
Graves Simcoe,[35] who proved just as ruthless but less clever.

His unit quickly morphed into the Queen's Rangers, a larger, more
cavalry-focused element than Rogers seemed to be planning. It was
designed to screen and work with the large foraging formations the
British were forced into for protection, and served as a prototype for
Banastre Tarleton's British Legion and Lord Rawdon's Volunteers of
Ireland—all of them Loyalist units and all noted for their brutality.
British regulars certainly maintained their bloodthirsty reputation (in
the early morning of September 1778, No-Flint Grey and his light
infantry managed to sneak up on the sleeping regiment of Colonel
George Baylor and stage another epic skewering, killing or wounding
at least sixty-nine with their bayonets),[36] but it was the Loyalist units
who were most notorious. Even Simcoe himself admits "a singular dislike of the Queen's Rangers had been occasioned by the frequent incursion that corps had made into the Jersies."[37] No surprise perhaps, he
was repeatedly ambushed and would be captured by whaleboaters in
October 1779, when his guide betrayed him.[38]

Dangerland was not a place Sir Henry Clinton enjoyed, but eliminating it demanded that he lure George Washington into decisive
combat, and this meant still more raiding. So on June 1, Clinton
pounced on two small forts on opposite sides of the Hudson at Verplanck's Point and Stony Point, just twelve miles south of the critical
American position at West Point.[39] He followed this up in early July
by sending former New York royal governor Major General William
Tryon on a six-day rampage along the Connecticut coast, during which
Norwalk, New Haven, and Fairfield were all burned, and at least one
mass rape took place.[40] Although GW did send some reinforcements
to Connecticut, he refused to march his army down to the coast or
anywhere Clinton could get at him.[41]

Instead, he responded with the same sort of large-scale raids the
British were perpetrating, and now he had the tactical tool he needed
to make a real impact. Since the beginning of the war, fast-moving
British light infantry had been responsible for much of the chaos and
casualties suffered by the Continental Army, the worst of it accom-

plished with bayonets. Nobody understood the damage inflicted better than GW, and his instinctive response was to acquire something similar, a process that began in the summer of 1777 and included Daniel Morgan and his rangers.[42]

Early in 1779 Washington consolidated all sixteen companies of light infantry into a single independent command, exactly the kind of unit Daniel Morgan wanted and expected to run. He was one of the heroes of Saratoga, and had consistently shown himself to be masterful with these kinds of troops. But he was a friend of Gates, ruled his units with a light hand, and maintained the same good-old-boy persona that scraped across Washington's class biases like fingernails on a blackboard; so Washington chose Anthony Wayne, a reliable henchman and martinet, instead.[43]

When he got the word Morgan immediately resigned his commission, which was impulsive, but Washington's later claim that "there was not, to my knowledge, the smallest cause for dissatisfaction"[44] was entirely disingenuous. Fortunately, Congress intervened and put Morgan on "an honorable furlough."[45] He was something close to a tactical genius and had proved it. Wayne was a human attack dog—a serviceable one, though, as he was about to demonstrate. And there was the matter of poetic justice.

Wayne's troops had been the victims of the Paoli Massacre, so when GW raised the possibility of the light-infantry corps scaling Stony Point's 150-foot cliff at night and pouncing on a fort full of sleeping British soldiers, he responded with almost canine enthusiasm: "I'll storm hell, sir, if you'll make the plans."

"Better try Stony Point first, General," Washington deadpanned. Wayne's problem was focus, never commitment.

Just past midnight on July 16, 1779, the 1,200 men of Wayne's light-infantry brigade began silently climbing Stony Point's face, "with fixed bayonets and muskets unloaded," at Washington's specific orders.[46] This was to be a No-Flint Grey–type of operation, and when advance parties reached the top and "forced their passage at the point of the Bayonet,"[47] they promptly began skewering the surprised occupants. But then they stopped. This was not to be Paoli redux, just a reminder. Only 63 redcoats met death at the end of a steel spike; 442 were taken prisoner and treated well, even according to the British.[48] This was retribution George Washington style: vengeful no doubt, but blood-thirsty never. Sir Henry Clinton was mortified, especially given the substantial efforts he'd made to re-fortify the place; but he was not about to overturn the results.[49]

Washington was invigorated and approved a similar raid, this time against British fortifications on Paulus Hook, a little peninsula on the Jersey shore just across from Manhattan. In the early morning dark-ness of August 19, Light-Horse Harry Lee led three hundred picked men in another "No-Flint" operation, during which fifty of the enemy were put to the bayonet. But Lee also took 158 prisoners and safely transported them to American lines after a difficult and daring retreat, an operation for which Congress awarded him a gold medal.[50] Once again Clinton failed to respond, and Paulus Hook turned out to be the last action fought by the central armies in 1779 before the big chill of winter. Washington was all about symbolism, and these two raids sent an undeniable message: Americans not only had bayonets, but they now could use them with skill and ruthlessness. Tactically, the one-sided war was over.

# 3

At the same time he was messaging the British in the East, George Washington was doing that and a whole lot more in the other realm of Dangerland, the domain of the Native Americans. In a larger sense what transpired was just one more chapter in the centuries-long saga of Indian removal; but in late 1778, GW was faced with an indigenous people problem that threatened the Continental Army where it was most vulnerable, its stomach. For Native American tribes, the out-break of the Revolutionary War could mean only trouble. The British at least had issued the Proclamation of 1763 aimed at barring Euro-pean settlement past the Appalachians, while the Americans in their Declaration of Independence referred to them as "merciless Indian savages." Most leaned toward the British, but that did not necessarily mean they wished to fight in British battles.[51]

One exception was the young Mohawk chief Joseph Brant, who was not only a charismatic leader among tribesmen, but tied to the British through the marriage of his sister Molly to Sir William Johnson, longtime superintendent of Indian Affairs.[52] Consequently, when the Revolutionary War shattered the initial neutrality of the six-nation Iroquois Confederation, only the Oneida and the Tuscarora failed to follow Brant down the warpath with the redcoats. By the end of 1778 this had resulted in a series of devastating raids led by Brant and British major John Butler in western Pennsylvania and upstate New York, the most notorious being the ones at Wyoming Valley near what is now Wilkes-Barre, and at Cherry Valley about fifty miles east of Albany. Sending waves of terror rebounding across the region, these raids caused significant depopulation in the very areas being tapped to feed the Continental Army.[53]

His lifeline threatened, Washington jumped on Congress's directive in late February 1779 to put together an expeditionary force for the "chastisement of the Savages."[54] Leading it would be a dirty job, so Washington first turned to Gates; then, when he not unexpectedly declined, pinned the tail on star-crossed John Sullivan.[55]

Although Greene had his reservations, Washington had every intention of closely supervising the accident-prone Sullivan. He knew how this was done. The Indians were magnificent fighters, but slash-and-burn agriculture left them never far from the edge of starvation. Interrupt the crop cycle and they were goners. So he carefully stipulated to Sullivan: "The immediate objects are the total destruction and devastation of their settlements and the capture of as many prisoners of every age and sex as possible. It will be essential to ruin their corps now in the ground and prevent their planting more."[56]

He gave Sullivan 2,300 Continentals and close instructions on how to use them. He was to proceed north and join with another 1,400 regulars at Tioga, and only then move into Iroquois country, remaining cautious at all times to avoid a Braddock-type ambush.

For once, Sullivan stuck to his mission statement. The Iroquois staged a few raids to divert him, and even took a brief stand at a village called Newtown on August 29.[57] But other than that, the Americans encountered pretty much nobody, since the Indians evacuated the local population long before they arrived. But that didn't matter to Sullivan. He spent the next five weeks of early autumn torching everything he could find: eighteen villages and 160,000 bushels of corn, in addition to girdling thousands of fruit trees.[58] He turned the place into a desert, for Native Americans at least.

The Iroquois would be back, staging devastating raids along the frontier in 1780 and 1781. But they were no longer occupants of the Mohawk Valley. Sullivan's raid had forced the tribes back to the shelter of the British forts at Niagara, and eliminated them as a factor in the fate of North America.[59] That was what Indian removal was all about, and exactly what George Washington wanted accomplished.

## 4

The American Revolution had a great many things going for it, but it would be hard to make a case that good fortune was one of them. Not only did a smallpox epidemic cast a shadow over all five years of the war, but on several occasions simple bad weather dealt the Glorious Cause injuries of the most serious sort.

Valley Forge was not an isolated occurrence. Living outdoors is always tough, but it got a great deal worse during the big chill of 1779–80, a winter recorded as one of the longest and coldest in U.S. history.[60] So at this juncture, when George Washington had the British more or less where he wanted them, the weather wrapped its icy, paralyzing claws around his army, and compounded his problems by allowing Sir Henry Clinton to slip out of New York Harbor with a major expedition against Charleston just before it froze solid.[61]

In November, Washington had decided to leave the defensive arc around the British with skeleton crews and consolidate the main army once again at Morristown for the winter. But as he moved his 8,500 men south, they were hit with a wall of unremitting sleet and snow that killed more than a few before they staggered into their former home in early December.[62]

Not much was left of it. So, just as at Valley Forge, they had to build huts while sleeping out in the cold. And it only got colder; the average temperature was ten degrees below freezing for the winter months.[63] Snow built up relentlessly until it reached between four and six feet. Soldiers struggled in vain to keep the roads open for supply wagons. But even the Greene-reformed quartermaster corps frequently couldn't force their teams through the masses of snow that seemed to pile up anew every night.

And that presumes they had something to deliver. The harvest of 1779 had not been a good one, and there were already grain shortages across the mid-Atlantic region. But that, in turn, presumes there was something to pay with. The Continental currency was in the midst of its final death spiral, hastened by a massive British counterfeiting effort, which the Culper Ring told Congress about.[64] This was the last straw, forcing the national legislature to retire and recall its notes in March 1780, effectively putting itself into bankruptcy.[65]

It's not an exaggeration to say this enraged Washington. In part he blamed financial manipulators; he talked about hanging them as examples, and called them "a host of infamous harpies, who to acquire a little pelf, would involve this great Continent in inextricable ruin."[66] But as time went on he was coming to understand the crisis was less a matter of nefarious financiers than it was of the system itself. "While our civil constitution rests upon its present basis, and the powers of Congress so incompentent to the duties requird of them," he told Greene when the terrible winter was finally over, "I have but little hopes that the face of our affairs will mend."[67]

Meanwhile, having absolved itself of financial responsibility, Congress charged each state to pay for and supply its own line in the Continental Army, a move guaranteed to produce noticeable disparities in the terms of reenlistment, which, GW reminded Congress, would affect at least half his army by January 1, 1781.[68] From this point forward Washington would have to go hat in hand to the various state governors and beg them directly for food, something he described as "pernicious beyond description."[69]

More to the point, there were no states willing or able to supply food to Washington's starving army in Morristown. He had already warned Congress in mid-December that "unless some expedient can be instantly adopted, a dissolution of the army for want of subsistence is unavoidable."[70]

Of course, everybody knew what that expedient was. "The distress has in some instances prompted the men to commit depredations on the Property of the Inhabitants," he told New Jersey magistrates, but then admitted it was "the effect of an unfortunate Necessity."[71] As an alternative he got them to agree to a requisitioning scheme with designated quotas for each county. But food was scarce and by February the troops were starving again and forced to fan out and take from the locals what they needed to stay alive. George Washington hated this, and was right to believe that it would ultimately undermine support for the Revolution.

But in this instance it doesn't seem to have happened. There was an apparent difference between how redcoats and Continentals in rags were treated when they showed up hungry. If the experience of good-natured Yankee Joseph Plumb Martin is any guide, they were likely greeted with a grumpy and reluctant generosity, not fear and loathing.[72] At any rate, unlike at Valley Forge, mortality rates never again rose to death-camp levels. Pretty much everybody seems to have gotten through the winter of Morristown II.

But spring didn't necessarily bring better conditions. On April 2, 1780, Nathanael Greene told Washington that "for want of sufficient support" his army could not be marched either north or south.[73] Stuck in Morristown, still on short rations, military life went on for the men. Steuben continued drilling them twice a day, with full battalions parading two times a week.[74] But the enthusiasm of Valley Forge seems to have vanished, replaced by an undercurrent of anger.

"We had borne as long as human nature could endure," remembered Joseph Plumb Martin, who was at Morristown in early May, when the men of his Connecticut regiment were preparing to drill, and an argument between the adjutant and one of the soldiers broke out. "Who will parade with me?" the infantryman yelled. "The whole regiment immediately fell in and formed," marching without their officers. When the regimental colonel tried to stop them, he was bayoneted in the resulting scuffle.[75] In the end it took an entire brigade of loyal, Patriot Pennsylvanians to lure the recalcitrants back to their huts, while a renewed food supply shortly brought them back under the discipline of their officers. The ringleaders were tried and sentenced to death; but Washington pardoned them all.[76] "The men have borne their distress with a firmness and patience," he told the governor of Connecticut, informing him of the mutiny. "But there are certain bounds, beyond which it is impossible for Human nature to go. We are arrived at these."[77] It was an ominous point, and Washington knew it.

Fighting this war for five long years had changed the generalissimo. He had been drawn into it by Country Party ideology, and as far as motivation went, he had not strayed far. But its strictures against taxation, standing armies, and the exercise of power by government in general had been obliterated in the face of Washington's actual wartime experience and the suffering of his men. GW was very bright, but he was never an intellectual. He learned by doing. Ideas were useful to him only if they mirrored reality, and these didn't.

Gradually, probably unconsciously, he had become a believer in a strong national government—something dealing with the French could have only reinforced. It was a competitive, dangerous world Washington saw out there. To survive, nations needed armies, taxes to pay for them, and money that was real. At this point all of this was self-evident to Washington. Others, Hamilton in particular, would run with these concepts, but it was GW's transformation that was central. He was on the road from generalissimo to Mr. President. But there were still lots of ditches and bad news ahead.

# 5

Sir Henry Clinton had been fortunate to sail out of New York before the big chill froze him in place, but removing almost 8,700 regulars, not to mention 5,000 sailors and 396 horses from Redcoat Central[78]— leaving the place vulnerable to Washington's army—constituted a big throw of the dice for the British commander, who had been initially wary of the southern strategy.[79] In fact, on January 15, 1780, Lord Stirling and 500 sleighs full of troops did come across the ice and stage a raid on Staten Island, but they couldn't get at the enemy behind fortifications and had to leave the next day.[80]

Anything bigger was out of the question for Washington, but Clinton couldn't take that as a given from the man who had shown up so unexpectedly at Trenton. Like GW, there may have been a little of the military groundhog—attacking the same target repeatedly—in Clinton; he had tried and failed to take Charleston in 1776. Now, with word of Savannah having been successfully defended, it was the obvious place to go. But then getting there turned into an adventure.

The weather at sea that winter was as foul as it was on land. On January 9 the fleet of ninety transports and ten warships was hit with a huge gale that literally blew it apart. To compound the difficulties, virtually all were caught in the Gulf Stream, running with unusual velocity. Ships would sail south all day, and actually end up farther north than when they started.[81] It was a testimony to British seamanship that the expedition didn't turn into a disaster at the outset. An ordnance vessel foundered, and all the cavalry horses were lost, but gradually the fleet pieced itself together and made land near Charleston in something over a month.

There wasn't even a horse for Sir Henry Clinton to ride when he arrived, but, now on familiar ground and scrutinizing the American position, he liked his chances. The earlier expedition had failed largely because it lacked a land component and the Americans in Fort Moultrie outgunned the attacking British ships. But now Clinton realized that because Charleston was located at the tip of a narrow peninsula between the Cooper and Ashley rivers, there was the opportunity of cutting off all land and water approaches and trapping the defenders inside.[82]

Perhaps because they had beat off the British before, the Americans, under General Benjamin Lincoln, were predisposed to take a stand. A Yankee farmer from Massachusetts, Lincoln was popular with militia, and Washington liked him; but he was clearly in over his strategic head, having never defended a city before.[83] Fort Moultrie on Sullivan's Island had fallen into disrepair since 1776, when Charles Lee had supervised the defenses. Lincoln put his efforts primarily here and into fortifications along the seaward side of the peninsula, where he expected the main British assault to come. But in doing so he failed to finish the land works across the northern neck. Perhaps his worst mistake was to commit 2,600 Continentals, including Washington's cherished Virginia Line, alongside another 1,000 militia, to the defense of the city, with no clear avenue of escape.

Clinton had simply to tighten the noose. On March 20, his naval colleague, Vice Admiral Mariot Arbuthnot, succeeded in sending five frigates over the bar that partially shielded Charleston. Five days later he landed 1,500 troops well to the north of the city, and by April 1, they had moved within one thousand yards of the defenders' unfinished works across the neck. It was the American army's last chance to evacuate, and they missed it.[84]

From this point it was an exercise in the geometric art of eighteenth-century military engineering, the methodical digging of parallel trenches supported by carefully calculated cannon emplacements (borrowed from Arbuthnot's warships). By late April, work on the third parallel was nearing completion. When that was finished direct bombardment of the city would become possible. Meanwhile, Banastre Tarleton's British Legion cavalry cleared out a six-mile zone behind Charleston, cutting off the possibility of relief from that quarter.[85]

The defenders inside put up a brave front; they had plenty of cannon and ammunition and fired relentlessly at the approaching sappers. On the night of April 24, a raiding party of two hundred Americans tried to cut the third parallel, but in the end were beaten back. It spooked the British and Germans, but they kept on digging. Washington had sent General Louis Lebègue Duportail, the able French military engineer,[86] but he arrived too late to do much more than get trapped, too. Meanwhile, Lincoln dithered in the face of civilian support for further resistance. Only when he realized he was snared did he offer to surrender on condition that his army could leave unconditionally—a free pass out.

Clinton would have none of it. He simply continued to pound the place until, on May 12, its citizens had had enough, and Lincoln surrendered with not much more than a fig leaf in terms of terms. The militia would be paroled, and officers were allowed to keep their swords—at least until their cries of "Long live Congress" put an end to that. Otherwise it was pretty much unconditional. A total of 2,571

Continentals were disarmed and taken prisoner, the largest loss of regulars in the entire Revolutionary War, along with a mammoth haul of nearly 350 pieces of artillery and almost 6,000 muskets.[87] And to make the process especially bitter, one of those muskets, apparently a loaded one, was tossed on a pile in an arsenal, setting off an explosion that killed an assortment of two hundred citizens and soldiers—British, German, and Continentals alike—and left up to sixty others horribly burned. "Half dead and writhing like worms," one German officer remembered.[88]

All of this Clinton had managed to accomplish at a cost of less than a hundred killed and two hundred wounded. In fact, his journal still leaves the impression that his subordinates gave Sir Henry more trouble than the Americans. He accused Lord Cornwallis of "UN-SOLDIERLY BEHAVIOR,"[89] and allowing his staff to "sneer" and encourage him to resign. As for his naval colleague Vice Admiral Arbuthnot: "In appearance we were the best of friends, but I am sure he is FALSE AS HELL."[90]

Throughout the campaign the misanthropic Clinton seems to have been in full "shy bitch" mode, his only friend being his adjutant, Major John André—the organizer of Howe's Mischianza having found a new patron. So Sir Henry, now the architect of a substantial victory, one that erased an earlier failure, and finding the social climate obviously uncongenial, was bent on leaving as quickly as possible.

On June 1, just over two weeks after the surrender, he and Arbuthnot had issued the same sort of proclamation Howe had proffered in New Jersey, offering full pardons in exchange for an oath of allegiance.[91] But then, two days later, without telling Arbuthnot, Clinton pulled a classic bait and switch by issuing a second proclamation demanding that oath takers "should take an active part in settling and securing His Majesty's government."[92] By the next week he was gone, taking André and four thousand troops back to New York and Redcoat Central.

On the voyage home he was probably feeling pretty good about the results of the campaign. But he might well have considered that he had evacuated Newport back in October in order to obtain more troops for the southern expedition.[93] Trading one city for another of approximately the same size did not necessarily constitute strategic progress.

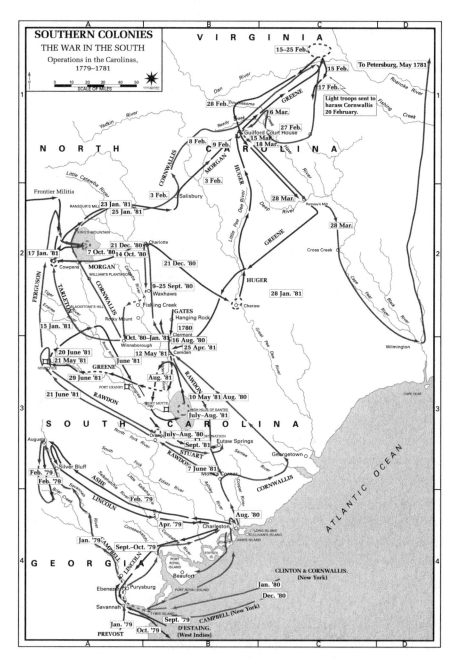

In spite of the bad blood between them, he left Lord Cornwallis in charge of Charleston. At this point Cornwallis was a veteran's veteran, a superb tactician and more than ready for an independent command. If not exactly a true believer,[94] he could hardly be called skeptical of the southern strategy, even though he had seen its critical supporting notion—that the countryside was packed with Loyalists—fall apart in New Jersey. Clinton left him specific instructions to pacify inland South Carolina, take North Carolina back, then march into Virginia to cooperate with elements supplied from New York.[95] Cornwallis's subsequent actions reflect him doing exactly what he was told. With a lot of help from his friends.

The resultant campaign would be dominated by a number of field-grade officers, all of them professionally ambitious, thoroughly experienced fighting Americans, and having become increasingly hard-line in their approach. Though he left for New York, John André was one of them, suggesting merchants trading with rebels be hanged and that fire "would be a telling weapon, applied to the homes and cornfields of rebel sympathizers."[96]

More notorious was Banastre Tarleton, the man who had captured Charles Lee. He was Oxford educated and, as immortalized by painter Joshua Reynolds, poster boy handsome, yet his aggressiveness and brutality would soon earn him a fearsome reputation.[97] Not far behind in this regard was his friend from Oxford days, Francis, Lord Rawdon, whom we last saw amused as his troops perpetrated gang rapes on Staten Island. Another Oxonian of the same ilk was John Graves Simcoe. And there was Patrick Ferguson, who at Brandywine disdained turning his technologically advanced rifles on a figure who may have been George Washington. He now told Clinton: "It is surely become necessary to exert a degree of severity, which would not have been justifiable at the beginning . . . if necessary lay waste the Country."[98]

During the southern campaign all of these men would command Loyalist units, and that was a significant factor in why things turned out as they did. After years of domination by Patriots, the Tories of South Carolina were lethally angry, and almost as soon as Charleston fell began conducting a campaign of murder, property confiscation, and irregular warfare, sanctioned and led by the British. During the early stages the Loyalists mostly held their own. But the process of stamping out the rebellion simply added fuel to the fire.[99] Thus two of the most talented irregular warriors in South Carolina, Thomas Sum-

*Banastre Tarleton:
as ruthless as he
was good-looking.*

JOSHUA
REYNOLDS/
WIKIMEDIA
COMMONS

ter and Andrew Pickens, were brought from retirement back into Patriot service after Loyalists trashed their plantations.

Banastre Tarleton had been literally making a name for himself. Shortly before Charleston fell, a Continental cavalry force under Colonel Abraham Buford arrived on the scene, saw that it was hopeless, and turned back for North Carolina. Cornwallis ordered Tarleton and the British Legion to run them down. On May 29, they caught up just south of the border at a place called Waxhaws, after riding 150 miles in fifty-four hours. The Americans hesitated to surrender, and Tarleton immediately launched an attack during which he was unhorsed—

a development he later claimed "stimulated the soldiers to a vindictive asperity not easily restrained."[100]

Less euphemistically speaking, out of a force of between 300 and 350, 113 Americans were killed and 150 wounded.[101] Henceforth Banastre would be known as "Bloody Tarleton," while "Tarleton's Quarter" was the term adopted for killing prisoners trying to surrender. The American commander was remembered as the victim of "Buford's Massacre." So it was that reputations were earned, and fear and loathing radiated outward.

Meanwhile, Cornwallis had moved promptly on Clinton's orders, marching up the Santee River to Camden, where he established his principal interior base. From there he set up a troop stronghold at Rocky Mount, along the Catawba River, which connected it to another redoubt in the far northwest known as Ninety Six. He also placed detachments at Cheraw, Hanging Rock, and Georgetown on the coast, so that by the end of June he could have had a map drawn showing he had restored royal authority to over fifteen thousand square miles of territory.[102]

But it would be at sharp divergence with what was actually happening. Over the summer of 1780, the brutal course of irregular warfare in rural South Carolina steadily ground down Loyalist units, exemplified by Tory colonel John Moore's force, which after one chaotic encounter with Patriot adversaries, went from twelve hundred to thirty stragglers he dragged back to Camden.[103] Everywhere Cornwallis looked, Loyalists were being suppressed or deserting to the other side. Whether his lordship wanted to admit it or not, the hills were not alive with the sound of Tories. Yet again the British had fundamentally overestimated the degree of Loyalist support, and then, as usual, compounded the problem with their own behavior.

One of Cornwallis's key henchmen, Lord Rawdon, was nearly archetypical in this regard. Hence in early July he attempted to deal with defections from his own unit, the Volunteers of Ireland, by offering ten pounds "for the head of any deserter," or five if he was delivered alive. When he called upon those living in and around Camden to join the militia and they refused, Rawdon arrested 160 of them, including 30 of the town's most prominent citizens.[104] On the other hand, it does seem likely that Rawdon and other British commanders were receiving intelligence from some of those citizens' slaves,[105] who might have seen the Patriot cause from a different perspective. At any rate, they had ample warning during the second week in August that a new American army was approaching Camden.

In the midst of all his problems, George Washington's reaction to the loss of Charleston was remarkably sanguine. "It will no doubt give spirit to our Enemies, and have a temporary effect upon our Affairs. But if extensively considered . . . it may be attended in the end by happy consequences. The enemy, by attempting to hold conquests so remote, must dissipate their force, and of course afford opportunities of striking one or the other extremity."[106] This constituted a rare glimpse at his cards, and these were not the words of a man playing a losing hand. Stay the course. Don't overreact.

Which is exactly what Congress did. The Carolinas and Virginia all seemed vulnerable, and the legislators wanted the southern army reconstituted. Washington recommended Nathanael Greene for the job.[107] Instead, they turned to Horatio Gates, a move that must have tested GW's composure. But Gates remained the architect of Saratoga, and he was known to be good with militia. The plan now was to rely heavily on such units, using them to build an army around the core of 1,400 Virginia and Maryland Continentals they had originally sent marching south under Johann DeKalb to rescue Charleston. So the choice seemed obvious, and GW was left to admonish Gates to keep him posted, which, of course, he didn't.[108]

Gates responded like a man floating on his own aura. As he headed south, about the only constructive thing he did was to call Daniel Morgan out of retirement and promise to make him a general, though, fortunately, it took Morgan time to gather his riflemen.[109] Meanwhile, on July 25, 1780, Gates caught up with the bedraggled Virginia and Maryland Continentals, tired and undernourished. He promptly dubbed them the "Grand Army"; he drilled them for one day, and the next morning put them on the road toward Camden. Twenty-one hundred North Carolina militia joined up on August 7, followed a week later by a pack of Virginia volunteers. As it neared its destination, what Gates had put together constituted a force structured on the fly, short on supplies, equipped with only eighteen cannon, and, after Buford's Massacre, pretty much devoid of cavalry in dangerously flat and lightly wooded terrain.[110] He would not be facing Gentleman Johnny Burgoyne this time; his opponents were world-class killers. But blinded, apparently, by self-confidence, Gates blundered on.

The British were waiting. Cornwallis, now back in Charleston, got word of the Americans' approach on August 9, and immediately headed for Camden and Rawdon.[111] He knew they were substantially outnumbered, but his troops were largely regulars and the Americans largely militia, so he wanted a fight.

On the night of August 15 he sent Rawdon forward with a substantial body of men on a reconnaissance in force, and around 2:30 A.M. they ran into the first of the Americans. Even though it was dark, Rawdon apparently knew the ground well enough to realize he was in an almost perfect position for a battle, the field being bordered on each side by swamps, which would prevent the larger American force from flanking.[112] He immediately sent word to Cornwallis, who agreed and set out to join him with the main body of troops.

Looking to devour what he thought was a much smaller British force, Gates had also ordered a night march. It was only after he did so that he learned, thanks to a count by his adjutant, that he had not the 7,000 troops he had assumed, but 3,052.[113] He was surprised but not deterred; so the army marched forward, and the dawn of a very hot August 16 found them lining up opposite British positions.

But unknowingly the Virginia and North Carolina militias had been placed directly in front of redcoat regulars, including the dreaded light infantry. Gates, who had been told there was disarray in the enemy lines, ordered them forward. When Cornwallis saw this, he responded by sending his men on the attack, causing the Americans to run, almost on first contact. Lieutenant Colonel James Webster quickly turned his victorious force and pounced on what was now the naked American flank made up of regulars under DeKalb, some of their ranks already collapsed by fleeing militiamen. The remaining Americans fought hard, but by noon this wing had disintegrated, leaving DeKalb mortally wounded by bullets, bayonets, and gun butts.

The other Americans didn't fare much better. Tarleton and his

Loyalist cavalry chased the survivors for twenty-two miles, killing and capturing as many as possible before darkness and exhaustion ended the pursuit.[114] The total casualties inflicted by the British remains uncertain, but several estimates, including Tarleton's, are as high as two thousand killed, wounded, or taken prisoner.[115] Gates wasn't one of them. Unlike DeKalb, he stayed on his horse and rode for dear life, arriving in Hillsborough three days and 180 miles later. He said he was there to rebuild his army. But there was nothing much to rebuild.

For the second time in three months British forces had obliterated a major American field army. In the terms of eighteenth-century European warfare, where ends were limited, this might have been considered a decisive development. But this was South Carolina, and as elated and confident as Cornwallis and his retinue now were that American resistance in the South had been shattered, the suspicion may have lingered that they were actually up to their necks in Dangerland.

Back at American headquarters the news of Camden was treated, it seems, with less consternation than derision, at least by GW's staff. "Was there ever an instance of a General running away, as Gates has done, from his whole Army?" Alexander Hamilton wondered. "One Hundred and eighty miles in three days . . . It does admirable credit to the activity of a man at his time of Life."[116] Washington himself remained stoic, blaming the defeat on the militia, and leaving it to Congress to dismiss Gates.[117] He was not the kind to gloat, and very soon he would have every reason to be distracted.

# 6

In addition to making him his adjutant, Henry Clinton had handed the intelligence portfolio to John André. Even in the decorous British Army, the theatrical major was not exactly a conventional choice as a spook, but he did clean up the administrative mess of his predecessors, and well before the two of them left for Charleston, he had developed a spectacular source.[118]

Benedict Arnold's gonzo heroics had been key to the victory at

Saratoga—acts accomplished while clashing repeatedly with his commander, Horatio Gates—not necessarily a bad thing in GW's eyes, but
actually a sign of his growing instability. He was also badly wounded,
his left leg again shredded by flying lead. Arnold was one of Washington's key battlefield paladins, and he was keen on keeping him in the
fold.[119] Military commander of Philadelphia, just vacated by the British, seemed an ideal posting—a place to recuperate and keep an eye on

*Benedict Arnold: the Revolution's available man.*

JOHN TRUMBULL/LIBRARY OF CONGRESS

residents with Loyalist sympathies. So this is where GW sent him,
and that is exactly what Arnold did.

Upon arrival he gravitated immediately toward the wealthy families who had positioned themselves just inside the Patriot line, at least

since the British had left. The Shippens were just such a family, oozing money and with a special treat, their coquettish youngest daughter Peggy. As a sixteen-year-old she had flirted with John André, who invited her to the Mischianza, though her father wouldn't let her attend. Now Judge Shippen was faced with an analogous problem. Though he initially welcomed Arnold into his home, he didn't expect the thirty-eight-year-old general to fall rapturously in love with and

*Peggy Shippen: bouffant and all,*
*captured by the hand of John André.*

YALE UNIVERSITY ART GALLERY

be matrimonially inclined toward his daughter; nor that she would reciprocate.

Meanwhile, carrying on a courtship at this level of society cost money. His only asset was his reputation and position. So he used them to capitalize himself through contractors, a practice not uncommon among American military administrators,[120] but on a sufficient scale to draw the ire of Patriot civilian authority. "I am told General Arnold is become very unpopular among you," Nathanael Greene wrote the always-alert John Cadwalader, "oweing to his associateing too much with Tories."[121] Soon after, Joseph Reed, now president of Pennsylvania's Supreme Executive Council, called him on it, publishing a scalding set of charges that accused Arnold of corruption and encouraging Loyalists.[122]

As he did on the battlefield always, Arnold took the offensive, responding with bluster and a demand for a court-martial to clear his name. In essence, he was seeking cover behind the military justice system, and Washington granted the request. After stalling through the summer of 1779, GW let the proceedings go forward.[123] The court verdict was negative but the punishment hardly severe: a reprimanding by Washington. No one could have been more diplomatic when he told Arnold, "The Commander in Chief would have been much happier in an occasion of bestowing commendations on an officer who has rendered such distinguished service to his Country."[124]

Or congratulating him on his marriage to Peggy Shippen, which took place that spring. His Excellency had known the family since the days of the First Continental Congress, and had watched their little girl turn into a beautiful young woman, no doubt with an approving eye.[125] He wanted his steadfast gladiator—some called him the American Hannibal—healed, happy, and back on the battlefield, and she looked like just the lass who could manage it. Unfortunately, this was hardly the case. The bride was a secret Tory, and the groom was looking to diversify.

There is little doubt that Arnold turned to the British almost immediately upon his marriage, making contact with John André through Peggy in May 1779.[126] His motives were clear. Whatever devotion Arnold may have once had to the Glorious Cause had been quenched by what he considered a long string of snubs, each one grating against his narcissistic personality—that, and the very American urge to Live Large. At this point he was all about the money, the proverbial thirty pieces of silver, which brings up an important point.

This was an unusual occurrence. The eighteenth-century European officer class was certainly an international one, and the system did allow service to foreign princes in wars not involving one's own monarch. But betraying one's own prince—in this case GW—and switching sides in the middle were strictly (that is, lethally) prohibited. This was not normal military behavior. Whatever his motivation, Arnold's act is best interpreted in another context entirely: that of revolutionary melodrama.

While it's hard to say if it's inevitable, modern revolutions have been shot through with betrayal, both real and imagined. Robespierre, Trotsky, and the Gang of Four are only at the head of a long line of true or reputed traitors whose function could be seen as a means of reenergizing revolutions in times of extended stress. In any case, because such acts so violently sunder the critical and perceived sacred bonds of revolutionary trust, they are likely to trigger exaggerated acts of retribution, not just to the perpetrator, but to thousands or even millions of innocents. In terms of potential for human devastation and its poisonous political legacy, the climate of perceived betrayal is one of the most dangerous of revolutionary conditions. That's why there was much more at stake here than just the military threat engendered by a turncoat general, although that was substantial.

Clinton had reservations from the beginning; but André's find in Arnold was too important to ignore. By the nature of the situation, and because there were so many of them, the Patriots always had a fundamental intelligence advantage, but now, with a steady stream of Loyalists being driven off the land and into New York, a potential beam of light into the inner workings of the rebel's military machine looked to be highly significant. Hence, Clinton didn't want Arnold to defect, but to resume active service and remain as a source.

Negotiations broke off for several months over money; Arnold didn't come cheap. Then in May 1780 they recommenced, this time employing code names and invisible ink (invented by John Jay's brother in England and first used by GW and the Culpers) to reach a deal: £6,000 (around $1 million today) and a British commission, should he end up defecting.[127] Clinton seemed satisfied, predicting in July "the Rebellion would end suddenly in a Crash,"[128] which remained to be seen.

George Washington was plainly puzzled by the apparently recuperated Arnold's behavior. His Excellency looked to him to take over the right wing of the Continental Army's main force and went to some trouble to have him appointed, only to discover Arnold didn't want an active command. Claiming ill health, he requested instead to be parked at West Point, the uppermost and key link in the American chain of fortifications guarding the vital Hudson River corridor.[129] GW wanted him back, but he was also indulgent toward his old warhorse. So, on August 3 he formally gave Arnold the command, along with specific instructions to work with the military engineers to refortify the place "to be ready against a sudden attack."[130]

The final act was at hand. Arnold informed Clinton that West Point's garrison was depleted, its fortifications in bad shape, and the great chain blocking the river rusted to the point that one heavy ship could snap it. But then he insisted that British good faith be verified up close and personal through a meeting with a high-ranking officer, specifically naming John André.[131]

Clinton plainly had reservations; besides being his chief administrator, André was just about his only friend. He warned him not to go behind enemy lines, to accept nothing on paper, and not to change out of his regimental uniform.

In short order the doomed André managed all three. He had sailed upriver on the aptly named HMS *Vulture*, and should have made Arnold come to him. Instead, he agreed to a rendezvous in the deep woods during the early morning hours of September 21. When Arnold offered the plans to West Point, André, dressed as a civilian, stuffed them in his boot. It was only around dawn, as he headed back in the direction of the *Vulture*, guided by Arnold's intermediary Joshua Smith and under Arnold's pass to travel unhindered, that André began to realize where he was. This was no Mischianza; this was Dangerland and he was in way over his head.

Things went steadily awry. The *Vulture* was gone, having been shelled and moved downriver. So the two headed overland back toward British lines. Anxious to avoid the various armed bands that roamed the trails, they traveled much more slowly than expected. Still fifteen miles from their objective, they were forced to spend the night in Crompond. The next morning, Smith, who did not realize who André actually was, left him to finish the remainder of the journey alone.[132]

André didn't make it far. Around Tarrytown he was accosted by three armed irregulars, possibly Loyalist Cowboys or maybe rebel Skinners. All he had to do was shut up and show them Arnold's pass; if they were Loyalists they would take him to British lines, if they were rebels, they would let him go. Instead, seeing one of them wearing a ragged British uniform coat, André blurted out: "My lads, I hope you belong to our party." They didn't; they were Patriots, but they were interested in shaking him down.[133] They took a special interest in his white-topped London-made boots, the contents of which caused them to shift back into Patriot mode, delivering André to Lieutenant Colonel John Jameson, who, after some deliberation, sent him and word of his capture back toward West Point. The letter arrived first at Arnold's desk, causing him to exit the scene like a dime-cinema villain, ordering a barge to row him to the *Vulture* and safety.

It was at this point that George Washington took the stage. He was returning from his pivotal meeting with Rochambeau in Hartford, and looking forward to breakfast with Benedict and Peggy, as were the members of his staff. "Ah, I know you young men are all in love with Mrs. Arnold,"[134] he teased. But upon arrival they got no reception at all. The general was gone, they were informed, and the lady of the house indisposed. Things got only murkier when GW got a look at West Point's defenses and realized nothing had been done to strengthen them.

In the afternoon, as Washington was resting before dinner, Hamilton delivered Jameson's letter along with André's incriminating packet full of information that could have come only from Arnold. He might as well have hit GW with a hammer; he was that stunned. This wasn't Thomas Conway, or Charles Lee, or even Horatio Gates; this was one of his stalwarts. "Arnold has betrayed us!" he moaned. "Whom can we trust now?"[135]

Not Peggy, for starters. She was still upstairs and now hysterical, the dazed military men were informed, calling out for George Washington. Along with Hamilton and Lafayette, he was the audience for one of the two truly bravura performances in a very theatrical series of events. Baby to her breast, nightgown arranged for easy viewing, the luscious Peggy played the role of the abandoned-wife-driven-insane to perfection. "General Arnold will never return. He is gone forever. He is gone there, there, there. The spirits have carried him up there. They have put hot irons in his head."[136] The boys backed off quickly, not suspecting what should have been obvious.

Only gradually did GW recover from his addled state. He had already ordered the place reinforced and would immediately send for more troops,[137] but he probably should have put West Point on alert and changed command at key posts, since he didn't know how far the conspiracy extended.[138] But as the situation became clearer, and Washington had time to regain his composure, shock gave way to monumental rage. Both contemporaries and historians have noted George Washington's capacity for anger on other occasions, but few would probably disagree that nothing made him madder than Arnold's defection. Behind the restored façade he was boiling.

He certainly wanted Arnold dead, and would soon personally sponsor a failed scheme to kidnap the defector so he could hang him.[139] But it's more important to recognize that it is at this point in the revolutionary drama sequence that paranoia and the urge for revenge can and frequently do take hold. Many another generalissimo would have reflexively sent to their deaths Peggy and her family, as well as all of Arnold's military associates—including, possibly, Daniel Morgan—and use the occasion to clean out those who inspired mistrust on other occasions, like Gates and all his colleagues, not to mention suspect civilians and on and on: There is no upper limit. And as each victim is added, the possibility for reconciliation and moderate post-revolutionary politics diminishes.

Not George Washington. "If we swallow the bait, no character will be safe. There will be nothing but mutual distrust."[140] When Arnold sent a letter from the *Vulture* proclaiming Peggy "Inocent as an Angel,"[141] GW promptly set her loose. He also spared André's guide Joshua Smith, who convinced him he believed he had been on a legitimate mission for a loyal American general.[142] Besides Arnold, GW's list of those proscribed consisted of a single English major.

Benjamin Tallmadge, GW's spy/special operator, volunteered to escort the British captive to Tappan, where his court-martial would be held. "Major Andre was very inquisitive to know my opinion as to the result of his capture. . . . I said to him that I had a much loved class mate in Yale College by the name of Nathan Hale, who entered the Army with me in the year 1776. . . . Do you remember the sequel of this story: 'Yes,' said Andre; 'he was hanged as a spy; but you surely do not consider his case & min alike.' I replied, 'precisely similar, and similar will be your fate!' "[143]

Hard words, but also obvious ones. Here was an enemy officer caught out of uniform behind enemy lines with incriminating evidence; realistically André's best hope was a gentleman's death before a firing squad, not a varlet's end on the gibbet. But even that was not to be. The one-day trial took place on September 29, and when some participants suggested bullets rather than manila for André, presiding officer Nathanael Greene sternly replied: "The mode of his death is prescribed by law."[144] He was judged a spy and he would hang.

The very next day George Washington informed Sir Henry Clinton to that effect.[145] Whether he knew of the general's affection for André or not, he must have known a letter announcing the prospective hanging of the adjutant general of the British Army would have some effect. Clinton immediately sent a three-man delegation upriver to try to save André. Lieutenant General James Robertson was the only one permitted ashore. After telling him there could be no official discussion of an acknowledged spy, Greene got to the unofficial point. The price for André's freedom was Arnold. This proposal Robertson didn't even bother answering but somehow left the meeting "persuaded" that no harm would come to André.[146]

His fate sealed, the theatrical young major once again found himself on familiar ground, and he would play out his last role with the performance of a lifetime. Everybody liked the unfailingly polite André—Hamilton was nearly gaga; even Tallmadge was fond of him—so they decided not to tell him that his personal request to GW for a firing squad was a nonstarter.[147] They knew that when George Washington really wanted to make a point, his ultimate recourse in terms of public ceremonies was to stage a hanging. And he meant this

*John André's self-portrait the night before his hanging.*

YALE UNIVERSITY ART GALLERY

one to be particularly impressive, even if the title role had to be played by an understudy, not the real culprit, Arnold.

Dressed in his full regimental uniform and, once again, his white-topped boots, André looked fully up to the part as he strode smiling onto the stage around noon on October 2, 1780, facing an audience of nearly all the Continental Army's generals—the organizer in chief chose not to attend—and several thousand troops. Only when he turned a corner through the multitude and saw the gallows did he falter and hesitate. But then André called forth his improvisational skills. "I am reconciled to my death, but I detest the mode," army surgeon James Thacher heard him say as he resumed his last march.[148]

He mounted the cart without assistance, even adjusted the noose before his arms were pinioned behind him. His last words were "I pray you bear me witness that I meet my fate like a brave man," before the whip cracked, the cart sprang forward, and André was launched into oblivion. Mercifully he lost consciousness almost immediately. They left him suspended for a half hour, a big red exclamation point.

Whether on the battlefield or the gallows, André was a brave man, there can be no question of that, but he was also an archetype of British misdirection. According to the exacting standards of an eighteenth-century military officer, he behaved properly, even admirably, from beginning to end. But this presupposed a highly circumscribed, aristocratic mindset, a cognitive framework nearly incapable of dealing with revolution on anything but the most repressive terms, and one too rigid to meet the ambiguous rigors of irregular warfare. Put him in Dangerland and he was lost, a bunny among wolves.

His fate was a sad one. But we shouldn't feel too sorry for André. That irrepressible wit Benjamin Franklin, whose house had been looted by the British major, didn't attend the send-off, but had he been there he might have thought, or even muttered to a confidant: "I say, André, before you swing, can you tell me what you did with my books and scientific instruments? How about my portrait?"

The offsite impresario was certainly satisfied with the performance. "Andre has met his fate," GW told John Laurens, "with that fortitude which was to be expected from an accomplished Man—and gallant Officer."[149] He had every reason to be gratified; the execution sent exactly the message he wanted to the British. Attempts to penetrate the Revolution's heart or its heartland are futile. This isn't necessarily civilized warfare; none of you are safe in Dangerland, good manners and breeding mean nothing here.

For their part the British seethed. Arnold threatened a "torrent of blood"[150] against American prisoners, and Clinton spoke of "dreadful consequences,"[151] but nothing like this was done. Actually, the mood of British officers in New York appeared less vengeful than deflated; to German officer Johann Ewald "it seemed as if all courage was gone with Major Andre's death."[152] They took to wearing black armbands for their departed compatriot, but it might as well have been for the British war effort.

Among Americans the episode had almost the opposite effect. Arnold's defection was universally reviled, his image hanged and burned.[153] Far from threatening the Glorious Cause, this act and his subsequent employment by the British as a military commander only energized it. Revolutions, it seems, need villains as well as heroes, and now the American version had both.

# CHAPTER 7

# The Long Goodbye

## 1

WHILE CERTAINLY BETTER THAN DEFEAT, THE STRATEGIC stalemate George Washington engineered and now had to manage was far from optimal. The war had gone on too long. His instincts and soon horrific reports from South Carolina told him that combat—formal battles and especially irregular warfare—was growing more vicious. Depredations and cycles of revenge were taking hold, and as they did the chances for reconciliation and the future of the Glorious Cause were jeopardized. He had to figure out a way to end it, to deliver the knockout blow.

Yet that required resources, and the Revolution, despite every sign of domestic prosperity, was flat broke.[1] Congress had already turned over the care and feeding of the Continental Army to the states, and in the fall of 1780 it was still months away from ratification of the Articles of Confederation, a step necessary for the quasi-cabinet system, creating secretaries of finance, war, and foreign affairs, that would eventually give it at least some effectiveness.[2] In the meantime—in fact, for a long time—the Revolution was carried by George Washington; after five long years of war he found the strength to drag it out of limbo and deliver it safely to the future. He became its chief diplomat, its essential generator of cash; whatever the job required he did, and all without sacrificing the principles of the Revolution. No generalissimo ever persevered better.

The relationship with the French was critical; they held the magic ingredients he needed for victory—warships and specie. The new French team had appeared in early July 1780, a naval expedition commanded by Admiral Ternay delivering five thousand soldiers under Jean-Baptiste Donatien de Vimeur, Comte de Rochambeau, to newly evacuated Newport, where they set up camp, though the British were soon hovering offshore.[3]

As we saw earlier in the same place, the initial attempts at Franco-American cooperation were painful, and despite having a smooth and influential interlocutor in Lafayette, Washington now realized that better results demanded direct contact. Yet he wanted it on his own terms. When Lafayette reported that Rochambeau was anxious to meet, GW hesitated, telling him instead that he was in desperate need of French guns and powder, and that "my presence here is essential to keep our preparations . . . going on at all."[4] The last thing the uniform-obsessed Washington wanted was fashion-conscious Gallic eyes reviewing his ragged troops; neutral ground at Hartford, Connecticut, was finally arranged.

By most accounts the meeting, which took place on September 22, was not a success. Washington arrived at the head of a retinue of twenty-two horsemen, including Hamilton, Knox, and Lafayette, but otherwise with only a scheme to send the French fleet to Boston, while using Rochambeau's troops to reinforce his own around New York so as to be ever ready to strike—the eternal assault-on-Manhattan dream. The grizzled Rochambeau, a thirty-seven-year veteran, his body a map of old war wounds, was not easily impressed by visionary schemes. He parried Washington easily by observing that both he and Ternay "had pointed instructions from their court for the fleet and the army to support each other."[5] But in doing so the normally crotchety Rochambeau didn't seem to hold it against the importuning American; perhaps through the eyes of a soldier, he recognized one of his own kind and also the basis of a working relationship. Meanwhile, his staff, perhaps partly to please the boss, was positively gaga with praise. Washington was not yet fifty and still a majestic physical specimen, so this was not surprising. But then something happened that transcended the man and the moment.

After the meeting broke up and the group rode away, Rochambeau's aide-de-camp, Guillaume-Mathieu, Comte Dumas, remembered passing through a nearby village:

> We arrived there at night, the whole of the population had assembled from the suburbs, we were surrounded by a crowd of children carrying torches, reiterating the acclamation of the citizens; all were eager to approach the person of him whom they called their father, and pressed so closely around us that they hindered us from proceeding. General Washington was much affected, stopped for a few moments, and, pressing my hands, said, "We may be beaten by the English; it is the chance of war; but behold an army which they can never conquer."[6]

If it wasn't an epiphany for the French, it should have been— a spontaneous demonstration that after all these years and so many setbacks the Glorious Cause still beat strong in the hearts of the people, and—of equal importance for the immediate future—that the Revolution and Washington were one. However impractical and self-serving his plans might be, it was hard to deny the obvious: GW was at the core of everything. Victory, if it was to be won, had to be pursued through him. Henceforth, the French proceeded pretty much on that basis.

The Hartford conference and the flash mob follow-up were fortunate in their timing, because there would be a lot of bad news that George Washington had to report to his alliance partners, and they scrupulously refrained from overacting. Consequently, only four days later, when Washington informed Rochambeau of Arnold's defection and explained a bit lamely that "traitors are the growth of every country and in a revolution of the present nature it is more to wondered at, that the catalogue is so small," the French general replied that the plot's discovery "plainly shews that the Divine Providence is favorable to Us and to our Cause."[7] It was a vote of confidence repeated in the face of even worse and more portentous news soon to come from the

Continental Army. From this point on, French faith in George Washington's leadership, if not his plans, remained unshaken and apparently unshakable.

This was important because Washington was about to open another front in his one-man war: financial rainmaking. Rochambeau's questions on recruitment and supply for the next year could not be answered, Washington had admitted, because of governmental uncertainty—that and the fact that money actually worth anything was virtually nonexistent. An army ultimately ran on cash. Since Congress had essentially abrogated its responsibilities in this regard, Washington was left with little choice but to become his own financier.

As always he scrupulously veiled the enterprise with republican propriety. Consequently, it was Congress in December 1780 that appointed John Laurens as special envoy with the mission of obtaining a mega-loan from France. His father had been president of Congress, so he certainly had political connections to the body. But everybody knew John Laurens was Washington's point man in a desperate mission to extract the specie necessary to restart the stalled and proverbially starving army.

The choice may have been telling in another respect—that it was not Alexander Hamilton. Both Hamilton and Laurens were the leading lights of GW's personal staff. Both were practiced and adept diplomats. Laurens spoke French fluently, but so did Hamilton. The two were the closest of friends, but no one was more competitive than Hamilton, and Washington's choice of Laurens over him for this most vital mission was bound to play on his tender ego, one more in a series of perceived slights that would lead him to leave the staff by the middle of February in what amounted to a temper tantrum.

Meanwhile, Washington demonstrated the importance he attached to the enterprise by huddling for three days in mid-January with Laurens and Thomas Paine, his designated secretary, to formulate strategy and produce detailed instructions.[8] At the core of everything was one gigantic proposition: "The absolute necessity of an immediate, ample and efficacious succor of money—large enough to be a foundation for substantial arrangements of finance, to revive public credit and give vigor to future operations."[9] Enough specie, in other words, to refloat the economy, or at least that part of it that had to do with the Revolution. As for the monumental task of convincing the French, Washington confidently placed it on twenty-seven-year-old shoulders.

John Laurens was not to be underestimated. A sort of MIA Founding Father, his fate was not to have the brilliant political career everybody predicted, but instead to be killed in a meaningless action at the very end of the war. Though his roots were in the South Carolina planter class, Laurens, along with Hamilton, hated slavery and made no attempt to hide his feelings—or his opinions about the contradictions it posed for the Revolution—from Washington. It's hard to say if their free-flowing "family" interactions over endless wartime meals were at the root of GW's slow transformation and postmortem emancipation of his own slaves, but it was unlikely he was ever subjected to two more intelligent and argumentative enemies of the peculiar institution. One thing was very clear and very tangible: this mission and its importance to Washington. "Colonel Laurens is so fully possessed of my ideas . . . that I should trouble you to no purpose by enlarging," he explained to Benjamin Franklin, America's man in Paris. "You may place entire confidence in him."[10] There was no missing that; Laurens and Washington spoke with one voice.

Still, it was hard from the beginning. Laurens arrived in Boston on January 25, 1781, only to find the frigate designated to carry him across the Atlantic was without crew or money to pay them. Fortunately, General Benjamin Lincoln, now paroled from his capture in Charleston, stepped in with a quantity of specie he managed to wheedle from the General Court and an innovative staffing solution—he recruited soldiers with nautical backgrounds from the Invalid Corps. So in early February, sailing on the first wind, John Laurens headed out into the bleak winter sea aboard a ship guided by the disabled and with absolutely no assurance, beyond his own determination, that the pot of gold at the end of the fleur-de-lis would ever materialize.[11]

## 2

Meanwhile, GW's worries had only compounded. Few things in wartime are harder than keeping an army trained and ready for combat, while locking them in a prolonged holding pattern, usually for strategic reasons. This one, the ring around Dangerland, had gone on for two and a half years. By this time it was eminently clear to Washington that in terms of further feats of privation the Continental Army was about at the end of its tether—something that terrified him. Though the winter of 1780–81 was a mild one, without money, food remained scarce.[12]

On New Year's Day the situation hit the combustion point among the troops of the Pennsylvania Line, many of them German immigrants, who had been repeatedly diddled over their terms of enlistment, something Washington knew about and had wanted concealed.[13] While the officers were off celebrating the thirty-sixth birthday of their new commander, Anthony Wayne, several hundred members under the leadership of a few sergeants and reinforced by several artillery pieces, persuaded or cajoled up to a thousand more to grab their muskets and march out of camp, heading for Philadelphia and the Congress.[14]

Washington was with the main army near Newburgh when he heard the news, and resisted the urge to ride south immediately, mainly because he feared leaving his own troops at such a moment. Instead, he told Wayne to stay close and use officers trusted by the recalcitrant troops to find out exactly what they wanted, and convey it forward to the civilian authorities.[15]

It didn't take Henry Clinton much longer to learn of the walkout, and he immediately sent out two emissaries with offers of pardons and protection in exchange for joining the British. They were greeted by the group's battle cry "We are not Arnold's," and promptly taken into custody. (They were later hanged.)[16] This was really less a mutiny than it was a military strike, a job action over really bad working conditions. Many of these Pennsylvanians were ready to stay in the army; they just wanted some justice.

In the end they got it, not from Congress, but from negotiations between Joseph Reed, the president of Pennsylvania, and a board of sergeants.[17] By the middle of January it was over. Half the soldiers were furloughed until April, and the rest allowed discharges, but enough seem to have returned for the line to remain basically intact and, most important, in camp.

Yet no sooner had this been resolved than a similar outburst took place among the men of the New Jersey Line. This time two hundred liquored-up troops were heading toward Trenton, the state capital. Washington was finished with negotiations. He ordered an immediate surrender, and sent five hundred Continentals under Major General Robert Howe marching from West Point in pursuit. On January 27 he caught and surrounded the vagabonds, who instantly gave up and repented. To discourage future unauthorized road trips, Howe lined up a firing squad of the twelve deemed most guilty to shoot two of the rebellious sergeants, kneeling before them at a range of a few yards. One was lucky and "sent into eternity in an instant"; the other required a second volley, which must have been messy.[18] But there would be no more trouble from the New Jersey Line, and this proved the last of the major troop disturbances.

But Washington couldn't know that, and this remained the worst and most difficult sort of news to convey to an alliance partner.[19] The revolts shocked Rochambeau, whose instructions from Paris, if the Continental Army fell apart, were to wait in Newport until his men could be withdrawn to the West Indies.[20] But he never panicked. Instead, he remained concerned but supportive of Washington, and when the cloud finally passed wrote him in early February: "I cannot not too much admire . . . the wisdom of the means employed by your Excellency. . . . I am in hopes that the causes of the want of Provisions, and most necessary things that your army Labours under, are going to be completely removed."[21] Not a guarantee, but an endorsement wrapped with the words Washington probably most wanted to hear.

Still, there remained several points of Franco-American friction, perhaps the thorniest being how and when to move south. A preview occurred in late December 1780, when newly minted British brigadier general Benedict Arnold sailed from New York to Portsmouth, Virginia, with a force of 1,500 to set up a base to rally local Loyalists, take pressure off Cornwallis in the Carolinas, and make it clear His Excellency's Virginia, filled with rivers leading inland, was no longer immune.[22] Who better to send that message? Clinton must have thought.

Arnold rampaged upriver as far as Richmond, burning tobacco and public buildings until mid-February, when a French ship of the line and two frigates that had slipped through the British blockade at Newport arrived, forcing him to concentrate behind his new defenses. One German officer remembered Arnold carrying two small pistols "as a last resource to escape being hanged," and on that day hardly seemed the "American Hannibal."[23] But when one of the frigates ran aground, the French withdrew into the Chesapeake and soon headed back toward Newport.

It was here, in February 1781, that nature jumped on the naval balance of power in the form of a giant storm that hit the British particularly hard since their anchorage at Gardiner's Bay at the eastern tip of Long Island was less protected than that of the French, snug in Newport. The damage done to the Royal Navy's warships in the form of broken masts and tattered lines was sufficient to give the French a sudden numerical advantage, a window of opportunity until repairs could be completed.

Both Washington and Rochambeau immediately realized that the time had come to send all the French warships and a substantial component of troops south to blockade and destroy Arnold's force. For safety's sake, though, time was of the essence. Washington moved quickly, sending Lafayette toward Virginia on February 20 with a force of 1,200 and instructions to execute Arnold "in the most summary way."[24] But the first week in March had passed before the naval element embarked. Ternay, who might have moved faster, was dead from typhus, replaced by Charles René Dominique Sochet, Chevalier Destouches, who waited too long. When he arrived at the mouth of the Chesapeake on March 16 he found Admiral Arbuthnot and an evenly matched British fleet waiting for him with the advantage of a following wind. After an indecisive few hours of combat, Destouches called a council of war and promptly sailed north on their advice to return to Newport.[25]

When the French slipped back into port on March 26, Washington responded with appropriate dip-speak, telling Rochambeau: "While I regret the disappointment of our plan I cannot but admire the good conduct and valour displayed by Mr Des Touche, The Officers and men of his Squadron in the course of the action."[26]

That was not the end of it. A month later GW received a follow-up from Rochambeau informing him, "The New-york Gazette has published a Supposed intercepted Letter wrote, as it says by your Excellency to Mr Land [Lund] Washington, and in which is this Paragraph: 'It was unfortunate—but I mention in confidence—that the French Fleet & detachment did not undertake the enterprize they are now upon, when I first proposed it to them—the destruction of Arnolds corps would then have been inevitable before the British fleet could have been in a condition to put to Sea.'"[27]

This was about as indiscreet as GW ever got, or at least was caught at, so it's interesting to see how he reacted. In his mea culpa to Rochambeau he first sought cover through obfuscation ("I assure you sincerely, that I have no copy of the original ... so that I am unable by a comparison to determine how far the publication may be just"); but finally owned up ("It would however be disingenuous in me not to acknowledge that I believe the general import to be true").[28] It was classic Washington: sly and cagey, but ultimately honest—the best reason for the French to continue believing in him. But this young marriage had plainly hit a low point.

Meanwhile, John Laurens's initial reception in Paris was not promising. In his first meeting with the foreign minister Comte de Vergennes, he learned Louis XVI was planning a gift of six million livres in specie, but when Laurens replied this was entirely insufficient, he was told "'public credit has its limits.' ... My only hope of obtaining addition succor is founded on the exalted opinion which the Ministers have of your Excellency and every thing which comes from you."[29] Since this included Laurens, his prospects were not entirely bleak.

By the end of the first week in April, Washington, still without news, was clearly frustrated but not without confidence. He told Laurens of Destouche's lassitude and its consequences "because we stood in need of something to keep us a float, till the result of your mission is known," but then added, "if it could be made to comport with the gen. plan of the War to keep a superior Fleet always in these Seas, and France would put us in a conditn to be active by advancing us—money. The ruin of the enemys schemes would then be certain."[30]

Two days later, his vision started to materialize; Laurens more or less broke the bank at Versailles. "Not to trouble Your Excellency," he began. "It is His most Christian Majestys determination, to guarantee a loan of ten millions of livres to be opened in Holland in favour of the United States—in addition to the gratuitous gift of six millions granted before my arrival—and four millions appropriated for the payment of bills of exchange drawn by Congress."[31] Just short of two weeks later he told that body's president he was about to return to America on a French frigate loaded with two million livres in specie along with another million aboard the frigate *Indien*.[32] The Glorious Cause hit the jackpot and this young man, barely remembered today, had shown up with the winning ticket. But instead of a number it simply read "George Washington." From this point it was only a matter of time and luck.

# 3

The fate of the British Empire in America continued to head south— literally, figuratively, and by now definitively. As late as October 1780 two times the number of redcoats remained in the New York enclave as were deployed in the Carolinas. But then Arnold's expedition and its apparent success led to a reinforcement of 2,600 more troops under a major general (William Phillips) who superseded him, to be followed by a third and a fourth installment in the winter and spring of 1781, shifting the majority of operational British forces and the entire center of gravity south.[33] In the face of all these new faces, the tide of battle, which reached its crest for the British at Camden, would ebb decisively into a long, grinding slide as inevitable as that of the real ocean.

An early illustration of the way down was provided by the sad fate of Patrick Ferguson. No favorite of Cornwallis, he had been given a corps made up only of Loyalist militia along with the dicey mission of traversing the backcountry between British strongpoints and protecting their flanks almost out to the North Carolina border.[34] Instead, he managed to infuriate just about everybody.

This was a very different Ferguson from the idealistic young commander who had refused to turn his high-tech rifles on what might have been Washington three years earlier. He now came equipped with two mistresses, Virginia Sal and Virginia Paul,[35] and what must have been a unique approach to generating support among the few Loyalists he encountered. "If you choose to be pissed upon forever and ever by a set of mongrels, say so at once and let your women turn their backs upon you, and look out for real men to protect you."[36] Just where they might be found he did not specify; but he had already stirred up a hornets' nest of lethally effective Patriots, especially among those living on the back slope of the Appalachians.

As a getting-to-know-you gesture he had proclaimed to the rebels that "if they did not desist from their opposition to British arms, he would march his army over the mountains, hang their leaders, and lay their country waste with fire and sword."[37] Threats like this were entirely reckless and not taken lightly along the frontier.

Ferguson was without the possibility of support. Almost immediately after Camden, Lord Cornwallis—acting on the theory that rebel support was not indigenous, but coming from North Carolina— gathered supplies and headed for Charlotte and eventually Hillsborough. By September 26, the van of an army sick enough to not proceed further reached Charlotte, nobody having the slightest idea where Ferguson was or what he was doing.[38]

Meanwhile, on the other side of the mountain, Ferguson's ill-considered threat led a mass of frontiersmen to self-organize around a number of Patriot leaders who had taken refuge among them after being ejected from South Carolina. There may have been over 1,500, mostly armed with long rifles and mostly on horseback, so they moved fast.[39]

Too fast for Ferguson. He learned of the threat only four days after it started heading toward him, and had just a vague impression of its magnitude. Apparently he had heard Cornwallis was in Charlotte, and started retreating toward him, but stopped when he came upon what looked like safety.[40] Kings Mountain was the pinnacle of a long ridge that separated North from South Carolina, and one that plainly dominated the surroundings. The textbook solution when facing a threat of unknown magnitude is to take the high ground, and that's what Ferguson did, pushing two hundred of his men out to forage, while sending the remaining nine hundred up the peak to establish themselves.

By late afternoon, October 7, 1780, the mountain men had arrived, tethered their horses, and began to infiltrate upward in what became a prototypical swarm.

There was a basic problem with Ferguson's position and with his reasoning. Kings Mountain was covered with old-growth pines, perfect to hide behind and take careful aim with a rifle. He had trained his Loyalists in volley fire and bayonet charges, and by doing so they were able to repeatedly chase off their sharpshooting assailants when they got too close. But the frontiersmen always scrambled back up to resume their lethal fire.

Finally, after about an hour of bloodshed, his men starting to waver badly, and Ferguson led a few officers in a last desperate effort to break out. The Patriots promptly shot him from his horse. The white flags of the remaining Loyalists were greeted with cries of "Tarleton's Quarter" and a number of those trying to surrender were shot dead. When it was over they stripped Ferguson naked, counted seven bullet wounds, and then urinated on his corpse.[41] The victors could hardly be restrained from murdering all the survivors and were satiated only by nine hangings, which took place over the next several days. The wounded were mistreated, neglected, and left to die.[42] In the end only a few hundred escaped alive, likely many of them being those originally sent out to forage.

Back in Charlotte the news of Ferguson's demise had a chastening effect on Lord Cornwallis. In the words of Banastre Tarleton: "The weakness of his army, the extent and poverty of North Carolina, the want of knowledge of his enemy's designs, and the total ruin of his militia presented a gloomy prospect. . . . He therefore formed a sudden determination to quit Charlotte."[43] But the grueling return to South Carolina was absolutely no picnic. A private in the Thirty-Third Regiment remembered: "We made our retreat like lost sheep, not knowing where to go, no forage, no provisions for our men, marching day and night. . . . Hard times with us indeed—a 16 days without a morsel of bread."[44] Finally, on November 1, Cornwallis reached Winnsboro, where he established winter quarters midway between the bases of Camden and Ninety Six, back from an invasion leading nowhere, and still surrounded by Dangerland.[45]

As the fated year 1781 began, the most characteristic aspect of the combat in the South was its growing cruelty. The British were up to their usual tricks, packing Patriot prisoners in pestilential hulks, where as many as eight hundred would die that year, and generally mistreating others. Future president Andrew Jackson was sword-slashed in the face for refusing to clean an officer's boots and made an Anglophobe for life.[46] But even the young "Old Hickory" had to admit, "In the long run, I am afraid the Whigs did not lose many points in the game of hanging, shooting and flogging."[47] That was the stark lesson of Kings Mountain, and the environment that greeted the new commander of the southern theater, Nathanael Greene.

After the Camden disaster, Congress didn't simply remove Gates from command; it rather abjectly ceded the choice of his replacement to GW. Characteristically, he demurred, preferring to simply "nominate" Greene, thereby preserving civilian supremacy and forcing them to ratify his choice.[48] In fact, they were sending the closest thing possible to Washington himself, a kind of doppelgänger at this point. At the core of both of them was a dogged decency that had guided and preserved them through the perilous course of war, and in the process forged a trust that was virtually absolute. This was critical because Greene's mission was critical: rebuilding the force structure in the Carolinas yet again. The South was descending into the kind of anarchy that might have befallen the larger environment had the Continental Army ever been shattered. The Revolution would have persisted, but the irregular warfare it generated would have eaten at its vitals.

That was exactly what was happening in South Carolina. "The division among the people is much greater than I imagined and the Whigs and Tories persecute each other, with little less than savage fury," Greene wrote back to headquarters and Hamilton, shortly after his arrival. "There is nothing but murders and devastations in every quarter."[49]

As he understood it, at the root of the problem were the rampaging militias, and Greene's solution proved to be an interesting hybrid born out of necessity. "This Country wants for its defence a small but well appointed Army; organized so as to move with great celerity." To build it, instead of excluding militias, he wanted to co-opt the most effective and controllable, citing elements led by Thomas Sumter, Francis Marion, and Elijah Clark, while avoiding those more inclined "to destroy provisions than oppose the Enimy."[50]

In terms of his own leverage to assemble and lead such a force, Greene left no doubt: "It is my opinion that General Washingtons influence will do more than all the Assemblies upon the Continent. I always thought him exceeding popular; but in many places he is little less than ador'd. . . . However I found myself exceedingly well received; but more from being the friend of the Generals than from my own merit."[51] That was the key to Greene's appointment and his success; he was programmed to act just like Washington.

In putting together his little army, Greene had several more tangible assets as well. GW immediately promised him Light-Horse Harry Lee and his legion of cavalry mixed with fast-moving light infantry, a force that proved ideally suited to the environment of continuous raids and ripostes, and one that meshed well with the indigenous partisan groups, particularly Marion's.[52]

Among the militias, the most effective and best led was certainly Francis Marion's. Unlike Sumter, who kept his men incentivized with Loyalist possessions,[53] Marion focused on British military supply lines, particularly the one leading from Camden back to Charleston.[54] His knowledge of the terrain, particularly the coastal wetlands, was encyclopedic, and over time he developed a dense and effective intelligence network that brought him word "of any small party of the enemy, or any escorts with stores," contemporary William Moultrie later wrote.[55] So successful was his campaign that by the end of 1780 it became common procedure for any British supply train headed for Camden to be accompanied by several hundred soldiers.[56]

This was an important trade-off numerically. Except for a small core, Marion's men came and went as their personal lives dictated. They might swarm for missions, but he could never be sure of an advantage in manpower or firepower. They arrived armed with a miscellany of shotguns, rifles, muskets, and homemade swords, but they usually shared one accouterment in common: They rode their own horses.[57]

Unlike the war in the North, where a combination of terrain and Washington's campaign to limit British access to forage minimized cavalry operations, much of the fighting in the South, where the land was significantly more open, took place on horseback. This was equine country—destined to become more so when the campaign moved into Virginia. The male inhabitants defined themselves in part by their skill in the saddle and the quality of their mounts. Since the Patriots continued to dominate the countryside, it follows that they had consistently better access to sturdier and faster horses, and that gave them a significant, though generally overlooked, advantage.

At least that's what happened to Banastre Tarleton in November 1780, when he decided to stamp out the Marion menace by luring him into an ambush with one of his own units as bait.[58] It surprised Marion enough to head for the swamps around the Santee River, and there ensued an epic twenty-six-mile chase at the end of which Tarleton was remembered as saying: "Come, my Boys! Let us go back, and we will find the Gamecock [Sumter], but as for this damned old fox, the Devil himself could not catch him."[59] So was born the legend of the "Swamp Fox" . . . but not his horses.

Greene had a still more important asset in his effort to forge an effective force out of the remnants of Camden and get control of the situation. Waiting for him in camp when he arrived was Daniel Morgan, back from retirement like a bear out of hibernation. Greene wanted to raid Winnsboro, where Cornwallis was preparing for another invasion of North Carolina. But when Morgan, along with Maryland general William Smallwood, urged caution, the "Old Wagoner" was gratified when the new boss actually listened.[60]

The two did not know each other well, Greene being in Washington's inner circle and Morgan burdened with the Gates connection, but the former's Quaker upbringing was more compatible than Washington's with the latter's backcountry demeanor. Besides, with Arnold gone, nobody had a better claim to the title of America's most successful combat general. This ursine hulk of a man—he never hesitated to assure anybody who would listen that "Old Morgan was never beaten"[61]—was exactly the tonic a shattered force needed. "Just do what Morgan tells you, boys, and we can't lose!"

And as it happened, he knew what he was doing. So did Greene. Though it did not seem so at the time.

# 4

In his first significant strategic decision of the campaign, Nathanael Greene made the kind of choice that either heralds disaster or the presence of a commander who is no longer in the slightest degree an amateur: He threw the military textbook out the window and split up his force.[62] To road-harden the troops he had inherited and help bring back their spirits, he personally marched the largest contingent southeast from Charlotte to Cheraw on the Pee Dee River. Meanwhile, he sent Daniel Morgan to the west side of the Catawba River with his own force of riflemen, several Virginia and Maryland militia elements, and a strong cavalry contingent under Colonel William Washington, a relative of His Excellency's, the intent being to harass the British strongpoints along the frontier, particularly the one at Ninety Six. "It makes the most of my inferior force," Greene wrote, "for it compels my adversary to divide his.... He cannot leave Morgan behind him to come at me ... and he cannot chase Morgan far ... while I am here with the whole country open before me."[63] Better yet, it actually worked.

Early in the new year Banastre Tarleton presented a plan to Lord Cornwallis aimed at running down Daniel Morgan and trapping him in the vicinity of Kings Mountain.[64] For all his good looks and Oxonian polish, Tarleton was a pretty predictable instrument militarily, relying primarily on his ever-aggressive instincts to guide him in combat. Cornwallis, a much better soldier, knew this, but was plainly frustrated by the chaotic environment surrounding him, and the prospect of crushing this incipient, almost insulting, little threat must have seemed appealing. Also, on January 4, he had been joined in Camden by 2,500 new redcoats from New York under Major General Alexander Leslie. So he confidently sent Tarleton on his way with a mix of around 1,100 regulars and Loyalists, cavalry heavy and featuring most of his light-infantry units[65]—an army built for predation.

With such a force it didn't take Tarleton long to catch up with Morgan. The former wagoner was traveling at a leisurely rate with his baggage and supplies and not apparently looking for a fight. On January 16, he was around forty miles to the southwest of Kings Mountain when he received word that Tarleton was six miles distant and closing fast. He quickly decided to make his stand in a wide, flat meadow called Cowpens with the Broad River in back, a choice that terrified some of his officers. The place seemed made for Tarleton and his cavalry, not this Patriot composite of militia from the Carolinas, Virginia, and Georgia, balanced only by Continentals from Maryland and Delaware. This was a mix that had led to disaster after disaster.

Yet Morgan had been in such situations before. He understood these men, especially the militia—knew their strengths and weaknesses, and, above all, their limits. He also spoke the language of the backcountry. He spent that night circulating among the campfires, telling them that he and they were invincible if they only did what he told them. Repeatedly, past thrashings had begun when the militia had broken and raced terrified toward and into other formations, who then joined the stampede. Morgan realized that to break the contagion more realistic expectations were required; he asked them to only face the enemy, fire two rounds, and then retreat in an orderly fashion. With these limited goals in mind, he set about arranging his other units in a fashion calculated to lure the ever-aggressive Tarleton forward, all the while decimating his attack into incoherence. Meanwhile, having a river at their backs pretty much ensured that everybody would stand and fight.

On January 17, 1781, it all came together at Cowpens. Tarleton lined up his force, which slightly outnumbered Morgan's, and went straight forward without hesitation. "Raised a prodigious yell, and came Running at us as if they Intended to eat us up," Morgan remembered.[66] One hundred and fifty riflemen stationed inconspicuously out front cut down the first fifteen British horsemen to enter Cowpens. Capable of loading on the run, they continued their lethal fire, and would shoot two-thirds of Tarleton's officers before the battle reached its climax.[67]

As the redcoats approached, militia commander Andrew Pickens got his men to hold fire until their targets were within range, and then unleashed a savage volley, which slowed the British sufficiently to allow for a second, before beginning what was mostly an orderly retreat. When British dragoons caught up with some on the far right, Morgan sent Washington's stalwart cavalry to quickly rescue them.[68]

Meanwhile, the main body of redcoats was nearing the composite Continental-militia line strung out on top of a hill transecting most of the battlefield; rather than waver, the Patriots delivered another round of fire, this one threatening to break up the entire British assault. Tarleton, being Tarleton, raised the stakes, calling forth his main reserve: a battalion of elite Highlander foot, which headed for the American right flank.

The commander of the American line, John Eager Howard, watched them come and ordered a militia company on the far right to pivot to meet them. Instead, they retreated back down the hill. Daniel Morgan asked Howard if his troops were under control, and when reassured that they were, ordered the entire line down the reverse slope, where they set up to take a stand hidden from British eyes.[69]

Seeing the Americans disappear convinced Tarleton and his troops that they were on the brink of a rout. In their eagerness to close, the British raced pell-mell over the crest, only to plunge into another thunderous American volley, soon followed by Washington's cavalry and Pickens's militia for a second time, the combined effect of which turned them into a helpless mob, begging for mercy. "Tarleton's Quarter" rang out, but Morgan and Howard would have none of it, shouting to their men not to kill those trying to surrender. This was an army of the United States of America, not a mob from the backcountry: Kings Mountain would not be repeated. Still, Tarleton himself, who raced from the battlefield with about 250 dragoons, was lucky to avoid capture, as it would have been a tough sell to keep the troops from applying "Tarleton's Quarter" to its namesake.

He left behind 110 dead, 200 wounded, and at least 525 prisoners,[70] in one of the few tactical defeats the British suffered in the Revolutionary War. But the win was really less important than the numbers and the implications.

The southern strategy was being bled white. From July to December 1780, Patriot partisans and militia managed to kill or wound 1,200 British and Loyalists and capture another 1,300, while losing only about a third of that number themselves.[71] At Cowpens, the Americans in a morning's work had eliminated what amounted to a sixth of Cornwallis's entire force at the cost of 12 killed and 60 wounded.[72]

Other British commanders would not prove so credulous and co-operative as Tarleton, but Morgan's approach to militia and other skittish troops was replicable. In the future exchange ratios might not be as spectacular, but they didn't have to be. So long as Americans were roughly holding their own in battle and inflicting casualties in the process, they were cementing the road to victory. In this way Cowpens was, as Henry Clinton later ruefully concluded, "the first link of a chain of events that followed each other in regular succession until they at last ended in the total loss of America."[73]

Daniel Morgan guessed an enraged Cornwallis wouldn't sit still when he heard the news. The battle was over at around ten in the morning, and shortly after noon Morgan was on the road with army, prisoners, and supplies, moving at a pace that would take him across a hundred miles and two rivers of North Carolina in a little more than five days.[74]

Cornwallis proved every bit as furious as expected; an American prisoner who witnessed Tarleton's debrief to his commander reported he leaned so hard on his sword that it broke in half, then swore he would recapture Morgan's prisoners no matter what it cost.[75] The next day, January 19, he set off on his fated pursuit, turning down the wrong road in the wrong direction, which, as one historian notes, captured the essence of British intelligence problems throughout the campaign.[76] He wasted an entire day before he got on the right route, and was increasingly frustrated at his army's failure to gain ground on Morgan. When he heard his quarry had already crossed the Catawba River, Cornwallis made a key decision in his forces' life expectancy: He stripped everybody—including himself, as a morale builder—of all baggage right down to the tents and most of the food, burning everything. His force would pick up speed and lose weight accordingly since his path through North Carolina would not prove promising for foragers.[77]

When Nathanael Greene heard about Cowpens, it was six days later and he was 125 miles away, camped along the Pee Dee River. But he realized he had to get involved immediately. Rescuing Morgan meant reuniting the two American forces, but that demanded he be found and told where to go. This was a mission too vital, apparently, to leave in anybody else's hands. He shifted command of his division to Isaac Huger, with instructions where to head for the linkup. Also, obviously thinking ahead, he told his quartermaster to begin gathering boats on the Dan River along the border between North Carolina and Virginia.[78] He then galloped off into the wilderness with a guide and a few cavalry, looking for Morgan.

He found him in just a few days—a mute testimony to the Patriot intelligence advantage—riding into Morgan's camp on January 31, just as Cornwallis was approaching. They held a brief council of war, plotting Morgan's escape and a deceptive path toward reuniting at Guilford Courthouse. Greene then stayed behind to organize his paladin's exit; he was almost captured, then headed back toward his army, having waged what amounted to a one-man war.

Morgan's progress was still slowed by his captives, so Cornwallis was now basically faster. But since he had little knowledge of the backcountry topography and virtually no intelligence information,[79] catching the wily wagoner proved impossible. On February 4 he moved northward as Cornwallis expected, but suddenly veered east in a forty-seven-mile march over two days that left him at Guilford Courthouse, reunited with Huger and the main element, and arriving almost simultaneously with Lee's Legion and Greene himself.[80] He had his army back together.

But Greene wouldn't have Morgan. A decade older than most of the key Continentals, Morgan had lived a hard life, and this last episode had left him racked with rheumatism, sciatica, and hemorrhoids. He would have to go back to Virginia to recover, effectively closing out a combat career that, with the exception of Quebec a long way back, had known only victory. Greene realized what he was losing. "Great generals are scarce—there are few Morgans to be found," he said when he left.[81]

But Greene was fully capable of proceeding without him. Like Washington, clear battlefield victories repeatedly eluded him, but now with Morgan's formula for redcoat reduction, he had a sure way to make combat count. Meanwhile, at the operational and strategic level he was sly and clever like his mentor GW, whom Cornwallis had previously chased without success. Now, in a series of moves worthy of his boss, he raced Cornwallis to the Dan, convinced him through false intelligence there were no boats downstream, and on February 13 succeeded in getting the last of his troops and the boats to the Virginia shore just as Cornwallis's soldiers arrived glowering, helpless to follow.

Without the prisoners he vowed to rescue, without equipment or supplies, Cornwallis apparently wanted to put the best face on another mission to nowhere, or at least Tarleton did. "The continentals being chased out of North Carolina, and the milita being awed . . . Earl Cornwallis thought the opportunity favourable for assembling the King's friends. With this intention he retired from the Dan, and proceeded by easy marches to Hillsborough, the capital."[82] Some hundreds of Loyalist sympathizers did filter in, but only out of curiosity, not to offer help, and in the full expectation that the rebels would soon be back.[83] Like the tide of an invisible ocean, Dangerland was inexorable.

Nathanael Greene shared Washington's brand of dogged aggressiveness; to him the fight had just begun. So after just ten days in Virginia to gather strength and receive a letter from Morgan again detailing his battlefield architecture,[84] he plunged back across the Dan and into North Carolina.

Two days later, on February 25, something happened that showed the way things were going. Pretending to be Tarleton and only a mile from his camp, Lee and the horsemen of his legion managed to line up in front of an equivalent band of Loyalist dragoons, and then without warning began hacking and shooting them until a hundred were dead and most of the other two hundred were seriously wounded.[85] Lee had once taken prisoners and treated them well. This was the sort of cruel trick the British had been perpetrating since Paoli; now Continentals could and would do the same, which testified to both their competence and the degeneration of the entire environment. And to bad days ahead for Cornwallis.

One of the worst came on March 15, 1781, at Guilford Courthouse, where the still-confident Cornwallis chose to fight Greene, on ground of the American's choosing, arranged according to Morgan's principles, while facing a two-to-one numerical disadvantage, roughly four thousand to two thousand.[86] One part of the militia's killing zone collapsed, but the rest mostly gave ground stubbornly, inflicting casualties all the way. The British finally bulled their way through and forced Greene to retreat, abandoning his artillery.[87]

Yet he had handed the British a classic pyrrhic victory. At a cost of 250 of their own casualties, the Americans killed or wounded 500 British and had bitten off another quarter of Cornwallis's army.[88] Washington understood exactly what had happened—"although the honors of the field did not fall to your lot, I am convinced you deserved them."[89] Greene put it more succinctly: "We fight get beat and fight again."[90] Yet this prolonged combat came at a cost morally. It should be noted that before Guilford Courthouse, in an effort to obtain intelligence Lee and his men applied a red-hot shovel to the feet of a Loyalist prisoner.[91]

But that was now combat reality, and over the next several months Nathanael Greene would advance into South Carolina, and, with a brilliant campaign of deception and sudden attack, gradually force the British, now commanded by the ineffable Lord Rawdon, back to Charleston. By July, Rawdon, his health shattered, was headed for England, but not before hanging a prominent citizen, Colonel Isaac Hayne, on trumped-up charges. When asked to spare Hayne's life, Rawdon supposedly responded with two words: "Major André."[92] For him and the British southern strategy, there remained only this pathetic act of revenge.

But it was Cornwallis's fate that dictated the collapse of the entire British North American war effort. Four days passed before he and his mangled army left Guilford Courthouse, and headed east toward the coast and the British enclave at Wilmington, marking their path with the graves of the wounded who died along the way.

Without provisions he reached Cross Creek, a settlement of Scots, who he hoped might feed them and even supply some recruits. He got neither and had to move on. American irregulars along the Cape Fear River made it impossible to ship food up from the coast. So it was a long, hungry march before around 1,400 of those still fit for duty made it to Wilmington on April 7. As usual, the British transatlantic link held firm; there were new uniforms, muskets, tents, and other items of military kit waiting. Yet this was the equivalent of slapping a new paint

job on a used-up beater of a car. After two weeks of rest, one of Cornwallis's cavalry officers wrote that "the Spirit of our little Army has
evaporated a good deal."[93]

But not Cornwallis's strategic vision, or what passed for it; he was
about to topple the last domino, the one that led to military oblivion,
on the grounds that Virginia was the real cause of problems in North
Carolina, just as he had reasoned North Carolina was at the root of his
difficulties in South Carolina. To his mind, Virginia looked like entirely greener pastures: full of good horseflesh to at last close the
equine-acquisition gap, with plenty of navigable rivers running east to
west to maximize the Royal Navy's usefulness; along with Massachusetts, it was at the core of the Revolution; and finally, and perhaps best
of all, given the state of his own army, there was already a substantial
number of redcoats in Richmond, Arnold's original force having been
reinforced by that of his friend Major General William Phillips, for a
total of around 2,600 relatively fresh bodies.[94]

It was so obvious, so logically irresistible, that Cornwallis crossed
into the Old Dominion in early April 1781, basically on his own authority, seeking to link up with Phillips, whom he ordered to meet him
near Petersburg.[95] Instead, Phillips died of a fever and it was Arnold
who delivered the reinforcements. Cornwallis apparently didn't share
Clinton's enthusiasm for turncoats, even effective turncoats, and Arnold soon headed back to New York and his sponsor in chief for further misdeeds.

Meanwhile, His Lordship—appropriately pumped up to around
five thousand troops—turned his attention to the small American
force of around three thousand that GW had sent to the Chesapeake
in March under Lafayette[96] to run down Arnold, which now seemed
ripe for destruction.[97] "The boy cannot escape me," Cornwallis supposedly crowed.[98]

That remained to be seen, but what was clear was Sir Henry Clinton's dismay at these developments. In the twenty-four months preceding May 1781, he had sent four separate detachments totaling nine
thousand troops—three-fifths of his entire force—to the Old Dominion, and watched helplessly as war's center of gravity slid inexorably
south until he could barely see it.

Clinton wanted those troops back, and made it clear to Cornwallis in a letter written two weeks earlier that found him in Williamsburg in early June, after letting Tarleton loose on the countryside, scattering Virginia's legislators, including Governor Thomas Jefferson, and generally rampaging through the Old Dominion's rickety defenses. After such manifest success, Cornwallis was disgusted to find that instead of a major campaign, Clinton wanted him to construct a naval station, a defensible redoubt along the Virginia coast to ship redcoats north.[99]

## 5

George Washington watched these developments with the inscrutable mask of a seasoned poker player—though it's also possible to make a case that he had to be dragged along the path to victory by the French. Assuming the former on the basis of a really cagey past, GW's apparent reluctance to see that the key to winning decisively lay in Virginia, not New York, still begs for explanation.

This all began in May 1781, when Washington learned that command of the French fleet in Newport was about to pass from the embarrassing Destouches to the more enterprising Jacques-Melchior Saint-Laurent, Comte de Barras; but more important was word that a much larger naval force under Admiral François-Joseph-Paul, Comte de Grasse, had departed from France. Its first destination was the West Indies, but after that, in the autumn, it might be available to sail north, should a suitable mission be found.[100]

Determining that mission was Rochambeau's intent when he invited Washington to confer at Wethersfield, Connecticut, in late May; but of equal importance, perhaps, the meeting was a signal that he was now willing to conduct true combined operations: French ground forces were no longer necessarily tethered to its fleet, which would be powerful enough to take care of itself.

Yet the whole thing turned into a bit of a charade. GW certainly attended, but he revealed himself fixated on using the French, both on land and sea, to attack and expel the British from Manhattan, the knockout blow par excellence. And one that would be very hard to accomplish. Amphibious operations are traditionally the most difficult and dangerous; French ships of the line were unusually large and might run aground; urban fighting was vicious and casualty-heavy—the list of challenges and imponderables continued right down to unknowns of tides and currents to compose a very ugly mission profile from a Gallic point of view.

It was always a nonstarter for Rochambeau: De Grasse was actually already under orders to sail to North America, and the general would soon pen him a secret message to ignore whatever alliance-speak boilerplate emerged from the meeting and set a course for the Chesapeake Bay.[101] Of course, Washington also knew most of this, courtesy of his budding and wine-stained friendship with Major General François-Jean de Beauvoir, Chevalier de Chastellux,[102] who even provided a memorandum suggesting he and Rochambeau should feign an attack on New York and then head for Virginia, close to what actually happened. What followed makes it even harder to believe Washington was ever really serious about a Manhattan showdown, especially since he told Noah Webster after the war that he considered it nothing more than a ruse for almost a year before the race south.[103]

Still, it seems that he was serious at the time. And that boiled down to realities of geography and motivation; he could probably get the Continental Army to contest nearby New York, but Virginia was a long way off, and they were about at the end of their collective rope. Two significant mutinies were just months in the past, and out of them emerged, it seems, a silent compact between Washington and the men in the ranks: They would remain loyal and would fight (they were, in fact, better than ever, after years of Steuben-inspired drills) but would no longer do it unpaid, half-naked, hungry, and forever. He knew Clinton's garrison was depleted. One good afternoon in the as-yet-to-be Big Apple could end it: finish Redcoat Central and the whole war. It must have been tempting at the psychological level of the Washington who kept revisiting the scenes of former defeats.

But he was a long way in every way from Fort Necessity. Experience had taught GW never to be without a Plan B, and it seems reasonable to conclude that the Virginia option was never far from his mind. As an experiment, it seems, Washington sent his least reliable unit, the formerly rebellious and now rebuilt Pennsylvania Line, marching toward Virginia under the guidance of his bluntest instrument, Anthony Wayne, with the aim of reinforcing Lafayette.[104] Along the way Wayne found it necessary to execute eleven, and move forward with the ammunition and bayonets of the rest under guard,[105] but he got them there by early June, and they proceeded to fight and fight hard to make sure "the boy" did indeed escape Cornwallis. Getting there would not be fun, but it could be done.

When considering the decision-making that led to the exquisite trap at Yorktown, it's also worth including the information and military-technical aspects of the environment—roughly speaking, two half-blind combatants wielding very heavy sledgehammers. Everything was time lagged and took place in agonizing slow motion, the most sluggish snare imaginable; but behind it all was an inexorable logic supported by one central possibility: Should de Grasse actually arrive, the naval balance of power would shift dramatically and potentially decisively in the direction of the Glorious Cause.

Still, there was the matter of luck—the manner in which events lined up, however sluggishly, out of the chaos of possibility. For example, Rochambeau had no way of knowing that Cornwallis would obligingly retreat to the coast and isolate himself at Yorktown when he told de Grasse to head for the Chesapeake. And from that point, events continued to break for the Revolution and its one and only generalissimo. No surprise here; he was, after all, destiny's child.

On August 14, GW received a letter from the Comte de Barras confirming that de Grasse had left the West Indies and was on his way with twenty-eight ships of the line, four frigates, and over three thousand troops.[106] Two days later a message from Lafayette in Virginia arrived informing Washington that Cornwallis was "throwing up works" at Yorktown.[107] That did it. He was familiar with the place and knew it could be cut off. In a joint letter the next day, GW and Rochambeau told de Grasse they would now "turn our attention towards the South. . . . For this purpose we have determined to remove the whole of the French army and as large a detachment of the American as can be spared to Chesapeak, to meet Your Excellency there."[108]

They had very little time. Barras also told Washington that de

Grasse would have to return to the Caribbean by mid-October, giving the Franco-American team approximately sixty days to move four thousand French and three thousand Continentals 450 miles with all their equipment, plus the cumbersome tools of siegecraft to Yorktown, then surround and batter Cornwallis's fortifications sufficiently to obtain his surrender before the admiral's deadline.[109]

The near impossible only brought out the best in Washington, by now a master of all aspects of his trade: working with Robert Morris, now officially installed as secretary of finance, to make sure enough French specie got distributed to lubricate the way south;[110] orchestrating the logistics so food and supplies were waiting at stopping points; coordinating with Barras, who was sailing down from Newport with siege cannon; and doing all of this while managing to befuddle Henry Clinton as to his operational intentions.

They began on August 19, marching south in three staggered columns, first using the Hudson as a shield, then, as they moved into Jersey, making it look like they might be headed for Staten Island or Sandy Hook, potential jumping-off points to assault Manhattan. Washington was almost out of the state before the British in New York realized he was not headed for them. Always the political animal, GW took time to march his army through Philadelphia, and that night the city was illuminated in his honor, as crowds pressed ahead to get a glimpse of their hero.[111]

It only got better. On September 5 a rider overtook Washington to inform him that de Grasse and his entire fleet had finally arrived at the Chesapeake Bay, which was certainly good news. But there was more to come. That same day, Sir Thomas Graves arrived off the Virginia Capes with nineteen ships of the line and promptly engaged the substantially larger French fleet. The action, which lasted until nightfall, was indecisive tactically, as most naval battles were, but definitive strategically—France's first major naval victory over the British since 1690. For Graves's ships were sufficiently damaged that he had to withdraw to New York for repairs.[112] Meanwhile, the Comte de Barras had entered the Virginia Capes with eight more ships of the line, making Chesapeake Bay effectively a French lake and the prospect of a redcoat rescue not much more than a mirage.

As Rochambeau approached on a barge: "I caught sight of General Washington waving his hat at me with demonstrative gestures of the greatest joy."[113] Since GW was plainly not into demonstrative gestures of any kind, this was probably a pretty accurate reflection of his mood. He knew then he had won. There were still difficulties to be encountered—troops at Head of Elk staged a sit-down strike for back pay, and when Robert Morris ran short of cash, GW had to turn to Rochambeau for 50,000 livres in coin to get them embarked and down the Chesapeake. But in the end, everybody reached Yorktown approximately together, this vast human migration skillfully and inevitably choreographed. Certainly it was a group effort. The French were military professionals and masters of siegecraft. GW's own staff was highly effective and his generals battle-tested. But all would have agreed that no matter how tortured the process, this was Washington's creation, his military masterpiece.

Because the land jaw of the great trap closed at a stately eighteenth-century pace, Washington had some time before all the pieces were in place and he could begin to preside over the bagging of Cornwallis. Very characteristically, he made a beeline for Mount Vernon, riding with a single aide sixty miles in one day to get there. He hadn't seen the place since the spring of 1775 and it was pretty dilapidated, but, for once, he barely noticed. For Martha was waiting, just as she had managed to spend fifty of the war's most miserable months in camp with her husband.[114] His spirits plainly soared in her presence, and were likely raised still higher by the apparent success of Jacky Custis's marriage in the form of four children GW had never seen. Jacky even showed an interest in accompanying Washington down to Yorktown, perhaps a last shot at a little martial ardor or out of sheer pride for his amazing stepfather. Either way it was a mistake, since he would quickly contract camp fever and die two months later, just short of his twenty-seventh birthday.[115]

Washington spent September 9 through 12 at Mount Vernon, obviously basking in Martha's warm company as the place gradually filled up with French and American officers. Seamlessly and in a manner that impressed even European eyes, the First Couple shifted from domesticity to ceremonial hospitality to war planning as the staffs of

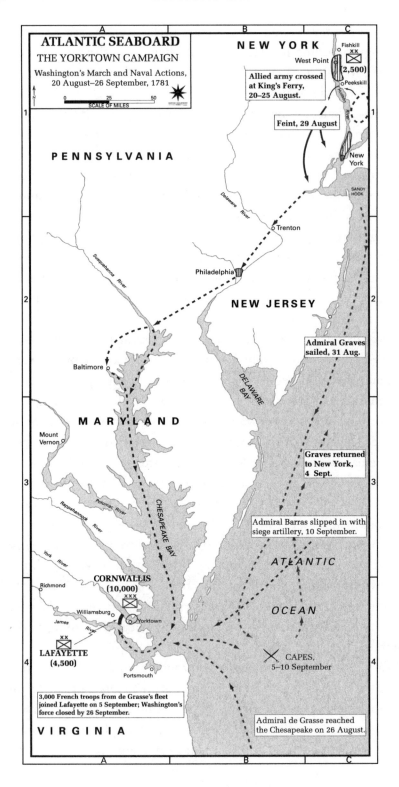

ATLANTIC SEABOARD
THE YORKTOWN CAMPAIGN

Washington's March and Naval Actions,
20 August–26 September, 1781

0        25        50
SCALE OF MILES

**NEW YORK**

Fishkill
West Point
Peekskill
(2,500)

Allied army crossed
at King's Ferry,
20–25 August.

Feint, 29 August

New
York

SANDY
HOOK

**PENNSYLVANIA**

Delaware River

Trenton

Philadelphia

Susquehanna River

**NEW JERSEY**

Admiral Graves
sailed, 31 Aug.

Baltimore

DELAWARE BAY

**MARYLAND**

Mount
Vernon

Graves returned
to New York,
4 Sept.

Potomac River

Rappahannock River

CHESAPEAKE BAY

Admiral Barras slipped in with
siege artillery, 10 September.

York River

**ATLANTIC**

**CORNWALLIS**
**(10,000)**

Richmond

Williamsburg
Yorktown

James River

**OCEAN**

**LAFAYETTE**
**(4,500)**

Portsmouth

CAPES,
5–10 September

3,000 French troops from de Grasse's fleet
joined Lafayette on 5 September; Washington's
force closed by 26 September.

**VIRGINIA**

Admiral de Grasse reached
the Chesapeake on 26 August.

Rochambeau and Washington began to sketch out the final details of the great trap.

The human components were still assembling when Washington reached the coastal lowlands and received word that de Grasse was getting impatient and maybe cold feet. You couldn't be French and be an admiral without worrying, and being cooped up in a bottlenecked body of water like the Chesapeake with the Royal Navy out there somewhere was bound to prey on his nerves. "The season is approaching when, against my will, I shall be obliged to forsake the allies for whom I have done my very best and more than could be expected."[116]

The dreaded deadline. Washington realized sieges took time, and he had to have more of it. As always in such emergencies, GW fell back on the majestic presence of George Washington to do his bidding; but it also said something that he went to de Grasse, not vice versa. Also, if this was a gravitas contest, he may have underestimated the competition.

On September 17 a boat picked up GW and Rochambeau and sailed for an entire day before reaching the French fleet, now anchored at Cape Henry, right at the bay's entrance as if poised to leave. Looming high out of the water, festooned with three decks of cannon ports, sailing battleships were by nature imposing. Seeing thirty-two of them lined up practically to the horizon must have caught George Washington's attention as he approached de Grasse's flagship, *Ville de Paris*, reportedly the biggest warship in the world with 110 guns and a crew of 1,300. But all this massiveness probably didn't prepare him for de Grasse himself, a huge, rotund figure, slightly taller than the American, who caught Washington in a bear hug, kissed him on both cheeks, and bellowed: *"Mon cher petit general!"*[117]

Not surprisingly in a negotiation where he was not only outweighed, but in which the other guy held thirty-two of the best cards, Washington had a great deal of trouble moving de Grasse. But ultimately he did get him to extend until November 1, which would prove to be the time needed. There was one more scare when the French admiral threatened to sail off to New York after Graves, but Washington was able to talk him out of it.[118] So, once again, largely due to the efforts of the generalissimo, the liquid hinge of the great trap held firm.

Meanwhile, on the British side, Cornwallis persisted in acting like Cornwallis and Clinton like Clinton, so they pretty much missed the significance of practically everything the French and Americans did until it was too late.

In early July, after getting Clinton's instructions to build a naval base, Cornwallis left Williamsburg and headed toward the coast, followed closely by Lafayette, now reinforced by Anthony Wayne's Pennsylvania Line. Almost reflexively the British general ambushed the Americans at Green Spring Plantation on July 9; but an unexpected bayonet charge by "Mad Anthony's" outnumbered Pennsylvanians held the redcoats back just long enough for Lafayette to rescue them. Another meaningless victory for the peerless earl; he likely left the encounter still thinking "the boy will not escape me . . . eventually."

But there was really little else for him to do but fortify Yorktown, which occupied him for the rest of the summer, enlisting the labor of the three to four thousand escaped slaves who now accompanied his army.[119] But it's important to realize that he did so in full expectation that the Royal Navy would send a decisive counterbalance to whatever threat the French mounted at sea, specifically the Caribbean fleet of George Rodney.[120] Cornwallis, like his counterparts in New York, was conditioned to believe Britannia ruled the waves and always would.

But instead, Rodney lingered for three months at Saint Eustatius, which he had conquered and was in the process of meticulously looting.[121] Worse still, he was not only slow sending Clinton and Graves intelligence of de Grasse's departure, but he left the impression that only a portion of the French fleet was headed for America. It was almost September before Clinton and Graves got word of the real size of the armada they faced.[122] On September 2, fully two weeks after the Franco-American march had begun, Sir Henry Clinton wrote Cornwallis, "It would seem that Mr. Washington is moving an army to the southward." He added that since Admiral Graves was on the way, "I flatter myself you will have little to apprehend from that of the French."[123] Self-flattery ended when Graves ultimately limped home bearing the scars of battle.

Knowing now that Cornwallis was in real danger, Clinton wasted little time putting together a rescue detachment and had them aboard transports by September 6, but Graves could not provide safe passage until his warships were repaired, which was bound to stretch on into October.[124] Clinton's response to the delay was similar to what had been emblematically British throughout the war. Hoping somehow to divert Washington's attention, he turned to his most reliable turncoat, Benedict Arnold, who obliged him with a ferocious raid along the Connecticut coast, featuring the torching of New London and the massacre of nearby Fort Griswold's defenders as they attempted to surrender.[125] Whatever the reverberations of what could now be called "Arnold's Quarter," they proved utterly without consequence—just gratuitously cruel. By the time Clinton's relief expedition arrived off the Chesapeake, Cornwallis had already surrendered, and the closest it got to contesting the high seas was a distant glimpse of French warships.[126]

Because his intelligence of what was going on in the countryside remained a dim and flickering flame, Cornwallis had no idea how outnumbered he was becoming as Washington, piece by piece, assembled his force until it reached nearly nineteen thousand, or more than a two-to-one advantage over the British, many of whom were sick.[127] On September 29, GW marched his entire army to Yorktown, where they occupied positions in a six-mile arc around the outer ring of British trenches. From this point it was, as it had been at Charleston, a matter of geometry.

At the juncture of the seventeenth and eighteenth centuries, Sébastien de Vauban, acknowledged master of siegecraft and faithful servant of Louis XIV, the Sun King, had reduced its practice to a matter of mathematics, literally, devising a system of parallel trenches minutely calculated to provide the best firing angles and maximum shelter for troops all the way to the point of attack.[128] Since that time French military engineers had gotten only more precise and relentless—hands down, the best in Europe. Sieges were not without episodes of vicious combat and occasional sallies leading to escape, but basically once French military engineers had an opponent cornered the way they had Cornwallis, there was no way out.

After the British outer defensive ring collapsed, and the first parallel was completed on October 9, Washington was given the honor of lighting the initial cannon in the coming barrage. Other than that, he didn't have to do much beyond a little cheerleading and his usual routine of exposing himself needlessly to enemy fire. Americans under Alexander Hamilton did take a key redoubt by swarming, while the French, using a more methodical approach against a similar but somewhat tougher target, suffered substantially higher casualties.[129] But otherwise it was a Gallic operation, designed and engineered to produce a predictable result.

Cornwallis probably knew he was finished as soon as Washington's army arrived, but he held out the hope of rescue by sea, one that grew dimmer daily, until on October 12 he wrote Clinton "nothing but a direct move to York River—which includes a successful naval action— can save me."[130] Three days later he told Clinton that his condition was so "precarious that I cannot recommend that the fleet and army should run great risk in endeavoring to save us."[131]

On the next night, October 16, he played his last card, ferrying troops across the York River to Gloucester and a land avenue out, but then nature intervened with a violent summer storm that sank some of the boats and blew the rest downriver.[132] The next morning, shortly after the last of the redcoats were retrieved, a British officer appeared waving a white handkerchief. It was October 17, marking the fourth anniversary of Burgoyne's surrender at Saratoga, and the second time an entire British army had been lost in the misguided attempt to subdue the American Revolution.

In an effort to save a little face, Cornwallis asked that his men be allowed to capitulate with full military honors. "The same honors will be granted to the surrendering army," GW informed Cornwallis coldly, "as were granted to the garrison of Charleston"[133]—basically, disarmament and internment. But Washington was never vindictive, so he allowed captured deserters from the Continental Army, along with John Graves Simcoe and his hated Queen's Rangers, to sail off toward New York before the formalities of surrender began.[134] It's safe to say the last thing he wanted to blemish the occasion were hangings, nonjudicial or otherwise, though it's worth noting that similar humanitarian concerns didn't deter him from rounding up and returning several hundred escaped slaves formerly under Cornwallis's protection.[135]

At around three in the afternoon of September 19, 1781, already an hour late, two columns of sullen British and German troops, ironically dressed in new uniforms, began trudging between a half-mile gauntlet of Americans and French lined up opposite each other—one splendid with polished boots and dress swords, the other "dirty and ragged, and a number of them . . . almost barefoot," remembered one observer, Baron Ludwig von Closen.[136] Many of the English avoided eye contact with the Americans, recognizing only the French, until Lafayette had the band strike up "Yankee Doodle," forcing them to acknowledge the obvious.

Waiting patiently astride their best horses at the end of the gauntlet, Washington and Rochambeau were expecting Cornwallis, but were informed by his second-in-command, Major General Charles O'Hara, that His Lordship was indisposed (perhaps an insufficiently stiff upper lip?) and could not attend. He then attempted to give Cornwallis's sword to Rochambeau, who refused. O'Hara was told, "The commander in chief of our army is to the right." Reluctantly, the British general then rode up to Washington with the proffered sword, only to be referred to his second-in-command, General Benjamin Lincoln, the same Lincoln who had been forced to surrender Charleston with such an ample portion of humble pie.

Sword presumably in hand, he then led the procession of captives to an open field where they ground their arms, many throwing their muskets on the pile "with violence, as if determined to render them useless," recalled the peripatetic Dr. James Thacher, who somehow managed to witness almost all of the Revolutionary War's big events. There was none bigger than Yorktown.[137]

Statistically, Washington and his army had captured more than eight thousand soldiers and sailors, all of their small arms, plus 244 pieces of artillery, not to mention a war chest packed with over £2,000 in specie (around $350,000 today).[138] A substantial haul certainly, but the true fortunes of war can't really be captured by numbers. Yorktown, coming after six years of military frustration, was a crushing defeat for Britain's efforts to subdue the American Revolution. That was obvious to Joseph Plumb Martin, standing in the ranks,[139] though probably less so to George Washington.

*Surrender at Yorktown: His Lordship was indisposed.*

JOHN TRUMBULL/LIBRARY OF CONGRESS

For like everything in the eighteenth century, the full impact of Yorktown proceeded at a stately pace. It was November 25 before word reached London. Lord North's reaction was immediate and correct: "O God! It's all over!"[140] But George III was ready to pour more resources into North America and stand staunchly behind the forever-militant George Germain.

The latter resorted to the King's domino imagery when he warned the House of Commons on the consequences of giving up on the American war: "We must not flatter ourselves that Canada would not immediately fall, and your fisheries in Newfoundland and all your possessions in the West Indies would also lie at the mercy of your enemies."[141] It didn't work; on December 14, after being attacked from all sides for continuing the war, North got up from the government bench and took a seat on a backbench, leaving Germain conspicuously alone.

The narrow power conduit that kept the unpopular war alive was essentially severed. Germain almost immediately retreated to his country home, and on February 27, 1782, the Commons voted to suspend hostilities in America.[142] North resigned soon after, replaced by the Marquess of Rockingham, committed to negotiating comprehensively with the Americans, and leaving the former Patriot King to reflect that "knavery seems to be so much the striking feature of its inhabitants that it may not be in the end an evil that they become aliens to this kingdom."[143] That spring Henry Clinton was recalled and replaced with Sir Guy Carleton, the same Carleton who had thwarted Arnold at Quebec and now, like Washington, had outlasted his third British commander in chief.[144]

Yet peace was still not clearly on the horizon. The struggle for and against American independence had metastasized into coalition warfare. So far, the potentially shaky alliance between the French and their junior partner Spain with the Americans had not only held firm; it prospered. The remarkable campaign of Bernardo de Gálvez, the Spanish governor of New Orleans, east along the shores of the Gulf of Mexico, had by May 1780 forced the British commander to officially surrender all of West Florida, leaving them without bases along that entire coast, which in turn had implications for the West Indies, much as Germain had suggested.[145]

As good as his word, de Grasse rejected Washington's request for further combined operations against Charleston and Savannah, and left instead directly for the Caribbean, where he worked out a plan with Gálvez's representative to capture the British Windward Islands and then Jamaica. This would have been an economic disaster. The sugar harvested from Jamaica alone was worth more to the British economy than all the thirteen colonies, five times as much as tobacco. George III had earlier told his first lord of the admiralty that he was willing to risk the naval security of Britain itself to protect his possessions in the West Indies.[146] As long as they were under threat there could be no peace.

Fortunately, into that breach sailed the Comte de Grasse, for the second time in American history arriving at exactly the right time and place to ensure U.S. independence—though the results weren't great if you were French. De Grasse's campaign in the Caribbean was a seagoing disaster. He did manage to invade and take the island of Saint Kitts in February 1782, but this minor success came at the cost of being totally outmaneuvered and significantly damaged by the much smaller fleet of Sir Samuel Hood, who then withdrew to join reinforcements. George III and the Royal Navy were not about to give up Jamaica, and they had sent back the errant George Rodney, still their best fighting admiral, and seventeen more ships of the line, all of them with copper-clad hulls to resist fouling, making them superior sailors in tropical waters.[147]

De Grasse didn't do much in March beyond repair his ships and wait for the invasion force to assemble. Finally, on April 7, he pulled out of Martinique with thirty-five ships of the line and a convoy of one hundred transports, intending to meet an additional twelve Spanish battleships, along with the invasion force of fifteen thousand waiting at Saint Domingue. He never made it. Rodney's copper-coated fleet ran him down in two days, and by nightfall of April 12 had virtually dismantled the French force, blowing up one battleship, capturing four, and scattering the rest. Among those taken was the giant *Ville de Paris* and de Grasse himself, the only officer on the command deck left standing. As many as three thousand French personnel may have been killed, with over five thousand soldiers and sailors captured. But more important, the threat to Jamaica had been obliterated. History could proceed.

# 6

What is clear today was far from apparent to George Washington, or so it seems. So long as the British presence persisted, he believed it was his job to keep the war and the Continental Army going, if necessary drag them along virtually single-handedly. To say he was suspicious of British intentions entirely understates the mood reflected in his correspondence.[148] "That the King will push the War as long as the Nation will find Men or Money, admits not of a doubt in my Mind,"[149] he told James McHenry in September 1782, almost a year after Yorktown. Yet the persistence of GW's urgency came in the face of Carleton's declaration ending active hostilities, along with the evacuation of Savannah and Charleston. Back in August, Carleton was even the first to tell

Washington that peace negotiation between American and British representatives had begun in Paris.[150]

Nevertheless, Washington remained haunted by the fear of somehow snatching defeat out of victory, so he defaulted to keeping the threat alive (at least in his own mind) and the Continental Army a functioning entity. Leveraging all this in the face of increasing apathy was not only extremely difficult, it was also dangerous, filled with possibilities for overstepping his authority and thereby endangering the Revolution itself—a period culminating in an episode that historian Joseph Ellis called "the Last Temptation of Washington."[151]

Strategically, since Yorktown and increasingly thereafter, the problem set for Washington was reduced to the British enclave on Manhattan, now more than ever Redcoat Central. Around that, Dangerland persisted, an area of irregular warfare intense enough to disrupt agriculture sufficiently to keep the English from feeding themselves except by transatlantic supply. Beyond that, in a great semicircle from the Hudson River into New Jersey and around to Connecticut, were the main elements of the Continental Army. Like juggling bowling balls, Washington had to keep everything and everybody more or less in motion and under control—that in the face of increasing fatigue and impatience for it all to be over. Fortunately for us, he never dropped the ball.

Washington remained intent on cutting British access to local food supplies, such as they were, and that entailed irregular warfare. As usual he turned to his most trusted special operator, Benjamin Tallmadge, as his enforcer. Once again utilizing whaleboat warriors, during the winter of 1782–83 they planned and executed several raids aimed at British food and forage, as well as maintaining a calorie cordon sanitaire as best they could through patrols.[152]

GW worried particularly over commerce along the Jersey coast, muttering about inflicting the death penalty on food traffickers.[153] It was exactly this area that epitomized Dangerland as well as the pitfalls associated with involvement. The career and demise of Joshua Huddy was a case in point.

Huddy had been a steady Patriot presence in the vicious struggle waged almost continuously along the Jersey shore, accused of hanging as many as fifteen Loyalists before he was captured, escaped, then was captured again on March 24, 1782, to be confined in a British prison ship. That didn't last long. He was turned over to a band of Loyalists under a Captain Richard Lippincott, ostensibly as part of a fake prisoner swap, and delivered by boat to a beachfront gallows, where he was promptly hanged with a note attached: "Up Goes Huddy for Phillip White."[154]

It didn't take long for GW to become involved. In an effort to prevent Patriot militias from taking independent reprisals, Washington ordered that a British officer of equivalent rank be chosen from the Yorktown detainees and executed,[155] subject only to Lippincott being turned over for trial. This was a serious mistake, one in clear contravention of the surrender agreement at Yorktown, which explicitly protected captured officers. Worse, the nineteen-year-old captain who drew the short straw, Charles Asgill, was a thoroughly sympathetic figure whose family had enough influence to arouse an international outcry.

Washington must have realized his error, but it was difficult to back down. As the date of execution approached he became increasingly uncertain,[156] and ironically it was the British who bought him some time by staging their own court-martial of Lippincott, only to acquit him. It didn't matter; by this time Louis XVI and Marie-Antoinette had become sympathizers, and the Comte de Vergennes was instructed to plead Asgill's case to GW. That provided sufficient cover. On November 7, 1782, the young officer was freed by an act of Congress, and GW could breathe a sigh of relief.[157] From beginning to end the episode illustrated that in the morally ambiguous territory of irregular warfare, even an operator as canny as Washington could stumble badly.

Yet his passion for things covert bordered on the reckless, as illustrated by his response to an even weirder undertaking hatched in late March 1782. Apparently out of misguided patriotic optimism, George III's son, seventeen-year-old Prince William Henry, had taken up residence in New York. Seeing the prince as a target of opportunity, Colonel Matthias Ogden proposed to GW that he lead a team across to Manhattan and kidnap him, along with the officer who was his custodian.

Likely envisioning walking bargaining chips, Washington could not hide his enthusiasm: "The spirit of enterprise so conspicuous in your plan for surprising in their quarters, & bringing off the Prince-William Henry & Admiral Digby, merits applause; and you have my authority to make the attempt; in any manner, & at such times as your judgment shall direct." But then, being George Washington, he thought to add: "I am fully perswaded, that it is unnecessary to caution you against offering insult or indignity to the persons of the Prince, or Admiral"[158]—a dignified kidnapping, almost an oxymoron, and much more likely to end in a bloody shoot-out. It's a good thing Ogden never attempted it, though GW was reportedly not happy that he did not.

Still, while tending to Dangerland was a consistent preoccupation, most of Washington's time and attention remained focused on the care and feeding of the Continental Army, its men in the ranks and its officers. Here, too, the road to the finish line was littered with pitfalls.

As far as the training and condition of Continental Army units, they had never looked better. Congress was less dysfunctional, and Robert Morris—whom Washington referred to as simply "the financier"—continued to allocate mostly French-derived specie effectively, so that by the summer of 1782 the force was considerably improved over the one at Yorktown.[159] Rochambeau's aide Baron von Closen was "struck by the sight of these troops, armed, in new uniforms, and with excellent military bearing."[160] Washington had them drilling continuously, and Steuben kept adding more complex evolutions, until one French general commented that they looked like Prussians.[161] There wasn't a trace of exaggeration in October when GW told John Jay in Paris at the negotiations: "I am certain it will afford you pleasure to know, that our Army is better organized, disciplined, & cloathed than it has been, at any period since the commencement of the War—This you may be assured is the fact."[162]

But there was a larger issue: Why were they still there? After nothing resembling large-scale combat since Yorktown, most of the men must have asked that question. But habit, a sense of duty, regular food, those new uniforms, pride in having become competent soldiers: Those, plus loyalty to the generalissimo himself kept them in camp and together, willing somewhat reluctantly to stick it out to the end as members of the Continental Army of the United States. At least there were no more big mutinies.

Yet there remains the still more fundamental question of how that army looked to the citizens of those amalgamated states. The psychological climate had changed; the threat of enslavement by Britain was a thing of the past, a shadowy memory; but this remained a public conditioned to be suspicious of standing armies—potentially even their own. During the fighting phase of the war, comparisons had been made between the Continental Army and Rome's legions under Caesar and the New Model Army of Cromwell, always with the implication that military dictatorship might also supplant the American republican experiment.[163] Now, as the months trailed on without combat and increasing numbers came to believe the war was over, Washington's determination to maintain the Continental Army at close to full strength was bound to raise further suspicions.

Washington knew that the idea of Washington as military dictator was real, and he was sensitive to it. Back in May 1780, he had questioned Hamilton over reports that he had suggested America would be better off if GW brought the Continental Army to Philadelphia and told Congress to go home.[164] But it's safe to say nothing prepared him for the proposal he received on May 22, 1782, from the head of the Invalid Corps, Lewis Nicola—a "representation I was deputed to make in the name of the field officers of the army." There followed a diatribe suggesting that both officers and men favored not disbanding at war's end until all grievances were addressed; asserting that "this war must have shewn to all, but to military men in particular the weakness of republicks," and then broadly hinting that the nation would be best served if Washington simply remained generalissimo "to conduct & direct us in the smoother paths of peace."[165]

GW was horrified, and that's putting it mildly. "Be assured, Sir, no occurrence in the course of the War, has given me more painful sensations than your information of there being such ideas existing in the Army as you have expressed." He offered to keep the letter confidential, "unless some further agitation of the matter shall make a disclosure necessary." He was also indignant that his entire persona of republican rectitude could be called into question: "I am much at a loss to conceive what part of my conduct could have given encouragement to an address which to me seems big with the greatest mischiefs that can befall my Country." He closed on almost a plaintive note, urging Nicola, "if you have any regard for your Country, concern for your self or posterity—or respect for me, to banish these thoughts from your Mind, and never communicate . . . a sentiment of the like nature."[166] If he believed that, he was kidding himself. There was a surly undercurrent of entitlement and disobedience growing inexorably, not among the men, but among his favorites: the members of the officer corps.

Nicola claimed to have spoken for them, although there was no way for GW, nor is there for us, to know how many. But from this moment Washington was put on notice that beneath what he considered the legitimate demands of his officers (he made a point of telling Nicola "no man possesses a more sincere wish to see ample Justice done to the Army than I do")[167] lay something far darker, a desire to take over. Washington was hardly politically naïve, but he really does seem to have had a blind spot when it came to the officer corps.

This had been building for a long time, since Valley Forge.[168] The idea that the danger and misery they faced had enhanced their revolutionary credentials beyond that of others had forged them into, if not exactly a nascent aristocracy, at least an available ruling class.[169] Yet Washington had remained largely oblivious; they were, after all, his kind of people. Now it had been shoved in front of his face, and still he did not react.

Instead, for the better part of eight months George Washington went about his business as if nothing was happening, while something like a real conspiracy took form—one with civilian backers in Congress who were among his closest associates, Robert Morris and Alexander Hamilton, now a member of Congress, having quit the army and taken up full-time politics.[170]

Events began to go critical in January 1783, when a three-man delegation of officers came down to Philadelphia from the main camp at Newburgh to present Congress a petition itemizing their perceived grievances, first among them their thwarted desire for a hefty postwar pension package. As usual Congress was long on sympathy but short on cash, which seems to have given the Hamilton–Morris confab the idea that the cumulative debt to the officers might be leveraged into a real capacity to collect taxes on a national basis, especially if the threat of a military coup was at least in the background.[171]

Hamilton could hardly have been more open with Washington over what was intended: "The claims of the army urged with moderation, but with firmness, may operate on those weak minds which are influenced by their apprehensions more than their judgments"; and about the commander in chief's perceived weakness in this regard: "An idea is propagated in the army that delicacy carried to an extreme prevents your espousing its interest with sufficient warmth."[172]

Washington's reply was far more orotund and circumspect than the one to Nicola, but he did finally get around to stating: "I shall pursue the same steady line of conduct which has governed me hitherto."[173] He plainly knew there was scheming afoot in the army, "the source of which . . . is again beginning to work under a mask of the most perfect dissimulation & apparent cordiality."[174]

To Alexander Hamilton, that could mean only one person: Horatio Gates was back. He had been removed from field command after Camden; in 1782 his New England supporters in Congress managed to repeal an earlier call for inquiry, and sent him back to Washington's staff at Newburgh, an apparently rehabilitated man. Not to GW. Even today the exact motives and identity of the conspirators remain murky, but to His Excellency, after all the bad blood between them, if anybody might be behind skullduggery in the army, it was Gates. There were even rumors that he led a faction favoring an actual rather than just a threatened coup, and it's hard to believe GW hadn't heard them.

Whatever the case, a final chain reaction began on March 10, 1783, when a document—probably authored by one of Gates's aides—brazenly called for a mass meeting of officers to air their grievances and plot strategy—in other words, to take the first step. It was at this point that the vulpine Washington kicked in; having drawn his prey out into the open, he pounced. There would be no meeting called by anybody but His Excellency, and he scheduled it for March 15.

It proved a command performance: Washington at his best and most masterful. He had toiled over his prepared remarks, writing them in his own hand for most of the previous day, until they read like a text in politico-military deprogramming. Before a packed audience in a wooden hall the officers had dubbed the Temple of Virtue,[175] he chastised them for ignoring his authority by calling an impromptu meeting; then he recalled their shared sacrifices to further soften them up, before getting down to destroying the opposition. "My God! What can this Writer have in view by recommending such measures? Can he be a friend of the Army? Can he be a friend to this Country? Rather, is he not an insidious Foe? Some Emissary, perhaps, from New York, plotting the ruin of both, by sowing the seeds of discord & separation between the Civil & Military powers of the Continent?" Having equated the plotters with the real enemy, Washington spelled out a final act of contrition he wanted from his audience: "to express your utmost horror & detestation of the Man who wishes, under any specious pretences, to overturn the liberties of our Country, & who wickedly attempts to open the flood Gates of Civil discord, & deluge our rising Empire in Blood."[176]

He probably had said enough, but his instincts told him he wasn't finished. He fished out a letter from Congressman Joseph Jones describing the body's fiscal challenges, but it was badly penned and even he was getting lost in its details. There was an instant's hesitation, followed by the spontaneity of genius. He put on a pair of new spectacles that few if any had seen him wearing and explained: "Gentlemen, you must pardon me. I have grown gray in your service and now find myself growing blind." That broke them, unleashed a flood of tears in many, such was his hold on them. He finished the letter and strode out.

But the meeting remained in session, and with Horatio Gates as chairman, passed a vote of thanks to the commander in chief, disavowed any coercive intentions, attested to their confidence in Congress, and requested that in the future GW handle all negotiations with that body. The vote was unanimous. The whole thing looked a little like the revolutionary show trials of the future. It helped that Congress came up with a plan to give officers five years' full pay in lieu of a pension, but the reality was that George Washington countered the threat of a military takeover with what amounted to a flick of the wrist. Symbolically, at least, this was the true measure of his influence over the fate of the American Revolution. Ultimate power had been waved in his face, and he only doubled down on republican principles and civilian supremacy, making it seem that the Last Temptation of Washington was no temptation at all.

Still, this whole unnatural situation had persisted for entirely too long; that was the reason the climate was radioactive in camp. French specie was running out, and that could only mean more trouble with the men. Yet the one thing Washington could not bring about was an official end to the war; civilian authority in Paris (basically Benjamin Franklin, John Jay, and John Adams)[177] had to do that. In February he learned that preliminary articles of peace had been signed, but nothing was official until they were finalized. A week passed after the Temple of Virtue showdown and still no news came in. It must have been a grim time for GW. Then a courier galloped into camp carrying a one-line letter dated March 24, 1783, from Anne-César, Chevalier de La Luzerne, the French minister in Philadelphia, announcing *"la conclusion de la paix."*[178] It was over at last.

In his formal Proclamation for the Cessation of Hostilities on April 18, a doubtless pheromone-soaked Washington, in congratulating those "who have performed the meanest Office, in erecting this *Stupendious Fabrick* of *Freedom* & *Empire,* on the broad basis of *Independency;* who have assisted in protecting the rights of human nature, and establishing an *Asylum* for the poor, and oppressed of all nations and Religions,"[179] made what may have been his most idealistic public statement. Yet it was also one that not only set a high standard for the future, but also a realistic vision of how the continent would be populated and controlled by Americans.

Perhaps prophetically, given the sorry history of imperialism, it was the Europeans who got the short end of the treaty negotiated in Paris. The British were the big losers, giving up in the Americas not only the original thirteen colonies, but also West and East Florida, plus Tobago.[180] But the ostensible winners, France and Spain, got little territory of permanent value, and were both on the brink of very bad times. A good case can be made that the debts accrued floating the Glorious Cause were a crucial factor in destabilizing the ancien regime and bringing about the French Revolution.

Franklin, Jay, and Adams did a lot better for the United States of

America, which emerged as independent state, sovereign over a huge block of territory from New England down to Florida and then west to the Mississippi River. Of course, the Treaty of Paris didn't do a thing for Americans not part, or fully part, of that newborn sovereign entity.

For African Americans, slavery persisted unabated. About the only positive postwar results for black people were British sponsored. As many as twenty thousand fugitive slaves may have left the Lower South when the English took leave of Savannah and Charleston.[181] Then there was Sir Guy Carleton's noble insistence on evacuating three thousand escapees who had gathered in New York, resolutely shipping them off to Nova Scotia in the face of vehement, if polite, objections from GW, whose maturation on this issue had not come far beyond some ambivalence over returning every one he caught to their owners.[182]

It was as bad, or maybe worse, for the Indians. It speaks volumes that in spite of having been involved continuously and in most regions of combat during the Revolutionary War, no Indian delegates were invited to participate in the talks at Paris.[183] In fact, American independence was negotiated on the basis of refusing to share the continent with its original inhabitants. George Washington, with his lifelong appetite for western acreage by the thousands, was an archetype of this approach, waging the war along the frontier ultimately on the basis of Indian removal. It's a sad fact, but for all his talk of "homelands" and eventual integration, for GW and for his fellow Americans, the future of the Indians was that they had no future.[184]

But if you happened to be a white American, almost any of the several million who had undertaken this perilous journey of revolution and survived, things turned out great, especially if you were George Washington. Approximately 200,000 actively served in some form of the Revolution's armed forces, and of those around 25,000 died.[185] This was a substantial harvest in blood, but hardly a puddle compared to what would come later, when it became practically the norm for wars associated with revolution to kill millions. We were fortunate, and a lot of that had to do with George Washington. He set the tone; it was his steadfast moderation that kept his colleagues in check and the Revolution under control. At this point, though, he must have felt mostly relief—that and continuing responsibility. There were only a few more things left to do, but they had to be done right.

Job one was disassembling the Continental Army he had built and tended since 1775. On this GW moved as decisively as his statement to Hamilton on April 4, 1783, indicated he would: "I have two reasons for mentioning this matter to you: the one is, that the Army (considering the irritable state it is in, its sufferings & composition) is a dangerous instrument to play with. The other, that every possible means . . . should be essayed to get it disbanded without delay."[186] He ignored his subordinates' petitions to postpone until accounts were settled, and, though he tried to get the men three months' pay before release, when that dwindled to a small parting gift from Congress, he showed no hesitation in letting the process go forward.[187]

By early June regiments from New Jersey, Massachusetts, New Hampshire, and Maryland marched out of camp and headed home with a furlough that was really a discharge. By the end of the year, the Continental Army was basically a memory. He dutifully submitted a plan for a substitute based on a federalized militia, one that Congress rejected, eventually cutting the remnant of the Continental Army to just eighty men.[188] That they dared to do such a thing pointed to one very obvious condition.

In revolutions, peace on paper and peace in reality often have turned out to be two different things. But not in America's. That, too, was Washington's responsibility. Under his final watch peace blanketed the country rapidly and decisively; Dangerland evaporated. Nearly fifty thousand Loyalists would exile themselves,[189] some presumably in fear for their lives, but the great majority stayed and, with the exception of property confiscation, suffered no harm. This would be remembered as a revolution without reprisals, and that stemmed in large part from the way George Washington had waged the war throughout. Certainly it had entailed violence, but he consciously and relentlessly kept it to a minimum consistent with military effectiveness. He was unfailingly more humane than his adversaries, and now his countrymen would reap the benefits of his moderation: real peace.

There remained only to cast aside the mantle of power that had weighed heavily on his shoulders for more than eight years. In early June he sent all the states his famous valedictory, which he began by stating: "The great object, for which I had the honor to hold an Appointment in the service of my Country being accomplished, I am now preparing to resign it into the hands of Congress."[190]

He then proceeded to wax lyrical about the future: "The Citizens of America, placed in the most enviable condition, as the sole Lords and Proprietors of a vast tract of Continent . . . are now, by the late satisfactory pacification, acknowledged to be possessed of absolute freedom and Independancy." Not only that, "but Heaven has crowned all its other blessings by giving a fairer opportunity for political happiness, than any other Nation has ever been favored with [since]. . . . The happy conjuncture of times and circumstances under which our Republic assumed its Rank among the Nations . . . was not laid in the gloomy Age of ignorance and superstition, but in an Epocha when the rights of Mankind were better understood and more clearly defined."[191]

Still, being Washington, he thought to warn his fellow citizens that the future was not assured. "This is the time of their political probation: this is the moment when the eyes of the whole World are turned upon them—This is the moment to establish or ruin their National Character for ever—This is the favorable moment to give such a tone to our federal Government, as will enable it to answer the ends of its institution—or this may be the ill fated moment for relaxing the powers of the Union, annihilating the cement of the Confederation and exposing us to become the sport of European Politicks."[192] Long years of war had made this self-evident to Washington: that the central government had to be able at the very least to raise revenues sufficient to secure its borders and field an army in times of danger. But these were matters for the future, and GW left no doubt he was stepping off the public stage.

The late fall of 1783 turned into his victory tour, capped by a memorable moment of political theater. On November 25 the British finally ended their long goodbye and set sail from what would never again be Redcoat Central. They were immediately followed by Washington, accompanied by thirteen cannon shots, at last taking Manhattan at the head of what was left of his army, soon joined by a crowd of boisterous civilians escorting them to an enthusiastic welcome, though from the thinned-out population of a very damaged city.[193] Still, firmly planted in what amounted to military groundhog heaven, Washington stayed eight event-packed days, the most memorable being his farewell to his officers at Fraunces Tavern. It was an emotional, tear-stained event, but GW must have noticed that of his closest wartime associates, only Steuben and Knox managed to attend.[194] Another reminder that the war and all that it had brought together was finished. Now it was his turn to stage the finale.

Washington left on December 4 and made his slow, well-wisher-clogged way south to Annapolis, where Congress was meeting. He could have just sent them a letter of resignation. But both Washington and the legislators understood that something more dramatic was demanded, a ceremonial demonstration of civilian supremacy over even the most powerful and revered of military commanders.

So on December 23 he stood before them in uniform one last time and delivered a short speech ending with: "Having now finished the work assigned me, I retire from the great theater of Action; and bidding an Affectionate farewell to this August body under whose orders I have so long acted I here offer my Commission and take my leave of all the employments of public life."[195] With that he pulled out the parchment document and handed it to Thomas Mifflin, the same Thomas Mifflin of the Conway affair, as if to show, in some accidental way, there were no hard feelings.

When George III, former Patriot King, heard GW might do such a thing he exclaimed: "If he does that, he will be the greatest man in the world." He did and maybe he was. At least great enough that America would never have, nor think it needed, another generalissimo.

# Conclusion

THE AMERICAN REVOLUTION WAS FAR FROM FINISHED WITH Washington, nor he with it. He would preside over its political phase, the state formation sequel that left us with the government we now have. Yet critically, he did so not as a war leader whose powers were only vaguely bound by necessity and his own good intentions, but as an elected official whose scope of responsibilities, while great, was tightly bound by a clearly defined governmental charter.

Now, it is possible to conceive of GW as a sort of godfather in this process, his hand quietly moving the principals from the inadequate Articles of Confederation toward the Constitutional Convention, presiding over it like a caudillo, then assuming power, elected with lockstep unanimity.

But nobody who has looked into his correspondence would take this interpretation seriously, if for no other reason than Washington plainly took every step back into public life with extreme reluctance. He also agonized over assuming the role of president, and in this case his reasons for not wanting to get involved were much more substantial and more personal.

For nearly six years after the war, he loved being home at Mount Vernon, beneath, as he called it "the vine and fig tree." Actually, through land acquisitions, he turned the place back into a little agricultural empire capable of consuming his vast energies, while Martha reconstructed his ultimate comfort zone, a semi-permeable membrane of hospitality to a constant stream of guests, while preserving his and her own privacy. Meanwhile, practically all of those guests were there because they agreed with George III's revised appraisal based on GW's dramatic resignation from the army; he was the new Cincinnatus, the Roman who twice became dictator only to retreat to his farm. He understood that his retirement had been the crowning act of his career, now the basis for his fame. Washington prized his own reputation, perhaps above all things, and in the end, pleas based on threats to that repute drove him to the Constitutional Convention, to the presidency, and finally to a second term. And in all cases that devotion held him in check and ensured that his honest commitments to republicanism and its corollary—that power stemmed ultimately from the people— were never compromised.

The focus here has been on Washington as generalissimo, and those days were over. Yet the experience had been profound, both for the man and the nation, and even after it was over, its impact lingered. First and foremost, not only was it assumed Washington would be the first president, but there is broad agreement the office itself was designed with him in mind.

For a republican government meticulously based on countervailing powers, the U.S. Constitution gave the chief executive extraordinary latitude in the fields of military and foreign affairs. This never would have happened without Washington and the presumption he would serve as president. And having assumed the office, GW plainly understood things on that basis. As he told Alexander Hamilton in 1794, well into his second term: "The powers of the Executive of the U. States are more definite, & better understood perhaps than those of almost any other Country; and my aim has been, & will continue to be, neither to stretch, nor relax from them."[1]

In this spirit he adopted a frankly hands-on approach to defending and consolidating the newborn state, and behind that was a calculated strategy worthy of a generalissimo. Roller-coaster relations with both France and Britain were certainly the attention getters, especially in Washington's second term, but it's also apparent that his primary objective was always to exert firm American control over the giant block of territory out to the Mississippi ceded to the United States by the Paris Treaty.

It's here that he explored the outer bounds of what might be the appropriate duties of a commander in chief under the Constitution. After two military expeditions into the upper midwest had ended in disaster at the hands of an amalgam of Native American tribes, Washington went into micromanagement mode. Once Congress voted funding for a temporary five-thousand-man Legion of the United States, GW carefully picked its commander—his favorite blunt instrument, Anthony Wayne—and kept an eagle eye on its training and deployment, all of which culminated in 1794 with the victory at Fallen Timbers, followed by the crop devastation that broke Indian power in the area forever.

The legion was expensive, and Washington probably hoped at least part of the cost would be defrayed by a new excise on whiskey, sold to Congress on the grounds it was a luxury tax. It was far from a luxury for farmers on the frontier; it was their only means of concentrating grain

*Washington reviewing militia assembled to
crush the Whiskey Rebellion.*

ATTRIBUTED TO FREDERICK KEMMELMEYER/
METROPOLITAN MUSEUM OF ART

crops sufficiently to earn them hard money. When the farmers of western Pennsylvania went into open revolt in the summer of 1794, and it looked like others to the south might be ready to follow, sixty-two-year-old George Washington not only considered the threat sufficiently serious to call up almost thirteen thousand militia, he put on a uniform and took the field himself; he rode out from Philadelphia in a coach, mounted his trademark white stallion, reviewed the troops, and left.

All of this sounds more than a bit like the sledgehammer anti-insurgent approach of the British, but there was one critical difference. GW left strict instructions that the rebels be dealt with gently as citizens of the United States. Resistance collapsed and there was no further violence. Two were tried and condemned to hang; Washington pardoned them both. Even in the face of a threat he considered critical enough to militarize himself, Washington behaved with emblematic moderation. He simply wanted to overawe and deter; it was all an exercise in political theater. He might have been ready to shed blood; but that was never his objective. He always minimized the violence, and that was at the heart of his genius as a revolutionary.

George Washington's political education had taken place during a time of revolution; he came to embody that revolution as its military leader, and it was at the heart of his life experience. For a man who learned by doing there was no escaping it. They were all revolutionaries, all the Founding Fathers, and each had to make his own accommodation with the new conditions of peace and consolidation at home and revolution abroad.

One elemental dynamic in this process was the growth of parties and their accommodation in the new constitutional system. It's interesting that it was Jefferson who said "If I could not go to heaven but with a party, I would not go there at all"[2] but then went on to found one. For Washington they were always "factions," antithetical forces threatening to tear apart the fabric of governance. Revolutions, almost by definition, are based on a single version of reality; believing anything else constitutes betrayal. Washington never got beyond that stage. Moreover, as he aged, it predisposed him to see his own personal view as the only politically correct one.

On the other hand, it was his commitment to revolutionary ideology that ultimately did not allow him to escape the contradictions imposed by owning other human beings. Unlike Jefferson, whose disembodied intellect permitted him to hate slavery while exploiting his slaves, Washington, because he learned through experience, found himself compelled to try to align his thoughts with his deeds. But given his prejudices and the momentum of a lifetime, the process was glacially slow. He plainly disliked slavery as an institution and wanted an end to it. But he understood the cost of southern allegiance to the Union was slavery, so he never did anything about it politically. Personally, he hated the system's inefficiency, but many of the slaves were Martha's, so he put off freeing them indefinitely. It was only in his will that George Washington brought himself to emancipate the hundreds of people he had for so long tyrannized. It's not much of a badge of honor, but it did put him at the last possible moment on the right side of America's greatest moral and political divide.

George Washington's steadfastness flattered him when he looked across the Atlantic and considered the fate of revolution in other hands. Already worried about France in the early summer of 1788, he warned Lafayette: "If I were to advise, I would say that great moderation should be used on both sides," but he may have already sensed that events were out of control, telling Madison earlier, "Liberty, when it begins to take root, is a plant of rapid growth."[3] After the Bastille had been stormed and Washington had been sent the key, he again admonished Lafayette that "the tumultuous populace of large cities are ever to be dreaded [for their] indiscriminate violence" and warned of the possibility of their being employed by "wicked and designing men . . . who will not hesitate in destroying public tranquility to gain a favorite point."[4]

Washington reacted with horror as excess piled upon bloody excess until he came to see the French Revolution as almost a visitation of hell, destined for tyranny and warfare, the exact opposite of what he wanted for America. Unfortunately, it was that version of revolution, not his own, that would mostly leave its bloody footprints smeared across the next two centuries. But that wasn't his fault. He remains, across all that time, a standard of how to bring about revolutionary change without killing too many people in the process. It's hard to say that's not his proudest legacy.

# ACKNOWLEDGMENTS

*REVOLUTIONARY*, BOTH ITS RESEARCH AND ITS WRITING, BEN-efitted greatly from a number of key intercessions. I originally told my editor Jonathan Jao that I wanted to attempt a military biography of a truly important American, and since the only soldier available on Mount Rushmore was George Washington, it had to be him. "Fine, but use your knowledge of irregular warfare to broaden your perspective and tell a more multidimensional tale."

I've seldom had better advice.

Until I ate lunch with Peter Onuf, a friend and truly eminent scholar of the period. Using the working title *George Washington: Accidental Insurgent*, I began to explain my concept for the book, when he interrupted: "Uh, Bob, he wasn't an insurgent. The revolution was an accomplished fact by the time he became General George, the leader of a sovereign state's army, or that's what they wanted everybody to believe." A humbling but vital course correction. Thanks, Peter.

As the project progressed, Jonathan moved to greener editorial pastures, and GW and I were eventually inherited by Molly Turpin, who adopted us both as if we were her own. Her energy and professional competence definitely made this a better book, while her wise-beyond-her-years advice smoothed the production process and kept everything moving in the right direction. Thanks, Molly.

Ditto for my agent, Henry Thayer, who did all the things agents are supposed to do with the contagious enthusiasm of a born problem solver. You and Molly were at your best in the debate over the title; but I can always depend on you for good advice and savvy negotiating.

On the academic side, I also owe a considerable debt of gratitude to Ed Lengel, although not the one I originally thought. At the time I began my research, Ed was the director of the massive Washington Papers project at the University of Virginia, and I introduced myself hoping he would help guide me through what promised to be a lot of paper. Instead, he pointed me toward a bonanza of electrons, the National Archives' Founders Online website. This is not only a wonderful resource for scholars, but a really user-friendly environment for people interested in learning about the Founding Fathers in their own words. So, thanks also, U.S. government.

Andrew Jackson O'Shaughnessy, whose book *The Men Who Lost America* provided me with a number of important insights into British thinking and behavior, took time from his busy schedule to talk to me at length on the topic, a session I found particularly productive.

I also want to thank my colleagues at the Naval Postgraduate School, Michael Freeman, Doug Borer, and Hy Rothstein, for giving the manuscript careful reads and a number of Why didn't I think of that? comments.

Closer to home, Sterling Deal, friend of forty-five years, gave chapters good reads as they were produced, along with much appreciated words of encouragement.

Still closer, wife Benjie was the first to hear every word. So as Director of Quality Control and Author Maintenance, along with a whole lot more, it's pretty obvious I can't thank you enough.

# NOTES

INTRODUCTION

1. Paul K. Longmore, *The Invention of George Washington* (Berkeley: University of California Press, 1988), 165.
2. Ron Chernow, *Washington: A Life* (New York: Penguin Books, 2010), 166.
3. John Shy, *A People Numerous and Armed: Reflections on the Military Struggle for American Independence* (Ann Arbor: University of Michigan Press, 1990), 175.
4. Andrew Jackson O'Shaughnessy, *The Men Who Lost America: British Leadership, the American Revolution, and the Fate of Empire* (New Haven, Conn.: Yale University Press, 2013), 115; Robert Middlekauff, *The Glorious Cause: The American Revolution 1763–1789* (New York: Oxford University Press, 2005), 254, 565; Stephen Brumwell, *George Washington: Gentleman Warrior* (New York: Quercus Press, 2012), 186–87.
5. John Adams to Hezekiah Niles, February 13, 1818, Papers of John Adams, Founders Online, National Archives.
6. Bernard Bailyn, "The Central Themes of the American Revolution: An Interpretation," in *Essays on the American Revolution*, ed. Stephen G. Kurtz and James H. Hutson (New York: W. W. Norton, 1973), 7–9.
7. Bernard Bailyn, *The Ideological Origins of the American Revolution* (Cambridge, Mass.: Belknap Press of Harvard University Press, 1992), xii.
8. GW to Bryan Fairfax, July 4, 1774, Papers of George Washington, Founders Online, National Archives, hereinafter cited as "GWP, Founders Online."
9. Kathleen DuVal, *Independence Lost: Lives at the Edge of the American Revolution* (New York: Random House, 2015), 63.
10. O'Shaughnessy, *Men Who Lost America*, 21–22, 132.

11. A letter from Philadelphia in 1775 warned Londoners "the Rage Militaire, as the French call a passion for arms, has taken possession of the Whole Continent," quoted in *Letters on the American Revolution, 1774–1776*, ed. Margaret Wheeler Willard (Boston: Literary Licensing, 1925), 101–2.

12. Middlekauff, *Glorious Cause*, 563–64.

13. Ibid., 36.

14. Matthew H. Spring, *With Zeal and Bayonets Only: The British Army on Campaign in North America, 1775–1783* (Norman: University of Oklahoma Press, 2008), 33; Bowler, *Logistics and the Failure of British Army in America: 1775–1783* (Princeton, N.J.: Princeton University Press, 1975), 6–7.

15. Cited in Alexander Rose, *Washington's Spies: The Story of America's First Spy Ring* (New York: Bantam Books, 2006), 55.

16. Middlekauff, *Glorious Cause*, 53, 145, 233.

17. Howard H. Peckham, ed., *Toll of Independence: Engagements and Battle Casualties of the American Revolution* (Chicago: University of Chicago Press, 1974), 132.

18. Carol Berkin, *Revolutionary Mothers: Women in the Struggle for American Independence* (New York: Knopf, 2005), 39.

19. James Thomas Flexner, *Washington: The Indispensable Man* (Boston: Little, Brown, 1974).

20. Chernow, *Washington: A Life*, xx–xxi; Carrie R. Barratt and Ellen Gross Miles, *Gilbert Stuart* (New York: Metropolitan Museum of Art, 2004), 137.

21. Longmore, *Invention of George Washington*, 51–52.

22. Alexander Hamilton to Tobias Lear, January 2, 1800, Alexander Hamilton Papers, Founders Online, National Archives.

23. See, for example, GW to George William Fairfax, July 10, 1783, GWP, Founders Online; Charles Royster, *A Revolutionary People at War: The Continental Army and American Character, 1775–1783* (Chapel Hill: University of North Carolina Press, 1979), 340.

24. Chernow, *Washington: A Life*, 243.

25. Don Higginbotham, *Daniel Morgan: Revolutionary Rifleman* (Chapel Hill: University of North Carolina Press, 1961), viii, 4.

26. "Memorandum on General Officers," March 9, 1792, GWP, Founders Online.

27. Joseph J. Ellis, *His Excellency: George Washington* (New York: Knopf, 2004), 86.

28. Cited in Longmore, *Invention of George Washington*, 29. This occurred to Washington early, as he marveled at his own survival of the Braddock disaster in 1755.

29. Flexner, *Indispensable Man*, 36–37.

30. Isaac Weld, Jr., "Early Descriptions Ante 1800," ca. 1796, Mount Vernon Library, cited in Chernow, *Washington: A Life*, 456.

## CHAPTER 1: THE GENTRIFICATION OF GEORGE

1. Ellis, *His Excellency,* 8; Brumwell, *Gentleman Warrior,* 15–18.
2. Ellis, *His Excellency,* 7; Longmore, *Invention of George Washington,* 1.
3. Flexner, *Indispensable Man,* 4.
4. Edward G. Lengel, *General George Washington: A Military Life* (New York: Random House, 2005), 8.
5. Chernow, *Washington: A Life,* 11, 157, 395–97.
6. Brumwell, *Gentleman Warrior,* 23.
7. John T. Phillips, ed., *George Washington's Rules of Civility: Complete with the Original French Text and New French to English Translations* (Leesburg, Va.: Goose Creek Productions, 2002), 11–12.
8. Ibid., 115.
9. William Fairfax to Lawrence Washington, September 9–10, 1746, in Moncure D. Conway, *Barons of the Potomack and Rappahannock* (New York: Grolier Club, 1892), 238.
10. Joseph Ball to Mary Washington, May 19, 1747, Joseph Ball Letterbook, George Washington Papers, Library of Congress, hereinafter cited as "GWP, Library of Congress."
11. Flexner, *Indispensable Man,* p. 6, describes George William as having "been beaten into a cringing weakling."
12. Ellis, *His Excellency,* 11–12.
13. Rowland Berthoff and John M. Murrin, "Feudalism, Communalism, and the Yeoman Freeholder: The American Revolution Considered as a Social Accident," in Kurtz and Hutson, *Essays on the American Revolution,* 266.
14. Flexner, *Indispensable Man,* 6.
15. Lengel, *General George Washington,* 13.
16. George Washington, "A Journal of My Journey Over the Mountains [. . .]," March 1748, GWP, Founders Online.
17. Ibid., journal entry, March 23, 1748.
18. Robert Stewart to GW, September 28, 1759, W. W. Abbot, Dorothy Twohig, and Philander D. Chase, eds., *The Papers of George Washington: Colonial Series* (Charlottesville, Va., University of Virginia Press, 1983) 6, 343.
19. GW, "Journal of My Journey," journal entry, April 4, 1748.
20. Ibid., journal entry, April 9, 1748.
21. See, for example, Ellis, *His Excellency,* 36–37. "Only someone dedicated to denying the full import of this evidence could reject the conclusion that Washington was passionately in love with Sally Fairfax."
22. Lengel, *General George Washington,* 15.
23. Ibid.
24. Ibid., 14–15.
25. Middlekauff, *Glorious Cause,* 58.

26. Lengel, *General George Washington*, 16.

27. GW, diary entry, November 4, 1751, Founders Online, National Archives.

28. *The Diaries of George Washington*, ed. Donald Jackson and Dorothy Twohig, 6 vols. (Charlottesville: University of Virginia Press, 1976–79), 1:82. Hereinafter cited as *Diaries of GW.*

29. Brumwell, *Gentleman Warrior*, 33.

30. *Diaries of GW*, 1:34, 114.

31. Cited in Fred Anderson, ed., *George Washington Remembers: Reflections on the French and Indian War* (Lanham, Md.: Rowman and Littlefield, 2004), 71.

32. Lengel, *General George Washington*, 16.

33. For background, see GW to Robert Dinwiddie, June 10, 1752, GWP, Founders Online.

34. Lengel, *General George Washington*, 17–18.

35. Ibid., 19–20.

36. Daniel K. Richter, *Facing East from Indian Country: A Native History of Early America* (Cambridge, Mass.: Harvard University Press, 2001), 168.

37. Earl of Holderness (Secretary of State) to Robert Dinwiddie, August 28, 1753, British National Archives, Colonial Office, 5–11, fols. 11–15; Brumwell, *Gentleman Warrior*, 37.

38. Journal of Governor's Council, cited in Longmore, *Invention of George Washington*, 18–19.

39. "Instructions from Robert Dinwiddie," October 30, 1753, GWP, Founders Online.

40. Chernow, *Washington: A Life*, 32.

41. Lengel, *General George Washington*, 20; Brumwell, *Gentleman Warrior*, 38.

42. *Diaries of GW*, 1:142.

43. Lengel, *General George Washington*, 26.

44. Christopher Gist, *Christopher Gist's Journals with Historical, Geographical and Ethnological Notes and Biographies of His Contemporaries*, ed. William Darlington (Pittsburgh: J. R. Weldin, 1893), 84.

45. Ibid., 85.

46. "Journey to the French Commandant: Narrative," 31, GWP, Founders Online.

47. Ibid.

48. Ibid.

49. GW to Richard Corbin, February–March 1754, GWP, Founders Online.

50. Robert Dinwiddie to GW, January 1754, "Instructs. To be observ'd by Majr Geor Washington on the Expeidtn to the Ohio," GWP, Founders Online.

51. Robert Dinwiddie to GW, June 1754, fn. 4, GWP, Founders Online.

52. GW to Robert Dinwiddie, March 20, 1754, GWP, Founders Online.

53. Brumwell, *Gentleman Warrior*, 50–51; Flexner, *Indispensable Man*, 15.

54. Lengel, *General George Washington,* 32–33.
55. GW to Horatio Sharpe, April 24, 1754, GWP, Founders Online.
56. Robert Dinwiddie to GW, May 15, 1754, GWP, Founders Online.
57. GW to Robert Dinwiddie, May 18, 1757, GWP, Founders Online.
58. Lengel, *General George Washington,* 34.
59. GW to Robert Dinwiddie, May 29, 1754, GWP, Founders Online.
60. Fred Anderson, *Crucible of War: The Seven Years' War and the Fate of Empire in British North America, 1754–1766* (New York: Random House, 2000), 52–59; Ellis, *His Excellency,* 13.
61. GW to Robert Dinwiddie, May 29, 1754, GWP, Founders Online.
62. GW to John Washington, May 31, 1754, GWP, Founders Online.
63. Cited in Lengel, *General George Washington,* 39.
64. Cited in Chernow, *Washington: A Life,* 45.
65. GW to Robert Dinwiddie, May 29, 1754, GWP, Founders Online.
66. Longmore, *Invention of George Washington,* 20.
67. Lengel, *General George Washington,* 40.
68. Longmore, *Invention of George Washington,* 22–23.
69. Lengel, *General George Washington,* 41.
70. Ibid., 42.
71. Flexner, *Indispensable Man,* 17.
72. "Account by George Washington and James Mackay of the Capitulation of Fort Necessity," July 19, 1754, GWP.
73. Brumwell, *Gentleman Warrior,* 62.
74. Robert Dinwiddie to GW, June 27, 1754, GWP, Founders Online.
75. John Robinson to GW, September 15, 1754; GW to John Robinson, October 23, 1754, GWP, Founders Online.
76. Authorities cited in Longmore, *Invention of George Washington,* 23.
77. Robert Dinwiddie to GW, August 1, 1754, GWP, Founders Online.
78. GW to John Augustine Washington, August 2, 1755, GWP, 1:206–8.
79. GW to William Fitzhugh, November 15, 1754, GWP, Founders Online.
80. Brumwell, *Gentleman Warrior,* 18.
81. Lengel, *General George Washington,* 54.
82. Ibid., 49.
83. Ibid., 50.
84. Brumwell, *Gentleman Warrior,* 69.
85. Ellis, *His Excellency,* 20.
86. Longmore, *Invention of George Washington,* 26–27.
87. GW to Fitzhugh, November 15, 1754, GWP, Founders Online.
88. GW to Robert Orme, March 15, 1755, GWP, Founders Online.
89. GW to John Augustine Washington, May, 14, 1755, Founders Online.
90. GW to John Augustine Washington, May 28, 1755, Founders Online.
91. GW to Thomas Lord Fairfax, May 6, 1755, GWP, Founders Online.

92. GW to Sarah Cary Fairfax, April 30, 1755, GWP, Founders Online.

93. GW to "Sally," 1749–50, GWP, Founders Online.

94. Cited in Flexner, *Indispensable Man*, 23.

95. Don Higginbotham, *George Washington and the American Military Tradition* (Athens: University of Georgia Press, 1985), 15.

96. GW to John Augustine Washington, June 28, 1755, GWP, Founders Online.

97. Walter Isaacson, *Benjamin Franklin: An American Life* (New York: Simon & Schuster, 2004), 166.

98. Brumwell, *Gentleman Warrior*, 73.

99. Ibid., 76.

100. GW to Robert Dinwiddie, July 18, 1755, GWP, Founders Online.

101. Higginbotham, *George Washington and the American Military Tradition*, 13.

102. Brumwell, *Gentleman Warrior*, 79.

103. David Humphreys, *Life of General Washington* (Athens: University of Georgia Press, 2006), 18.

104. Longmore, *Invention of George Washington*, 31–32.

105. Lengel, *General George Washington*, 60; Brumwell, *Gentleman Warrior*, 80; Ellis, *His Excellency*, 22.

106. Cited in Chernow, *Washington: A Life*, 61.

107. Flexner, *Indispensable Man*, 28.

108. GW to Adam Stephen, September 11, 1755, GWP, Founders Online; Brumwell, *Gentleman Warrior*, 93–94.

109. GW to Andrew Lewis, September 6, 1755, GWP, Founders Online.

110. GW to Christopher Gist, October 10, 1755, GWP, Founders Online.

111. See, for example, GW to Robert Dinwiddie, April 24, 1756; May 3, 1756, GWP, Founders Online.

112. GW to Adam Stephen, November 18, 1755, fn. 3, GWP, Founders Online.

113. Robert Dinwiddie to GW, January 22, 1756, GWP, Founders Online.

114. Longmore, *Invention of George Washington*, 37–38.

115. Brumwell, *Gentleman Warrior*, 95–96.

116. GW to Robert Dinwiddie, July 1, 1756, GWP, Founders Online.

117. Higginbotham, *George Washington and the American Military Tradition*, 34–37.

118. Robert Dinwiddie to GW, February 2, 1757, GWP, Founders Online.

119. Brumwell, *Gentleman Warrior*, 106.

120. Higginbotham, *George Washington and the American Military Tradition*, 32–33.

121. Middlekauff, *Glorious Cause*, 8.

122. "Instructions to Company Captains, Fort Loudoun," July 29, 1757, GWP, 4:341–45.

123. Ibid.

124.  See, for example, GW to Robert Dinwiddie, December 4, 1756; July 11, 1757, GWP, Founders Online.

125.  GW to Robert Dinwiddie, September 17, 1757, GWP, Founders Online.

126.  GW to Robert Dinwiddie, August 3, 1757, GWP, Founders Online.

127.  Robert Stewart to GW, September 28, 1759, GWP, 6:343.

128.  GW to Robert Dinwiddie, June 12, 1757, GWP, Founders Online.

129.  GW to Robert Dinwiddie, April 22, 1756, GWP, Founders Online.

130.  Flexner, *Indispensable Man*, 32.

131.  Brumwell, *Gentleman Warrior*, 119.

132.  GW to Sally Fairfax, September 12, 1758; September 25, 1758, GWP, Founders Online.

133.  John Forbes to John Blair (acting Virginia governor), March 20, 1758; cited in Lengel, *General George Washington*, 70.

134.  Ibid.

135.  Ellis, *His Excellency*, 32.

136.  GW to John Robinson, September 1, 1758, cited in Lengel, *General George Washington*, 72.

137.  Forbes to Bouquet, September 4, 1758, cited in Brumwell, *Gentleman Warrior*, 133.

138.  Flexner, *Indispensable Man*, 34; Lengel, *General George Washington*, 75.

139.  Lengel, *General George Washington*, 73.

140.  Flexner, *Indispensable Man*, 34.

141.  Brumwell, *Gentleman Warrior*, 148.


CHAPTER 2: LIVING LARGE

1.  Brumwell, *Gentleman Warrior*, 156; see also, for example, Ellis, *His Excellency*, 40.

2.  Flexner, *Indispensable Man*, 39.

3.  GW to Robert Cary & Company, September 20, 1759, GWP, Founders Online; Chernow, *Washington: A Life*, 97.

4.  GW to Eliza Powel, March 26, 1797, GWP, Founders Online.

5.  GW to Sally Fairfax, May 16, 1798, GWP, Founders Online.

6.  Cited in Chernow, *Washington: A Life*, xxi.

7.  Douglas Southall Freeman, *George Washington* (New York: Charles Scribner, 1948), 2, 283; see also Brumwell, *Gentleman Warrior*, 157.

8.  Chernow, *Washington: A Life*, 92.

9.  Flexner, *Indispensable Man*, 51.

10.  Chernow, *Washington: A Life*, 122.

11.  Ellis, *His Excellency*, 49.

12.  Thorstein Veblen, *The Theory of the Leisure Class* (New York: Macmillan, 1899).

13. See "How Mount Vernon Grew," in Flexner, *Indispensable Man*, 45.

14. Ellis, *His Excellency*, 41.

15. An excellent selection of invoices and correspondence between George Washington and Robert Cary & Company are available at the National Archive's Founders Online. See in particular GW to Robert Cary & Company, September 20, 1759; August 10, 1760; September 28, 1760; April 3, 1761; May 28, 1762; September 18, 1762.

16. "Invoice from Robert Cary & Company," September 28, 1768, GWP, Founders Online.

17. GW to Robert Cary & Company, January 25, 1769, GWP, Founders Online.

18. GW to Robert Cary & Company, May 1, 1764, GWP, Founders Online.

19. Gordon S. Wood, *The Radicalism of the American Revolution* (New York: Knopf, 1992), 134.

20. Ellis, *His Excellency*, 52–53.

21. Longmore, *Invention of George Washington*, 85.

22. Middlekauff, *Glorious Cause*, 61–62. The exact figures as of January 6, 1763, were £122,603,336 with an interest of £4,409,797.

23. Ibid., 23.

24. Jack P. Greene, "An Uneasy Connection: An Analysis of the Preconditions of the American Revolution," in Kurtz and Hutson, *Essays on the American Revolution*, 46.

25. Middlekauff, *Glorious Cause*, 22–24.

26. Ibid., 28.

27. Longmore, *Invention of George Washington*, 68.

28. Ibid., 103.

29. Middlekauff, *Glorious Cause*, 55.

30. Longmore, *Invention of George Washington*, 120.

31. Flexner, *Indispensable Man*, 242–43.

32. Longmore, *Invention of George Washington*, 120–21; Bailyn, "Central Themes of the American Revolution," 7–9.

33. Trenchard, quoted in Bailyn, *Ideological Origins of the American Revolution*, 61–62.

34. Bailyn, "Central Themes of the American Revolution," 9.

35. Bolingbroke, cited in Longmore, *Invention of George Washington*, 184.

36. Longmore, *Invention of George Washington*, 121.

37. GW to William Crawford, September 17, 1767, GWP, Founders Online.

38. Ellis, *His Excellency*, 55–56; Shy, *People Numerous and Armed*, 100–101.

39. Ellis, *His Excellency*, 56.

40. Brumwell, *Gentleman Warrior*, 185; Ellis, *His Excellency*, 58.

41. GW to Thomas Lewis, February 17, 1774, GWP, Founders Online.

42. Cited in Longmore, *Invention of George Washington*, 67.

43. Richard R. Beeman, *Patrick Henry: A Biography* (New York: McGraw-Hill, 1974), 13–22.

44. Excerpted from Virginia Resolves as printed in *The Journal of the House of Burgesses,* cited in Middlekauff, *Glorious Cause,* 84.

45. GW to Robert Cary & Company, September 20, 1765, GWP, Founders Online.

46. Middlekauff, *Glorious Cause,* 86.

47. *New London Gazette,* September 20, 1765, reprinted in Bernard Bailyn, "Religion and Revolution."

48. Middlekauff, *Glorious Cause,* 134.

49. Longmore, *Invention of George Washington,* 100.

50. Shy, *People Numerous and Armed,* 92–93.

51. GW to Robert Cary, July 21 1766, GWP, Founders Online.

52. Of recent attempts to come up with a general theory of revolution, Ted Robert Gurr's "relative deprivation" model has proved most influential and long-lasting. See Ted Robert Gurr, "Why Men Rebel Redux: How Valid Are Its Arguments 40 Years On?" *E-International Relations,* November 2011.

53. Wood, *Radicalism of the American Revolution,* 169.

54. Ibid., 51.

55. Bailyn, *Ideological Origins of the American Revolution,* 47.

56. Ibid.

57. Email from Bernard Bailyn, September 20, 2014.

58. Middlekauff, *Glorious Cause,* 154–55.

59. Charles F. Hoban, ed. *Pennsylvania Archives,* 8th ser., vol. 7 (Harrisburg, Penn.: J. Severns, 1935), 6189–92.

60. Ellis, *His Excellency,* 61.

61. Longmore, *Invention of George Washington,* 96.

62. GW to George William Fairfax, June 27, 1770, fn. 1, 2, GWP, Founders Online.

63. Berkin, *Revolutionary Mothers,* 17–18.

64. Middlekauff, *Glorious Cause,* 187.

65. Longmore, *Invention of George Washington,* 119.

66. Chernow, *Washington: A Life,* 146.

67. GW to George Mason, April 5, 1769, GWP, Founders Online.

68. Cited in Brumwell, *Gentleman Warrior,* 180.

69. Ibid., 181.

70. Douglas S. Freeman, *George Washington: A Biography,* 7 vols. (New York: Scribner, 1948), 3:292.

71. Chernow, *Washington: A Life,* 166.

72. Middlekauff, *Glorious Cause,* 53.

73. Greene, "An Uneasy Connection," 42.

74. Middlekauff, *Glorious Cause,* 56, 78–80.
75. Cited in Middlekauff, *Glorious Cause,* 115.
76. Middlekauff, *Glorious Cause,* 233.
77. Richards J. Heuer, *Psychology of Intelligence Analysis* (Washington, D.C.: Center for the Study of Intelligence, 1999), 33.
78. Bailyn, "Central Themes of the American Revolution," 13.
79. Brumwell, *Gentleman Warrior,* 183
80. Ibid.
81. Middlekauff, *Glorious Cause,* 234.
82. Ibid.
83. Cited in Shy, *People Numerous and Armed,* 102–3.

CHAPTER 3: RAGE MILITAIRE

1. Adolf Hitler, Speech, Munich Exhibition Halls, March 14, 1936, Max Domarus, *Hitler: Speeches and Proclamations 1932–1945,* 4 vols. (Wauconda, Ill.: Bolchazy-Carducci Publishers, 1992), 2:790.
2. Chernow, *Washington: A Life,* 162.
3. GW to Robert Carey & Co., November 10, 1779, GWP, Founders Online.
4. GW to Bryan Fairfax, July 20; August 24, 1774, GWP, Founders Online.
5. Longmore, *Invention of George Washington,* 124–25, 127.
6. Fairfax Resolves, #12, George Washington Papers, Library of Congress Digital Collection.
7. Cited in James MacGregor Burns and Susan Dunn, *George Washington* (New York: Times Books, 2004), 21.
8. Cited in Patricia Brady, *Martha Washington: An American Life* (New York: Penguin, 2006), 92.
9. Middlekauff, *Glorious Cause,* 240–42.
10. Longmore, *Invention of George Washington,* 137.
11. Middlekauff, *Glorious Cause,* 247.
12. Ibid.
13. Cited in Longmore, *Invention of George Washington,* 138.
14. Ibid.
15. Ibid.
16. Shy, *People Numerous and Armed,* 175.
17. Middlekauff, *Glorious Cause,* 253.
18. Worthington C. Ford et al., eds., *Journal of the Continental Congress, 1774–1789* (Washington, D.C., 1904–27) 1:5–80.
19. Longmore, *Invention of George Washington,* 143–44.
20. Ibid., 145.
21. Middlekauff, *Glorious Cause,* 254.
22. Brumwell, *Gentleman Warrior,* 186–87.

23. Robert McKenzie to GW, September 13, 1774, GWP, Founders Online.

24. GW to Robert Mckenzie, October 9, 1774, GWP, Founders Online.

25. Ellis, *His Excellency*, 65.

26. Middlekauff, *Glorious Cause*, 263.

27. Longmore, *Invention of George Washington*, 147.

28. Ibid., 149.

29. Chernow, *Washington: A Life*, 175.

30. Ibid., 182.

31. Shy, *People Numerous and Armed*, 139.

32. Flexner, *Indispensable Man*, 63.

33. GW to John Jay, April 14, 1779, GWP, Founders Online.

34. Middlekauff, *Glorious Cause*, 565–66.

35. Shy, *People Numerous and Armed*, 151, 154, 176; Scott D. Aiken, *The Swamp Fox: Lessons in Leadership from the Partisan Campaigns of Francis Marion* (Annapolis, Md.: Naval Institute Press, 2012), 21.

36. O'Shaughnessy, *Men Who Lost America*, 11.

37. Middlekauff, *Glorious Cause*, 563–64.

38. Ibid., 273.

39. Ibid., 274.

40. Peckham, *Toll of Independence*, 3.

41. GW to George William Fairfax, May 31, 1775, GWP, Founders Online.

42. Lengel, *General George Washington*, 88.

43. Longmore, *Invention of George Washington*, 182; Chernow, *Washington: A Life*, 183.

44. Longmore, *Invention of George Washington*, 161; Middlekauff, *Glorious Cause*, 286.

45. GW to Joseph Warren, President Pro Tem, Provincial Convention of Massachusetts, June 2, 1775, Avalon Project, Yale Law School.

46. Ford, *Journal of the Continental Congress*, 2:56.

47. Ibid., 2:68–70; Middlekauff, *Glorious Cause*, 286.

48. Brumwell, *Gentleman Warrior*, 192–93.

49. They include James Thomas Flexner and Douglas Southall Freeman.

50. See, for example, Lengel, *General George Washington*, 86; Ellis, *His Excellency*, 68; Chernow, *Washington: A Life*, 185–86.

51. Longmore, *Invention of George Washington*, 171–72.

52. "Washington Accepts His Appointment as Commander of Continental Army," June 16, 1775, GWP, Library of Congress.

53. GW to Martha Washington, June 18, 1775, GWP, Founders Online.

54. Ellis, *His Excellency*, 71.

55. Higginbotham, *George Washington and the American Military Tradition*, 43.

56. Chernow, *Washington: A Life*, 237.

57. Middlekauff, *Glorious Cause*, 269.

58. O'Shaughnessy, *Men Who Lost America*, 83.
59. Cited in Shy, *People Numerous and Armed*, 110–11.
60. Paul David Nelson, *Francis Rawdon-Hastings, Marquess of Hastings: Soldier, Peer of the Realm, Governor-General of India* (Madison, N.J.: Fairleigh Dickinson University Press, 2005), 26–27.
61. Benjamin Hichborn to John Adams, November 25, 1775, Papers of John Adams, Founders Online, National Archives.
62. GW to Samuel Washington, July 20, 1775, GWP, Founders Online.
63. Lengel, *General George Washington*, 105.
64. O'Shaughnessy, *Men Who Lost America*, 86.
65. Cited in Alexander Rose, *American Rifle: A Biography* (New York: Delacorte, 2008), 46.
66. Edmond S. Morgan, "Conflict and Consensus in the American Revolution," in Kurtz and Hutson, *Essays on the American Revolution*, 303, 304–5.
67. Middlekauff, *Glorious Cause*, 287.
68. Cited in Rose, *American Rifle*, 46.
69. GW to Philip Schuyler, July 28, 1775, GWP, Founders Online.
70. Middlekauff, *Glorious Cause*, 528.
71. See, for example, GW to Charles Lee, May 9, 1776, GWP, Founders Online; Chernow, *Washington: A Life*, 191.
72. James Thacher, *Military Journal of the American Revolution* (Plymouth, Mass.: First Rate Publishers, 1823; 2014 reprint), July 20, 1775.
73. Chernow, *Washington: A Life*, 195.
74. GW to Philip Schuyler, July 28, 1775.
75. Cited in Flexner, *Indispensable Man*, 68.
76. Thacher, *Military Journal*, August 1775.
77. Trask, cited in George Athan Billias, *General John Glover and His Marblehead Mariners* (New York: Henry Holt, 1960).
78. Ibid.
79. Lengel, *General George Washington*, xxviii.
80. Don Higginbotham, *Daniel Morgan: Revolutionary Rifleman* (Chapel Hill: University of North Carolina Press, 1961), 119.
81. GW to John Hancock, March 18, 1777, GWP, Founders Online.
82. Terry Goldway, *Washington's General: Nathanael Greene and the Triumph of the American Revolution* (New York: Henry Holt, 2005), 42.
83. Ibid., 196.
84. John Sullivan to GW, August 2, 1775, GWP, Founders Online.
85. Middlekauff, *Glorious Cause*, 310.
86. Shy, *People Numerous and Armed*, 114.
87. Middlekauff, *Glorious Cause*, 302.
88. Ibid., 525.
89. Lengel, *General George Washington*, 113.

90. Roger F. Duncan, *Coastal Main: A Maritime History* (New York: Norton, 1992), 217.

91. Joseph Conforti, *Creating Portland: History and Place in Northern New England* (Durham, N.H.: University of New Hampshire Press, 2007), 60; Thacher, *Military Journal,* August 1779; Brumwell, *Gentleman Warrior,* 215.

92. Middlekauff, *Glorious Cause,* 544–55.

93. GW to Philip Schuyler, October 26, 1775, GWP, Founders Online.

94. Bowler, *Logistics and the Failure of the British Army,* 150.

95. GW to Joseph Reed, November 30, 1775, GWP, Founders Online.

96. Flexner, *Indispensable Man,* 68–69; Lengel, *General George Washington,* 109; GW to Jonathan Trumbull, February 8, 1776, GWP, Founders Online.

97. GW to John Sullivan, January 10, 1776, GWP, Founders Online.

98. Ellis, *His Excellency,* 86; see also Elizabeth A. Fenn, *Pox Americana: The Great Smallpox Epidemic of 1775–82* (New York: Hill and Wang, 2001).

99. Middlekauff, *Glorious Cause,* 532.

100. Lengel, *General George Washington,* 114.

101. Longmore, *Invention of George Washington,* 191.

102. Ellis, *His Excellency,* 76–77.

103. Ibid., 83.

104. GW to Lund Washington, August 20, 1775, GWP, Founders Online.

105. Ellis, *His Excellency,* 84; Brumwell, *Gentleman Warrior,* 218.

106. GW to Joseph Reed, November 28, 1775, GWP, Founders Online.

107. Chernow, *Washington: A Life,* 213.

108. GW to John Hancock, January 4, 1776, GWP, Founders Online.

109. Chernow, *Washington: A Life,* 207; Lengel, *General George Washington,* 115.

110. Middlekauff, *Glorious Cause,* 314.

111. GW to Philip Schuyler, January 18, 1776, GWP, Founders Online.

112. O'Shaughnessy, *Men Who Lost America,* 141; see also, for example, GW to Philip Schuyler, October 4, 1775, GWP, Founders Online.

113. Higginbotham, *Morgan,* 62.

114. Middlekauff, *Glorious Cause,* 311.

115. Higginbotham, *Morgan,* 38.

116. GW to Benedict Arnold, December 5, 1775, GWP, Founders Online; Brumwell, *Gentleman Warrior,* 218.

117. Higginbotham, *Morgan,* 41.

118. Jeremiah Greenman, *Diary of a Common Soldier in the American Revolution, 1775–1783: An Annotated Edition of the Military Journal of Jeremiah Greenman,* ed. Robert C. Bray and Paul E. Bushnell (DeKalb, Ill.: Northern Illinois University Press, 1978), 23.

119. Middlekauff, *Glorious Cause,* 313.

120. Ellis, *His Excellency,* 86.

121. Higginbotham, *Morgan,* 47–48.

122.  Berkin, *Revolutionary Mothers,* 70.
123.  Higginbotham, *Morgan,* 25.
124.  Ellis, *His Excellency,* 81.
125.  Chernow, *Washington: A Life,* 214–15.
126.  GW to Joseph Reed, January 31, 1776, GWP, Founders Online.
127.  Lengel, *General George Washington,* 118–19.
128.  Gates, cited in ibid., 120.
129.  GW to John Hancock, February 26, 1776; GW to Philip Schuyler, February 27, 1776, GWP, Founders Online.
130.  Lieutenant Colonel Rufus Putnam to GW, February 11, 1776, GWP, Founders Online.
131.  Brumwell, *Gentleman Warrior,* 315.
132.  Middlekauff, *Glorious Cause,* 316.
133.  Chernow, *Washington: A Life,* 227.
134.  GW to John Augustine Washington, March 31, 1776, GWP, Founders Online.
135.  J. Hancock to GW, April 2, 1776, GWP, Founders Online.

CHAPTER 4: AMATEUR HOUR

  1.  Flexner, *Indispensable Man,* 77.
  2.  Charles Lee to GW, February 14, 1776, GWP, Founders Online.
  3.  Charles Lee to GW, February 19, 1776, GWP, Founders Online.
  4.  Cited in David Lee Russell, *Victory on Sullivan's Island: The British Cape Fear/Charles Town Expedition of 1776* (Haverford, Penn.: Infinity Press, 2002), 98.
  5.  GW to Knox, April 3, 1776, GWP, Founders Online.
  6.  Lengel, *General George Washington,* 131.
  7.  GW to Joseph Reed, April 1, 1776, GWP, Founders Online.
  8.  Ibid. See also GW to Israel Putnam, August 25, 1776, GWP, Founders Online.
  9.  Lengel, *General George Washington,* 132.
 10.  Chernow, *Washington: A Life,* 232–33; Longmore, *Invention of George Washington,* 199.
 11.  Ibid.
 12.  "General Orders," June 28, 1776, *The Papers of George Washington,* Revolutionary War Series, ed. David R. Hoth, 22 vols. (Charlottesville: University of Virginia Press, 1985), 5:239. Hereinafter cited as "GWP, Revolutionary War Series."
 13.  Chernow, *Washington: A Life,* 230.
 14.  GW to Generals Greene, Sullivan, and Stirling, April 27, 1776, GWP, Founders Online.

15. Chernow, *Washington: A Life*, 242.
16. GW to John Hancock, May 5, 1776; GW to Jonathan Trumbull, April 22, 1776; Jonathan Trumbull to GW, April 27, 1776; GWP, Founders Online.
17. Royster, *Revolutionary People at War*, 77–78.
18. Middlekauff, *Glorious Cause*, 347.
19. Nathanael Greene to GW, August 1, 1776, GWP, Founders Online.
20. James H. Edmondson, "Desertion in the American Army During the Revolutionary War" (PhD diss., Louisiana State University, 1971), 240, ch. 8.
21. GW to John Hancock, July 11 and July 17, 1776, GWP, Founders Online.
22. Lengel, *General George Washington*, 164.
23. Ibid., 140.
24. Nathanael Greene to GW, August 15, 1776, GWP, Founders Online.
25. GW to Hancock, June 17, 1776, GWP, Founders Online.
26. Ellis, *His Excellency*, 93.
27. GW to Philip Schuyler, December 18, 1775, GWP, Founders Online.
28. Howe, cited in Rose, *Washington's Spies*, 25.
29. GW to Hancock, July 3, 1776, GWP, Founders Online.
30. Spring, *With Zeal and with Bayonets Only*, 17–18.
31. O'Shaughnessy, *Men Who Lost America*, 50.
32. Cited in Mark Urban, *Fusiliers: The Saga of a British Redcoat Regiment in the American Revolution* (New York: Walker, 2007), 81.
33. Brumwell, *Gentleman Warrior*, 183.
34. Middlekauff, *Glorious Cause*, 269–70.
35. O'Shaughnessy, *Men Who Lost America*, 21–22; 28–29.
36. Ibid., 25.
37. Ibid., 11; Charles P. Neimeyer, *America Goes to War: A Social History of the Continental Army* (New York: NYU Press, 1997), 61.
38. Chernow, *Washington: A Life*, 234.
39. Lengel, *General George Washington*, 134; Chernow, *Washington: A Life*, 235.
40. O'Shaughnessy, *Men Who Lost America*, 176.
41. Captain Johann Ewald, *Diary of the American War: A Hessian Journal*, trans. and ed. Joseph P. Tustin (New Haven, Conn.: Yale University Press, 1979), 183.
42. Spring, *With Zeal and with Bayonets Only*, 161.
43. Lengel, *General George Washington*, 135.
44. GW to Charles Lee, August 12, 1776, Founders Online.
45. Francis, Lord Rawdon, to Francis Hastings, tenth Earl of Huntingdon, August 5, 1776, Hastings Collection, Huntingdon Library.
46. GW to John Hancock, July 14, 1776, GWP, Founders Online.
47. Ambrose Serle, cited in Chernow, *Washington: A Life*, 249.
48. Chernow, *Washington: A Life*, 241.
49. Joseph Reed, "Memorandum of an Interview with Lieutenant Colonel James Paterson," July 20, 1776, GWP, Revolutionary War Series, 5:400–401.

50. GW to Colonel Adam Stephen, July 20, 1776, GWP, Founders Online.

51. The Declaration of Independence, UShistory.org/declaration/.

52. Benjamin Rush to John Adams, July 20, 1811; Thacher, *Military Journal*, July 18, 1776.

53. Lengel, *General George Washington*, 136; Longmore, *Invention of George Washington*, 100.

54. GW to Lund Washington, August 19, 1776, GWP, Founders Online.

55. Lengel, *General George Washington*, 139.

56. O'Shaughnessy, *Men Who Lost America*, 215.

57. Middlekauff, *Glorious Cause*, 349.

58. Joseph Ellis, *Revolutionary Summer: The Birth of American Indpendence* (New York: Knopf, 2013), 113.

59. Chernow, *Washington: A Life*, 248.

60. Lengel, *General George Washington*, 146.

61. John Adams to Abigail Adams, October 8, 1776, Adams Family Papers: An Electronic Archive, Massachusetts Historical Society.

62. William Howe to Germain, April 26, 1776, Historical Manuscripts Commission, *Stopford-Sackville Manuscripts* (London: Eyre and Spottiswoode, 1904), 2:30; O'Shaughnessy, *Men Who Lost America*, 100.

63. The secretary, Ambrose Serle, cited in O'Shaughnessy, *Men Who Lost America*, 99.

64. Cited in Lengel, *General George Washington*, 146.

65. Middlekauff, *Glorious Cause*, 353.

66. Lengel, *General George Washington*, 148.

67. Chernow, *Washington: A Life*, 251.

68. Lengel, *General George Washington*, 150.

69. Ibid.

70. GW to Hancock, September 6, 1776, and Nathanael Greene to GW, September 5, 1776, GWP, Founders Online.

71. Ford, *Journals of the Continental Congress*, 5:749.

72. Lengel, *General George Washington*, 152.

73. *Diary of Frederick Mackenzie*, 45, cited in Middlekauff, *Glorious Cause*, 354–55.

74. Chernow, *Washington: A Life*, 253.

75. GWP, Revolutionary War Series, 6:58.

76. GW to John Hancock, September 16, 1776, GWP, Founders Online.

77. Tench Tilghman, *Memoir of Lieutenant Colonal Tench Tilghman, Secretary and Aid to Washington* (Whitefish, Mont.: Kessinger, 2010), 137.

78. Lengel, *General George Washington*, 154.

79. Chernow, *Washington: A Life*, 353.

80. Ibid.

81. Spring, *With Zeal and with Bayonets Only*, 187.

82. *Life and Correspondence of Joseph Reed,* ed. William B. Reed (Chestnut Hill, Mass.: Adamant Media, 2001), 1:237.

83. Lengel, *General George Washington,* 156.

84. GW to Philip Schuyler, September 20, 1776, GWP, Founders Online.

85. William Tryon, cited in Chernow, *Washington: A Life,* 255.

86. GW to Lund Washington, October 6, 1776, GWP.

87. Rose, *Washington's Spies,* 27–30.

88. Ibid., 31.

89. Nathanael Greene to GW, July 28, 1776, fn. 1, GWP, Founders Online.

90. GW to Thomas Jefferson, September 26, 1785, GWP, Founders Online.

91. Ibid.

92. James Thacher, *Military Journal,* October 1776.

93. GW to John Hancock, September 8, 1776, GWP, Founders Online.

94. Chernow, *Washington: A Life,* 258.

95. Lengel, *General George Washington,* 161.

96. Ibid.

97. GWP, Revolutionary War Series, 7:52.

98. Chernow, *Washington: A Life,* 259; Lengel, *General George Washington,* 163.

99. O'Shaughnessy, *Men Who Lost America,* 141.

100. Flexner, *Indispensable Man,* 86–87.

101. Ford, *Journals of the Continental Congress,* 6:866.

102. Lengel, *General George Washington,* 164.

103. Flexner, *Indispensable Man,* 87.

104. GW to Nathanael Greene, November 8, 1776, GWP

105. Nathanael Greene to GW, November 9, 1776, GWP.

106. Lengel, *General George Washington,* 166.

107. Chernow, *Washington: A Life,* 162.

108. James Grant to Edward Harvey, November 22, 1776, James Grant Papers, Library of Congress.

109. Brumwell, *Gentleman Warrior,* 261. It has been estimated that around 57 percent of the 3.3 million Soviet prisoners of war died in captivity, while around 381,000 of the 2.2 million German POWs (around 14 percent) held by the Russians did not survive. These figures are clearly approximations, but the point here is to provide a basis for comparison.

110. Peckham, *Toll of Independence,* 132.

111. Chernow, *Washington: A Life,* 239.

112. Charles Lee to GW, November 19, 1776, GWP, Founders Online.

113. Cited in Chernow, *Washington: A Life,* 263.

114. Ibid.

115. GW to John Hancock, September 2, 1776; GW to Jonathan Trumbull, September 20, 1776; GW to Hancock, December 5, 1776, and December 16, 1776, GWP, Founders Online.

116. GW to Charles Lee, November 21, 1776, GWP, Founders Online.

117. Joseph Reed to Charles Lee, November 21, 1776, GWP, Revolutionary War Series, 7:238.

118. Ibid., 7:237.

119. Memo of Conversation, February 7, 1776, cited in O'Shaughnessy, *Men Who Lost America*, 11.

120. Shy, "The American Revolution: The Military Conflict Considered as a Revolutionary War," in Kurtz and Hutson, *Essays on the American Revolution*, 133–34.

121. Brumwell, *Gentleman Warrior*, 264.

122. Ibid., 266.

123. Charles Lee to GW, GWP, Founders Online.

124. GW to Charles Lee, December 11, 1776; Charles Lee to GW, December 11, 1776, GWP, Founders Online.

125. Chernow, *Washington: A Life*, 267; Thacher, *Military Journal*, February 1, 1777.

126. Cited in Lengel, *General George Washington*, 177.

127. O'Shaughnessy, *Men Who Lost America*, 96, 101; Brumwell, *Gentleman Warrior*, 272.

128. GW to Hancock, December 20, 1776, GWP, Founders Online.

129. Lengel, *General George Washington*, 175.

130. This story was remembered by Washington's friend William Gordon in *The History of the Rise, Progress, and Establishment, of the Independence of the United States of America: Including an Account of the Late War, and of the Thirteen Colonies, from Their Origin to That Period* (London: Dilly and Buckland, 1788), 2:354.

131. James Thacher, *Military Journal*, January 14, 1777; Royster, *Revolutionary People at War*, 110–11.

132. Royster, *Revolutionary People at War*, 110–11; Berkin, *Revolutionary Mothers*, 39–40.

133. Ewald, *Diary of the American War*, 43.

134. Middlekauff, *Glorious Cause*, 365.

135. Brumwell, *Gentleman Warrior*, 267, 273; Lengel, *General George Washington*, 178–79.

136. Lengel, *General George Washington*, 179–80.

137. GW to Joseph Reed, December 23, 1776, GWP, Founders Online.

138. Brumwell, *Gentleman Warrior*, 280.

139. Cited in Bruce Burgoyne, ed., *Enemy Views: The American Revolutionary War as Recorded by the Hessian Participants* (Bowie, Md.: Heritage Books, 1996), 185.

140. Lengel, *General George Washington*, 186–87; Brumwell, *Gentleman Warrior*, 281–82.

141. Thacher, *Military Journal,* January 5, 1777.
142. Lengel, *General George Washington,* 188.
143. Sergeant R., "The Battle of Princeton," *Pennsylvania Magazine of History and Biography* 20 (1896), 515–16.
144. Brumwell, *Gentleman Warrior,* 284; Lengel, *General George Washington,* 196.
145. Undated Intelligence Assessment, James Grant Papers, reel 37, Library of Congress.
146. Lengel, *General George Washington,* 200.
147. Brumwell, *Gentleman Warrior,* 287.
148. Lengel, *General George Washington,* 204.
149. Flexner, *Indispensable Man,* 97–98.
150. Sergeant R., "Battle of Princeton," 517.
151. O'Shaughnessy, *Men Who Lost America,* 102.
152. Lengel, *General George Washington,* 206; Chernow, *Washington: A Life,* 282.
153. Lengel, *General George Washington,* 207.
154. Cited in Chernow, *Washington: A Life,* 283.
155. GW to Jonathan Trumbull, January 10, 1777, GWP, Founders Online.
156. Varnum Lansing Collins, ed., *A Brief Narrative of the Ravages of the British and Hessians at Princeton in 1776–1777* (New York: New York Times, 1968), 14, 15. To cite one example, the *Pennsylvania Evening Post* provided a dramatic account of rapes by British soldiers in New Jersey to include sixteen women being carried off, and one man who reported both wife and ten-year-old daughter raped.

CHAPTER 5: OUT IN THE COLD

1. James Grant to Edward Harvey, January 15, 1777, James Grant Papers, reel 38, Library of Congress; Lengel, *General George Washington,* 210.
2. GW to John Hancock, December 20, 1776, GWP, Founders Online.
3. Ibid.
4. Royster, *Revolutionary People at War,* 190.
5. Spring, *With Zeal and with Bayonets Only,* 278.
6. Cited in Terry Golway, *Washington's General: Nathanael Greene and the Triumph of the American Revolution* (New York: Henry Holt, 2005), 120.
7. Shy, "American Revolution," 134.
8. Golway, *Washington's General,* 119.
9. Ibid., 120.
10. Ford, *Journals of the Continental Congress,* 6:1043–46.
11. GW to John Sullivan, July 25, 1777, GWP, Founders Online.
12. Middlekauff, *Glorious Cause,* 371; Chernow, *Washington: A Life,* 294.
13. GW to John Hancock, February 14, 1777, GWP, Founders Online.
14. Middlekauff, *Glorious Cause,* 532; GW, cited in Joseph Plumb Martin, *Pri-*

vate Yankee Doodle; Being the Narrative of Some of the Adventures, Dangers and Sufferings of a Revolutionary Soldier, ed. George E. Scheer (Boston: Little, Brown, 1962) 65, fn. 5.

15. GW to Jonathan Trumbull, February 10, 1777, GWP, Founders Online; Middlekauff, Glorious Cause, 532.

16. Middlekauff, Glorious Cause, 405.

17. GW to Jonathan Trumbull, March 29, 1777; Nathanael Greene to GW, March 24, 1777, GWP, Founders Online.

18. Neimeyer, America Goes to War, 117.

19. Royster, Revolutionary People at War, 190.

20. GW to Joseph Reed, February 23, 1777, GWP, Founders Online.

21. Flexner, Indispensable Man, 101.

22. Higginbotham, Morgan, viii.

23. GW to John Hancock, September 28, 1776, GWP, Founders Online.

24. GW to Adam Stephen, May 12, 1777, GWP, Founders Online.

25. GW to Jonathan Trumbull, June 23, 1777, GWP, Founders Online.

26. Brumwell, Gentleman Warrior, 301.

27. O'Shaughnessy, Men Who Lost America, 142–43.

28. Middlekauff, Glorious Cause, 374.

29. Ibid., 375.

30. GW to John Hancock, July 2, 1777, GWP, Founders Online.

31. GW to John Hancock, July 10, 1777, GWP, Founders Online.

32. GW to George Clinton, August 13, 1777, GWP, Founders Online.

33. GW to George Clinton, August 16, 1777, GWP, Founders Online.

34. Brumwell, Gentleman Warrior, 301–2.

35. GW to Daniel Morgan, August 16, 1777; GW to Israel Putnam, August 16, 1777, GWP, Founders Online.

36. GW to Philip Schuyler, May 3, 1777, GWP, Founders Online; New England Delegation to GW, August 2, 1777, JAP; Thacher, Military Journal, August 31, 1777.

37. GW to Horatio Gates, August 4, 1777, GWP, Founders Online.

38. Middlekauff, Glorious Cause, 391.

39. GW to George Clinton, August 1, 1777, GWP, Founders Online.

40. GW to General Artemas Ward, August 11, 1777, GWP, Revolutionary War Series, 10:589.

41. Lengel, General George Washington, 221.

42. Middlekauff, Glorious Cause, 391.

43. Lengel, General George Washington, 222.

44. Johann Ewald, Diary of the American War, 76.

45. William Howe to George Germain, August 30, 1777, Historical Manuscripts Commission, Stopford-Sackville Manuscripts, 2:75, cited in O'Shaughnessy, Men Who Lost America, 117.

46. Ewald, *Diary of the American War*, 81, 91.

47. GW to John Hancock, August 23, 1777, GWP, Founders Online.

48. Cited in Middlekauff, *Glorious Cause,* 292.

49. Washington's General Orders, September 5, 1777, "American Memory Timeline," GWP, Library of Congress.

50. Lengel, *General George Washington,* 226; Brumwell, *Gentleman Warrior,* 304; Middlekauff, *Glorious Cause,* 393.

51. Lengel, *General George Washington,* 231.

52. Ibid., 239.

53. Brumwell, *Gentleman Warrior,* 305–6.

54. GW to Hancock, September 11, 1777, GWP, Founders Online.

55. Lengel, *General George Washington,* 241.

56. Flexner, *Indispensable Man,* 2:224.

57. Cited in David Patten, "Ferguson and His Rifle," *History Today* 28 (1978): 451.

58. Robert L. O'Connell, *Soul of the Sword* (New York: Free Press, 2002), 163.

59. Ellis, *His Excellency,* 103.

60. Jefferson, *Writings* (New York: Library of America, 1984), 1318.

61. GW to Anthony Wayne, September 18, 1777, GWP, Founders Online.

62. "Massacre at Paoli," *Historical Magazine* 4 (November 1860): 346; Lengel, *General George Washington,* 247.

63. Ibid.

64. September 11, 1777, *John Peebles' American War: The Diary of a Scottish Grenadier, 1776–1782,* ed. Ira D. Gruber (Mechanicsburg, Penn.: Stackpole, 1998), 137.

65. Cited in Lengel, *General George Washington,* 249.

66. Nelson, *Francis Rawdon-Hastings,* 57.

67. O'Shaughnessy, *Men Who Lost America,* 117. The portrait remained in the ancestral home of the Greys for over a century. In 1906 it was returned to America and now hangs in the White House.

68. O'Shaughnessy, *Men Who Lost America,* 154.

69. Middlekauff, *Glorious Cause,* 388.

70. Flexner, *Indispensable Man,* 104.

71. General Orders, October 3, 1777, GWP, Revolutionary War Series, 9:373.

72. Ibid., 9:308.

73. Cited in Lengel, *General George Washington,* 254.

74. Charles Cotesworth Pinckney, "The Battles of Brandywine and Germantown," *Historical Magazine* 10 (July 1866), 203–4.

75. Ewald, *Diary of the American War,* 93–94.

76. Brumwell, *Gentleman Warrior,* 310.

77. Lengel, *General George Washington,* 259.

78. Ibid., 260.

79. GW to John Hancock, October 5, 1777, GWP, Founders Online.

80. Court-Martial and Dismissal, General Orders, November 20, 1777, in GWP, Revolutionary War Series, 12:327–28.

81. Royster, *Revolutionary People at War,* 149.

82. Ewald, *Diary of the American War,* 96, 104; *John Peebles' American War,* 146.

83. Bowler, *Logistics and the Failure of the British Army,* 70–71.

84. Lengel, *General George Washington,* 262–63; October 31, 1777, Greenman, *Diary of a Common Soldier,* 83.

85. Lengel, *General George Washington,* 309; James Thacher, *Military Journal,* February 10, 1778.

86. Ibid.

87. Martin, *Private Yankee Doodle,* 87.

88. GW to John Hancock, October 18 and 24, 1777; GW to Israel Putnam, October 26, 1777, GWP: Revolutionary War Series, 12: 305–7.

89. William Alexander "Lord Stirling" to GW, November 3, 1777, GWP, Revolutionary War Series, 12:111.

90. GW to Thomas Conway, November 5, 1777, Flexner, *Indispensible Man,* 113.

91. Richard M. Ketchum, *Saratoga: Turning Point of America's Revolutionary War* (New York: Henry Holt, 1997), 385–87.

92. Nathanael Greene to GW, December 1, 1777; Henry Knox to GW, December 1, 1777, GWP, Founders Online.

93. Lengel, *General George Washington,* 266.

94. Ibid., 267.

95. General Orders, December 17, 1777, GWP, Revolutionary War Series, 12:620.

96. Royster, *Revolutionary People at War,* 190–91; Flexner, *Indispensable Man,* 110; Chernow, *Washington: A Life,* 333.

97. GW to Henry Laurens, December 23, 1777, GWP, Founders Online.

98. Chernow, *Washington: A Life,* 32.

99. GW to Brigiadier General John Lacey, January 23, 1778, GWP, Revolutionary War Series, 13:323.

100. Ford, *Journals of the Continental Congress,* 6:1043–46.

101. Middlekauff, *Glorious Cause,* 419; Flexner, *Indispensable Man,* 109–10.

102. GW to Johanthan Trumbull, February 6, 1778; GW to William Livingston, February 14, 1778; GWP, Founders Online.

103. Middlekauff, *Glorious Cause,* 423.

104. Golway, *Washington's General,* 163.

105. James K. Martin and Mark E. Lender, *A Respectable Army: The Military Origins of the Republic, 1763–1789* (London: Wiley-Blackwell, 2005), 100–103.

106. Cited in Royster, *Revolutionary People at War,* 179.

107. Flexner, *Indispensable Man,* 113.

108. Ellis, *His Excellency*, 107; see also Lengel, *General George Washington*, 278; Chernow, *Washington: A Life*, 320–21.

109. *Diary and Autobiography of John Adams*, ed. L. H. Butterfield, 4 vols. (Cambridge, Mass.: Belknap Press of Harvard University Press, 1961), 4:5.

110. James Craik to GW, January 6, 1778, GWP, Founders Online.

111. Thomas Conway to GW, January 10, 1778, GWP, Founders Online.

112. See, for example, GW to Lafayette, December 31, 1777, GWP, Founders Online.

113. James Thacher, *Military Journal*, May 5, 1778.

114. Royster, *Revolutionary People at War*, 180.

115. Flexner, *Indispensable Man*, 115

116. GW to Horatio Gates, February 9, 1778, GWP, Founders Online.

117. Flexner, *Indispensable Man*, 115.

118. Thomas Conway to GW, July 23, 1778, GWP, Founders Online.

119. Brumwell, *Gentleman Warrior*, 325.

120. Higginbotham, *Morgan*, 78–79.

121. Ibid., 79.

122. Cited in Richard N. Rosenfeld, *American Aurora* (New York: St. Martin's, 1998), 345.

123. Lengel, *General George Washington*, 290.

124. Middlekauff, *Glorious Cause*, 423.

125. John McAuley Palmer, *General von Steuben* (New Haven, Conn.: Yale University Press, 1937), 157.

126. Lengel, *General George Washington*, 282.

127. William H. McNeill, *Keeping Together in Time: Dance and Drill in Human History* (Cambridge, Mass.: Harvard University Press, 1997).

128. Royster, *Revolutionary People at War*, 129; Ellis, *His Excellency*, 113; Wayne E. Lee, *Barbarians and Brothers: Anglo-American Warfare: 1500–1865* (New York: Oxford University Press, 2011), 205.

129. Neimeyer, *America Goes to War*, 83.

130. Shy, *People Numerous and Armed*, 171; Greenman, *Diary of a Common Soldier*, 8; Martin, *Private Yankee Doodle*, 111–12.

131. Middlekauff, *Glorious Cause*, 420.

132. Royster, *Revolutionary People at War*, 195.

133. GW to George Clinton, February 16, 1778, GWP, Founders Online.

134. Ellis, *His Excellency*, 114.

135. Royster, *Revolutionary People at War*, 208.

136. Brumwell, *Gentleman Warrior*, 335.

137. Middlekauff, *Glorious Cause*, 410–11.

138. Cited in Samuel Flagg Bemis, *The Diplomacy of the American Revolution*, (Bloomington: Indiana University Press, 1965), 61–65.

139. Thacher, "Biographical Sketches: La Fayette," in *Military Journal*.

140. Shy, *People Numerous and Armed,* 131.

141. GW to Henry Laurens, May 18, 1778, GWP, Founders Online.

142. Cited in Lengel, *General George Washington,* 283.

143. Chernow, *Washington: A Life,* 336.

144. Lengel, *General George Washington,* 285.

145. Shy, "American Revolution," 140; George III to Lord North, June 11, 1779, *Correspondence of King George the Third,* ed. John W. Fortescue, 6 vols. (London, 1928), 4:350.

146. O'Shaughnessy, *Men Who Lost America,* 68.

147. George Germain to Henry Clinton, March 21, 1778; cited in Lengel, *General George Washington,* 285.

148. GW to Henry Laurens, April 30, 1778, GWP, Founders Online.

149. O'Shaughnessy, *Men Who Lost America,* 210.

150. Middlekauff, *Glorious Cause,* 558; Lengel, *General George Washington,* 286–88.

151. O'Shaughnessy, *Men Who Lost America,* 214.

152. O'Shaughnessy, *Men Who Lost America,* 221.

153. Ewald, *Diary of the American War,* 138–39.

154. Ibid.

155. GW to Henry Laurens, May 28, 1778; GW to William Livingston, June 1, 1778; GW to William Livingston, June 22, 1778, GWP, Founders Online.

156. Higginbotham, *Morgan,* 87.

157. Chernow, *Washington: A Life,* 339.

158. Council of War, June 24, 1778, GWP, Library of Congress.

159. Ibid.

160. Lafayette to GW; Nathanael Greene to GW, June 24, 1778, GWP, Founders Online.

161. Lengel, *General George Washington,* 294.

162. Middlekauff, *Glorious Cause,* 429–30.

163. O'Shaughnessy, *Men Who Lost America,* 221.

164. Brumwell, *Gentleman Warrior,* 342.

165. Lengel, *General George Washington,* 299.

166. Martin, *Private Yankee Doodle,* 110–11.

167. Cited in Chernow, *Washington: A Life,* 342.

168. Lengel, *General George Washington,* 302.

169. Ibid., 303.

170. See, for example, Charles Lee to GW, June 30, 1778, GWP, Founders Online.

171. "Account of a Duel Between Major General Charles Lee and Lieutenant Colonel John Laurens," December 24, 1778, GWP, Founders Online.

172. Lengel, *General George Washington,* 304.

173. Middlekauff, *Glorious Cause,* 434.
174. Flexner, *Indispensable Man,* 124; Rose, *Washington's Spies,* 68.


CHAPTER 6: DANGERLAND

1. GW to Brigadier General Thomas Nelson, Jr., August 20, 1778, GWP, Founders Online.
2. Nelson, *Francis Rawdon-Hastings,* 63.
3. Middlekauff, *Glorious Cause,* 436.
4. Ibid.
5. Flexner, *Indispensable Man,* 126.
6. Brumwell, *Gentleman Warrior,* 346.
7. September 5, 1778, *John Peebles' American War,* 215; Brumwell, *Gentleman Warrior,* 347.
8. Nathanael Greene to GW, August 28–31, 1778, GWP, Founders Online.
9. John Laurens to GW, September 2, 1778, GWP, Founders Online.
10. Theodore Ropp, *War in the Modern World* (New York: Collier Books, 1962), 54; Robert L. O'Connell, *Of Arms and Men: A History of War, Weapons and Aggression* (New York: Oxford University Press, 1989), 165.
11. John Laurens to GW, September 2, 1778, GWP, Founders Online.
12. GW to John Sullivan, September 1, 1778, GWP, Founders Online.
13. Lengel, *General George Washington,* 308.
14. GW to Henry Laurens, November 11, 1778, GWP, Founders Online.
15. GW to Henry Laurens, November 14, 1778, GWP, Founders Online.
16. George Germain to Henry Clinton, March 21, 1778, cited in Lengel, *General George Washington,* 285.
17. February 3, 1779, *John Peebles' American War,* 247; Lengel, *General George Washington,* 321.
18. Campbell, cited in O'Shaughnessy, *Men Who Lost America,* 223.
19. Middlekauff, *Glorious Cause,* 438.
20. Brumwell, *Gentleman Warrior,* 356; Chernow, *Washington: A Life,* 366.
21. Lengel, *General George Washington,* 321.
22. E. K. Davies, ed., *Documents of the American Revolution, 1770–1783,* 21 vols. (Shannon: Irish University Press, 1972–81), 17:224.
23. Ibid.
24. Ellis, *His Excellency,* 122; Brumwell, *Gentleman Warrior,* 348.
25. Ibid., 347.
26. See, for example, GW to Lord Stirling, January 8, 1779, GWP, Founders Online.
27. Bowler, *Logistics and the Failure of the British Army,* 118; see also Ewald, *Diary of the American War,* 157.

28. Charles Royster, *Light-Horse Harry Lee and the Legacy of the American Revolution* (New York: Knopf, 1981), 206.

29. Rose, *Washington's Spies*, ch. 3.

30. GW to Benjamin Tallmadge, July 5, 1779; Rose, *Washington's Spies*, 112.

31. GW to Benjamin Tallmadge, November 11, 1780, GWP, Founders Online.

32. Benjamin Tallmadge to GW, November 25, 1780, GWP, Founders Online.

33. Rose, *Washington's Spies*, 28.

34. Alexander Innes, Inspector General of Provincial Forces, January 1777, cited in J. R. Cuneo, *Robert Rogers of the Rangers* (New York: Oxford University Press, 1959), 274–75.

35. John Graves Simcoe, *Simcoe's Military Journal: A History of the Operations of a Partisan Corps, the Queen's Rangers* (New York: Bartlett and Welfore, 1844), 18.

36. Spring, *With Zeal and Bayonets Only*, 233–34.

37. Simcoe, *Simcoe's Military Journal*, 316.

38. Ewald, *Diary of the American War*, 173; Simcoe, *Simcoe's Military Journal*, 117.

39. *John Peebles' American War*, 263; Lengel, *General George Washington*, 318.

40. *John Peebles' American War*, 273–76; Berkin, *Revolutionary Mothers*, 40.

41. Brumwell, *Gentleman Warrior*, 351.

42. GW to Daniel Morgan, June 13, 1777, GWP, Founders Online.

43. GW to Anthony Wayne, July 1, 1779, Hamilton Papers, Founders Online.

44. GW, cited in *The Writings of George Washington*, ed. John C. Fitzpatrick, 39 vols. (Washington, D.C.: Government Printing Office, 1921–44), 19:226.

45. Don Higginbotham, *Morgan*, 97.

46. GW to Anthony Wayne, July 10, 1779, GWP, Founders Online.

47. Anthony Wayne to GW, July 16, 1779, GWP, Founders Online

48. *John Peebles' American War*, 283.

49. Ewald, *Diary of the American War*, 168.

50. Lengel, *General George Washington*, 318.

51. Middlekauff, *Glorious Cause*, 574–75; Berkin, *Revolutionary Mothers*, 111–12; Jared C. Lobdell, ed., *Indian Warfare in Western Pennsylvania and North West Virginia at the Time of the American Revolution* (Bowie, Md.: Heritage Books, 1992), 41–42; DuVal, *Independence Lost*, 76, 78.

52. Berkin, *Revolutionary Mothers*, 112.

53. Wayne E. Lee, *Barbarians and Brothers: Anglo-American Warfare, 1500–1865* (New York: Oxford University Press, 2011), 218–19; George Clinton to GW, October 15, 1778; GW to George Clinton, March 4, 1779, GWP, Founders Online.

54. Ford, *Journals of the Continental Congress*, 13:252.

55. GW to Horatio Gates, March 6, 1779; Nathanael Greene to GW, April 26, 1779; GW to Nathanael Greene, May 4, 1779, GWP, Founders Online.

56. GW to John Sullivan, May 31, 1779, GWP, Founders Online.

57. Lee, *Barbarians and Brothers*, 212.

58. James Thacher, "Biographical Sketches: John Sullivan," in *Military Journal;* Lee, *Barbarians and Brothers,* 214.

59. Lengel, *General George Washington,* 312–13.

60. Ibid., 319; Chernow, *Washington: A Life,* 368.

61. O'Shaughnessy, *Men Who Lost America,* 230.

62. Lengel, *General George Washington,* 319.

63. Ibid.

64. Rose, *Washington's Spies,* 180–81.

65. Ibid., 184.

66. GW to William Fitzhugh, April 10, 1779, GWP, Founders Online.

67. GW to Nathanael Greene, May 21, 1780, GWP, Founders Online.

68. GW to S. Huntington, April 2, 1780; August 20, 1780, GWP, Founders Online.

69. Quoted in Higginbotham, *George Washington and the American Military Tradition,* 90.

70. Cited in Chernow, *Washington: A Life,* 367.

71. GW to Magistrates of New Jersey, January 8, 1780, GWP, Library of Congress.

72. Martin, *Private Yankee Doodle,* 104, 111–12, 114.

73. Nathanael Greene to GW, 2 April 1780

74. May 1780, Greenman, *Diary of a Common Soldier,* 171; Martin, *Private Yankee Doodle,* 187–88.

75. Martin, *Private Yankee Doodle,* 182–84.

76. Lengel, *General George Washington,* 321.

77. GW to Jonathan Trumbull, Sr., May 26, 1780, GWP, Founders Online.

78. O'Shaughnessy, *Men Who Lost America,* 230.

79. Ibid., 223–24.

80. Nelson, *Francis Rawdon-Hastings,* 69; Thacher, *Military Journal,* January 17, 1780.

81. January 1, 9, and 20, 1780, *John Peebles' American War,* 387–88.

82. *John Peebles' American War,* 335.

83. Middlekauff, *Glorious Cause,* 448.

84. *John Peebles' American War,* 335.

85. Banastre Tarleton, *A History of the Campaigns of 1780 and 1781 in the Southern Provinces of North America* (London: T. Cadell, 1787), 16–17.

86. GW to S. Huntington (now President of Congress), March 27, 1780; GW to Benjamin Lincoln, March 30, 1780, GWP, Founders Online.

87. O'Shaughnessy, *Men Who Lost America,* 231.

88. Middlekauff, *Glorious Cause,* 455; Ewald, *Diary of the American War,* 239.

89. William T. Bulger, ed., "Sir Henry Clinton's 'Journal of the Siege of Charleston, 1780,'" *The South Carolina Historical Magazine* 66, no. 3 (July 1965): 149.

90. Ibid., 165.
91. Middlekauff, *Glorious Cause*, 455.
92. Tarleton, notes from first chapter of *History of the Campaigns of 1780 and 1781*.
93. October 1779, Greenman, *Diary of a Common Soldier;* October 27, 1779, *John Peebles' American War*, 302.
94. O'Shaughnessy, *Men Who Lost America*, 250.
95. Middlekauff, *Glorious Cause*, 456.
96. Robert M. Hatch, *Major John André: A Gallant in Spy's Clothing* (Boston: Houghton Mifflin, 1986), 82.
97. O'Shaughnessy, *Men Who Lost America*, 257.
98. Cited in Shy, *People Numerous and Armed*, 187.
99. Middlekauff, *Glorious Cause*, 456.
100. Tarleton, *History of the Campaigns of 1780 and 1781*, 30.
101. Ibid., 32.
102. Nelson, *Francis Rawdon-Hastings*, 73–74; Middlekauff, *Glorious Cause*, 459.
103. Middlekauff, *Glorious Cause*, 258; Nelson, *Francis Rawdon-Hastings*, 75.
104. Nelson, *Francis Rawdon-Hastings*, 87.
105. See, for example, Tarleton, *History of the Campaigns of 1780 and 1781*, 16–17.
106. GW to Jonathan Trumbull, Sr., June 11, 1780, GWP, Founders Online.
107. Middlekauff, *Glorious Cause*, 459.
108. GW to Horatio Gates, July 18, 1780; August 12, 1780, GWP, Founders Online.
109. Higginbotham, *Morgan*, 102.
110. Middlekauff, *Glorious Cause*, 460.
111. Ibid.
112. O'Shaughnessy, *Men Who Lost America*, 257.
113. Middlekauff, *Glorious Cause*, 461.
114. Tarleton, *History of the Campaigns of 1780 and 1781*, 108–9.
115. Ibid.; Chernow, *Washington: A Life*, 374.
116. Cited in Ron Chernow, *Alexander Hamilton* (New York: Penguin, 2004), 138.
117. GW to Samuel Huntington, September 15, 1780, GWP, Founders Online.
118. Rose, *Washington's Spies*, 200–202.
119. GW to Benedict Arnold, August 3, 1778, GWP, Founders Online.
120. Claire Brandt, *The Man in the Mirror: A Life of Benedict Arnold* (New York: Random House, 1994), 148–49.
121. Nathanael Greene to John Cadwalader, November 10, 1778; *The Papers of Nathanael Greene*, ed. Richard Showman, 13 vols. (Chapel Hill: University of North Carolina Press, 1983), 3;58.
122. Flexner, *Indispensable Man*, 142.

123. GW to Benedict Arnold, July 20, 1779, GWP, Founders Online.

124. Cited in Flexner, *Indispensable Man,* 142.

125. Chernow, *Washington: A Life,* 173, 381–82.

126. Flexner, *Indispensable Man,* 143; O'Shaughnessy, *Men Who Lost America,* 234; Rose, *Washington's Spies,* 196.

127. O'Shaughnessy, *Men Who Lost America,* 235.

128. Ibid.

129. Flexner, *Indispensable Man,* 142–43; James Thacher, "Biographical Sketches: Arnold," in *Military Journal.*

130. GW to Benedict Arnold, August 3, 1780, GWP, Founders Online.

131. Henry Clinton to George Germain, October 11, 1780, cited in O'Shaughnessy, *Men Who Lost America,* 235.

132. Rose, *Washington's Spies,* 204–5.

133. Chernow, *Washington: A Life,* 381.

134. Flexner, *George Washington,* 2:384.

135. Ibid., 2:386.

136. Ibid., 2:389.

137. GW to Nathanael Greene, September 18, 1780; GW to Anthony Wayne, September 26, 1780, GWP, Founders Online.

138. Flexner, *Indispensable Man,* 146.

139. Rose, *Washington's Spies,* 216–22.

140. GW cited in Flexner, *Indispensable Man,* 148.

141. Benedict Arnold to GW, September 25, 1780, GWP, Founders Online.

142. Rose, *Washington's Spies,* 211; James Thacher, *Military Journal,* October 2, 1780.

143. Benjamin Tallmadge to Jared Sparks, February 17, 1834, *The Public Papers of George Clinton: First Governor of New York, 1777–1795, 1801–1804,* ed. H. Hastings and J. A. Holden, 10 vols. (Albany: 1899–1914), 6:263–64.

144. Nathanael Greene, cited in Golway, *Washington's General,* 230.

145. GW to Henry Clinton, September 30, 1780, GWP, Founders Online.

146. James Robertson to Henry Clinton, October 1, 1780, cited in Carl Van Doren, *Secret History of the American Revolution* (New York: Viking, 1941), 488–89.

147. John André to GW, October 1, 1780, *Major André's Journal* (CreateSpace Independent Publishing Platform: 2016), 72.

148. Thacher, *Military Journal,* October 2, 1780.

149. GW to John Laurens, October 13, 1780, GWP, Founders Online.

150. Benedict Arnold to GW, October 1, 1780, GWP, Founders Online.

151. "Clinton's Narratives," Van Doren, *Secret History of the American Revolution,* 494–95.

152. Ewald, *Diary of the American War,* 251.

153. Thacher, "Biographical Sketches: Arnold"; Flexner, *Indispensable Man,* 148.

CHAPTER 7: THE LONG GOODBYE

1. E. James Ferguson, *The American Revolution: A General History, 1763–1790* (Homewood, Ill.: Dorsey Press, 1974), 145.
2. Ellis, *His Excellency*, 131.
3. Flexner, *Indispensable Man*, 137.
4. GW to Lafayette, July 22, 1780, GWP, Founders Online.
5. "Answers to Queries by the Comte de Rochambeau and the Chevalier de Ternay," and "Conference at Hartford," September 22, 1780, in *Papers of Hamilton*, ed. Harold C. Syrett, 27 vols. (New York: Columbia University Press, 1961), 2:435–38.
6. Gilbert Chinard, *George Washington: As the French Knew Him* (Whitefish, Mont.: Literary Licensing, 2013), 40.
7. GW to Rochambeau, September 26, 1780; Rochambeau to GW, September 30, 1780, GWP, Founders Online.
8. Chernow, *Washington: A Life*, 391.
9. GW to John Laurens, January 15, 1781, GWP, Founders Online.
10. GW to Benjamin Franklin, January 15, 1781, Benjamin Franklin Papers, Founders Online.
11. John Laurens to GW, February 4, 1781, GWP, Founders Online.
12. Royster, *Revolutionary People at War*, 303–4.
13. Ibid., 202–3.
14. Lengel, *General George Washington*, 326.
15. GW to Wayne, January 3, 1781, GWP, Founders Online.
16. Thacher, *Military Journal*, January 4, 1781.
17. Royster, *Revolutionary People at War*, 303.
18. Thacher, *Military Journal*, January 27, 1781.
19. GW to Rochambeau, January 20, January 24, January 29, 1781, GWP, Founders Online.
20. Lee Kennett, *The French Forces in America, 1780–1783* (Westport, Conn.: Praeger, 1977), 83–84.
21. Rochambeau to GW, February 2, 1781, GWP, Founders Online.
22. Lengel, *General George Washington*, 328.
23. Ewald, *Diary of the American War*, 295.
24. GW to Lafayette, February 20, 1781, GWP, Founders Online.
25. Brumwell, *Gentleman Warrior*, 377.
26. GW to Rochambeau, March 21, 1781, GWP, Founders Online.
27. Rochambeau to GW, April 26, 1781. For clarity's sake I have substituted Rochambeau's actual quotation, which was plainly a bad translation of the article, with the actual words of GW in his letter to Lund Washington of March 18, 1781, GWP, Founders Online.
28. GW to Rochambeau, April 30, 1781, GWP, Founders Online.

29. John Laurens to GW, March 24, 1781, GWP, Founders Online.

30. GW to John Laurens, April 9, 1781, GWP, Founders Online.

31. John Laurens, April 11, 1781, GWP, Founders Online.

32. John Laurens to Huntington, April 24, 1781, in Francis Wharton and John Bassett Moore, *The Revolutionary Diplomatic Correspondence of the United States,* 6 vols. (Wentworth Press, 2016), 4:382–84.

33. Shy, *People Numerous and Armed,* 197.

34. Tarleton, *History of the Campaigns of 1780 and 1781,* 86–87; Nelson, *Francis Rawdon-Hastings,* 74.

35. Berkin, *Revolutionary Mothers,* 65–66.

36. Cited in Lyman C. Draper, *King's Mountain and Its Heroes: History of the Battle of King's Mountain, October 7th, 1780, and the Events Which Led to It* (Cincinnati: P. A. Thomson, 1881), 169.

37. Ibid.

38. Middlekauff, *Glorious Cause,* 464–65.

39. O'Shaughnessy, *Men Who Lost America,* 264.

40. Middlekauff, *Glorious Cause,* 467.

41. Spring, *With Zeal and with Bayonets Only,* 260.

42. Middlekauff, *Glorious Cause,* 468.

43. Tarleton, *History of the Campaigns of 1780 and 1781,* 166.

44. Cited in Spring, *With Zeal and with Bayonets Only,* 36–37.

45. Higginbotham, *Morgan,* 112.

46. Middlekauff, *Glorious Cause,* 456; O'Shaughnessy, *Men Who Lost America,* 259.

47. Cited in Aiken, *Swamp Fox,* 23.

48. Chernow, *Washington: A Life,* 375–76.

49. Nathanael Greene to Alexander Hamilton, January 10, 1781, GWP, Founders Online, GWP.

50. Ibid.

51. Ibid.

52. GW to Nathanael Greene, October 22, 1780, GWP, Founders Online.

53. O'Shaughnessy, *Men Who Lost America,* 265.

54. Aiken, *Swamp Fox,* 28.

55. William Moultrie, *Memoirs of the American Revolution, So Far as It Related to the States of North and South Carolina, and Georgia* (New York, 1802), 293.

56. Aiken, *Swamp Fox,* 81.

57. Ibid., 4–5.

58. Tarleton, *History of the Campaigns of 1780 and 1781,* 172.

59. Ibid., 14.

60. Higginbotham, *Morgan,* 120.

61. Ibid., 139.

62. Middlekauff, *Glorious Cause,* 474–75.

63. Cited in Lengel, *General George Washington,* 325.
64. Middlekauff, *Glorious Cause,* 476.
65. O'Shaughnessy, *Men Who Lost America,* 267.
66. Higginbotham, *Morgan,* 137.
67. Spring, *With Zeal and with Bayonets Only,* 172–74.
68. Middlekauff, *Glorious Cause,* 479.
69. Ibid.
70. O'Shaugnessy, 267; Middlekauff, *Glorious Cause,* 480.
71. Aiken, *Swamp Fox,* 16.
72. O'Shaugnessy, *Men Who Lost America,* 267.
73. Chernow, *Washington: A Life,* 391.
74. Higginbotham, *Morgan,* 145.
75. Ibid., 147.
76. Middlekauff, *Glorious Cause,* 481.
77. Tarleton, *History of the Campaigns of 1780 and 1781,* 223; Spring, *With Zeal and with Bayonets Only,* 26–27.
78. Higginbotham, *Morgan,* 149.
79. O'Shaughnessy, *Men Who Lost America,* 268.
80. Middlekauff, *Glorious Cause,* 484.
81. Higginbotham, *Morgan,* 155.
82. Tarleton, *History of the Campaigns of 1780 and 1781,* 229.
83. Ibid., 230–31.
84. Higginbotham, *Morgan,* 156.
85. Charles Royster, *Light-Horse Harry Lee and the Legacy of the American Revolution* (New York: Knopf, 1981),
86. Lengel, *General George Washington,* 326.
87. Middlekauff, *Glorious Cause,* 488–92.
88. O'Shaughnessy, *Men Who Lost America,* 271; Golway, *Washington's General,* 266–69.
89. GW to Nathanael Greene, April 18, 1781, GWP, Founders Online.
90. Nathanael Greene to GW, May 1, 1781, GWP, Founders Online.
91. Royster, *Light-Horse Harry Lee,* 37.
92. Nelson, *Francis Rawdon-Hastings,* 102–3.
93. Cited in Middlekauff, *Glorious Cause,* 493.
94. O'Shaughnessy, *Men Who Lost America,* 273.
95. Simcoe, *Simcoe's Military Journal,* 203–4.
96. GW to Lafayette, March 8, 1781, GWP, Founders Online.
97. Cornwallis to Henry Clinton, May 26, 1781, GWP, Founders Online.
98. Lengel, *General George Washington,* 330.
99. Middlekauff, *Glorious Cause,* 581.
100. Lengel, *General George Washington,* 331.
101. Flexner, *Indispensable Man,* 155–6.

102. Brumwell, *Gentleman Warrior*, 381–82.

103. Ibid., 393.

104. GW to Anthony Wayne, Febrary 26, 1781, GWP, Founders Online.

105. Brumwell, *Gentleman Warrior*, 387.

106. Middlekauff, *Glorious Cause*, 583.

107. *Diaries of GW*, 3:411.

108. GW to Rochambeau, August 17, 1781, GWP, Founders Online.

109. Lengel, *General George Washington*, 335.

110. GW to Robert Morris, August 17, 1781, GWP, Founders Online.

111. Chernow, *Washington: A Life*, 408.

112. O'Shaughnessy, *Men Who Lost America*, 312.

113. Cited in Chernow, *Washington: A Life*, 409.

114. Chernow, *Washington: A Life*, 409; Lengel, *General George Washington*, 336.

115. Chernow, *Washington: A Life*, 421.

116. Cited in Flexner, *George Washington*, 2:449.

117. Ibid.

118. Chernow, *Washington: A Life*, 412.

119. O'Shaughnessy, *Men Who Lost America*, 276–77.

120. Tarleton, *History of the Campaigns of 1780 and 1781*, 363–64.

121. Ibid., 308–9.

122. O'Shaughnessy, *Men Who Lost America*, 309.

123. Letter cited in Tarleton, *History of the Campaigns of 1780 and 1781*, 416.

124. *John Peebles' American War*, 450.

125. Ibid., 472–73; Brumwell, *Gentleman Warrior*, 395.

126. *John Peebles' American War*, 450.

127. Lengel, *General George Washington*, 337;

128. Robert L. O'Connell, *Soul of the Sword: An Illustrated History of Weaponry and Warfare from Prehistory to the Present* (New York: Free Press, 2002), 170.

129. Lengel, *General George Washington*, 340.

130. Cited in Richard Ketchum, *Victory at Yorktown: The Campaign That Won the Revolution* (New York: Henry Holt, 2004), 235.

131. Cited in Chernow, *Washington: A Life*, 416.

132. Lengel, *General George Washington*, 341.

133. Flexner, *George Washington*, 2:460.

134. Simcoe, *Simcoe's Military Journal*, 254; Ellis, *His Excellency*, 136–37.

135. Ibid.

136. Cited in Chernow, *Washington: A Life*, 418.

137. James Thacher, *Military Journal*, October 19, 1781.

138. Flexner, *Indispensable Man*, 164; Tarleton, *History of the Campaigns of 1780 and 1781*, 391.

139. Martin, *Private Yankee Doodle*, 240–41.

140. Golway, *Washington's General*, 289.

141. O'Shaughnessy, *Men Who Lost America*, 200.

142. Brumwell, *Gentleman Warrior*, 410.

143. Gordon S. Wood, "The Making of a Disaster," *New York Review of Books*, April 28, 2005.

144. Flexner, *Indispensable Man*, 167.

145. DuVal, *Independence Lost*, 186, 214–15.

146. O'Shaughnessy, *Men Who Lost America*, 343.

147. Brian Lavery, *Empires of the Seas: How the Navy Forged the Modern World* (London: Conway Maritime Press, 2009), 144–45.

148. See, for example, GW to Nathanael Greene, November 16, 1781; GW to Lafayette, November 15, 1781; GW to John Hancock, May 4, 1782; GW to Nathanael Greene, August 6, 1782; GWP, Founders Online.

149. GW to James McHenry, September 12, 1782, GWP, Founders Online.

150. Lengel, *General George Washington*, 344–45.

151. Ellis, *His Excellency*, 141.

152. Benjamin Tallmadge to GW, December 8, 1782; Benjamin Tallmadge to GW, February 21, 1783; GW to Benjamin Tallmadge, January 4, 1783; GWP, Founders Online.

153. GW to William Livingston, January 12–13, 1782, GWP, Founders Online.

154. *The People's History of America, from the Earliest Discoveries to the Present Day* (New York: Henry Allen, 1875), 484.

155. GW to Moses Hazen, May 3, 1782, GWP, Founders Online.

156. GW to Benjamin Lincoln, June 5, 1782, GWP, Founders Online.

157. GW to Benjamin Lincoln, October 7, 1782, GWP, Founders Online.

158. GW to Matthias Ogden, March 28, 1782, GWP, Founders Online.

159. Brumwell, *Gentleman Warrior*, 411.

160. Baron Ludwig von Closen, *The Revolutionary Journal of Baron Ludwig von Closen, 1780–1783* (Williamsburg, Va.: Omohundro Institute, 2012), 239–40.

161. James Thacher, "Biographical Sketches: Steuben," in *Military Journal*.

162. GW to John Jay, October 18, 1782, GWP, Founders Online.

163. Ellis, *His Excellency*, 138–39.

164. GW to Alexander Hamilton, May 2, 1780, GWP, Founders Online.

165. Lewis Nicola to GW, May 22, 1782, GWP, Founders Online.

166. GW to Lewis Nicola, May 22, 1782, GWP, Founders Online.

167. Ibid.

168. Ellis, *His Excellency*, 114.

169. Royster, *Revolutionary People at War*, 208.

170. Richard H. Kohn, "The Inside History of the Newburgh Conspiracy: America and the Coup d'Etat," *William and Mary Quarterly*, 3rd ser., 27 (1970): 187–220.

171. Ibid.; Chernow, *Washington: A Life*, 432; Lengel, *General George Washington*, 346; Ellis, *His Excellency*, 141.

172. Alexander Hamilton to GW, February 13, 1783, GWP, Founders Online.
173. GW to Alexander Hamilton, March 4, 1783, GWP, Founders Online.
174. Ibid.
175. Brumwell, *Gentleman Warrior,* 415.
176. GW to Officers of the Army, March 15, 1783, GWP, Founders Online.
177. Middlekauff, *Glorious Cause,* 591.
178. Chevalier de La Luzerne to GW, GWP, Founders Online.
179. GW, "Proclamation for the Cessation of Hostilities," April 18, 1783, GWP, Founders Online.
180. DuVal, *Independence Lost,* 236.
181. Berkin, *Revolutionary Mothers,* 126–27.
182. Chernow, *Washington: A Life,* 440–42.
183. DuVal, *Independence Lost,* 229.
184. Ellis, *His Excellency,* 212–14; DuVal, *Independence Lost,* 340; Lengel, *General George Washington,* 355–56.
185. Shy, *People Numerous and Armed,* 248–50.
186. GW to Hamilton, April 4, 1783, GWP, Founders Online.
187. Royster, *Revolutionary People at War,* 344; GW to Morris, June 3, 1783, GWP.
188. Brumwell, *Gentleman Warrior,* 420–21.
189. Berkin, *Revolutionary Mothers,* 105.
190. GW "To the States," June 8, 1783, GWP, Founders Online.
191. Ibid.
192. Ibid.
193. Flexner, *Indispensable Man,* 178.
194. Lengel, *General George Washington,* 351.
195. "Address to Congress on Resigning Commission," December 23, 1783, GWP, Founders Online.

CONCLUSION

1. GW to Alexander Hamilton, July 2, 1794, Hamilton Papers, Founders Online.
2. Cited in Chernow, *Washington: A Life,* 669.
3. GW to Lafayette, June 18, 1788; GW to James Madison, March 2, 1788, GWP, Founders Online.
4. Cited in Flexner, *Indispensable Man,* 256.

# INDEX

*Page numbers of illustrations appear in italics.*
*Key to abbreviation:* GW = George Washington

Adams, John, xiv, 73, 77, 88, 133, 137, 177, 193, 194, 294–95
Adams, Samuel, 73, 85, 193
Addison, Joseph, *Cato*, 109, 143
Albemarle, Lord, 27
Allen, Ethan, 86
Allentown, Pa., 207
American Revolution, xiv–xv, xvii–xxvii
  Arnold's perfidy as energizing, 249
  the Association and, xiv, 78–80, 82–84
  Britain's blunders leading to, 68–74
  Britain's epic failure and, 90, 91, 165
  British cut off from local supplies, xviii, xxii–xxiii, 122, 123, 128, 189, 219, 221, 271, 287
  British forces unable to win, xvii–xviii, 128–29, 202, 213
  British misperceptions, 71, 102, 116, 125
  British mistakes, 123–29, 164–65
  British occupation of six cities, xviii, 71, 126, 153, 182–84, 189, 191, 214, 217–19, 233, 271, 287 (*see also* Boston, Mass.; Charleston, S.C.; Newport, R.I.; New York City; Philadelphia, Pa.; Savannah, Ga.)
  British pardons offered, 127, 133, 152, 232, 255
  British prolonging of, 127, 203
  British surrender, 282–84, *284*
  British tyranny and atrocities as motivation, xix–xx, 128–29, 150, 164–65, 213
  Carlisle Peace Commission and, 204–5
  casualties (*see specific battles*)
  conspiracy theories and fear as motivation, xvi–xvii, 62–65, 71, 75–76, 77, 79, 84, 86, 124, 125, 155
  Continental Army created, 87–88 (*see also* Continental Army)
  core element, 77, 98
  Country Party ideas and, xv–xvi, xix, xxvi, 57, 61–65, 67, 73, 124
  death toll, total, 295
  depredations and cycles of revenge, 250
  French military alliance, 87–88, 201–3, 214–18, 231, 251, 285
  French monetary support, 253–54, 258–59, 294
  German mercenaries, 125–26 (*see also* Hessians)
  as the Glorious Cause, xv, xviii, 75, 89, 101, 116, 122, 150, 200, 249, 251
  growing cruelty of, 202, 262, 270, 271
  GW as heart and soul of, xiii–xiv, xxvi, 75, 114, 118, 194, 250–51

American Revolution (*cont'd*)
  GW's prevention of mass slaughter,
    xx–xxii, xxvi, 295–96
  hatred of Britain and, 182, 202
  individual rights and, 64–65
  inspirational rhetoric for, 109
  Intolerable Acts triggering, xiv,
    71, 90
  irregular warfare (Dangerland) and,
    xx–xxxi, 68, 81, 85, 89, 102, 122, 123,
    128, 155, 178, 189, 207, 218–21, 234–35,
    236, 239, 245, 249, 250, 262, 271, 287,
    288
  lack of funds, 80, 192, 250, 253, 254,
    255
  local militias, xiv, xvii, 78, 82, 83, 85,
    86, 93, 94, 119, 140, 146, 151, 152, 155,
    156, 157, 163, 167, 168, 169, 174, 176,
    184, 186, 187, 207, 214, 215, 217, 230,
    231, 237, 238, 239, 262, 263, 265,
    266–68, 270–71, 288
  lowest point, 155
  myths about, 35, 92, 127
  number of troops in active service,
    295
  peace conference with Howe, 137
  Proclamation for the Cessation of
    Hostilities (April 18, 1783), 294
  "Rage Militaire" and, xv, 83–84, 91,
    92, 96, xvii, 129, 157
  "shot heard round the world," 85
  stalemate years, 213–50
  suddenness of, 75
  Treaty of Paris (1783), 287, 294
  war in the South, 217–18, 229–39, *233*,
    259–73
  *See also specific battles and leaders*
  —**battles**
  Bennington (1777), 174, 183
  Brandywine (1777), 178–80, *178, 179*
  British evacuation of Boston (1776),
    113
  Bunker Hill (1775), 90–91, 113
  Camden (1780), 237–39, 259, 262
  Charleston (1780), 230–32, *233*
  Cowpens (1781), 266–67

Fort Washington (1776), 148–49
  Green Spring (1781), 280
  Guilford Court House (1781), 271
  Harlem Heights (1776), 140–42
  Kings Mountain (1780), 260–61
  Lexington and Concord (1775),
    84–85, 91
  Long Island (1776), 134–37, *135, 136*
  Monmouth (1778), 207–12, *209, 211*
  Moores Creek Bridge (1776), 129
  Paulus Hook (1779), 224
  Princeton (1777), *158*, 160–64, *162*
  Quebec (1775), 108–10
  Rhode Island (1778), 214–15
  Saratoga (1777), 183–84
  Stony Point (1779), 223–24
  Trenton (1776), 156–59, *157*
  Valcour Island (1776), 146–47
  White Plains (1776), 146
  Yorktown (1781), 281–82
André, John, 127, 183, 232, 234, 241
  Benedict Arnold and, 242, 244, 247
  capture by Patriots, 245
  convicted as a spy and hanged,
    246–49
  Howe's Mischianza and, 205–6, 232
  portrait of Peggy Shippen, *241*
  self-portrait, night before hanging,
    *248*
Arbuthnot, Mariot, 231, 232, 257
Arnold, Benedict, 86, 101, *240*, 249
  André's life offered in exchange for,
    247
  Battle of Saratoga, 184, 190–91,
    239–40
  Battle of Valcour Island, 146–47
  as British brigadier general, 256
  charges of corruption against, 242
  Clinton and, 272
  Connecticut raids by, 281
  Cornwallis's dislike of, 272
  failed attack on Quebec, 108–10
  falling-out with Gates, 190
  Fort Griswold massacre and, 281
  GW's letter to, 109
  instability of, 239–40

invasion of Canada and, 101
marriage to Peggy Shippen, 241–42
posting to Philadelphia, 240–42
reviling of, 249
sent to fight Burgoyne, 174, 175, 184
Ticonderoga and, 86, 101
as traitor, 101, 242–45, 252
Virginia expedition, 256–57, 259, 272
wounding of, 240
Articles of Confederation, 212, 250, 299
Asgill, Charles, 288
Association, xii, 78, 79, 80, 82–84
Aung San Suu Kyi, xxvii

Bailyn, Bernard, xv, 57
Baker, James, 40–41
Baltimore, Md., 85, 153
Barras, Comte de, 273, 275–76
Basking Ridge, N.J., 154
Beaujeu, Daniel de, 33–34
Beaumarchais, Pierre, 169, 201
Bennington, Battle of, 174, 183–84
Bolingbroke, Viscount, 56, 57, 67
Boston, Mass.
    Boston Massacre, 68
    Boston Port Bill, 71, 77
    Boston Tea Party, xiv, xvi, 56, 68–69
    British evacuate, 113, 124
    British occupy, xvi, 71
    British ships arrive in, 90
    British troops in, 66–67, 102
    Dorchester Heights, 107, 111–12, 113
    epicenter of resistance and
        suspicion, 67
    rioting against Stamp Act, 61
    Siege of, 71, 102–14, *103*
    slaves in, 64
Botetourt, Lord, 58, 67
Bouquet, Henry, 43, 44, 45
Braddock, Edward, 29–35
    Battle of the Monongahela, 33–35
    GW and, 30–35, 50, 308n28
    wounding and death of, 34–35
Bradford, William, 32
Brandywine, Battle of, 178–80, *178, 179*

breech-loading rifle used, 181
casualties, 180
GW's brush with death, 181
Brant, Joseph, 225
Brewster, Caleb, 220–21
Britain
    blunders and misperceptions, 68–74,
        102, 116
    Boston Tea Party, news of, and, 71
    bureaucracy of, 55
    colonial policy, 51–53, 55
    Country Party, xv, 56–57, 61–62, 63,
        64, 65, 67, 69, 73, 77–78, 86, 124
    Fairfax family, power of, 6
    France's rivalry with, 56, 169, 215
    Glorious Revolution of 1688, 56
    GW's rage against, 50–51
    Highland revolt of 1745–46, 71
    Industrial Revolution and, 54–55
    losses in Treaty of Paris, 294
    mercantile system, 53, 55
    national debt, 54, 57
    patronage jobs in, 55
    rights of Englishmen and, xv,
        56–57, 62
    Seven Years' War, 24, 28–46, 54, 55
    as superpower, 54–55
    suppression of rebellion by, xvii, 71,
        124–25, 152
    taxation and unrest in, 54, 57
    Treaty of Paris (1783), 287
    Walpole political machine, 56
    *See also* George III, King of
        England; *specific leaders*
British Army, 84–85, 90–91
    aristocracy and, xviii, 127
    atrocities and retribution against
        colonials, xvii, xix–xx, 85, 91, 102,
        124, 127, 128–29, 131, 149–50, 167, 182,
        213, 236, 262, 325n156
    best units, 209
    in Boston, 102
    brutal officers of, 234
    casualties, 85, 91, 167, 184, 188, 232,
        267–68, 271
    Coldstream Guards, 209, 211

British Army (*cont'd*)
commander's personal staff and, 170
desertions, 207
disdain toward Patriots, xvii, 91, 127,
   156, 283
evacuation of Boston, 112–13
Franklin on, 35
French and Indian War and, 25,
   33–35
Hessians and, 125–26, 129, 155, 156–59,
   167, 231
Highlanders, 267
horses lost, effect of, 176, 230
interdiction of local food supplies
   and, xviii, xxii–xxiii, 122, 123, 128,
   189, 219, 221, 287
light infantry and grenadiers, 85, 90,
   115, 141, 152, 182, 186, 197, 209,
   222–23, 238, 263, 265
logistics chain, tethered to coast,
   xviii, 128, 155
long-term enlistment in, 128
myths about, 127
Native Americans and, 225
in New Jersey, 151, 152, 155, 160,
   164–65, 167, 207–9, 325n156
occupation of six cities, xviii, 71, 126,
   153, 182–84, 189, 191, 214, 217–19, 233,
   271, 287
officers of, xviii, 89, 131, 206, 249 (*see
   also specific officers*)
pounds sterling as currency, 192
punitive agenda, xix, 124–25, 127,
   149
reasons they could not win against
   the Patriots, xvii–xix, 128–29, 202,
   213
retreat from Philadelphia and Battle
   of Monmouth, 207–12
size of, 156, 160, 207
as skilled professionals, 89, 127–29
spies for, 102
stationed in the American colonies,
   56, 61, 66–67, 70
strategic plan for 1777, 172–73
surrender at Yorktown and, 283

treatment of prisoners, xix, 149–50,
   323n109
war in the South, xx, 230–39, *233*, 256,
   265–72
Washington, Lawrence, in, 3–4, 5
wilderness fighting and, 43
*See also specific battles*
British Parliament
American colonies reject taxation,
   60, 73
American Revolution and mistaken
   strategies by, 123–29
blunders leading to the American
   Revolution, 70–74
Boston Port Bill, 71
coercion-based strategy, 71
Country Party critique of, 57
debates over fractious colonies,
   xviii–xix
"decisive blow" strategy, 124, 126–29
declaration ending hostilities, 286
doves vs. hawks on continuing the
   war (1778), 203–4
Franco-American alliance and, 203
ideological abhorrence of the
   American Revolution, 127
Intolerable Acts, xvi, 71, 90
no seats for colonials, 70
peace commissions and, 126, 204
Pitt's compromise, 125
"southern strategy," 116, 126, 129–30
Stamp Act of 1765, 59–61, 70
taxation without representation, 70
Townshend Acts, 65–68
troops placed in the Americas by, 70
Vandalia colony and, 58
vote to end hostilities in America, 284
*See also* Germain, George; *specific
   members*
Brooklyn Heights, 115, 121, 137, 138
Battle of Long Island and, 137
GW and evacuation of troops from,
   138
Buford, Abraham, 235
Buford's Massacre, 236, 237
Bunker Hill, Battle of, 90–91, 113

Burgoyne, John, 90, 125, 146–47, 238
  Battle of Saratoga, 183–84
  capture of Fort Ticonderoga, 174
  strategy to cut off New England,
    173–74
  surrender at Saratoga, 189, 201, 282
Bushnell, David, 143–44, 181, 189–90
Butler, John, 225
Byng, Admiral John, 39
Byron, "Foul-Weather Jack," 73, 215,
  218

Cadwalader, John, 156, 157, 161, 163, 242
  duel with Conway, 195–96
Cambridge, Mass., 93, 100
  GW's headquarters in, 104, 110
  rifle companies' snowball fight, 96–97
Camden, S.C., 236, 265
  Battle of, 237–39, 259, 262
  casualties, 239
Campbell, Archibald, 217
Canada, 15–16, 28, 115
  Battle of Quebec, 108–10
  colonial forces and invasion of, 87,
    101
  Congressional plan to reinvade,
    216–17
Carleton, Sir Guy, 109, 146–47, 173, 285
  declaration ending hostilities, 286
  evacuation of fugitive slaves, 295
Carlisle, Lord, 204–5
Cary, Robert, 52–53, 54, 60, 75, 314n15,
  314n22
*Cato* (Addison), 109, 143
Chadds Ford, Pa., 178, 179, 180
Chappel, Alonzo, 136
  *Lord Stirling at the Battle of Long
    Island, 136*
Charleston, S.C., 116, 129, 217–18
  British evacuation of, 286
  British occupation, xviii, 233, 271
  British raping of women and, 131
  British victory at, 230–32, 283
  GW's reaction to loss of, 237
  Rawdon's hanging of citizen Hayne,
    271

Charlotte, N.C., 260, 261, 265
Chastellux, Chevalier de, 274
Chernow, Ron, 80
Cherokees, 40–41, 44
Chesapeake Bay, 176
  Cape Henry, 279
  French fleet in, 274, 275, 276, 279
Chew, Benjamin, 186
Church, Benjamin, 102
Civil War, xix
Clark, Elijah, 263
Clausewitz, Carl von, 214
Clinton, Sir Henry, 90, 116, 125, 127,
  134–35, 173, 204, *206*, 206–7
  army's New Jersey march, 207–9, 221
  Arnold's betrayal and, 243–44
  attempts to draw GW into combat,
    222
  Battle of Monmouth and, 209
  Battle of Rhode Island and, 215
  Charleston expedition, 226
  GW's irregular combat against, 218
  GW's Yorktown campaign and, 276,
    280–81, 282
  hanging of André and, 247, 249
  "hearts and minds" strategy, 152
  in New York City, 213, 218, 232
  offer of pardons by, 255
  recall of, 285
  recall of troops from Virginia, 272–73
  southern strategy and, 116, 126, 129,
    217, 272
  strategic plan for 1778 and, 204
  war in the South and, 217–18, 229–33,
    *233*, 259–73
Closen, Baron Ludwig von, 283, 289
Coercive Acts. *See* Intolerable Acts
College of William and Mary, 11
Colonial America (under Britain)
  British authorities, cluelessness of, xv
  British ban of westward expansion, 58
  British colonization and, 3
  British mercantile system and, 53, 55
  British misperceptions, 71, 102, 116,
    125
  British policy and, 55

Colonial America (under Britain)
    (cont'd)
  British taxation of, xiv, xvi, 59–61,
    65–68, 70, 71
  British troops in, 56, 61, 66–67
  British unfair economic practices,
    53–54
  commerce and trade, 51
  expansion westward and, 15, 55
  fears of enslavement by England, xvi,
    54, 61–64, 67, 71, 79, 84, 86
  indentured servitude in, 64
  Intolerable Acts and, 71
  land speculation, Ohio Valley, 12
  literacy rate, xv
  Mennonites and Anabaptists in, 9
  militias of, xiv, xvii, 80, 82–84
  organized dissent in, 66
  Patriot-Loyalist split, xvii
  population of, 28
  power structure, xxi
  "the Rage Militaire" and, xvii, 82–84
  religious enthusiasms in, xvi
  replacing royal governance in, xiv, 77,
    79, 83–84, 86, 87
  rights of Englishmen and, 64, 70
  Shirley as head of British Forces, 36
  Stamp Act of 1765, 59–61
  taxation without representation, 70
  tea tax and, 66
  tobacco crop, 51, 53
  Townshend Acts, 65–68
  trade restrictions with Britain and, 78
  undermining royal authority and, 79
  Washington family, land
    acquisition, 3
Common Sense (Paine), 111
Congress. See Continental Congress
Conjugal Lewdness; or, Matrimonial
    Whoredom (Defoe), 49
Connecticut, 66, 117, 118, 119, 143, 144,
    164, 168, 219, 221, 222, 287
  Arnold's torching of New London
    and Fort Griswold massacre, 281
  Continental Regiment mutiny,
    228–29

GW-Rochambeau meetings, 251–53,
    273
  Royal Navy coastal attacks, 104
  Tryon's rampage, 222
Connecticut Light Horse, 120
Constitutional Convention, 299,
    300
Constitution of the United States, xvi,
    xxvi
  executive powers and GW, 300–301
Continental Army, xviii, xx, xxii–xxiii
  African Americans in, 199, 200
  as amateurs, xxiv, 93, 98, 99, 102, 107,
    116, 137, 143, 147, 154, 186
  bayonets and, 92, 104, 119, 127,
    223–24
  bounty for (New Year's Day, 1777),
    160
  carelessness with weaponry, 119
  combat-hardened core, 169, 178, 200
  creation of, 87–88
  defeat at Brandywine, 178–80
  Delaware Continentals, 137, 146, 156,
    266
  demographics of men, 199
  desertions, 111, 120, 151, 200
  disassembling (1783), 296
  discontent in (1780), 228–29
  enlistment term changes and other
    reforms (1777), 166–67
  flying camp reinforcement scheme,
    119
  French supplies for, 169, 178, 202
  funding for, 213–14, 227–28
  green troops, 169, 178
  GW address to the troops (Dec. 29,
    1776), 159–60
  GW as brake on excess, xiii, 159
  GW as commander in chief, xi, 87,
    88–89
  GW on sedition and mutiny, 118
  GW on soldiers and lewd women,
    118–19
  GW's leadership cadre and inner
    circle, 80–84, 97–101, 170–72, 177,
    196, 254

GW's view of the common soldier, xxiv, 40, 94
as homegrown manpower, 128, 146
idleness of (1782), 289–90
incorporation by Congress (July 4, 1775), 94
largest loss of regulars, 232
Marblehead men, 95, 96–97, 138, 145, 157, 169, 214
march from Boston to New York, 116–17
Maryland Continentals, 137, 146, 156, 168, 237, 266, 296
Massachusetts Continentals, 145
military engineering and, 145
militiamen in, 151
modeled on British Army, xxiv, 116
Morristown hardships (1779–80), 226–29
myths about, 91
New England Continentals, 163, 200
New England militias and, 93, 94, 95–96, 106
officer corps, xxiv–xxv, 95, 97, 200–201, 290–91
one-year term of duty and reenlistment crisis, 105–6, 109, 152, 154
original stratagems, 143–44, 183–84
panic under fire, 140, 151, 178, 187, 238
Pennsylvanians in, 179, 229, 255, 275
powder shortage, 104, 111, 119, 120
raiding and skirmishes (winter 1777), 167
recruitment of troops, 168
refusal to follow orders, 120
revolutionary principles and, 167
revolutionary state of mind of, 128–29
rifle companies and, 91, 95–96, 161
size of, 156, 160, 168, 207
smallpox and disease casualties, 105, 110–11, 120, 146, 168, 226
smallpox inoculations of, 168
as standing army, 105, 166

Steuben and, xxiv, 198–99, 203, 207, 274, 289
supply problems, 99, 225, 289
training and discipline, 91–97, 105, 119–20, 169, 178, 289
uniforms and, 119, 169
Valley Forge hardships (1777–78), 191–93
Virginians in, 95–96, 141, 157, 161, 210–11, 231, 237, 238
walkouts (winter 1780–81), 255–56, 274
war of attrition by, 184, 188
weapon shortage, 104, 119
weather problems, 226–27
winding down of war and last acts, 287
See also specific battles
Continental Congress (First), xiv, 59, 76–79, 81, 100
Continental Congress (Second), xiv, 85–90
bankruptcy and, 227, 250, 253
Carlisle Commission rejected by, 204
currency problems, 192, 227
Declaration of Independence, 133
European recognition and, 87
expansion of GW's powers and army reforms, 166
flying camp reinforcement scheme, 119
functioning of, 289
GW appointed army commander, 88, 317n49
GW arrival in uniform, 68, 86
GW's resignation speech, 298
GW's role in, 86–90
invasion of Canada and, 87, 216–17
meeting in Baltimore, 153
meeting in York, 191
national army created, 87–88
officers' grievances and, 290–93
rejection of federalized militia, 296
Contrecoeur, Claude Pierre Pécaudy de, 22, 23, 33

Conway, Thomas, 179, 180, 190, 193–96
  shot in duel with Cadwalader, 195–96
Conway Cabal, 194, 196
Cornwallis, General Lord Charles, 99,
  127, *161*, 188, 275
  Battle of Camden, 238
  Battle of Green Spring, 280
  Battle of Guilford Court House,
    270–71
  Battle of Long Island, 135
  Battle of Monmouth, 209, 211
  Battle of Princeton, 160–64
  collapse of British war effort and, 271
  escaped slaves with, 282
  Ferguson and, 259, 260, 261
  Greene and Morgan escape, 269–70
  GW's Yorktown campaign and, 280,
    281
  march from Guilford Courthouse to
    Wilmington, 271–72
  pursuit of GW by, 152–53, 160, 164
  pursuit of Morgan by, 265, 268, 269
  Royal Navy and, 280
  southern strategy and, 129
  at Trenton, 137
  troops killed or wounded, 267, 271
  Virginia plan of, 272–73
  war in the South and, 232, 233–34,
    236, 256, 265
  winter quarters in Winnsboro, 261,
    264
Coulon de Villiers, Louis, 26–27
Country Party, xv, 56–57, 61–62, 63, 64,
    65, 67, 69, 73, 77–78, 86
  American Revolution and, xv–xvi,
    xxi, xxvi, 57, 61–62, 63, 64–65, 67, 73,
    124
  GW's revolutionary thinking and,
    67, 77–78, 86, 229
  GW's role cast by, 67, 77–78, 88
Cowpens, Battle of, 266–67
  casualties, 267
  implications of British defeat,
    267–68
Craik, James, 21, 41, 39, 82, 194
Culloden, Battle of, 124

Culper Ring, 220–21, 227, 243
Cumberland, Duke of, 29, 43
Custis, John Parke "Jacky," 48, 68, 75,
    180, 277
Custis, Martha Parke "Patsy," 48, 75

Dagworthy, John, 36
Dartmouth, William Legge, Lord, 59
Davidson, John, 17
Deane, Silas, 77
Declaration of Independence, xii,
    133–34
Defoe, Daniel, *Conjugal Lewdness; or,
    Matrimonial Whoredom*, 49
de Grasse, Comte, 273, 279
  arrival in Chesapeake Bay, 276
  British capture of, 286
  campaign in the Caribbean, 285–86
  flagship of, *Ville de Paris*, 279, 286
  GW meets with, 279
  naval battle with British, 276
  Yorktown Campaign and, 275, 279
DeKalb, Johann, 237, 238, 239
Delaware Continentals, 137, 146, 156,
    266
Delaware River
  Battle of Princeton and, 161, *162*
  Battle of Trenton and, 157, 159
  blocked to the British, 189
  British reopen access to, 190
  Forts Mifflin and Mercer and, 189
  Howe's Philadelphia plan and, 175
Delawares, 16, 17, 40, 45
d'Estaing, Charles-Hector, Comte,
    214–15, 217–18
Destouches, Chevalier, 257–58, 273
Dickinson, John, *Letters from a Farmer
    in Pennsylvania*, 67
Dinwiddie, Robert, 14, 15–16, 32
  GW and, 14, 15, 27–28, 36, 37, 38, 41
  GW's mission for (1753–54), 16–20
  Virginia Regiment and, 35, 36
Drew, James, 91
Dumas, Guillaume-Mathieu, Comte,
    251
Dunmore, John Murray, Earl of, 76

Duportail, Louis Lebègue, 231
Duquesne, Marquis, 15–16, 23, 29

East India Company, xiv, 68
*Easy Plan for a Militia, An*
    (Pickering), 119–20
Elk River, Md., 176, 277
Ellis, Joseph, 106, 287
Emerson, Ralph Waldo, 95
Emerson, William, 95
Ewald, Johann, 127, 155, 176–77, 249

Fairfax, George William, 7, 41, 309n11
    GW and, 7, 9, 31, 85
    marriage to Sally Cary, 10, 20, 31, 41
    surveying expedition (1748), 9–10, 18
Fairfax, Sally Cary, 10, *11*, 20, 31, 41–42,
    47, 49, 180, 309n21
Fairfax, Thomas, Baron, 6, 8–9
Fairfax, William, 5–6, 7, 20, 41
    mentoring of GW, 7–8, 11, 27
Fairfax Resolves, 76, 80
Fallen Timbers, Battle of, 301
Falmouth, Mass., burning of, 102–3
Ferguson, Patrick, 127, 181, 234
    fate of, 259–61
Ferry Farm, Va., 4, 5
Fielding, John, Cornwallis portrait,
    *161*
fire ships, 143–44
Fitzgerald, John, 163
Fitzhugh, William, 28
Flexner, James Thomas, xx
Florida, 55, 204, 285, 294, 295
Forbes, John and Forbes expedition,
    43–46, 50
    veterans of, in GW's circle, 82
Fort Cumberland, 36, 38, 41
Fort Duquesne, 29, 32, 33, 38, 43, 46
    Battle of, 45–46
Fort Griswold, 281
Fort Le Boeuf, 17, 18
Fort Lee, 121, 147, 148–51
Fort Ligonier, 45
Fort Mercer, 189, 190
Fort Mifflin, 189, 190

Fort Moultrie, 230–31
Fort Necessity, 23, 25, 26, 27, 28, 29, 32
    veterans of, in GW's circle, 82, 97
Fort Pitt, 46
Fort Ticonderoga, 43, 87, 107, 147
    Arnold and Allen capture, 86, 101
    artillery moved from, 107, 117
    Burgoyne captures, 174
Fort Washington, 99, 121, 145, 147
    Battle of, 148–49
    Greene and loss of, 150
    GW's reaction to loss of, 149
    Hessians bayoneting of wounded
        Americans/killing prisoners, 149
Fort William Henry, 39
Founding Fathers, xxi, 65, 302
Fox, James, 125
France
    alliance with the Americans, 87–88,
        169, 201–3, 214, 215–16, 231, 251, 285
    American loan from, 253–54, 258–59,
        294
    attack at Great Meadows, 25–27
    British rivalry with, 56
    conflict in the Ohio Valley and GW,
        15–20, 22–27
    Franco-American friction, 256–58
    French and Indian War (Seven
        Years' War), 28–46, 169
    gains from Treaty of Paris, 294
    GW's wariness about, 216, 217
    Lafayette and GW, 181
    military engineering and, 281
    Napoléon's defeat by Britain, 54–55
    Native American allies, 16, 23, 25, 45
    population of American colonies, 28
    Robespierre and, 101, 243
    siegecraft and, 281
Franklin, Benjamin, 70, 73
    on British regular troops, 35
    confiscated portrait, 183, 327n67
    French alliance and, 201–2
    house occupied by André, 183, 248
    Howe peace conference and, 137
    Laurens seeking French loan and,
        254

Franklin, Benjamin (*cont'd*)
  peace negotiations and, 294–95
  response to André's hanging, 248
  Steuben and, 198
  warning Braddock about Indians, 32
Frederick the Great, 39, 164
French and Indian War (Seven Years'
    War), 24, 28–46
  Battle of Fort Duquesne, 45–46
  Battle of Minden, 126
  Battle of the Monongahela, 33–35
  Braddock and, 29–35
  Braddock's defeat, 33–35, 37, 43, 80–81
  British four-pronged plan, 29
  British war debt and, 54
  casualties, 35, 45, 46
  Forbes expedition, 43–46
  as global conflict, 24
  GW and, xxii, xxiv, 28–46
  GW and start of war (1754), 21–27
  GW's pre-war mission, 16–20
  Loudoun relieved of command, 39
  Montcalm's campaign, 39
  murder of Jumonville, 23–24, 26,
    216
  Native Americans and, 32–33, 34,
    40–41, 44, 45–46
  Pitt and, 39, 43
  Rogers and, 122–23
French Navy, 202, 214
  capture of Grenada, 218
  cost and construction of ships, 216
  failed pursuit of Arnold and,
    257–58
  fleet arrives in Delaware Bay, 212
  fleet under de Grasse, 273, 274
  fleet under d'Estaing, 214–15, 217–18
  fleet under Destouches, 257–58, 273
  fleet under Ternay, 251, 257
  largest warship in the world, 279
  loss of ships to Rodney, 286
  size of ships, logistics and, 214,
    274
  West Indies and, 285–86
French Revolution, xxi, 294, 303
Fry, Joshua, 21, 22, 25

Gage, Thomas, 61, 71, 73, 90, 102
  Battles of Lexington and Concord,
    84–85
  French and Indian War, 31, 33
Gálvez, Bernardo de, 285
Gandhi, Mahatma, xxvii
Gates, Horatio, 31, 82, *83*, 110–11, 112,
    171, 225
  as adjutant general, 110
  Arnold and, 190
  backbiting by, 150
  Battle of Camden, 237–39
  Battle of Saratoga, 183–84
  Congress dismisses, 239
  Conway Cabal and, 194, 195
  coup against GW and, 292–93
  forces of, delivered to GW, 156
  GW and, 82, 174–75, 237
  as hero of Saratoga, 189, 190, 195, 237
  intrigue surrounding, 190
  Morgan and, 196, 223
  Northern Department and, 174–75
  war in the South and, 237
George II, King of England, 24
George III, King of England, xvii, 59,
    61, *62*, 74, 111, 125, 127, 134
  alternative scenario for, 73–74
  British Army and, 56, 61
  Colonial petitioning of, 79
  colonials seen as children, 70, 125
  GW replaces in America, 89, 114
  GW's resignation, response to, 298,
    300
  as Patriot King, 57, 61, *62*, 71, 73, 74,
    79, 111, 133, 134, 203, 285, 298
  plot to kidnap his son, 288–89
  prolonging of war and, 203–4, 213
  strategic plan for 1777, 173
  surrender at Yorktown and, 284
Georgia, 77, 217, 266. *See also*
    Savannah, Ga.
Germain, Lord George, 123, 126–27,
    138, 142, 176, 204, 213, 285
  "southern strategy," 217, 218
  strategic plan for 1777, 173
  surrender at Yorktown and, 284

Germantown, Battle of, 184–88, *185*
  assault on Chew House, 186–88, *187*
  casualties, 188
  Fourth Virginia captured, 188
  Mount Airy, 186
Gerry, Elbridge, xiii, 89
Gist, Christopher, 17, 18–20, 23, 36, 39
Glover, John, 138, 145
  Battle of Trenton and, 157
  Marblehead men and, 138, 145, 157,
    169, 214
Gordon, Thomas, 56, 67
Grant, James, 45, 124, 135, 149, 156, 187
  Battle of Princeton and, 160
  on GW in Morristown, 166
Graves, Sir Thomas, 276, 280–81
Great Awakening, xvi
Greene, Caty, 99–100, 196
Greene, Christopher, 189
Greene, Nathanael, xx, xxv, 99–100,
    *100*, 120, 121, 135–36, 147, 148, 193,
    196
  advance into South Carolina, 271
  aggressiveness of, 270
  on Arnold, 242
  Battle of Brandywine, 180
  Battle of Germantown, 186, 187, 188
  Battle of Guilford Court House,
    270–71
  Battle of Monmouth, 210
  Battle of Princeton, 163
  Battle of Rhode Island, 215
  Battle of Trenton, 158
  commander, southern theater,
    262–65, 268–72
  Cornwallis and, 269–70
  decency of, 262
  defense of the Hudson River, 147, 148
  GW and, 99, 171
  hanging of André and, 247
  loss of Fort Washington and, 150, 151
  Morgan and, 264, 268–69, 270
  as quartermaster general, 193, 227, 228
  race to Dan River, 269–70
  report on British/Hessian atrocities,
    167

  treatment of prisoners and wounded,
    267
  Valley Forge and, 191
  war councils of June 1778 and, 208
Greenman, Jeremiah, 109, 200
Green Spring, Battle of, 280
Grey, Charles "No-Flint," 182, 183
  bayoneting of colonials, 182, 183, 222
  burning of New England coast, 215
  portrait of Franklin and, 183, 327n67
Guilford Court House, Battle of, 271
Gurr, Ted Robert, 315n52

Hackensack, N.J., 150
Hale, Nathan, 142–43, 219, 247
Half-King, 16, 17–18, 20, 22, 23–25, 27
Halifax, Nova Scotia, 117, 129
Hamilton, Alexander, xxi, 170, *171*,
    245–46, 247, 251, 262, 300
  Battle of Germantown, 186
  Battle of Trenton, 158
  Battle of White Plains, 146
  competitiveness of, 253
  defense of Philadelphia and, 177
  discharge of troops and, 296
  on Gates, 239
  on GW's staff, xxiii, 170, 196, 253, 290
  political ideas of, 229
  rumors of coup against GW and,
    291–92
  at Valley Forge, 196
  Yorktown Campaign and, 282
Hancock, John, 73, 85, 88, 106, 112, 122,
    139, 140, 145, 154, 170, *171*, 180
Hand, Edward, 161
Harlem Heights, Battle of, 140–42, 145
  casualties, 142
Havel, Václav, xxvii
Hayne, Isaac, 271
Heister, Philip von, 135
Henry, Patrick, 59–60, 76, 77, 172
Hessians, 125–26
  Battle of Brandywine and, 179–80
  Battle of Long Island and, 126, 135
  Battle of Princeton and, 161–64
  Battle of Trenton and, 156–59

Hessians (*cont'd*)
  with Cornwallis, 152–53
  desertions, 207
  Jägers, 152–53, 176
  killing frenzy of, 149
  looting, burning, rape, and
    mistreatment of civilians, 126, 155,
    167, 325n156
  in New Jersey, 155–59, 167
  in New York City, 145
  number of troops, 125–26, 129
  Patriots' conspiracy theories and, 125
  surrender at Trenton, GW's
    treatment of, 159
  surrender at Yorktown and, 283
  taking no prisoners, 140, 149
  war in the South and, 231
Hickey, Thomas, 117–18
HMS *Cerberus*, 90, 173, 206, 207
HMS *Eagle*, 129
HMS *Vulture*, 244, 245
Hood, Sir Samuel, 286
Howard, John Eager, 267
Howe, Admiral Richard, 125, 126, 127,
    129, *130*, 138, 173, 205
  Battle of Rhode Island and, 214–15
  congressional delegation and, 137
  flagship of, 129
  flotilla against Philadelphia, 175–76
  Kips Bay Landing and, 140–41
Howe, General William, 90, 113, 123,
    125, 126, 129, *132*
  Battle of Brandywine, 178–80, *178*,
    *179*
  Battle of Bunker Hill, 90–91, 113, 134,
    138
  Battle of Germantown, 184–88
  Battle of Long Island, 134–37, *135*, *136*
  Battle of Trenton, 160
  counterinsurgency strategy, 173
  departure (Mischianza), 205–6, 232
  division of his army, 184
  encounters enmity of locals, 176
  failure to stop the rebellion, 183
  GW returns lost dog of, 205
  habit of "stopping short," 137, 141

"hearts and minds" strategy, 152
  horses lost, effect of, 176
  leaves New Jersey with troops, 172
  Loyalists used by, 221–22
  mistress of, 150
  in New Jersey, 154
  pardons offered by, 152
  peace offer and GW, 131–33, 134
  in Philadelphia, 191
  Philadelphia plan, 173, 175–76, 182–83
  private secretary for, 137, 322n63
  pursuit of GW, 145–46, 147
  relieved of command, 204
  taking Brooklyn Heights and, 137–38
  traps set for GW by, 172
  treatment of prisoners and, 150
Howe, Robert, 256
Huddy, Joshua, 287–88
Hudson River
  defense of, 147–48
  strategic importance of, 146
  Verplanck's and Stony Point forts,
    222
  *See also* Fort Lee; Fort Washington
Huger, Isaac, 269
Huntingdon, Earl of, 131
Hutchinson, Thomas, 61

India, as British colony, 39
*Indien* (French frigate), 259
Industrial Revolution, 54–55
Intolerable Acts, xvi, 71, 90
Invalid Corps, 254, 290–91
Iroquois, 17, 45, 225–26
irregular warfare, 82, 85, 128, 142, 239
  André capture by irregulars, 245, 249
  Boston resistance and, 102
  British harassed/mauled by, 155, 207,
    271, 287
  Continental Army and, 178
  as Dangerland, xxi, 218–21, 249, 287
  GW and use of, xiv, xx, 35, 68, 81, 89,
    122, 189, 219, 220, 221, 288
  inherent danger of using, 262, 288
  Loyalist bands, 123, 143, 213, 221,
    234

war in the South and, 234–35, 236,
  250

Jackson, Andrew, 65, 262
Jameson, John, 244–45
Jay, John, 243, 289, 294–95
Jefferson, Thomas, xxvi, 76, 273, 302,
  303
  Declaration of Independence and,
    133
  *Notes on the State of Virginia*, 8
Jefferis Ford, Pa., 178
Johnson, Sir William, 225
Joncaire, 17, 18
Jones, Joseph, 293
Jones, Thomas, 167
Jumonville, Joseph, 23–24, 26, 216

Kemmelmeyer, Frederick, *Washington
  reviewing militia assembled to crush
  the Whiskey Rebellion, 301*
Kings Mountain, Battle of, 260–61,
  262
Knowlton, Thomas, 141–42
Knox, Henry, 98–99, *98*, 117, 131–32, 191,
  251, 298
  artillery and, 99, 121, 161
  Battle of Germantown, 186, 188
  Battle of Monmouth, 210
  Battle of Princeton, 161
  Battle of Trenton, 158
  fortification of Dorchester Heights,
    107
  in GW's inner circle, 171, 194
  at Valley Forge, 196
  war councils of June 1778 and, 208
Knyphausen, Wilhelm von, 179, 180,
  181

Lafayette, Marquis de, 170–71, 202,
  245–46, 251
  Battle of Brandywine, 180
  Battle of Green Spring, 280
  Battle of Monmouth, 208–9, *209*, 211
  Battle of Rhode Island, 215
  bravery under fire, 180

defense of Philadelphia and, 177
  failed pursuit of Arnold and, 257, 272
  French Revolution and, 303
  given Stephen's division, 188
  GW's affection for, 180–81
  GW's Yorktown campaign and, 280
  as liaison with the French, 181, 215, 216
  surrender at Yorktown and, 283
  talent as a commander, 208
  at Valley Forge, 196, *197*
  war councils of June 1778 and, 208
  Wayne and escape from Cornwallis,
    275
Lake Champlain, 29, 101, 115
  Battle of Valcour Island, 146–47
  Fort William Henry, 39
Lake George, 107
Laurens, Henry, 170, 177, 192, 205,
  216–17
Laurens, John, xxi, 170, 180, 196, 216,
  249, 254
  French loan and, 253–54, 258–59
*Lee* (privateer), 104
Lee, Charles, xxiv, 31, 80–82, *81*, 88, 95,
  98, 146
  Battle of Monmouth, 208–10, *209*
  as British informant, 197
  capture of, 154, 234
  as commander, 116, 129
  court-martial of, 211–12
  death of, 212
  as de facto second-in-command, 110
  duel with John Laurens, 212
  forces of, delivered to GW, 156
  fortification of New York and, 115–16
  GW and, 82, 151, 197–98, 210
  as hero of Charleston, 129–30, 145
  military engineering and, 145
  at New Castle, 147
  treachery and insubordination, 110,
    150–52, 153
  at Valley Forge, 198
  war councils of June 1778 and, 208
Lee, Henry "Light-Horse Harry," 82,
  193, 220, 224
  war in the South and, 263, 270, 271

Lee, Richard Henry, 77, 193–94
Legion of the United States, 301
Leslie, Alexander, 265
*Letters from a Farmer in Pennsylvania*
    (Dickinson), 67
Lincoln, Benjamin, 217, 218, 230–31, 254
    surrender at Charleston, 231–32, 283
    surrender at Yorktown and, 283
Lippincott, Richard, 288
Lloyd Loring, Elizabeth, 150
Lloyd Loring, Joshua, 150
Lloyd's Neck, N.Y., 221
Locke, John, xv
Long Island, 121, 122, 123
    Battle of, 134–37, 135, 136, 140
    casualties, 140
    Hessians shooting of surrendering
        Patriots, 140
Longmore, Paul, 77
Loudoun, Lord, 38, 39, 43
Louisiana, 28
Louis XIV of France, 281
Louis XV of France, 26
Louis XVI of France, 258, 288
Lovell, James, 193
Loyalists (Tories), xiv
    the Association and, 83
    atrocities and retribution by, 213
    Battle of Camden and, 237–39
    Battle of Kings Mountain and,
        260–61
    British commanders of, 234
    British evacuation of Boston and, 113
    British Legion, 222, 231, 238–39
    British misperception of, 116, 164,
        176, 236
    brutality and, 222
    desertions of, 236
    fate of John Moore's force, 236
    GW's treatment of, 117, 296
    irregulars under Rogers, 143
    irregular warfare and, 262
    Lee's cruel trick on, 270
    as minority, xvii
    in New Jersey, 154, 167
    in New York, 117, 142, 221–22, 243

    in Philadelphia, 182
    post-war exile of, 296
    Queen's Rangers, 176, 221–22, 282
    raiding by, 222
    Rogers and, 221–22
    in the South, 116, 129, 217, 218, 234,
        236, 260–61, 262, 270, 271
    as spies, 102, 117
    suspicions about, 84
    Volunteers of Ireland, 222
Lynch, Michael, 117

Mackay, James, 25, 27
Mandela, Nelson, xxvii
Manley, John, 104
Mao, Madame, 101
Marblehead, Mass.
    Glover's regiment, 138, 145, 157, 169,
        214
    troops from, 95, 96–97
Marie-Antoinette of France, 288
Marion, Francis, 263, 264
Martin, Joseph Plumb, 200, 210, 228,
        283
Marye, Reverend, 6
Maryland, 22, 25, 27, 35, 36, 38, 58, 176,
        264
    Continentals, 137, 146, 156, 168, 237,
        266, 296
    militias of, 265
    rifle companies and, 87, 92
Mason, George, 67, 76, 80
Mathews, David, 117
Maurice de Saxe, 113
Maxwell, William, 180
McHenry, James, 286
McKenzie, Robert, 79
Mercer, Hugh, 39, 82, 148, 163
Mercer, John, 37
Middlekauff, Robert, 61
Mifflin, Thomas, 82, 98, 193, 195, 298
militias, 296
    Battle of Bennington, 174
    Battle of Cowpens, 266–68
    Battle of Germantown, 184, 186,
        187

Battle of Guilford Courthouse,
270–71
Battle of Princeton, 163
Battle of Rhode Island, 214–15
Battle of Trenton and, 156, 157
Battles of Lexington and Concord, 85
at Boston, 93
British bad behavior and increase in,
155
Clinton's march encountering, 207
Continental Army and, 94, 168, 169
discipline and training problems,
119–20, 140, 146, 151
"flying camps" and, 119
French and Indian War, 15, 21, 32, 37
GW and Fairfax County militia, 86
GW prevents reprisals by, 288
Loyalist, 259, 261
Maryland, 176, 265
New England, 174
New Jersey, 152, 155, 167
Pennsylvania, 119, 163, 195
Philadelphia's, 156
raising, 82–84
revolutionizing of, xiv, xvii, 78, 82, 83
Virginia, 80, 265
war in the South and, 217, 230, 231,
237–39, 262, 263, 265–68, 270–71
Whiskey Rebellion and, 301, 302
Minden, Battle of, 126
Mingos (migrant Iroquois), 16, 17
Mississippi Company, 58
Mohawks, 225
Monmouth, Battle of, 207–12, 209, 211
casualties, 212
GW rallies the troops, 210–11, 211
Monongahela, Battle of the, 33–35
Montcalm, Louis-Joseph de, 39
Montesquieu, xv
Montgomery, Richard, xxvi, 101, 108–9
Montreal, 108, 109
Moore, John, 236
Moores Creek Bridge, Battle of, 129
Moravians, 45
Morgan, Daniel, xxx, 31, 68, 91, 95, 96,
97, 171, 190, 246, 264

Battle of Cowpens, 266–67
Battle of Quebec, 108, 109, 171
formula for redcoat reduction, 269
Gates and, 196, 223, 264
Greene rescuing, 268–69
GW's view of, 171, 196
as hero of Saratoga, 223
passed over by GW and furloughed,
223
prisoners taken by, 267, 268
pursued by Cornwallis, 268
Rangers, 171–72, 174, 184, 196, 207, 265
rank, Eleventh Virginia, 171
retirement of, 269
at Valley Forge, 196
war in the South and Greene, 264,
265
Morris, Gouverneur, 50
Morris, Robert, 276, 277, 289, 291
Morristown, N.J., 153
GW's headquarters (1776–77), 164,
166–67
GW's headquarters (1779–80), 226–29
smallpox inoculations at, 105, 168
Moultrie, William, 263
Mount Vernon, Va., 5, 12, 14, 49, 53, 67
GW changes crops and
management, 53
GW expands, renovates, 52–53
GW leaves (May 5, 1775), 85
GW preparing for coming conflict
and visitors at (1774–75), 80–82
GW returns, Yorktown Campaign
and, 277–78
GW's return post-war, 299–300
Mowat, Henry, 103
Muse, George, 21, 25, 26
Musgrave, Thomas, 183, 186

Nancy (British supply ship), 104, 107,
112
National Archives, Founders Online
program, xxii
Native Americans
American Revolution and, 224–26
attacks on Virginia frontier, 37–38

Native Americans (cont'd)
  claims on the Ohio Valley and, 16
  Creek uprising in Georgia, 77
  Fallen Timbers breaking power of,
    301
  as French allies, 16, 23, 25
  French and Indian War and, 32–33,
    34, 40–41, 44, 45–46
  fur trading and, 16
  GW and, 9, 17–18, 19, 25, 35, 40–41, 44
  GW and Indian removal, 295
  GW as "the Great Knife," 40
  as losers in the Treaty of Paris, 295
  Ohio Valley treaty, 58–59
  Pontiac's War, 58
  smallpox and, 13
  Sullivan Expedition against, 225–26
  Wyoming and Cherry Valley
    massacres, 225
  See also Half-King; specific tribes
New Brunswick, N.J., 153, 163–64
New Hampshire regiments, 210–11
New Jersey
  Battle of Monmouth, 207–12, 209,
    211
  Battle of Paulus Hook, 224
  Battle of Princeton, 158, 161–64, 162
  Battle of Trenton, 156–59, 157
  British and Hessian atrocities in, 155,
    164–65, 167, 325n156
  British campaign in, 151, 155
  British in (winter 1777), 167
  British pardons offered to Patriots,
    152
  Clinton's march across (1778), 207–9
  food traffickers along the coast, 287
  GW decamps to, 147, 150
  GW's starving troops and, 228
  hanging of Joshua Huddy, 288
  Howe's protection of Loyalists in,
    154
  Howe's strategy in, 154
  local resistance against the British,
    155
  Loyalists in, 154, 164
  militias of, 152, 155

Saw Mill Road, 161–62
Stony Creek bridge, 162
Newport, R.I.
  Battle of Rhode Island, 214–15
  British evacuation of, 232
  British occupy, xviii, 153
  French in, 251, 257, 276
Newtown, Battle of, 225
New York City
  arson and burning of, 142
  Battle of Harlem Heights, 140–42
  British evacuation of, 46, 297
  British landing, Kips Bay, 139, 140–41
  British occupy, xviii, 126, 212, 214,
    218–19, 287
  British ships at, 115–16, 123, 129
  as British target, 115, 124, 126–29
  Brooklyn Heights and, 115, 121, 137
  Bushnell's submarine and fire ships,
    144
  Declaration of Independence read,
    134
  defense of, orders of Congress and,
    139
  feigned attack on, 274
  Governors Island, 121
  GW and troops escape, 138–42, 145
  GW's defenses for, 120–21
  GW's mistakes and, 121–22, 137
  GW's spies and, 219–21
  GW's victory tour, 297–98
  Hessians in battle for, 126, 135, 136
  intrigue in, 142, 143
  Knox's artillery and, 121
  Loyalists in, 117, 122–23, 142, 221–22,
    243
  Pell's Point and, 145
  size of British forces, 128
  Stamp Act Congress, 60
  statue of George III and, 61, 134
  Stirling raid on Staten Island, 229–30
  whores at Holy Ground, 119
New York state, 86
  Battle of Fort Washington, 148–49
  Battle of Long Island, 134–37, 135, 136
  Battle of Saratoga, 183–84

Battle of Stony Point, 223–24
Battle of White Plains, 146
Brant and Butler raiding in, 225
Cherry Valley massacre, 225
*See also* Fort Ticonderoga; Hudson
   River; West Point
Nicola, Lewis, 290–91
Niles, Hezekiah, xiv
non-importation agreements, 60,
   65–66, 78
North, Lord, 126, 203, 204, 284
   "Americans must fear you," 124
   surrender at Yorktown and, 284
North Carolina
   Battle of Kings Mountain, 260–61
   Cornwallis detachments in, 236
   Cornwallis in Charlotte, 260, 261
   fate of Ferguson in, 259–61
   Greene in Charlotte, 265
   militias of, 237, 238, 260–61
   Ninety Six, 236, 261, 265
   war in the South and, 236
*Notes on the State of Virginia*
   (Jefferson), 8
Nova Scotia, 29, 117, 129, 295

Ogden, Matthias, 288, 289
O'Hara, Charles, 283
Ohio Company, 12–13, 14, 21–23, 25, 27
   GW as Dinwiddie messenger, 16–20
Ohio Valley
   Braddock's defeat, 33–35
   British ban on westward
      expansion, 58
   Forbes expedition, 43–46
   Forks of the Ohio, 14, 44, 46
   French fort and ambitions, 15, 16,
      21, 25
   Great Meadows and, 32
   GW and bounty land in, 58–59
   GW's Great Meadows expedition,
      21–27
   GW's pre-war mission, 16–20
   Monongahela River and, 33, 34
   Native Americans and, 32
   Pontiac's War, 58

*See also* Fort Duquesne; Fort
   Necessity; French and Indian War
Oneidas, 225
Orme, Robert, 30

Paine, Thomas, 253
   *Common Sense*, 111
Paoli Massacre, 182, 183, 186, 223, 270
Parker, Peter, 116, 126, 129
Paterson, James, 132
Paulus Hook, Battle of, 224
Peale, Charles Willson, 68, 156
   Morgan's portrait, *96*
   Washington's portrait, 68, *69*
Peebles, John, 204
Pendleton, Edmund, 76
Penn, William, 27
Pennsylvania
   Battle of Brandywine, 178–80, *178*,
      *179*
   Brant and Butler raiding in, 225
   Conway's Brigade, 179
   legislature moves to Lancaster, 191
   militia under Cadwalader, 156, 163
   Paoli Massacre, 182, 183, 186, 223, 270
   Patriot troops of, 179, 229, 255, 275
   rifle companies and, 87, 161
   Wyoming massacre, 225
   *See also* Philadelphia, Pa.
Perth Amboy, N.J., 153, 172
Philadelphia, Pa.
   British evacuate, 207, 222
   British occupy, xviii, 182–84, 189, 191
   Congress evacuates (1776), 153, 183
   Continental Congresses in, 76–79,
      85–90, 119, 122, 133
   Declaration of Independence and,
      133
   GW marches through, 276
   GW's defense of, 177
   GW's popularity in, 85–86
   Howe's grand departure, 205–6
   Howe's offensive plan and, 173
   Loyalists in, 182–83
Phillips, William, 259, 272
Pickens, Andrew, 235, 266, 267

Pickering, Timothy, 119
  *An Easy Plan for a Militia*, 119
Pigot, Sir Robert, 215
Pitt, William, 39, 43, 54, 70, 71, 73, 125,
  203
Pontiac's War, 58
Powel, Eliza, 49
Princeton, N.J., 153, 164
  Battle of, *158*, 160–64, *162*
prisoners
  "Arnold's Quarter," 281
  British prison ships, 149, 262
  deaths among, 149
  GW's treatment of, 159, 164, 205, 224,
    246, 282
  Patriots captured, xix, 149–50
  Soviet and German prisoners vs.
    Patriots taken prisoner, 149,
    323n109
  "Tarleton's Quarter," 236, 261, 267
privateers, 104, 169
Putnam, Israel "Old Put," 93, 113, 141,
  144, 147, 148
Putnam, Rufus, 112

Quakers, 45, 99, 141, 176, 264
Quebec, 101
  Battle of (1775), 108–10

"Rage Militaire," xvii, 83–84, 91, 96,
  101, 111, 129, 157, 308n11
Rall, Johann, 156, 158–59
Randolph, Peyton, 76, 77
Rawdon, Francis Lord, 127, 131, 183, 234
  Battle of Camden, 238
  revenge and, 271
  Volunteers of Ireland and, 222, 236
  war in the South and, 236–37
Reading, Pa., 182, 191
Reed, Joseph, xxiii, 82, 98, 117, 132, 141,
  155, 170, 242, 255
  treachery and insubordination, 150–52
Revere, Paul, 85
revolution
  American as different, xxvi–xxvii, 65
  Argentina's, xix

Bolshevik, xxvii
Chinese Gang of Four, 243
Chinese aftermath, as neo-dynastic,
  xxvii
conspiracy theory fomenting, 63
Czech Republic, xxv
difficulty of sustaining, 129
economic disparities and, 63
ending of apartheid, South Africa,
  xxvii
India, xxvii
lack of permanent change from, xxv
leaders of, illusion and bluffing by, 94
Marxist-Leninism and, 63
Myanmar/Burma, xxvii
rage and, 50
"relative deprivation" model, 315n52
retribution and, xxvii, 159, 243
Russian revolution aftermath, xxvii
single vision of, 302
towering individual and prevention
  of bloodbath, xxvii
treachery and, 101, 243
"Velvet" type of, xxvii
Reynolds, Joshua, Tarleton portrait,
  234, *235*
Rhode Island, Battle of, 214–15
riflemen and companies, 87, 91, 95–96
  Battle of Quebec and, 108
  breech-loading rifle, 181
  Morgan's Rangers, 171–72, 174, 184,
    196, 207, 265
  New Jersey Campaign, 161
Robertson, James, 247
Robespierre, Maximilien, 101, 243
Rochambeau, Comte de, 251, 256, 258,
  289
  GW meetings with, 251–53, 273–74
  GW's criticism of Destouches and,
    257–58, 336n27
  surrender at Yorktown and, 283
  Virginia strategy and, 274
  Yorktown Campaign and, 275, 277,
    279
Rockingham, Lord, 285
Rodney, George, 280, 285–86

Rogers, Robert, 122–23, 142, 143, 221–22
Royal Navy
  aristocracy and, 127
  Battle of Rhode Island and, 214–15,
    216
  battle with de Grasse, 276
  burning of Falmouth, 102–3
  Bushnell's submarine and, 144
  Colonial America and, 55
  confined to seacoast, 128
  Cornwallis's Virginia plans, 272
  Franco-American alliance and, 204,
    215
  French and Indian War and, 28, 43, 45
  French in the Caribbean and, 285–86
  GW offered position in, 6–7
  in Halifax, 117
  Howe as commander, 125
  Hudson River and, 147–48
  in New York Harbor, 115–16, 123
  privateers used against, 104
  Rodney in Saint Eustatius, 280
  seacoast raids and bombardment,
    102–4
  Southern Loyalists and, 116
  storm of Feb. 1781, and, 257
  transatlantic passage, 130–31
  transport of Clinton's forces, 212
*Rules of Civility and Decent Behavior in
  Company and Conversation, The,* 6, 8
Rush, Benjamin, 86, 133–34
Rutledge, John, 137

Saint-Pierre, Jacques Legardeur de,
    18, 21
Sandy Hook, N.J., 211, 212
Saratoga, Battle of (Bemis Heights
    and Freeman's Farm), 183–84
  Arnold and, 184, 190–91, 239–40
  British casualties, 184
  Burgoyne's surrender, 189, 201, 282
  Gates as hero of, 189, 190
  Morgan's Rangers, 184
Savannah, Ga., xviii, 217, 218, 230, 286
Schuyler, Philip, 98, 101, 108, 142, 174,
    190

Scotland: revolt of 1745–46, 71, 124
Scott, Bill, 200
Scott, Charles, 39, 82, 161, 210, 220
Scott, Winfield, 210
Sergeant, Jonathan, 193
Serle, Ambrose, 137, 322n63
Seven Years' War. *See* French and
    Indian War
Sharpe, Horatio, 27
Shawnees, 16, 40
Shenandoah Valley, 8, 9–10, 37–38
  GW's land acquisition in, 11
  GW's surveying trip (1748), 9–10
Shippen, Peggy, *241,* 241–42, 245–46
Shirley, William, 36–37
Shuldham, Molyneux, 113
Simcoe, James Graves, 183, 234, 282
  Queen's Rangers and, 222, 282
Six Nations of the Iroquois
    Confederation, 16, 225
slavery
  in Barbados, 14
  British evacuation of fugitive slaves,
    295
  in Colonial America, xvi, 63–64
  Custis family slaves, 47, 303
  GW and, 4, 14, 37, 200, 254, 295, 303
  Hamilton and, 254
  indentured servitude as, 64
  Laurens and, 254
  slaves as informants for the British,
    237
  Stirling as slave owner, xxv
smallpox, 13, 105, 226
  GW contracts (1751), 13
  GW inoculates Continental Army
    troops, 13, 105, 168
  inoculation of Martha Washington,
    168
Smallwood, William, 264
Smith, Joshua, 244, 246
Sons of Liberty, 61
South Carolina, 270
  Battle of Camden, 237–39, 259, 262
  British victories in, xxx
  Buford's Massacre, 236, 237

South Carolina (*cont'd*)
  Cornwallis in Winnsboro, 261, 264
  fighting on horseback and, 264
  Greene's advance into, xx, 271
  increasing brutality of war in, 262
  irregulars, 234–36, 239, 250, 262, 263
  Loyalists in, 164, 234, 262
  rice exports, 78
  Virginia Regiment fighting in, 38–39
  war in the South and, 230–36
  *See also* Charleston, S.C.
Spain, 5, 285, 294
spies
  André and, 239, 242, 243, 244–45
  Arnold's betrayal, 242–43
  code names and invisible ink, 243
  Culper Ring, 219–21
  in GW's secret council of war,
    156–57
  Hale hanged as, 142–43
  Loyalists as, 102, 117
  Patriots' advantage, 243, 269
  Rogers as double agent, 123
Stamp Act Congress, 60
Stamp Act of 1765, xiv, 59–61, 70, 134
Staten Island
  British raping of women on, 131
  British troops on, 129, 130–31, 134
Stephen, Adam, 21, 39, 82, 133, 153
  Battle of Brandywine, 179
  Battle of Germantown, 187
  Battle of Trenton, 157–58
  court-martial of, 188
  loss at Bergen, 172, 188
Steuben, Friedrich von, xxiv, 198–99,
    *199*, 203, 208, 207, 274, 289, 298
Stirling, Lord William Alexander, xxv,
    97, 153, 156, 172
  Battle of Brandywine, 179
  Battle of Long Island, 136–37, *136*
  Battle of Monmouth, 210
  in GW's inner circle, 171, 190
  raid on Staten Island, 229–30
  at Valley Forge, 196
  war councils of June 1778 and,
    208

Stony Point, N.Y., 222
  Battle of, 223–24
Stuart, Gilbert, xxii, *48*, 50
Stuart, John, 3rd Earl of Bute, 73
Sullivan, John, xxv, 100–101, 104, 156
  Battle of Brandywine, 179, 181
  Battle of Germantown, 186, 187, 188
  Battle of Long Island, 135–37
  Battle of Newtown, 225–26
  Battle of Princeton, 163
  Battle of Rhode Island, 214–15
  Battle of Trenton, 158
  diplomatic gaffes of, 215, 216
  in GW's inner circle, 171
  GW warns about troop behavior,
    167–68
  Sullivan Expedition, 225–26
Sullivan's Island, S.C., 129, 230
Sumter, Thomas, 234–35, 263
Sun Tzu, 113

Talbot, Silas, 144
Tallmadge, Benjamin, 220–21, 247, 287
Tarleton, Banastre, 127, 154, 183, 220,
    234, 235–36, 261, 264, 270
  Battle of Cowpens and, 266–67
  as "Bloody Tarleton," 236
  British Legion and, 222, 231, 238–39
  pursuit of Morgan by, 265–66, 268
  Virginia rampage, 273
Ternay, Admiral, 251, 257
Thacher, James, 94, 155, 248, 283
Tilghman, Tench, 140
Townshend, Charles, 65
Townshend Acts, 65–68
Trask, Israel, 96–97
Treaty of Paris (1783), 287, 294, 301
Trenchard, James, *100*
Trenchard, John, 56, 57, 67
Trenton, N.J., 153
  Battle of, 156–59, *157*
  Cornwallis and, 137, 161
Trotsky, Leon, 101, 243
Trumbull, John
  *Battle of Princeton*, 158
  portraits by, *171*, *240*

Trumbull, Jonathan, 144, 164, 229
Tryon, William, 116, 117, 142, 222
*Turtle* (submarine), 144
Tuscaroras, 225

United States
  Articles of Confederation, 212, 250,
    299
  Constitutional Convention, 299,
    300
  Declaration of Independence, 133
  European recognition of, 87–88
  fears of military dictator and, 290–92
  French contributions to creation of,
    202
  GW as first President, 299–303
  nascent aristocracy and, 291
  national elections, xxiv
  popular sovereignty and, xxiv
  as sovereign, independent state, 132,
    295
University of Virginia, Washington
    Papers project, xxii

Valcour Island, Battle of, 146–47
Valley Forge (1777–78), 191–203, *197*
  death toll at, 193
  dueling and, 201
  food shortage at, 192–93
  French aristocrats at, 201
  GW announces French alliance,
    202–3
  GW's change of attitude toward
    rank and file, 40, 94, 200
  leadership cadre and inner circle at,
    196
  military notables at, 196–201
  Steuben training at, 198–99, 203
  weather problems, 226
Van Braam, Jacob, 17, 18, 21, 26, 27, 116
Vandalia colony, 58
Vauban, Sébastien de, 281
Veblen, Thorstein, 51
Vergennes, Comte de, 201, 258, 288
Vernon, Edward, 5, 6
Verplanck's Point, N.Y., 222

Virginia
  adjutant general, 12, 14–15
  Continentals, 95–96, 141, 157, 161,
    210–11, 231, 237, 238
  Cornwallis plan and, 272–73
  Fairfax County and Association, 80
  Fairfax County militia, 80, 86
  Fairfax family and, 6, 8
  Fairfax Resolves, 76, 80
  gentry class and, xxiv, 3, 30
  Indian attacks on the frontier,
    37–38
  as key to winning the war, 273–74
  local takeover of, 80
  Mason raising voluntary infantry
    in, 80
  militias of, 80, 265
  Natural Bridge, GW, Jefferson,
    and, 8
  as Revolutionary hotbed, 272
  rifle companies and, 87, 95–96, 108
  Stamp Act of 1765 and, 59–60
  Yorktown Campaign and Cornwallis
    surrender, 275–84, *284*
Virginia Convention, 76
Virginia: House of Burgesses, 12,
    67, 76
  funding of Fry expeditionary
    force, 21
  GW as member of, 46, 59, 88
  GW proposes boycott of British
    goods and slave trade, 66
  Henry's Resolves, 59–60
  non-importation agreements and,
    66, 76
Virginia Regiment, 27, 35–40, 43–46,
    68, 79, 82, 120
  Forbes expedition, 43–46
  GW's attempts to make them a
    regular British Army unit, 36–37,
    38, 44
  GW's leadership team, 39–40
  McKenzie's letter to GW, 79
  Ohio Valley land promised to, 58
  rank and file, 40
  veterans of, in GW's circle, 82

Walpole, Robert, xv, 24, 56
Ward, Artemas, 88, 93, 94, 113
War of Jenkins' Ear, 5
Warren, Joseph, 91
Washington, Augustine (father), 3, 4
Washington, George
  as archetype, xxvii
  as exemplary person, xxiii
  first portrait, by Peale, 68, 69
  image of, xxii, 159, 177
  as "indispensable man," xx
  journals of, 9
  letters of, xxii–xxiii, 31, 42, 47, 89, 214
  as new Cincinnatus, 300
  popularity of, 85–86, 251
  stature of, xxiii, xxvii
—character and characteristics
  appearance of, 8, 77, 86, 88, 94
  athleticism, strength, 8, 77, 96–97
  bluffing and deception, 6, 94, 106,
    122, 216–17
  bravery, xxv–xxvi, 34, 210, 308n28
  as bulwark of decency, 89, 159, 167–
    68, 262
  conspicuous consumption by, 51–53
  called "Caunotocarious," 9, 17–18, 22
  contradictions of, xxii
  as controlled and calculating, 152
  deliberation in pursuing objectives, 31
  dress and clothing, importance of, 6,
    68, 86, 88, 94, 119, 132, 251
  diplomacy and statecraft, xxii, 132–33,
    214, 216–17
  fox hunting and horsemanship, 8, 9,
    51, 94
  as gentry, class consciousness and,
    xxiii–xxiv, xxv, 6, 67, 196, 200–201
  holding a grudge, 50
  image of, 47, 89
  intelligence of, 67
  lack of education, 67
  luck of, xxv–xxvi, 34, 114, 137, 156, 210,
    275, 308n28
  Martha's view of, xx
  mask of and concealed emotions, xxii,
    xxvii, 10, 41, 47, 50, 106, 160, 220

  as merciful, 19, 159, 164, 205, 224, 246,
    282, 302
  personal magnetism, 39, 98, 210, 279,
    293
  politeness, xxiii, 6, 8
  as politician, 59
  as public speaker, 59
  rectitude and moderation, xx, xxii,
    xxvii, 47, 77–78, 88–89, 113
  religious beliefs, xxiv
  response to appointment to head the
    army, 88–89
  ruthlessness of, xxi, xxiii
  self-control, 6, 10, 49–50
  shifting of blame and, 27, 151, 188
  solid and conscientious, 79
  strategic, 6
  talent for choosing men, 17, 39,
    97–101, 170
  travel with pomp and ceremony, 37
  values instilled in childhood, 6, 8
  wrath of, 188, 195, 246
—family and personal life
  Barbados trip (1751), 13–14
  birth, 3
  brother Lawrence as role model,
    surrogate father, 3–4, 6, 7, 9
  death of stepdaughter Patsy, 75
  death of stepson Jacky, 277
  debt and, 53, 75
  education, 6
  Fairfax family and, 6, 7–12, 31, 38, 42
  family as gentry, 3
  father's death, 4
  first exposure to Native Americans, 9
  inheritance from Patsy's death, 75
  knowledge of the frontier and, 9–12
  Lafayette as surrogate son, 180–81
  land acquisition by, 11, 52, 58, 295, 299
  living large and, 51–54, 314n15, 314n22
  love for Sally Cary Fairfax, 10, 11, 20,
    31, 41–42, 47, 49, 309n21
  marriage to Martha Custis, 46, 47–51
  mother and, 5, 47
  sex life, 42, 49
  ship purchased, The Farmer, 53

siblings of, 3
slaves and, 14, 37, 200, 254, 295, 303
spending habits, 51–53
as surveyor, 9–12, 58
wealth of, and Martha's dowry, 47–48
—health
bleeding of, 41
Craik as physician, 41
dysentery (1755), 33
dysentery (1757), 41
smallpox (1751), 13
sterility of, 42, 48
—military career as Colonial, xx
ambitions of, 5, 12, 30, 36–37, 41
attitude toward war, 24, 40, 41
band of brothers for, 39
Battle of Fort Duquesne and, 45–46
as Braddock aide-de-camp, 30–35
as champion of the victims, 41
commander in chief, Virginia's
    forces (1755), 35
courage and leadership talents,
    39–40, 50–51
Dagworthy dispute, 36–37
departures from European
    practices, 36
Dinwiddie and, 14, 15, 16–20, 27–28,
    36, 37, 38, 41
disciplining of men and, 40
early inexperience of, 21–22, 27
Fairfax mentoring of, 27
fellow officers who are later
    enemies, 31
Forbes expedition and (1758),
    43–46
Fort Necessity and, 23, 25, 26, 27, 28
French and Indian War and, 28–46
Fry's death and promotion to full
    colonel, 25
Great Meadows expedition and start
    of French and Indian War (1754),
    21–27
initial military career, 10
irregular warfare and, 35
Lawrence's influence, 12
as lieutenant colonel, under Fry, 21

as messenger for Dinwiddie, Forks
    (1753–54), 16–20
murder of Jumonville and, 23–24, 26
Native Americans and, 17–18, 19, 25,
    37–38, 40
observations in Barbados, 13–14
rank's importance to and, 28, 30
Ohio Company and, 12–13, 14
psychology used with the common
    soldier, 40
renown after Braddock defeat, 37
replaces Lawrence as adjutant
    general, 15
rise in the military, 41
royal commission denied, 37, 38, 44,
    50, 94
Royal Navy appointment thwarted,
    6–7
Virginia Regiment and, 35–40, 43–46
—Revolutionary General
address to officers (Mar. 15, 1783),
    292–93
address to the troops (Dec. 29, 1776),
    159–60
as amateur, 89–90, 93, 116, 147, 178–79
as America's "Patriot King," 67, 88,
    89, 114
announces French alliance to the
    troops (May 5, 1778), 202–3
appointment to the head the army,
    88–89, 317n49
Arnold's betrayal and, 240, 244,
    245–46
Asgill affair and, 288
bayoneting and, 223–24
betrayal and treachery against, 98,
    117–18, 150–52, 190, 193–94, 292–93
blame for the defeat at Camden, 239
blind spots regarding commanders,
    xxv
bravery under fire, 163, 210
British diplomatic efforts and, 131–33
British peace commission and, 204–5
British retreat from Philadelphia
    and Battle of Monmouth, 207–12,
    *209, 211*

Washington, George
—**Revolutionary General** (*cont'd*)
  British strategy in 1777 and, 173–76
  British withdrawals for American
    cities and, 286
  Bunker Hill, response to, 91
  Burgoyne's surrender and, 189
  at Cambridge, 93, 96–97, 100, 104, 110
  changes to the Army and, 166–67
  "chastisement of the Savages," 225–26
  Congress consulted on strategy, 122
  Congressional critics of, 193–95
  Congress strikes medal for, 114
  Cornwallis in pursuit of, 152–53
  Cornwallis surrender, 282–84, *284*
  court-martial of Lee, 211–12
  court-martial of Stephen, 188
  cutting British off from local
    supplies, xviii, xxii–xxiii, 122, 123,
    128, 189, 219, 221, 287
  as dangerous when cornered, 138, 155
  defeat at Brandywine, 178–80, 181, 183
  defense of New York and, 116–17
  defense of New York mistakes,
    121–22, 137
  defense of Philadelphia and, 177–80,
    189–90
  defense of Philadelphia mistakes,
    178–79
  delegating authority and, 121–22
  desertions, anger at, 120
  diplomacy of, 214, 250, 257–58, 336n27
  ending the war, 250–98
  ethical high ground taken by, 117,
    192
  evacuation of Brooklyn Heights and,
    138
  execution of André, 249
  farewell to officers (1783), 298
  fears of military dictator and,
    290–92
  fortification of Dorchester Heights,
    107
  French allies and, 214, 216, 217, 231,
    251–54, 273–82
  French faith in, 252–53

  as Generalissimo, xiii, xxiii, 7, 89,
    93–94, 97, 114, 116, 118, 170, 183, 229,
    279, 298
  Germantown attack and defeat,
    184–88
  gestures by, 205
  hangings and, 40, 118, 247–48
  Harlem Heights and escape from
    New York, 140–42, 145
  hatred of Conway, 195
  Hickey and plot against, 117–18
  as "His Excellency," xiii, xxv, 110, 132
  horse of, 160, 177, 210
  innate talents and, 89–90, 94
  irregular warfare and, xx, 68, 218, 219,
    220, 221, 236, 287
  leadership cadre and inner circle, xxiii,
    80–84, 97–101, 170–72, 177, 196, 254
  leaves Mount Vernon (May 5, 1755), 85
  loss at Quebec and, 110
  loss of Charleston, reaction to, 237
  luck of, 114, 137, 156, 163, 210, 275
  Manhattan showdown and, 273–74
  as marked man, 90
  Monmouth, rallying the troops at,
    210–11, *211*
  nadir of war and, 155, 324n130
  New England militias and, 106
  New Jersey campaign, achievement
    of, 164
  New York City loss and, 134–42
  officer corps and, xxiv–xxv, 95, 97,
    200–201, 290–91
  original stratagems and devices,
    143–44, 189–90
  "penmen" for, xxi, 98, 170
  plot to kidnap Prince William
    Henry, 288–89
  practical ideology of, 229
  preparing for the role (1774–75), 79,
    80, 82
  prevention of mass slaughter and,
    xx–xxii, xxvi, 295–96
  Princeton, rallying the troops at, 163
  problem of temporary army, 105–6,
    109, 152, 154, 159–60

Proclamation for the Cessation of
Hostilities (April 18, 1783), 294
raiding strategy, 222–23
real peace and, 296–97
reinvasion of Canada opposed, 216–17
resignation as commander, 298, 300
response to news of Lexington and
Concord, 85
revolutionary principles and, 116,
167–68, 192, 200, 229, 251, 294,
302–3
Rochambeau conferences, 251–53,
273–74
on Royal Navy's bombardment, 104
siegecraft and, 99
as spymaster, 143, 219–21, 288
stalemate years of the war, 213–50
standing army desired by, 105, 229
struggle to get resources from
Congress, 213–14, 227–28, 250
supply system and, 86
surprise as strategy, 107, 138, 156–58,
184
symbolism of Stony Point and
Paulus Hook, 224
training and discipline of troops,
93–97, 105, 116, 119–20, 167, 254–55,
289
treatment of Arnold's wife and
cohorts, 246
treatment of prisoners and enemy
wounded, 159, 164, 205, 224, 282
Trenton surprise attack and, 156–58
use of long rifles, 68
valedictory address, 297
victory along the Hudson, 184
victory tour, 297–98
view of the common soldier, xxiv, 40,
94, 200
visionary leadership, xxv
war council, 1776, Battle of Trenton,
156–57
war council, 1777, deliberation on
British strategy, 175–76
war council, 1777, Battle of
Princeton, 162

war councils, 1778, Battle of
Monmouth, 207–8
White Plains and, 146
winding down of war and last acts,
287–94
winter headquarters, Morristown,
164, 166–67, 226–29
winter headquarters, Valley Forge,
183, 191–93, 194–201, 197
Yorktown Campaign, 275–82
—social issues and politics
belief in strong national government,
229, 297
British banning of westward
expansion and, 58
as center of resistance, 66
Constitutional Convention and, 299,
300
Country Party ideas, 67, 77–78, 86,
229
Fairfax Resolves and, 76, 80
fears of enslavement by England
and, xiv, 75–76, 77, 205
First Continental Congress and,
76, 77
as first President, 299–303
individual rights and, 65
member, House of Burgesses, 46,
59, 88
as militant, 67–68
Mississippi Company and, 58
Native Americans and, 44, 295
path toward rebellion, 58, 59, 79
proposes boycott of British goods
and slave trade, 66, 67
rage against Britain, 50–51, 59
raising a voluntary force in
Virginia, 80
Second Continental Congress,
85–90
Stamp Act of 1765 and, 60
unfair British economic practices
and, 53–54
Virginia Convention and, 76
Washington, Jack (brother), 28, 30, 31,
113

Washington, John (great-
    grandfather), 3
  called "Caunotocarious," 3, 9, 18
Washington, Lawrence (half-brother),
    3–7, 4, 12–15, 22
  British Army and, 3–4, 5, 50
  as father figure for GW, 3–4, 6, 7,
    9, 12
  marriage to Anne Fairfax, 5–6
  Mount Vernon and, 5, 12
  Ohio Company and, 12–13
  siege of Cartagena and, 5, 13, 15
  as Virginia's adjutant general, 12,
    14–15
  War of Jenkins' Ear and, 5
Washington, Lund (cousin), 134, 142,
    258, 336n27
Washington, Martha Custis (wife), xx,
    48, 48–49, 75, 277, 299–300
  burning of GW's letters, xxii
  at Cambridge and, 100, 110
  extant letter from GW, 89
  First Continental Congress and, 76
  marriage to GW, 46, 47–51
  Mount Vernon and, 49, 277, 279
  slaves and, 47, 303
  smallpox inoculation of, 168
  at Valley Forge, 196
  wealth of, 46, 47–48
Washington, Mary Ball (mother), 3, 4,
    5, 7, 47
Washington, Samuel (brother), 91
Washington, William, 265, 266, 267
Wayne, Anthony, 180, 193, 210, 255
  Battle of Foreign Timbers, 301
  Battle of Germantown, 187
  Battle of Green Spring, 280

  Battle of Stony Point, 223–24
  GW's Yorktown campaign, 280
  Paoli Massacre and, 182, 186, 223
  Pennsylvania Line and, 255, 275, 280
  Virginia expedition, 274–75
  war councils of June 1778 and, 208
Webb, Samuel, 132
Webster, James, 238
Webster, Noah, 274
West Indies, 204, 256, 273, 275, 284, 285
  Jamaica, 286
  Saint Eustatius, 280
  Saint Kitts, 285
West Point, N.Y., 219, 222
  Benedict Arnold given command at,
    244
  GW arrives at, Arnold's betrayal
    and, 245–46
whaleboat wars, 221, 222, 287
Whiskey Rebellion, 301–2, 301
  GW pardons leaders of, 302
White Plains, Battle of, 146
  casualties, 146
William Henry, Prince, 288–89
William of Orange, xxvii
Williamsburg, Va., 14, 16
Wilson, Benjamin, 183, 327n67
Winnsboro, S.C., 261, 264
Wood, Gordon S., xv
Wyoming massacre, 225

Yorktown Campaign, 275–82
  arms and men captured at, 283
  Cornwallis surrender, 282–84, 284
  as crushing defeat for Britain, 283
  full impact of, 284
  Siege of Yorktown, 281–82

ABOUT THE AUTHOR

ROBERT L. O'CONNELL received a Ph.D. in history at the University of Virginia. Subsequently, he spent thirty years as a senior analyst at the National Ground Intelligence Center, followed by fourteen years as a visiting professor at the Naval Postgraduate School. He is the author of numerous books, two of which, *The Ghosts of Cannae: Hannibal and the Darkest Hour of the Roman Republic* and *Fierce Patriot: The Tangled Lives of William Tecumseh Sherman,* were national bestsellers, the latter winning the 2015 William H. Seward Award for Excellence in Civil War Biography. He lives in Charlottesville, Virginia.

ABOUT THE TYPE

This book was set in Caslon, a typeface first designed in 1722 by William Caslon (1692–1766). Its widespread use by most English printers in the early eighteenth century soon supplanted the Dutch typefaces that had formerly prevailed. The roman is considered a "workhorse" typeface due to its pleasant, open appearance, while the italic is exceedingly decorative.